Cultural
Aesthetics

CULTURAL AESTHETICS

Renaissance Literature and the Practice of Social Ornament

PATRICIA FUMERTON

The University of Chicago Press

CHICAGO AND LONDON

Patricia Fumerton is associate professor of English at the
University of California, Santa Barbara.

The University of Chicago Press, Chicago 60637
The University of Chicago Press, Ltd., London
© 1991 by The University of Chicago
All rights reserved. Published 1991
Printed in the United States of America

00 99 98 97 96 95 94 93 92 91 5 4 3 2 1

ISBN (cloth): 0-226-26952-3

Library of Congress Cataloging-in-Publication Data
Fumerton, Patricia.
Cultural aesthetics : renaissance literature and the practice
of social ornament / Patricia Fumerton.
p.   cm.
Includes bibliographical references and index.
1. English literature—Early modern, 1500–1700—History and
criticism.   2. Manners and customs in literature.   3. Literature and
society—England—History—16th century.   4. Literature and society—
England—History—17th century.   5. Literature and anthropology—
England—History.   6. Aristocracy in literature.   7. Culture in
literature.   8. Renaissance—England.   9. Aesthetics, British.
I. Title.
PR428.M35F86   1991
820.9′355′09024—dc20   91-14320

For my parents

Through whose large bountie poured on me rife,
In the first season of my feeble age,
I now doe liue.

Contents

Illustrations

Acknowledgments

Much is owed. I am indebted to the community of colleagues who generously offered comments on parts of my manuscript; their support made my project feel like it "belonged": Heather Dubrow, Stephen Greenblatt, Linda Gregerson, Donald Guss, Jonathan Haynes, Richard Helgerson, Stephen Orgel, Patricia Parker, George Pigman III, Mark Rose, Peter Stallybrass, Leonard Tennenhouse, Don Wayne, and Andrew Weiner. I owe special thanks to Leah Marcus for her enthusiastic, critical, and unflagging encouragement through more versions of my manuscript than either she or I would care to remember. For Alan Liu, thanks unspeakable. He is the "ABSENT presence" at the heart of this book.

My colleagues and students at the University of Wisconsin, Madison, and at the University of California, Santa Barbara, provided me with fertile soil in which to nurture my project. I am especially grateful to my 1987 graduate class at UCSB, the "first seminarie" and testing ground for many an idea. I have been aided in the difficult task of collecting permissions and prints by Emma Lipton, Mark Girouard, John Murdoch, Patrick Noon, and Lee Bliss. Shannon Miller and Simon Hunt courageously helped me check the mass of notes and historical data (all errors of fact, of course, are theirs).

Chapter 2 appeared in an earlier version in *ELH* 53 (1986) and chapter 3 appeared in an earlier version in *Representations* 15 (1986). Parts of the book were presented as talks at the International Congress on Medieval Studies (1984), the Renaissance Society of America Conference (1988), and the Modern Language Association Convention (1987 and 1988). I have greatly benefited from the (often anonymous) responses of the audiences.

Finally I must acknowledge gifts of the market: financial support for my project was given by the Academic Senate of the University of Wisconsin, Madison; the Academic Senate, Faculty Career Development Program, and Interdisciplinary Humanities Center of the University of California, Santa Barbara; and the National Endowment for the Humanities. Much thanks to all.

1

INTRODUCTION
A Still Life: Clock, Jewel, Orange

This book is about the fragmentary, the peripheral, and the ornamental—what may be called, in terms specific to the culture I am dealing with, the *trivial*. My focus is the trivial selfhood of the aristocracy in the English Renaissance: a sense of self, as we will see, that was supported and, indeed, constituted by bric-a-brac worlds of decorations, gifts, foodstuffs, small entertainments, and other particles of cultural wealth and show.[1]

My correlative interest is the way this sense of self arose at the intersection between historical and aesthetic arenas of life. "Trivial" is my general term for an analytic of the fragmentary, peripheral, and ornamental addressed at once to the context of historical fact and to the texts of aesthetic artifact. Under the rubric of the trivial, I consider first a primary level of past existence where historical context appeared to the aristocratic self as radical disconnection. The luxurious bric-a-brac of the aristocrat's everyday life was one with a cosmos in which even central historical configurations seemed broken apart and marginalized in incoherence, and where self was thus fixed in fracture. History, we may say, was a broken confectionary plate whose sweet pieces (which we will come upon later) might be puzzled back together again by the shattered self but *never* in such a way as to recover the fancied roundedness of original unity.

To study history as a broken confection or disjointed pile, as I intend to do, will seem trivial to historians seeking mainstreams and currents of development (or in the *Annales* variant: deep structures of the *longue durée*).

To think in Braudel's terms, indeed, I wish to study a layer of history even more superficial than the "surface disturbances, crests of foam" of *l'histoire événementielle*."[2] Over the transitory foam of political events rises my *métier:* an even more ephemeral foam of culture whose waves are only as substantial as a wave machine in an Inigo Jones masque. But while I embrace "trivial" as a concept, I reject its derogatory connotation. Any such derogation, I believe, is at last only a repression pinpointing the anxiety of both mainstream and *Annales* history: the fear of the naked datum, of the fact that seems *mere* fact unsupported by any continuous structure or ground. How did the past itself think its naked facts so that a sense of identity, of selfhood, could arise even amid historical incoherence?

Here lies the design of my sliding scale of triviality: the fragmentary and peripheral were at last also ornamental. My answer is that the past aestheticized itself. It was precisely the broken, disconnected, and "detached" quality of historical fact that enabled the Renaissance to achieve an aesthetic understanding of itself as cultural *artifact*. A truly historical view of Renaissance aristocracy will therefore be one that recognizes the necessity of aesthetics in understanding past culture. When approached in a historicized manner, aesthetics provides a mediation between the Renaissance and our own age of postmodernity that is not a dismissal of history but precisely a representation or interpretation of history.[3]

Imagine, then, that on his way to die a king carries a silver clock to present to a favorite, that on the scaffold he hands a jeweled locket to an advisor, and that after his blood is spilled a spiced orange issues from his pocket. Imagine also the kingly "self" that arises to sustain itself (even past death) on the mythic basis of such trivial bric-a-brac embedded at the heart of great historical moments—arises as if each dismembered part and possession, each essential fragment, were a bit of its lasting art. Or again (to look forward to a realm of visual artifact we will consider), imagine a self that paints its portrait not in full-length but in miniature, or perhaps as a still life in which the fragmented and peripheral ornaments of life (and death)—a clock, a jewel, an orange—are caught in strange juxtaposition.

Cultural Aesthetics is about the life of subjectivity caught in the trivial intersection between the historical and the aesthetic. It is about the historically "useless" arts of gifts, chivalric romances, miniatures, sonnets, banqueting-house desserts (with their confectionary plates), court masques, and the trade exotica of the East Indies. These merely decorative or delicious fragments limn in the medium of aesthetics what I will finally call a vast system of "oblique" historical reference in the social practice of the English Renaissance. There are many Renaissance trifles that may be considered, of course, and other critics prefer to study alternative specks of curiously meaningful insignificance (Jeffrey Knapp, for instance, privileges "trifling" tobacco).[4] But I have chosen to focus on the above trifles because each engages the literary in a way that foregrounds a different aspect or problem of aristocratic subjectivity: the self as collective (chapter 2), as secret (chapter 3), as void (chapter 4), and as foreign or strange (chapter 5). Each of the above "mere" ornaments indexes a phase of historical incoherence in which we can watch the fictional making of the aristocratic self.

The Paradigm

Well! we are all *condamnés,* as Victor Hugo says: we are all under sentence of death but with a sort of indefinite reprieve . . . : we have an interval, and then our place knows us no more.

Walter Pater, *The Renaissance*[5]

The following tells the story of one self facing an actual interval between sentence of death and that moment when our place knows us no more. It is a detailed, full-bodied paradigm, whose methodology I will defend.

On January 27, 1649, in Westminster Hall Charles I was condemned "to be putt to death by the severinge of his head from his body . . . In the open Streete before Whitehall."[6] Edmund Ludlow, Lieutenant-General of the Horse, recalled the next moment: "The King would have spoken something before he was withdrawn; but being accounted dead in law immediately after sentence pronounced, it was not permitted."[7] Instead, Charles was hustled away by the guard and taken to St. James's Palace, to await his death in fact.

In the remaining interval Charles spent much time in seclusion with Bishop Juxon reaffirming his life in God.[8] But on his final full day (January 29), he sought those secular extensions of his being yet remaining in England: his two youngest children, Princess Elizabeth (aged thirteen) and Henry, Duke of Gloucester (aged nine). Charles had messages for his family, but worried that his final words to Elizabeth would be forgotten. "'Sweetheart,' he said, 'you'll forget this.' 'No,' she answered, 'I shall never forget it while I live,' and pouring

forth abundance of tears promised him to write down the particulars."
The King then took young Henry upon his knee:

> "Sweetheart, now they will cut off thy father's head. Mark, child, what I
> say, they will cut off my head and perhaps make thee a king. But mark
> what I say; you must not be a king so long as your brothers Charles and
> James do live. For they will cut off your brothers' heads, when they can
> catch them, and cut off they head too, at the last. And therefore, I charge
> you, do not be made a king by them."

The child earnestly replied: "I will be torn in pieces first." Charles at
the same time took pains to reassure his children "not to grieve for
him, for he should die a martyr."[9]

As Sir Thomas Herbert (Groom of the Bedchamber during the
King's captivity) recalled, the King then shared amongst them "all the
wealth now in my power to give my two children." This consisted of
"diamonds and jewels, most part broken Georges and Garters," which
had been secreted in "a little cabinet . . . closed with three seals."[10]
The same day Charles entreated Herbert to distribute most of his remaining belongings amongst family and friends: books, largely religious (Charles's personally annotated Bible was to go to the Prince,
along with the same message the King had communicated to Elizabeth), as well as James's *Works,* and a romance called *Cassandra.* He
also gave away, with one important exception, his personal jewels, including "a large ring sun-dial of silver—a jewel his Majesty much
valued" and his gold watch. As the afternoon wore on, Charles sent for
Colonel Tomlinson, his kindest keeper, and gave him a "legacy" of "a
gold tooth-picker and case that he kept in his pocket."[11]

On January 30 Charles awoke to the dawn of his death. He took
care that he would look and act his best. He instructed Herbert to
make his beard "trim" and called for a shirt "more than ordinary, by
reason the season is so sharp as probably may make me shake, which
some observers will imagine proceeds from fear. I would have no such
imputation." He put in his pocket a clean handkerchief and an orange
stuck full of cloves.[12]

Around 10 A.M. the King's stern keeper, Colonel Hacker, knocked on
the door to summon him to Whitehall. "The King bade him go forth,"
recalled Herbert, "he would come presently." Taking along "the silver
clock that hung by his bed-side," Charles began the short journey
through St. James's Park. Along the way, he asked Herbert "the hour
of the day; and taking the clock into his hand, gave it him, and bade

him keep it in memory of him."[13] Once at Whitehall, they proceeded to the King's bedchamber "where he used to lye" to await the final summons.[14] About noon, though the King had not wanted to eat after taking the Sacrament, he consumed half a manchet and a glass of claret "in case some fitt of fainting might take him upon the scaffold."[15] Charles refused the offer of some Puritan ministers to pray with him, however, though he did ask them in their prayers to remember him.[16] The last knock finally came. The King ordered, "'Open the door,' Herbert remembered, "and bade Hacker go, he would follow."[17]

The route the King followed to the scaffold was exactly the same as that he would have taken, in better days, to a masque (fig. 1). Charles

1. Plan of Whitehall Palace by G. P. V. Akrigg (buildings re-numbered and "Whitehall Highway" added). Based chiefly on the survey of the ground level made by John Fisher shortly before 1670 and published by George Vertue in 1747. Photo from G. P. V. Akrigg, *Jacobean Pageant; or, The Court of King James I* (Cambridge: Harvard University Press, 1962), pp. 398–400.

2. George Vertue's print of H. Terrason's drawing of Whitehall Banqueting House, 1713.
Vertue added in his own hand the initials C. R. and a crown above the first-floor window as
well as the date 1648 (Old Style) below it. He also appended the note in the bottom right
margin, which reads: "Tis according to the truest reports, said that out of this Window
K. Charles went upon the Scaffold to be beheaded. the window frame being taken out
purposely to make the passage on to the Scaffold, which is equal to the landing place
of the Hall within side." Photo from John Charlton, *The Banqueting House, Whitehall*
(London: Her Majesty's Stationery Office, 1964), p. 22.

proceeded from his private chambers, down his privy gallery, and into
his Banqueting House. Rather than sitting in his chair of state at the
south end of the hall, however, where he would have watched a masque
entertainment, the King traveled the length of the Banqueting House to
its north (or stage) end, where he passed through a hole "broken,"
Herbert said, "through the wall" into the adjoining staircase. He then
stepped out the staircase window onto the scaffold, which faced the public highway of Whitehall in front of the Banqueting House. (George
Vertue inscribed over the fatal porthole Charles's signature: a crowned
"C. R." [fig. 2].)[18]

On this scaffold, Charles appeared on stage as the actor in his own, last
masque. One witness, indeed, viewed the scene as a kind of mirror to the
masquings the King once participated in. Charles, he observed, exited the
Banqueting House "with the same unconcernedness and motion, that he

usually had, when he entered into it on a Masque-night."[19] We will later need to explore more fully the contemporary perception that the King went to his death as if in a masque. For now, we can merely notice some of the features of the scaffold scene that reinforced the resemblance. To begin with, the very design of the scaffold gave Charles an enclosedness similar to that of the masque stage, which temporarily shut its masquers away behind arbors, rocks, mountains, and other machinery. "The breast-high railing of the scaffold was draped in black cloth, so that all the dense crowds in the street would see would be the bright flash of the axe at the top of its swing." But just as the unruly crowds at a masque at last broke in visually (and, as we will see in a later chapter, even physically) upon the enclosed masquers, here too massed spectators finally intruded. Throngs packed the roofs of the neighboring buildings, peering over the scaffold's railing to view the entire grisly act of execution.[20] And perhaps most specifically reminiscent of a masque: the executioner and his assistant wore fantastic disguises of black masks, wigs, and false beards akin to the get-ups of antimasquers. Their tight-fitting costumes were those of sailors or of butchers.[21] The latter costume would have been grotesquely fitting for the unusually low block, apparently "a quartering-block on which the bodies of traitors were dismembered."[22]

Before laying his head on this block, Charles wished to act his last speech. But since he found it impossible to speak loud enough for his public audience, he turned his words instead to the more intimate gathering of spectators on the scaffold, including a group of shorthand reporters (one such reporter is pictured, notebook propped on knee, in a contemporary rendering of the scaffold scene [fig. 3]). The speech was published the same day.[23] In it Charles affirmed his innocence and, excusing Parliament, laid blame on the army. He forgave all, however, praying "that they may take the right way to the Peace of the kingdom. . . . So, Sirs, I do wish with all my soul, and I do hope there is some here* that will carry it further." He spoke for the law of kings; of the "liberty" and "freedom" of the people (which "consists in having of government; those laws by which their life and their goods may be most their own"); and against power: "If I would have given way to an arbitrary way, for to have all laws changed according to the power of the sword I needed not to have come here. And, therefore, I tell you, and I pray God it be not laid to your charge, that I am the martyr of the people." The pronoun "I," as heard

*The text adds a note that Charles here turned "to some gentlemen that wrote."

3. The execution of Charles I. Bishop Juxon, immediately behind the shorthand reporter (kneeling, left), holds the King's Order of the Garter, or "George." Photo from Charlton, *Banqueting House,* p. 26.

here, dominated throughout in preference to the royal "we." Indeed, "I," "me," and "myself" appear in forty of the forty-nine sentences of Charles's last speech (often repeatedly in the same sentence).

After making this speech, the King arranged with the executioner a signal for the stroke—"when I thrust out my hands"—and tucked his hair under a white, satin night-cap, which he had brought along.[24] Turning to Bishop Juxon, he said:

> I have a good cause, and a gracious God on my side.
>
> *Doctor Juxon:* There is but one stage more. This stage is turbulent and troublesome; it is a short one. But you may consider, it will soon carry you a very great way. It will carry you from Earth to Heaven. And there you shall find a great deal of cordial joy and comfort.
>
> *King:* I go from a corruptible to an incorruptible crown; where no disturbance can be, no disturbance in the world.
>
> *Doctor Juxton:* You are exchanged from a temporal to an eternal crown, a good exchange.

The King now removed his cloak and gave the Bishop his St. George medallion—his last and most valued jewel, which he wore every day.[25] (The trinket dangles from Juxon's outstretched hand in the picture of the scaffold scene.) On handing over this George, Charles spoke to Juxon his last, enigmatic word: "Remember."

The King then laid his neck upon the block. But readiness was all. When the executioner stooped to put some hair under his cap, Charles, "Thinking he had been going to strike," spoke sharply: "Stay for the sign." The executioner's quick reply: "Yes I will and it please your Majesty." A very little time elapsed. At last "the King stretching forth his hands, the executioner at one blow severed his head from his body." The head was held up for full view, and immediately troops of soldiers drove the crowds in opposite directions "purposely to disperse and scatter the people."[26]

Struggling hordes nevertheless clamored cannibalistically to gather up pieces of the King. Sir Roger Manley recorded:

> They were inhumanely barbarous to his dead corpse. His hair and his blood were sold by parcels. Their hands and sticks were tinged by his blood and the block, now cut into chips, as also the sand sprinkled with his sacred gore, were exposed for sale. Which were greedily bought, but for different ends, by some as trophies of their slain enemy, and by others as precious reliques of their beloved prince.[27]

The executioner, who had secured from the King's pocket the clove-scented orange and the handkerchief, was offered twenty shillings for the orange "by a gentleman in White-hall, but refused the same; and afterwards sold it for ten shillings in Rose mary Lane."[28]

Mementos proliferated after the event. Disraeli mentions a poem "upon the King's Book (the Icon Basilike) bound up in a cover, coloured with his blood." Allan Fea, a fond recorder of Charles I relics, notes a little volume of *Les Heures royalles, dediées au Roy* (Paris, 1657), "the binding of which was made of Charles the Martyr's hair, interwoven with gold and silver thread." Bits of hair as well as of blood-stained sand and cloth were often inserted in lockets and rings bearing commemorative mottoes. Figure 4, for example, shows an enameled locket with a portrait of Charles done on hair, a skull and crossbones marking its memorial character. Secreted in the back is "a piece of linen stained with blood" thought to have come from the "martyred" King. Finally, such remembrances evolved into miniatures of Charles reputed to be worked in needlepoint wholly from his own hair. As Charles's martyrdom gained fashion, the number of such relics grew, as did the magical, life-giving powers they were said to possess.[29]

At the time of the execution itself, though, the army worked hard to keep the King, and his blood lineage, firmly dead. A proclamation was issued that very afternoon prohibiting anyone from declaring Prince Charles the successor. But just as the executioner failed verbally to confirm the truncation of Charles's kingship after decapitating his body (neglecting, on holding up the severed head, to cry the customary phrase, "Behold the head of a traitor"), so too efforts to truncate the succession lacked full voice. In both Ireland and Scotland, with the death of Charles I, Charles II was at once proclaimed King.[30]

4. Enameled locket with a portrait of Charles I, done on hair, said to have belonged to Lady Janet Murray. The skull and crossbones mark the locket as a memorial piece; in the back is a fragment of linen stained with blood, supposedly of the King. Photo: Trustees of the National Museums of Scotland.

The Paradigm of Truncation: Culture as Fragment

I have told this story detailing an "interval" of life "under sentence of death" in order to stage at the start what I mean by the aristocratic self. As proclaimed in the "I's" of his scaffold-speech, Charles responded to the imminent truncation of his body by stressing personal subjectivity rather than his political embodiment as the royal "we." Yet what such self-assertion witnesses, I would argue, is not selfhood conceived as a unified or single "I" so much as selfhood in all its experiential fragmentariness—selfhood, that is, at once succumbing to discontinuity and conscious enough of its truncation to desire transcendence.

But before we can more fully assess such fragmentary subjectivity, we need to take into account the lens—the "paradigm"—I have used to bring it into focus. Recently, the opening paradigm—especially as practiced in Renaissance new historicist studies—has come under attack. The new historicism's predilection for reading whole histories within isolated, "thickly described" historical moments, critics say, is *fragmentary*. Carol Thomas Neely, for instance, condemns such method as the (male) mastery of the literary text through "a brief, fragmentary reading" of culture. Robert N. Watson, reviewing Stephen Greenblatt's "Invisible Bullets," argues that the "historical data" presented through paradigms "may be so fragmentary as to be worthless for characterizing the crucial activities of an entire culture." For Walter Cohen, paradigmatic "fragmentariness" risks an "arbitrary connectedness" lacking any "organizing principle" able to sustain consistent readings. And for Edward Pechter, the missing organizing principle of the method is "community."[31]

In response, we might note that much of literary criticism has always been paradigmatic. After all, it would seem that the charge of fragmentariness applies not just to historical exempla but potentially to *any* passage or even canon of works nominated as representative.[32] To invert the terms of the critique: what would a total, wholly representative, or nonfragmentary reading of history and/or literature look like? Or again: would such "representative" reading reminiscent of the great, inaugural works of historicism and literary history in the nineteenth century (in the era of Taine) really be desirable?[33] What we face here, in sum, is a criticism of new historicist paradigmatism that does not address the total scope of the problem. Enacted in paradigmatism is the problematics of interpretation or understanding *generally*—especially in regard to the gap between parts and wholes.

The assumption of the critiques of the paradigm rehearsed above is that historical understanding requires the discernment of historical continuity—of an underlying continuum in which the "representativeness" of parts can be plotted by measuring how near or far each lies to some central norm prescriptive of the "whole." Implicit in the charge of fragmentariness or arbitrary connectedness, in other words, is the belief that history develops on something like a ground plane of integral space or, thinking temporally, as a unified process—a rationalist view of history, we may speculate, that originally arose through the substitution of worldly causality for divine agency in Enlightenment historiography and that achieved perhaps its highest cogency in our own century in positivistic history of ideas (e.g. Lovejoy's "unit-ideas" combining as if physically in space and time). The paradigm is a violation of such belief—and ultimately of the historiography premised upon reason's detection of cause within a unified nature—because it is truncated. It is cut short. It shares in the sharp, heavy force of interregnum that breaks up any cohesive ground plane of history.

In sum, that part of us that hearkens back to a continuous historical universe *wishes* to say, "The King is dead; long live the King." But continuity, I would argue, is not history as Charles lived it or as our own scholarship has most recently tried to understand it in breaking with traditional intellectual history. As epitomized in my story of Charles's life and death, history can also be perceived as truncation. At every moment, history is the interregnum felt within the continuum.

Such, in any case, is the essential revisionism of a new historicist method conditioned by its own postmodern moment to break with the historical continuum (and often, it seems, single culture) of the older historiography.[34] To make a paradigm is to affirm that the Interregnum or—to choose an example of discontinuity with equal resonance in both British and American contexts—Civil War *has* occurred, and that such a break cannot be thought away through a logic of connection unwilling to address the very fact, the felt experience, of breakaway history. Or more fully: it is not the case that the breakaway moments in history that have always been the great motivators of new historical methods inhere only in such loud political events as interregnum or civil war. Rather, the moment of fragmentary history I seek to elucidate saturates cultural and literary history even in its quietest and smallest events. Interregnum, that is, is to be found in the detachment of Charles's head; but it may also be found, with just as much lived momentousness, in the detachment of a child from its family (the "child-giving" I will study), in the detachment of a jeweled locket from the portrait it contains, or in the less literal detachment that is the hallmark of aesthetic experience.

To come back to Charles, then, the execution at Whitehall merely heads the list of paradigms I offer to demonstrate the thesis of history as truncation or fissure. To expand upon Charles's execution in its context, indeed, is to realize that the problem of historical break or interruption was very much on the minds of the participants themselves. Our spokesmen here might be the Independents who ushered in the Interregnum. The Independents heralded a millennial reinstatement of originary unity or continuity. But, as Noel Henning Mayfield shows, they also grounded their actions on a believed fragmentariness: (1) on an emphasized gap between the "law" of the Old Testament and the "grace" of the New (which allowed them confidently to hold an "illegal" trial and execution of a king); and (2) on the conviction that, in executing Charles, the Antichrist, they would cut off contemporary history.[35] It was out of such affirmed rupture that the fantasized continuum could be realized. In sentencing Charles to die "by the severinge of his head from his body" and in truncating any answer he could make to his sentence—"being accounted dead in law immediately after sentence pronounced"—the Independents made of Charles the very em*bodi*ment of faith based on detachment from the past.

But it is Charles's own actions, in the gap of life remaining to him between sentencing and execution, that best brings the sense of detached, truncated, or fragmentary history home to us. This is so despite the fact that his actions in this interval of suspension were deliberately calculated to *extend* his life-principle and identity.

Let me first catalog the methods Charles used to extend himself before, like Atropos, severing the thread. Charles not only wished to sustain a continuum of self in the afterlife through "martyrdom"—a role he assumed in his meeting with his children ("he should die a martyr") and reiterated on the scaffold ("I am the martyr of the people")—but also by living on in the world itself through cultural memory. With an intense craving Charles needed to be remembered: he feared that his daughter would forget his parting words and so repeated them to Herbert for transmission to his son; he gave souvenirs to Tomlinson and Herbert to keep "in memory of him" (e.g., the silver clock marking each segment of irrecoverably passed time); he asked the Puritans, whom he scorned, to remember him in their prayers;[36] he hoped the shorthand reporters on the scaffold would promulgate his last speech; and just before laying his head on the block, he left his listeners with the single, resonant command: "Remember."

In particular, Charles tried to make a memorable, lasting whole of himself by implementing two related strategies of self-memorialization. We can take our first cue from his highly dramatic command to "remember," which may have been exactly dramatic. We know that Charles read Shakespeare's plays during the latter part of his captivity. The possibility arises, therefore, that in his last moments he may consciously have been echoing the ghost of Hamlet's father crying from limbo: "remember me."[37] King Hamlet, of course, was asking his son for revenge, whereas King Charles spoke to his children and people of forgiveness. Yet both monarchs were attempting to sustain their ghostly selves among the living through memory. Their fear, we may say, was one of death as an abrupt termination, as a kind of cutting off or chopping up of the self—"Cut off even in the blossoms of my sin," King Hamlet laments to his son.[38] Charles's parting words to his own son Henry conjure up such fear vividly in their mesmerizing image of rampant beheading: "they will cut off thy father's head. . . . they will cut off my head. . . . they will cut off your brothers' heads, when they can catch them, and cut off thy head too." The very rhythm of the language succumbs to the chopping ax. Only Charles's reiterated call to remember what he is saying can seem to ward off the blow of truncation: "Mark, child, what I say. . . . But mark what I say." To be forgotten is to be cut up, made fragmentary. Only in memory are we whole.

What the comparison to Shakespeare cues us to is the fact that one of Charles's strategies of self-memorialization was self-*dramatization*—a studied performance of kingly self-possession designed to stamp his un-changed identity into the minds of all spectators at the execution. Shake-speare, we may say, was only prologue to the main performance. Here I return to the resemblance between Charles-going-to-death and Charles-going-to-masque. As remarked by the witness who thought the King exited his Banqueting House onto the scaffold with the same "uncon-cernedness and motion" with which "he entered into it on a Masque-night," Charles at last staged himself for the benefit of cultural memory through conventions that may best be understood as masquing. He wrote for himself what we might call his Execution Masque.[39]

As a precise comparison, I invoke the last of the actual court masques, *Salmacida Spolia* (1640). In *Salmacida Spolia,* Charles had rehearsed his im-pending role as martyr in the character of the ruler Philogenes, a "lover of the people" whose populace becomes villainous and literally foreign to him in the antimasque. True to the form of the masque, however, these antimas-quers are at last easily displaced—with a mere change of stage machinery. Yet the subsequent scene reveals the masquers (Philogenes/Charles and his noble "heroes") not so much triumphant as withdrawn within an "inac-cessible" mountain of the mind.[40] Able to draw only on "inward helps, not outward force," Philogenes/Charles suffers with Christ-like "patience to outlast / Those storms the people's giddy fury raise."[41]

In his Execution Masque, Charles rewrote this role. He played a lover of the people sacrificed by antimasquing subjects (the executioners in their "terrifying disguise")[42] who this time could not be dispelled. Yet if the Execution Masque was a masque awry, Charles himself remained the true masquer—embodying order and law—until the very end. Indeed, as the witness previously cited confirms, everything about Charles's actions suggested the measured "staging" of a masquer: his concern with looking "trim," with wearing an extra garment and eating a light meal so that he would not shiver from apparent fear on the stage, and, of course, his extraordinary control. It was Charles who gave orders to Hacker (by responding to each summons with a countercommand: "go, he would follow"), who thought to bring along a proper cap to hold up his hair, and who determined the exact moment of truncation with his deliberate "sign." So authoritative was Charles's order to await his direction that the executioner knee-jerked recognition of control: "Yes I will and it please your Majesty." In this moment of control, the unruly world of the antimasque was in fact dispelled by the kingly masquer—a feat of majesty that can be seen to have held its own even after Charles's death in the omission of the cry of "traitor." Even the sense of mystery of the masque universe was recreated. The inscrutable word "Remember," which so troubled both contemporaries and later historians, recalls not only *Hamlet* but the enigmatic signs and emblems of a masque.[43]

Milton, we can thus say, had the wrong dramatic genre in mind when he attacked Charles's extraordinary composure on the scaffold as "a vizor of courage" of the kind extolled by "bad poets, or stage-players [who] are very ambitious of being clapped at the end of the play."[44] He hit closer to the mark in his criticism of the frontispiece to Charles's memorial, *Eikon Basilike:* "A masking scene," he scoffed, decked out with "quaint emblems and devices, begged from the old pageantry of some Twelfthnight's entertainment at Whitehall."[45] For Charles, the execution was analogous to a Whitehall masque. Charles depended on his final appearance on the stage to create a lasting vision of personal authority. Performed before the backdrop of the Banqueting House, his Execution Masque was, without doubt, to have been memorable.

Complementing the method of self-dramatization was Charles's second strategy of self-memorialization: gifts. To follow Charles's progress in the interval between his sentencing and execution is to watch not just a masquer but a gift-giver. Indeed, masquing and gift-giving were by tradition homologous rituals. Gift-giving was integral with the origin of masque art: the ancient mummery in which strangers arrived at court bearing gifts for the sovereign. The very occasion of masques—most importantly, Twelfth Night or the Feast of Epiphany—is telling. Twelfth Night commemorated the arrival of Eastern travelers bearing such gifts as spice (we remember the spice that perfumed Charles's orange) for another king, the Christ child. Descended from such levels of tradition, court masques in Charles's day were generous manifestations of the principle of gift, often in the form of prayers or offerings to the king from his admiring courtiers.

The variation that Charles improvised in his Execution Masque (and its preceding actions) was to reverse the roles of gift-giver and recipient. His Eastern traveler—Herbert—*received* from a king rather than rendered to him. Charles alone gave gifts, that is, and a lot of them. The broken valuables in the cabinet, the books and personal jewelry, the gold toothpick case, the clock, the George—all were precious gifts that Charles dispensed, we might say, as reverse-memento-mori, as reminders not of his death but of his life. Indeed, it is chillingly strange to hear in Herbert's account that the King, on the way to death, thought to bring along an ultimate memento for a gift: his clock. One would think he had other things on his mind. But the gift was part of those other things. Each gift was a medium of memory. Each was an attempt by Charles to tie himself to friends and enemies in a temporal, allusive exchange charged with the promise of continued life. In this light, indeed, his very "martyrdom" could be seen as an extension of the principle of gift. When the Bishop Juxon tells Charles on the scaffold, "You are exchanged from a temporal to an eternal crown, a good exchange," he crowns the sequence of gift exchanges that ensure the continuity of Charles's life-principle.

I will reserve fuller study of Renaissance gift-giving for later. Here, I will simply sketch a preliminary understanding of the strange semiotics and economy of the gift to help us phrase more precisely the way Charles hoped to be memorialized. The gift, we may say, was how Charles wished to *allude* to himself. The notion that language is referential is in economic terms a market notion. A name "stands for" something as if a contract were drawn between signifier and signified. By contrast, allusion deflects direct reference: at best there exists but a mediated and uncontracted (or unnegotiated) chain of reference between names. This is what makes allusion a resource for the kind of "gifted" language we ordinarily account to the "literary." It is the allusive sign-system of gifts—of tokens that do not so much refer to "Charles" as allude to him in an unnegotiated bond of trust—that Charles attempted to invoke in his masque-like performance on the scaffold. Just as the King's behavior and setting in his last moments alluded to the universe of the masque, in short, so the gifts he dispensed were to be allusions to himself. Together, masquing and gift-giving created a self-propagating structure of memorialization designed to ensure the continuance of Charles's "I" among the spectators/receivers to whom he "presented" it.

Such, then, were Charles's efforts to extend himself—efforts we must now cut off to resume the theme of truncation and discontinuity. For in the end, I suggest, all the King's strategies for sustaining himself as a whole presence in cultural memory were indeed cut off. The terrific irony of the carefully managed death by which Charles sought continuum in this world was that he could only sustain life and wholeness at the cost of terminal fragmentariness. After all, if Charles successfully created an enduring, whole self out of the artistry of masque and gift exchange, how are we to read the fact that he was rent piecemeal by a devouring mob? Rather than given as gifts, each royal morsel, like Charles's pocketed spiced orange, was bought with hard cash.[46] Scattered all over Britain—nowhere better illustrated than in the multiple pictures representing the many relics of the King in Fea's book—Charles became truncation personified. So, too, the binding of the book of the King's "martyrdom," *Eikon Basilike* (in "a cover, coloured with his blood") and of the other book covered by "Charles the Martyr's hair, interwoven with gold and silver thread" seem mockeries of the power of the masque and gift to extend the life-principle and identity. The King who would continue in memory came to be chopped up (again we hear the rhythm of Charles's "chopping" admonition to his son) for piecemeal distribution.

But to strike the home chord of my argument: such fragmentation was ultimately also a strange manner of redemption. Each tidbit of a relic saved from Charles's execution held for its possessor a whole story—a whole paradigm, we might say—about the King (however incommensurable the story might have been with other such bric-a-brac stories). Meaning lay deep and mysterious, simultaneously secular and divine, in the iconic pieces of Charles. Each piece—a lock of his hair, a thread of his clothing, a drop of his blood—served for the faithful, superstitious, or merely curious as a window opening upon his identity. The relics of Charles, in sum, were exempla of the way Charles successfully communicated a memorable sense of whole self through shards and fragments of himself—through, that is, discontinuities that shatter any continuum. It is in such fragments no matter how "unrepresentative," therefore, that we must look to find Charles's history. Such is the rationale for my opening paradigm of Charles's execution and for the other bits and pieces of context and text I will pick up and examine in this book. I create a mosaic or collage of broken history from passages and events that are often themselves *about* the broken, the detached, or the trivial. And I use my collage to model history *as* brokenness rather than to reach back to some impossibly whole scene in the background.

To sum up my position: history is a sense of meaningful and subjective existence distributed among discrete cultural frames (family, society, politics, etc.); and it is the nature of those frames to have overlapping and sometimes contestatory boundaries marked by fragmentary "little things" that do not seem to fit in any one frame, that do not cohere around any central rule, that feel frustratingly trivial—but also somehow most important—to the "self." In our postmodern age, of course, we are especially sensitive to the fragmentary and discontinuous, to what Naomi Schor has called "detailism." As Schor explains, we experience the "pervasive valorization of the minute, the partial, and the marginal."[47] However, as exemplified by the revolutionary Independents, and more personally by Charles himself, the sense of truncated history is not an exclusively postmodern phenomenon. Indeed, in many ways the aristocracy of the English Renaissance (an age constituted from the late sixteenth to early seventeenth centuries in a world-shaking series of gaps that we call a "transitional period") lived the discontinuous, fragmentary detail more intensely than we.

From the Fragmentary to the Peripheral and Ornamental

As we have seen in Charles's execution, the cultural history of the Renaissance may be understood as fragmentariness attempting futilely to sustain a coherent identity in cultural memory. But the problematics of memory, mediated by the experience of temporality, is not the only way to approach the trivial selfhood of the English Renaissance. I will also want to draw upon spatial or synoptic modelings of fragmentariness.

One such conceptual model is the "peripheral." Fragments are to a unified sense of self, we may say, as the peripheral is to the central. What is the Renaissance self in these terms? My answer is that it is the identity whose central awareness is that it is peripheral. Like strands of Charles's hair on a book cover, the fragmentary history of the aristocratic subject is not so much a text within as a weaving *outside*. It is a sense of identity estranged from the center. Indeed, we may adopt Steven Mullaney's descriptor for the liminal place of the stage in Renaissance England: "strange."[48] The strangeness of the history of the subject is that seemingly peripheral facts or artifacts can suddenly become signs of *alternative* central meaning.

As an initial example, consider once more the clock that Charles brought along on the way to his execution. It is strange that Charles would have thought to bring a clock, an artifact that the circumstances made entirely useless and peripheral to the central event of his martyrdom. Yet the very peripherality of the clock suggests it held important meaning. The clock—and the gift Charles made of it—pointed to a central significance alternative to that of martyrdom: the drive to preserve identity in the world of the here and now that contradicted the King's desire for eternal sacrifice. This is the deeper strangeness of the clock.

Or consider a more difficult, layered case of peripherality and alternative central meaning: Charles's George, as sketched by the contemporary Hollar (fig. 5). At first glance, we would again seem to be dealing with an insignificant, peripheral artifact. Certainly the George was valuable—Herbert reported that it was "cut in an onyx with great curiosity, and set about with twenty-one fair diamonds, and the reverse set with the like number."[49] Yet it was only a trinket, a decoration, worn on the outside of Charles's person. It seems strange that Charles would have given it such moment, holding onto the jewel to the very end, and—when he did finally surrender it to Juxon—speaking the momentous word, "Remember." But the peripheral held alternative central meanings for Charles. Or more fully, if we take as central his desired martyrdom, then the complex and multiple significances focused in the case of the jewel make us see that the central was itself just one of a succession of alternative centralities.

I mean "case" here literally. To begin with, the front case of the jewel shows St. George slaying the dragon, and thus represents the values of the Order of the Garter that Charles avidly patronized: friendship, sincerity, faithfulness, peace, fidelity, Christianity, majesty, bravery.[50] These, we might say, were central to Charles because they were the virtues by which he wanted to be remembered. The masque *Coelum Britannicum* (1634) confirms the importance to him of such values linked with the Order of the Garter: in concluding upon representations of virtues like those just listed, it included "Eternity on a globe . . . bearing in his hand a serpent bent into a circle, with his tail in his mouth," about which shone stars figuring the stellified King and his fellow "heroes," and below which opened up "the prospect of Windsor Castle, the famous seat of the most honourable Order of the Garter."[51]

5. Wenceslaus Hollar's drawing of the "George" (Order of the Garter) given by Charles I to Bishop Juxon on the scaffold. Contains a portrait of Henrietta Maria, far right; front of locket, center; back, far left. Photo from Fea, ed., *Memoirs of the Martyr King,* facing p. 136.

Open the case, however, and the masculinist Garter ornament of George slaying the dragon begins to reveal a further central meaning—one linked not to the masque but to romance, and not to men-at-arms but to the women they served. Virtually every explanation of the origin of the Order of the Garter alluded to a woman. The most popular explanation had Edward III gallantly picking up a lady's garter and reproving the lascivious thoughts of bystanders with the words—which became the motto of the Order—*Honi soit qui mal y pense* (Evil be to him who thinks evil).[52] Both this legend and the myth of St. George, whose dragon-slaying exploits also served a lady, thus point to the tradition of romance. Have we here, in this originary telling, penetrated closer to Charles's central vision of himself? After all, a romance, *Cassandra,* was one of the gifts Charles dispensed before his execution (along with his clock), and during his captivity he read Spenser's *The Faerie Queene* (book 1 of which, of course, was based upon the St. George legend).[53]

Or is the association with romance—most certainly a trivial genre— only another peripherality that points to still further centers of concern? Here we come to the religious crux of Charles's vision of himself as martyr. We would do well to remember that the romance of the knight George can itself be considered only an allegory for the complex story of *Saint* George. The problems that the religious figure of George posed for Protestant England led to a system of allegorization, Roy Strong notes, that could "ascend from the struggle of a Christian against the Antichrist of Rome to that of Christ versus the Devil."[54] Nor was this all, for the allegory of St. George was itself only Charles's screen for an even more problematic, because implicitly Catholic, *image* of St. George.[55] A complex weave of issues inhered in the icon that Charles-as-martyr wore on his jewel and blazoned in his masque.

But lest we think that by penetrating successively through the Order of the Garter and romance we have at last reached a secure, central meaning in the allegory/icon of religion, we need now only gaze into the literal center of the jewel to see how undecidable centrality becomes. What is the central meaning of Charles's jewel? Just as each cover or layer of meaning is at once peripheral and an alternative central significance, I suggest, so the central meaning of the jewel is that the alternatives never settle into a stable configuration. At the jewel's heart, in the center of its (peripheral) centers, limned in the rich conventions of miniature painting, we see a face. The significance of the face is that it combines without decidable priority all the cover meanings—Order of the Garter, romance, feminine, Catholic—we have turned up. The face is that of Henrietta Maria, Charles's Catholic ladylove.

Layer within layer, then: the artifacts and ornaments that encrust the surface of history are at once peripheral and strangely central. As we will see, the Renaissance aristocrat's identity was suspended within intricate and endless regressions of artifacts (rooms in a house, miniatures, jewels, poems, masques, even meals at a banquet) each of which was pivotal precisely to the extent that it was marginal.

To come to my second synoptic model for the fragmentary history of aristocratic subjectivity, we need now only emphasize what has already been intimated above in the richly worked case of the jewel and decorative limning of Henrietta Maria: "ornamentation." In the aristocratic context, the peripheral was also that which was decorative. Strangely fragmentary and peripheral history, I suggest, is finally as trivial as the history of ornament. Or rather, history in the view I offer *is* ornament—a notion I offer for the express purpose of taking us from historical to aesthetic experience.

I mean by this a version of Angus Fletcher's concept of *kosmos,* the Greek word for ornament.[56] Fletcher's analysis takes any particular ornament—a George hung from a Garter ribbon or, to adopt a modern example, an alligator on a shirt—to be insignificantly decorative when considered by itself. It is not expressive of anything in particular. What the ornament *is* expressive of cannot be seen: the overall order or cosmos that the wearer inhabits (e.g., the upper class). Decoration, in other words, allegorizes or alludes to a world of cultural value that could not otherwise be represented *except* by means of oblique, allusive adornment. What I argue based on Fletcher's model is that we must open up the cosmos of Renaissance ornaments to reveal the great allegory of history they harbor: the "meaningfulness" of an experiencing subject whose total "meaning" is embeddedness in a culture inexpressible except in token fragments.

The ornamental urge, in sum, is one with the historical urge: the drive to be part of the cultural whole (if only a part as fragmentary and peripheral as a link in a jeweled necklace). That urge is especially marked in the plethora of trivial ornaments surrounding the aristocracy of the English Renaissance. Whenever we see a piece of such ornament—a jewel, an epic simile, any peripheral fact or artifact that merely "adorns" the center—behind it lies the historical. There is no such thing, in other words, as "pure" ornament. Pure ornament, pure aestheticism, always hangs around the bespangled neck of history; and, reciprocally, history never appears naked of ornamentation.

Charles himself, of course, dedicated most of his life to severing the relationship between ornament and history. He embraced ornament, that is, to deny history. His participation in court masques is exemplary. Collaborating with the great spectacle-man, Inigo Jones,[57] Charles essentialized masque ornament. His masques were everywhere embellished with glorious scenery, glittering costumes, decorative dance, and iconic emblems that Charles worked hard to keep "purely" ornamental. Only the antimasques with their topical references were clear evidence of a larger historicity; and they were carefully dispelled, often, as in Jonson's *Love's Triumph Through Callipolis* (1631), in a rite of purification or expiation.[58] Left at the sterilized center were Charles and Henrietta hermetically sealed with their private band of followers in an "inaccessible" mountain of adornment.[59]

Yet even for Charles it was at last not that easy to write himself into a world of purified ornament. In fact, his masques continually acknowledged the historicity of ornament even in the process of denying it. Such explains the odd proliferation of antimasques in the Caroline masque. On the one hand, the court wanted the antimasque-like qualities of history purged; on the other, it seemed impelled to create a horde of topical antimasques that kept resurfacing. Though condemned as trivial nothings—mere peripheralities—antimasques continually badgered Charles's closed, ornamental circle and demanded, if only through allusion, due recognition and action. Indeed, the extent to which they were actually a *part* of Charles's self-created and self-creating ornament is evident in their repeated and anxious evocation of his father, James. Here lies another sense in which the antimasques were historical: not only *"anti*-masques" (defined against Charles's masques) but also *"ante*-masques" (defined by a prior masque reign).

The antimasques in Charles's masques repeatedly and nervously invoked the unruly history of James's reign. In *Chloridia* (1631), for instance, the Saturnalian underground world of the antimasque smacked of the ingestive and economic (as well as possibly also sexual) incontinence of James's court. In particular, the figure of Tantalus pointed to James: "Half famished Tantalus is fallen to his fruit with that appetite as it threatens to undo the whole company of costard-mongers, and has a river afore him running excellent wine."[60] James was renowned for his excessive consumption of fruit (to the dismay of his doctors and in violation of all the medical books) as well as for overindulging in drink, especially at parties like the topsy-turvy one being described.[61] Again, James's court seems to have been the target of the "story" of *Coelum Britannicum*. Issuing a proclamation that told of the reformation of Jove for his past sins—"all the lascivious extravagancies and riotous enormities of his forepast licentious life" —the masque spoke with little indirection about the "forepast" bedroom proclivities that had governed James's political appointments: "Ganymede is forbidden the bedchamber, and must only minister in public. The gods must keep no pages nor grooms of their chamber under the age of 25, and those provided of a competent stock of beard."[62] Again and again, Charles's masques invoked and then tried to adorn with order and permanence the topical misrule of James's court.

The only way Charles could prevent the history of James's reign from intruding too strongly in his masques was at last to have his father raised literally to the status of pure art: into the rich paintings of James's rule and apotheosis by Rubens that decorated the Banqueting House ceiling. Here James was caught in ornament at the moment of being elevated from this life. Transcendentalized in art, he was safely sealed away. Yet the fact that James—and the unruly historicity his rule embodied—could only be contained by ornament *in death* makes an ironic statement about the encroaching historicity of Charles's masques. For at the very moment James was raised to "pure" ornament, Charles's masques faced their end. During the years 1636–37 all productions ceased "by reason the room where formerly they were presented having the ceiling since richly adorned with pieces of painting of great value figuring the acts of King James of happy memory, and other enrichments . . . might suffer the smoke of many lights."[63] Fearing that Rubens's art would be mortally harmed by the black smoke from masquing candles, Charles removed the remaining few masques of his reign to a hastily built, temporary building. Pure art, in other words, brought the experience not of permanence ("happy memory") but of transience and decay—and ultimately of historical process. Pure art, we may say, punched a hole in the secure Banqueting House wall and revealed the chopping block beyond.

Cultural Aesthetics

Here I arrive upon the aesthetic stage of my argument. We have seen that truly to think the aristocratic self of the age, we require a logic of the trivial that can be developed in terms of the fragment, periphery, and ornament. The last piece of this logic falls into place when we realize that in speaking of the fragmentary and peripheral *as* ornamental we are already in the realm of the special province of literary criticism: the critique of "literary" and, more broadly, aesthetic sensibility.

To put the issue succinctly: I suggest that art that seeks to purify and conserve is not so much the opposite as the uncanny double of the destructive truncating, chopping, and fragmenting of history. That is, Charles's desire to give permanence to the ornament of his masques, to collect pieces of art—to turn his own life into a piece of art—was born of the same energies of the Interregnum that anatomized or tore apart. In the most obvious sense, this is because the desire to conserve derives from a heightened awareness of mutability. But in another sense it is because to turn life into art is to take life apart and select only the fragments that are best (most beautiful, sublime, moving, disturbing, etc.). Charles's artistry of self, in this sense, is a forerunner of nineteenth-century aestheticism, which I intrude here not as an automatic recourse of literary or artistic sensibility, but as a historically specific go-between by which to think the relation/difference between the Renaissance and our present sensibility.

Walter Pater's aesthetic critic, for example (described in his collection of essays, *The Renaissance*), also takes apart in the service of self. The critic asks, "What is this song or picture, this engaging personality presented in life or in a book, to *me?*" and seeks to grasp the quintessence of his experience of the pleasurable—of the ideal, the beautiful, art for art's sake—by submitting it to the ax: "by analysing and reducing it to its elements." All things

> are valuable for their virtues, as we say, in speaking of a herb, a wine, a gem; for the property each has of affecting one with a special, a unique, impression of pleasure. Our education becomes complete in proportion as our suscepti- bility to these impressions increases in depth and variety. And the function of the aesthetic critic is to distinguish, to analyse, and separate from its adjuncts, the virtue by which a picture, a landscape, a fair personality in life or in a book, produces this special impression of beauty or pleasure, to indicate what the source of that impression is, and under what conditions it is experienced. His end is reached when he has disengaged that virtue, and noted it, as a chemist notes some natural element, for himself and others.[64]

As the above passages declare, the urge to dismember in the service of art— "to distinguish, to analyse, and separate," to "disengage"—applies to liv- ing beings and artifacts equally: to pleasing personalities "in life or in a book," Pater twice affirms. In fact, for Pater, as for Charles, life *is* art. Yet here again beauty can be lived only through a consuming anatomization by and of the subjective (born of the fractured age Pater calls "modern"). Ev- erything comes to the individual as a composite of fleeting, fragmentary impressions, the quintessence of which the seer must seize as a "relic":

> Analysis . . . assures us that those impressions of the individual mind to which, for each one of us, experience dwindles down, are in perpetual flight; that each of them is limited by time, and that as time is infinitely divisible, each of them is infinitely divisible also; all that is actual in it being a single moment, gone while we try to apprehend it, of which it may ever be more truly said that it has ceased to be than that it is. To such a tremulous wisp constantly re-forming itself on the stream, to a single sharp impression, with a sense in it, a *relic* more or less fleeting, of such moments gone by, what is real in our life fines itself down. It is with this movement, with the passage and dissolution of impressions, images, sensations, that analysis leaves off—that continual vanishing away, that strange, perpetual, weaving and unweaving of ourselves. (My emphasis)[65]

This passage could well serve as epitaph for Charles—for a monarch who sought to conserve his self in a "pure" art removed from life, from mutability, while simultaneously dispersing the self and being received in bits and pieces as a "relic." Charles's very act of writing himself, of making himself into art, involved the act of self-dismemberment. But what Charles's aestheticism did not (until too late) recognize, Pater's—at least obliquely—does. Pater's aes- thetic of good "taste,"[66] focused on fragments or peripheralities ("a herb, a wine, a gem") that somehow contain the essence of "what is real in our life," acknowledges *history*. His art for art's sake points obliquely to "The Renaissance," which titles his book. The gesture is not merely decorative. As Carolyn Williams argues, for Pater "the 'aesthetic' and the 'historicist' are mutually implicated, generated as correlative functions, and represented in the same set of figures." The result: an "aesthetic historicism," to borrow Williams's phrase, whereby the subjective experience of the Renaissance "spirit" continually revivifies an otherwise passed away or dead art.[67]

Behind "pure" art, then, or at least behind the ornamental that hopes to stay the sentence of death, the historical stands in oblique view. There are certainly many intellectual "scaffolds" or stages upon which we could set the Renaissance in order to see it as a distinct historical period. We could, for instance, place it upon the stage of intellectual history as it evolved from Enlightenment historiography through post-Hegelian *Geistesgeschichte* (the vision of the world as activated by collective Self, Spirit, or Mind) all the way to Lovejoy's Chain of Being or Tillyard's World Picture. However, the stage upon which I will at last set the Renaissance for critical appreciation will not be the "worldview" of idealist philosophy and its descendants but the correlative one of aestheticism. It is through a critical understanding of aestheticism that we can begin to think about Renaissance subjectivity—a self like a multifaceted jewel in an ornamental setting.

Charles, of course, merely tops the class of aristocratic subjects whose intense concentration upon "trivial" aesthetic forms signposts the emergence of the kind of historical subjectivity that will be my topic. During the series of transitional gaps in the late sixteenth and early seventeenth centuries, we will see, the nature of the English aristocratic "self," in both its private and public aspects, became especially problematic in ways that at last embraced other classes as well. Historical transition brought about social, political, economic, and other displacements of aristocratic "place" that destabilized the self in its delicate balance between private and public presence and fomented the need for a renegotiation of the meaning of selfhood. The aristocratic self needed to be reinvented to claim a new position able to overcome marginality by making marginality one with cultural centrality. And it was the play of ornaments swirling all around the aristocratic self that marked the parameters of the conflict. The Elizabethan and Jacobean aristocracy occupied the uneasy interface between the historical and the aesthetic, the central and the peripheral, the unified and the fragmentary. They lived the practice of social ornament.

In the following chapters, I detail the cultural aesthetics of the Renaissance according to an itinerary of topics illustrating the aristocracy's richly ornamental ambience and the discontinuous development of trivial subjectivity within that ambience. Our shifting story will modulate between historical fact and aesthetic artifact: between such "practical" ornaments (as they might be called) as detachable living spaces, dispensable gifts, expendable children, and insubstantial or "airy" foodstuffs and such artistic decorations as pretty trinkets, bejewelled miniatures, conceited banquets, and "toyish" or "gifted" poetry. Ultimately, such modulation should be heard as a single, historical/aesthetic note. That note rings distinctly in the genre upon which I close this book: the Jacobean masque, an ornamental but also highly topical and historically situated genre providing one of our best arenas for observing the trivial details of cultural aesthetics.

The way to the masque will be diverse. In chapter 2, I will first of all create a background for my overall argument about subjectivity: collectivity. The chapter studies the processes of cultural exchange that fostered a sense of Elizabethan social solidarity or common (rather than subjective) identity. "Foster" is descriptive. To trace the essential lineaments of Elizabethan social exchange, I observe the culture of "giving" as epitomized in the fostering of children; and I match such fostering to an aestheticization of the spirit of the gift, Spenser's *Faerie Queene*. As we will see, Elizabethan gifts—even if they were children or epic romances—were trivial. But they were also crucial to the creation and expression of an ideal commonality or grand "we."

It is against the backdrop of Elizabethan collectivity that in chapter 3 we can see a characteristic temper of subjectivity emerging. The "I" arose amid the flux of exchangeable cultural and aesthetic trivialities expressive of the "we," but did so in such a way that it at once incorporated and divested itself of the feeling of solidarity. On the one hand, it faced outward with a full sense of itself as public figure; on the other, it looked inward "secretly" into ever more hidden recesses of private identity. By studying such fancy ornamental gifts as the miniatures of Nicholas Hilliard and the sonnets of Sir Philip Sidney, I will argue that the subjectivity that formed within the collective cosmos of Elizabethan cultural exchange was deeply divided between public and private sensibilities. It wished at once to exist in exchange with others and to bar all exchange capable of unlocking its closed miniature or sonnet of meaning—an experience of self-splitting, as we will see, both like and crucially unlike our modern sense of self.

What happened when the private self attempted to break away completely from the public self that still faced outward to the collective world of cultural exchange? It is here that I come to the masque. Chapter 4 looks into the reign of James to view the ultra-fragmentary, -peripheral, and -decorative ornaments of masques and their associated banqueting houses (both filled with tidbits of sugar-spun conceits). Here we will recognize that the result of the threatened split between public and private selves was the "void." The delicious art forms I sample demonstrate vividly that the self, as if making a chocolate mold of privacy, at last hollows itself out. Public and private selves were both facades for a detached particle of nothingness, a truly alien or existentially alienated self, lurking within.

Chapter 5, my conclusion, then continues the study of the masque form in order to reflect on the relation between history and aesthetics. Employing the model of strange or foreign trade (specifically the alien trade of the East India Company), the chapter proposes a model of history and subjectivity that is also literary. Here I will broach a notion of literary reference—implicit in all my discussion of fragmentary, peripheral, or ornamental history—as "oblique topicality." Subjectivity, we may say, is a self-reference generated from oblique references to history—as if the self stood before a mirror to see both itself and (straining to look past or around its image) the world over its shoulder.

Addendum. If I were to write as an intellectual historian dedicated to a continuous model of history, I might summarize my argument thus: *Cultural Aesthetics* is the history of the rise of the "self" in English Renaissance aesthetics, particularly as such aesthetics arose alongside economics, politics, and other cultural phenomena from an underlying cause that . . .—but I truncate this.

2

Exchanging Gifts: The Elizabethan Currency of Children and Romance

> from your selfe I doe this vertue bring,
> And to your selfe doe it returne againe:
> So from the Ocean all riuers spring,
> And tribute backe repay as to their King.
> Right so from you all goodly vertues well
> Into the rest, which round about you ring,
> Faire Lords and Ladies, which about you dwell,
> And doe adorne your Court, where courtesies excell.[1]

In the proem to book 6 of *The Faerie Queene,* Spenser inaugurates his book's virtue, courtesy, by imagining an intimate exchange of gifts between "I" and "your selfe," poet and Queen Elizabeth. The closed circuit of prestation, however, soon opens up through figuration ("So") to reveal a cosmic cycle of reciprocity between the ocean and its tributary rivers—a rain cycle that in its turn flows through further figuration ("Right so") into what might be called the social "reign cycle": the "ring" of lords and ladies centered on the Queen. The proem thus creates from the act of exchange a whole *kosmos*—physical, social, and at last also *ornamental*. Embodied in the "Faire Lords and Ladies," "courtesies" "doe adorne" the "Court."

Cosmic exchange is then recapitulated later in book 6 in another episode peripheral to the plot: Mount Acidale in canto 10. There the Graces who "adorne" Venus (st. 21)—and most especially the three Graces or "daugh-

ters of delight" (15)—dance round an unnamed, crowned maid. The dance
is an intimate act of reciprocal exchange: the three Graces (whose motto in
the episode is that "good should from vs goe, then come in greater store"
[24]) "graced [the maid] so much to be another Grace" (26). But again, the
episode goes on to expand this intimate round outward into a fully public
circle of giving. Generalizing, the poet declares that the three Graces "on
men all gracious gifts bestow" (23); emphasizing the social and political
parameters of this universe of grace, he ends by laying the whole scene of
prestation at the feet of the Fairy Queen (28). Once more, then: a whole
cosmos of courteous exchange. And once more, the cosmos is all ornament.
The maid around whom the Graces dance is a "precious gemme" set
"Amidst a ring most richly well enchaced" (12); and the general population
to whom the Graces bring their gifts is "decked" in body and "adorned" in
mind (23). The ideal *court*-esy, or "Ciuility," of Queen Elizabeth becomes a
cosmic and ornamental ring of gifts generating ever "greater store" (23, 24).

We will need to reserve a place in the next chapter for the "gemme" of
unnameable intimacy at the center of the Elizabethan cosmos of ornamental exchange. Here we need to recreate the setting for such precious
identity. That is, we need to trace the Elizabethan expanded identity or collective cultural surround as it was constructed in a ring of ornamental
exchange akin to that of Spenser's Graces.[2] I refer to the seminal give-and-
take that engendered aristocratic society through a circulation of the minor
artifacts, creatures, and ideas that were the body politic's "daughters of delight" (to use Spenser's epithet for the Graces): its *children,* literal and
poetic. Specifically, my concern is with the practice and aesthetics of child
gifts: the exchange or "presentation" of minor children (implying by
"minor" also conceptual triviality) under the matronage of Queen Elizabeth and the *re*presentation of such exchange in the "first seminarie" of the
Garden of Adonis in *The Faerie Queene* (3.6.30). What is at stake here in
both context and text is a cultural fiction: the ability of trivial, fragmentary,
peripheral, or ornamental experience—what I have suggested is the constitutive basis of history—to foster the ideal commonality. In examining
such fiction, we can for the moment be kind. Our concern is not with the
way gift exchange did or did not "actually" create commonality, but rather
with the way Elizabethans were able to fictionalize such exchange, to turn
it into a practice and discourse charged with the task of securing culture.
Any suspicions we may have about the efficacy of the fiction can be deferred
(or at least not foregrounded) until chapters 4 and 5, where we will turn to
the reign of James and a different, darker side of gift exchange.

My particular thesis, then, is twofold. First, Elizabethan aristocratic society created itself in great part by transcending fragmentary experience through an imaginative re-creation of its practice of exchanging trivial things (especially children). But second, faith in a unitary society required that legitimate exchange repress divisive otherness. As we will see, the system of gift exchange helped the aristocracy subdue the broken and peripheral divisions of culture it called foreign, primitive, childish, *Irish*. The overall result was a specifically English fiction of culture-as-gift that sanitized the other at its margins, that made the other seem merely alien rather than a part of the peripheral and fragmented Elizabethan polity itself. Thus was England's public identity graced with "civility."

But we cannot fully understand the cultural and poetic gifts of Elizabethan civilization, nor its negotiations with the alien, until we recover the primitive gift embedded within civility.

The Ring of Gift

I receive as my pattern—or *donnée*—the Kula ring. The Kula ring's application to my historical and poetic concerns, however suggestive, will be inexact. But the Kula has the advantage of having been studied to such an extent that the main lineaments of the cultural fact I bring to bear on the Elizabethan state and on Spenser's poetry will stand out starkly.[3]

The gifts of the Kula ring, an exchange carried on by tribes in a circle of Pacific islands, are primarily of two kinds: red shell necklaces and white shell bracelets. As figure 6 illustrates, these trinkets circulate in opposite directions from island group to island group in a wide orbit. Along this route (complemented by the orbits-within-orbits of an intratribal form of Kula), red shell necklaces always move clockwise and white shell bracelets always move counterclockwise. As Bronislaw Malinowski visualized it: imagine a participant turned toward the center of the ring; "he receives the arm-shells with his left hand, and the necklaces with his right, and then hands them both on. In other words, he constantly passes the arm-shells from left to right, and the necklaces from right to left."[4]

The essential feature of such circular exchange is that it is a systematic expression of what Marcel Mauss analyzed as the three ethical coordinates of the spirit of the gift: the obligations to give, to receive, and to repay.[5] Each of these is a distinct obligation, and yet each implies the others in a regulated progression whose outcome is the complete circulation of the gift. To have is to be obliged to give. In the Kula social code, as Malinowski puts it, "to possess is to give. . . . A man who owns a thing is naturally

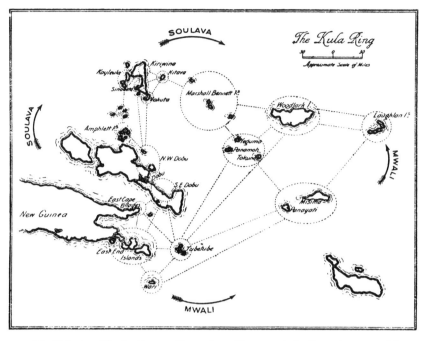

6. The Kula ring. "Soulava" are necklaces; "mwali" are armshells. From *Argonauts of the Western Pacific* by Bronislaw Malinowski.

expected to share it, to distribute it, to be its trustee and dispenser. And the higher the rank the greater the obligation."[6] Second, to be given a gift is to be obliged to receive. That is, reception of the gift in such a system is in itself an obligation tantamount to the original donation. Finally, to receive is to be obliged to give back. In a reciprocal exchange between two parties, for example (a model we will soon need to broaden), a gift must be not only accepted but also repaid with an equivalent gift, or else the giver incurs insult and the receiver loses face. The extreme interdependence of such giving and receiving in gift economies appears clearly in the Toaripi and Namau languages (the former Papuan, the latter Melanesian), which have "only a single word to cover buy and sell, borrow and lend."[7]

Ultimately, such a system of ethical regulations propels the gift in a process of *circulation,* rather than simply of tidal flux between two parties, because it enmeshes two-party exchange within the chain of exchanges that is the whole society and, indeed, cosmos (insofar as nature itself is person-

ified as gift partner). This is possible because the final step of exchange—
repayment—is not necessarily directed toward the original donor. The obligation of reciprocation can be fulfilled by passing on a gift one has
received to a third party. This can be well seen in a parallel to the Kula, the
hunting customs of the New Zealand Maori. After hunting birds in the
forest, the Maori give a portion of their kill to the priests, who eat part of
the catch and then prepare a talisman that, placed in the forest, "causes
birds to be abundant . . . , that they may be slain and taken by man."[8] This
is a three-party cycle of exchange in which repayment takes the form of
passing on the gift: the forest gives to the hunters, who give to the priests,
who in turn (translating the original gift into artifact) complete the cycle
by giving back again to the forest. The gifts of the Kula or Maori thus circulate expansively and ceaselessly. "They never stop," Malinowski says, "it is
the fact . . . that no one ever keeps any of the Kula valuables for any length
of time." In essence, Mauss adds, the gift received "is at the same time property and a possession, a pledge and a loan, an object sold and an object
bought, a deposit, a mandate, a trust; for it is given only on condition that it
will be used on behalf of, or transmitted to, a third person."[9]

By this system of gift exchange, human society arises as the alternative to
the submerged genesis of gift: the state of war. In the state of war (which,
Marshall Sahlins points out, is the Hobbesian foundation of Mauss's concept of the gift), every man is potentially an enemy. But enemies can be
converted into friends by means of gifts such that, for example, the overseas
Kula partner becomes a "patron and ally in a land of danger and insecuri-
ty."[10] Gift exchange, in other words, marks what is essentially a grand,
imaginative leap from violence between enemies to an otherwise unimagin-
able peace. The threat of war is contained. Though never wholly van-
quished or made invisible, its antagonisms are sublimated into the energies
attendant upon the decorous handling of the gift. Failure to give, accept, or
repay, Mauss suggests, now subsumes antagonism to such an extent that it
becomes in itself "the equivalent of a declaration of war; it is a refusal of
friendship and intercourse." The threat of war, that is, becomes no more
than the fear always latent in gift exchange: worry, for instance, over
whether one can adequately reciprocate the gift received, whether one will
be equally repaid for the gift given, or whether one will win the best gift
partner.[11] The hostilities of warfare, indeed, are literally buried within the
ceremonies of the gift in the form of mock violence, magical spells, and
pointed language. One term, for instance, for the Kula return gift—
kudu—means "the tooth which bites, severs and liberates."[12] In part as an

expression of these tensions, and as a reaction against the pressures of obligation, givers in the Kula will belittle the return gift and fiercely throw it on the ground. "Pains are taken to show one's freedom and autonomy as well as one's magnanimity," Mauss notes.[13]

Ultimately, such ritualized self-interest and antagonism displace not only physical warfare but its economic embodiment, the competitive money market. A strictly economic market (a topic I return to in later chapters) voices the suspicion and rivalry of war: it demands immediate exchange as well as open bargaining and weighed values. On the contrary, gift exchange transmits the trust and generosity of friendship: the gift obligates delayed reciprocation and free giving, without ever negotiating terms or values.[14]

Instead of war or competition, then, there arises trust and its greatest source, the spirit of generosity. And instead of death—of which war is the collective perpetuation—there arises life. In fact, the "spirit" of the gift ethic of generosity is just that: a spiritual as much as ethical force, a life force that should remind us that "generosity" is rooted in the Latin *genere,* meaning "to beget" or "to produce." Invariably, Hyde affirms, "either the bearers of the gift or the gift itself grows as a result of its circulation."[15] In the Kula, the cycle of generous exchange begets an increase of vitalism both in the fellowship of gift partners and in the gifts themselves: armshells and necklaces accumulate names, personalities, and magical powers. The Maori ring of gift, which embraces both nature and human society, similarly reaps an increase of generosity by regenerating what would otherwise be consumed by the hunters of birds: the forest *hau* (its "spirit" or "fecundity").[16] Death—not only of the birds and forest but also, by implication, of the society built around the forest—is contained: "The gift and its bearers share a spirit which is kept alive by its motion among them, and which in turn keeps them both alive."[17]

Epitomizing the ability of gifts to subsume death is the first of the three gift obligations: free, unnegotiated giving. By freely giving up the gift, the giver always experiences a kind of death. The gift, in essence, dies to him when it departs from his hands; and since a part of him is invested in the gift (he gives his trust in giving his gift), a part of him dies as well. But the paradox of gift exchange is that such death or loss actually begets greater life in the increased value attached to the gift and in increased good feeling between gift participants. In fact, Hyde argues, because gifts chronicle simultaneously a kind of death and a kind of new life, they are frequently exchanged at liminal moments in human lives, times of transformation such as births, marriages, and (as in the case of Charles I) deaths:

It might be said that the gifts we give at times of transformation are meant to make visible the giving up we do invisibly. And of course we hope that there will be an exchange, that something will come toward us if we abandon our old lives. So we might also say that the tokens we receive at times of change are meant to make visible life's reciprocation. They are not mere compensation for what is lost, but the promise of what lies ahead. They guide us toward new life, assuring our passage away from what is dying.[18]

The gift, in sum, ensures peace in the face of war, trust in the face of fear, life in the face of death. Nor is the cost freedom or individuality. The self asserts itself in gift-giving through the lack of declared rules and the ceremonial expression of personal aggression and self-interest.[19] Nevertheless, the gift participant only gains liberty and identity through bondage to a larger body that dilates and mingles selves. Through the generosity and trust required by gift-giving, a sociable merging of personalities occurs, which is reflected in the language describing the gifts exchanged. "When two of the opposite valuables meet in the Kula and are exchanged," Malinowski observes, "it is said that these two have married. The armshells are conceived as a female principle, and the necklaces as the male."[20]

The confusion here of objects, values, contracts, and sexes (establishing the further etymological link between "generosity" and "gender") characterizes all systems of gift. For the gift ring is a complete cultural experience (what Mauss calls "total prestation") that through the act of donation at once generates, expresses, and contains every aspect of the community: economic, legal, social, political, religious, and—not the least—aesthetic.[21]

Indeed, we would do well to close our view of the Kula ring by highlighting aesthetics: emphatically, the necklaces and bracelets that articulate total cultural prestation are *ornamental*. We might think here of the etymological link between "decorate" and "decorum."[22] The Kula ring is an elaborate decorum or ceremony in which prestation regenerates the cosmos of culture as a decorative pattern—a sort of gigantic necklace or bracelet linking all the tribes. Seemingly removed from the realms of the useful or practical, the decorous and decorative instill a value in Kula ornaments that a Western sensibility would call art.[23] Or rather, the artful cosmos of gift is not ignorant of the more utilitarian exchanges—including economics—necessary to any culture. Prestation or presentation discriminates itself from the utilitarian for the purpose of *framing* it (as in a painting) and thus of re-presenting it in a revisionary manner. As Malinowski notes, Kula participants sharply distinguish gift exchange from a form of barter, *gimwali*, that takes place on the same expeditions where Kula gifts are circulated.

"Often, when criticising an incorrect, too hasty, or indecorous procedure of Kula, they will say: 'He conducts his Kula as if it were *gimwali*'."[24] Such distinction creates a "framework" of decorum within which to represent the indecorous. As Malinowski came finally to realize, "in the *kula* the most important economic fact is that the nonutilitarian exchange of valuables provides the driving force and the ceremonial framework for an extremely important system of utilitarian trade."[25]

Through the Kula, to invoke Pierre Bourdieu's description of archaic societies, living is thus "raised to the level of an art for art's sake" distinguished from "self-evident realities such as the 'business is business' or 'time is money' on which the unaesthetic life-style of the *harried leisure classes* in so-called advanced societies is based."[26]

The Ring of Elizabeth

With the Kula ring given to us by the anthropologists in hand—not as a model whose precise shape we are contracted to follow, but as itself simply an initial gift to be passed on with new and surprising variation—I present the total prestation of Elizabethan society and its greatest example, "fosterage" or "placing out": the exchange of children.[27] Elizabethan children were the human equivalent to Kula gift trinkets (and, as we will see, Elizabethan gift trinkets as well). They were little, peripheral, detached, and—though initially unformed or even ugly—ornamental.

In multiple ways, children were peripheral to, or detached from, the practical adult world. To begin with, as Lawrence Stone notes, infants were considered essentially inhuman: "smelly and unformed little animals lacking the capacity to reason." Even as they matured—and despite growing attention given to them in the late sixteenth century—children were treated much as domestic pets. On the one hand, they were affectionately coddled as pet-like "playthings, toys to divert the mind," and, on the other, they were directly equated with animals in need of strict training, to be "broken in just as one would break in a puppy, a foal or a hawk." Even when serving a utilitarian role, aristocratic children remained outside their to-be-assumed societal position: they were servants. Aristocratic children served the daily meals to their parents and other adults, standing silent—as a kind of ornamental border—at the edges of the dinner table. Finally, children were peripheral or marginal in their ephemerality. Indeed, the extraordinarily high death rate of children made them in a literal sense "expendables." The child, in Philippe Ariès's summation, "was such an unimportant thing, so inadequately involved in life."[28]

What we shall trace is the way gift exchange fashioned these living trivialities into meaning-filled ornaments as valuable as jewels. Faced with the child's disconnection or detachment from civilized society, the Renaissance made of the child a kind of aesthetic artifact whose very detachedness *in the form of circulation* rendered it immensely precious: each exchanged child became a link in a grand circle or necklace of culture signifying the very status of society as civil. Exchangeable children were prized ornaments that—like the personified trinkets of the Kula ring—performed a generative cultural function.

But we will need to make a crucial variation from the Kula in elucidating the aesthetic of Elizabethan child exchange. That variation will be to mark the nationalization of what in its "primitive" roots was a tribal and sept concept. By this I mean that the English *nation* at the time of Elizabeth constituted itself not as something akin to septs in a "primitive" culture, but as precisely the "civilized" state that suppressed what it saw to be the merely primitive—and especially *Irish*—practice of total prestation. As in the bridling of the child's animal or aboriginal nature, that is, the English nation sought to suppress the cultural earliness it saw in the Irish. We must thus observe not only the English system of child exchange but the repression within that system of its uncanny look-alike, the "barbaric" Irish system of child exchange.

I nominate as the centerpiece of English prestation the Kula ring of actual child exchange between five English families and the Elizabethan court. I select these aristocratic families in particular because at least two of them, as we will see, were patrons of Spenser: the Manners (earls of Rutland), the Russells (earls of Bedford), the Hastings (earls of Huntingdon), the Herberts (earls of Pembroke), and the Sidneys (knights). The ring of child exchange between these five families and the court is not perfect (there is an indirect link, for instance, between the Pembroke and Sidney families), but the essential circularity is clear.

As mapped in figure 7, the route of exchange was one in which individual children (tracked by my arrows) flowed to other families to fill what were in essence vacancies created by the prior transmission of children—the whole system comprising a sort of cascade of children, one after the other, in series.[29] Entering the circle of exchange at the point of its intersection with the court, we observe that circa 1590 Queen Elizabeth's Court of Wards gave the wardship of Robert Tyrrwhit to the countess of Rutland. The latter countess had in 1588 given away her own daughter (eleven-year-old Bridget Manners) to the Bedfords. The heir of the Bedfords, thirteen-

year-old Edward Russell, had in 1585 himself been given away to the Huntingdons (so, too, William Russell's daughter, Katherine, had been given to
the Huntingdons in the 1560s). And the Huntingdons themselves—a family constantly taking and giving children—had sometime after 1577 given
away one of their charges (the earl of Rutland's sister) to the Pembroke family. The first four links in our circle, then, are a perfect match.

To trace the next link, however, requires that we describe a different sort

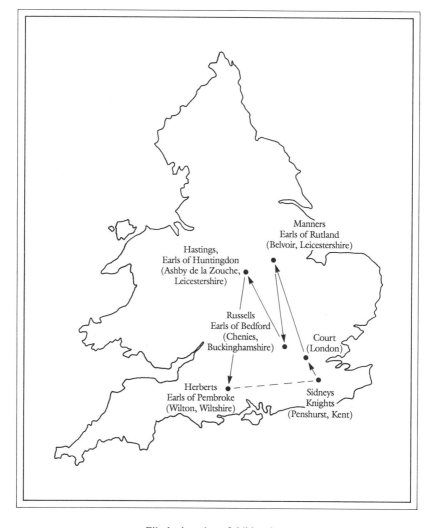

7. Elizabethan ring of child exchange.

of exchange—though one sufficiently related to carry my point. The Pembrokes had not, so far as I can find, earlier given away a child of their own. But they had allied themselves to the Sidney clan when, in 1577, Mary Sidney had been given to Pembroke in marriage. Of course, however young the bride was (then only sixteen), such exchange was not formally an instance of child-giving. But the exchange of Mary Sidney had much the same significance because the marriage system was the larger system of exchange within which child gifts operated. The relatedness of youthful marriage and child exchange is confirmed when we then move past the Sidneys on our map to close the total child-gift circle. At the age of fourteen (in 1575), Mary Sidney had herself been a child-gift of the Sidneys to court.[30]

In essence: the Kula ring. Virtually all the important features of the Kula appear in the above circle of children and the widespread system of fosterage it exemplifies. First, we can stress that the English Kula was indeed a circle of exchange even though in this particular culture, as opposed to the actual Kula, the circle had a center: Elizabeth. Indeed, Elizabeth's centrality in what may be conceived as English "centripetal" child-giving seemed to encourage rather than diminish free circulation. Consider, for example, that the Queen's participation tended to be just the climax of a process in which an individual child passed through two or more stages of exchange. Penelope Devereux was circulated in this way: as a thirteen-year-old, she was bequeathed by her father to the Huntingdons, raised by the countess of Huntingdon until the age of eighteen, and only then given as Maid of Honor to Elizabeth. Bridget Manners was similarly circulated before ending up in court. Given by her mother, the countess of Rutland, to the Bedfords, Bridget was kept by the Bedford countess until the age of twelve and then passed along to the Queen as Maid of Honor. "Her Majestie acknowledgeth she hath cause to thanck you for her," the Queen's representative wrote to Rutland.[31] The Queen's commendation to Rutland here, we may say, completes the circle of exchange because it was itself a kind of gift.

Tangent to such child-gift circles centered on the Queen (some themselves tangent to the larger orbit I mapped in fig. 7) were more limited spin-offs or epicycles of child-giving. Thus, for example, the Rutland-Bedford-Elizabeth exchange described above intersected with another gift circle—restricted but intense—located in the reciprocal giving of children between just the Bedfords and the court. The second earl of Bedford gave his daughter Anne in service to Elizabeth (probably in the early 1560s) "when she was very young." Then in 1570, as if in exchange, there returned to Bedford from court—at the express command of Elizabeth— the wardship of the eleven-year-old George Clifford. Later still, as if in reciprocation, the Bedfords gave more children to the Queen: Elizabeth and Ann, the granddaughters of Bedford, who were placed as Maids of Honor in attendance upon Elizabeth circa 1590.[32] As "natural mother" of both her maids and wards, in sum, Elizabeth was the center of aristocratic child-gift circles;[33] yet the center did not at all inhibit the capillary circulation of children in extensive circles-upon-circles.

Second, the role of wardships in Elizabethan child exchange demonstrates particularly well another resemblance to the Kula: the imaginative use of gift circulation to substitute human society—*culture*—for the state of war. Wardships were microcosms of court-centered child rings since they always involved a three-party exchange, with the court acting as second or central partner. On the death of the head of a family, the dependent minor would be given to the Court of Wards, which would then give the child to a third party, which in turn (at least theoretically) returned the child at its coming of age to the parent family. The two wardships included in the circle of families in fig. 7 show that families entered into wardships much like Kula gift partners reaching out to hostile lands: in the hope of rising above war. The countess of Rutland requested the wardship of Robert Tyrrwhit in order to marry Tyrrwhit to her daughter, Bridget, and so end a feud between the Rutland and Tyrrwhit families. And Queen Elizabeth had the same idea in mind for the Clifford ward, the heir of one of the northern Catholic earls (Cumberland) who rebelled against her. Indeed, by awarding to Bedford the Clifford boy (who subsequently married one of Bedford's daughters), Elizabeth drew the Cliffords not only into the three-party exchange of wardship but into the entire society of child-giving we saw in fig. 7, a Protestant circle loyally centered on Elizabeth's court.[34] As if acknowledging that Elizabeth's gift of the ward displaced inclinations to war or rebellion, Clifford's mother then generously supplemented with a further gift the allowance she paid Bedford for maintaining her boy.[35]

Such generosity invested in wardship suppressed warfare in its form of competitive economics as well. Of course, as the great taker and giver of children, the Court of Wards was in reality a business operation by which children were bought and sold for profit. Yet Elizabeth, through Burghley (master of the wards, 1561–98), deliberately resisted market values. Prices were kept exceedingly low so that the granting of a wardship as well as the many ritual steps involved in obtaining the ward remained tied to the heart of court patronage: the gift. Burghley emphasized the gift spirit of generosity by receiving into his own household at least eight crown wards of the aristocracy whose education he carefully supervised for no financial profit. In the final analysis, it was this spirit of generosity, not mercenary or financial motives, that contemporaries imaginatively foregrounded.[36]

Indeed, the language and spirit of generosity repeatedly surfaced in the giving of children, whether the children were given as wards, Maids of Honor, servants, relatives, or family friends. Lady Hoby, for example (herself at an early age given by her parents to the Huntingdons), reported in her diary that a "Mistress Bell" came "to *offer* me the saruice of one of hir Daughters," and that her "Cossine Gates" brought her his thirteen-year-old daughter, "who, as he saied, he *freely gaue* me" (my emphases). As late as the eighteenth century, Roger Sydenham readily gave the gift of his thirteen-year-old son when a wealthy relative appeared at his door, requesting, "Roger, will you give me your elder son? You have three sons. I fear mine will be dead before I get home. Give him to me fresh and part with him willingly, and I will take good care of him." Facing his own death in 1572, Alderman William Carre similarly invoked the generosity of the gift, particularly emphasizing that the gift-child was something freely passed along. He bequeathed his six children to six different relatives, desiring that "etche of them will be so good as to take one of my childer . . . to whom I will gyve them as frelye as God haith sente or geaven them to me."[37]

In the same spirit, the earl of Essex in 1576 bequeathed his son Robert to Burghley, "Master of the Wardes":

> uppon the assured Confidence that your love to me shall dissend to my Childrenne, and that your Lordship will declare yourself a Friend to me, both alive and dead, I have willed *Mr Waterhouse* to shew unto you how you may with Honor and Equity do good to my Sonne *Hereford,* and how to bind him with perpetual Frendship to you and to your House. And to the Ende I would have his Love towardes those which are dissended from you spring up and increase with his Yeares, I have wished his Education to be in your Household, tho' the same had not bene allotted to your Lordship as Master of the Wardes.[38]

The assurance with which Essex bequeathed his son to Burghley is rooted in the ethic of gift, which obliges the recipient to accept the gift offered. By accepting the gesture and freely repaying it with Robert's education, Burghley as well as Essex reaped the "increase" of generosity—the "Confidence," "Love," and "perpetual Frendship"—that would "bind" their houses together.

Given the explicitly generous ethic of Elizabethan child exchange, then, a third major resemblance to the Kula ring emerges. As in the Kula, the design of English child-giving was ultimately to elevate generosity into what may be called a *spiritual* fact. In freely giving children, that is, the English aristocracy generated social bonds that communicated a mystical force seeming to sustain life even in the face of death. Death was everywhere in the child ring we traced in fig. 7. It was on the death of her husband, for instance, that the countess of Rutland gave away her daughter Bridget to the Bedfords. Again, death—of the father in a border skirmish with the Scots—impelled the Bedfords to give their boy Edward Russell to the Huntingdons.[39] And, of course, death always triggered child-giving in the case of such wardships as those of Tyrrwhit and Clifford. It was such unsparing and pervasive death that the giving of children denied. Through the spirit of generosity evoked by giving his son to Burghley, Essex on the threshold of his own death seemed to achieve continued life: "your Lordship," he said to Burghley, "will declare yourself a Friend to me, both alive and dead." The wealthy relative who asked Roger Sydenham for his elder son thought the same way: given "fresh" and "willingly," the boy would compensate for his own child, dying. Though children themselves were mortal—indeed, the most ephemeral of all—the very dispensability that allowed them to be circulated as gifts promised life.

The single most telling demonstration I have found of the life-giving spirit of generosity in Elizabethan child exchange (projected in defiance of all political "realities") is a letter written by Queen Elizabeth to Sir Henry Sidney in 1575. In her double capacity as foster mother and Queen, Elizabeth wrote to console Sidney for the death of his youngest child, Ambrosia, and to offer in compensation to receive into service his yet-living daughter, Mary (thus inviting the completion of the family circle in fig. 7). The Queen opens her letter by affirming her trust that "Good Sidney" will bear his losses as acts of God, "which He hath lately showed by taking unto Him from your company a daughter of yours," and she assures Sidney, "we would not have you ignorant (to ease your sorrow as much as may be) how we take part of your grief upon us." She then offers to receive into her care Sidney's daughter, Mary:

> He hath yet left unto you the comfort of one daughter of very good hope, whom, if you shall think good to remove from those parts of unpleasant air (if it be so) into better in these parts, and will send her unto us before Easter, or when you shall think good, assure yourself that we will have a special care of her, not doubting but as you are well persuaded of our favour toward yourself, so will we make further demonstration thereof in her, if you will send her unto us.
> And so comforting you for the one, and leaving this our offer of our good-

will to your own consideration for the other, we commit you to Almighty God.[40]

Like all gift exchange, the transaction proposed in this letter blurs donation and reception: the gift given invokes the gift returned. Elizabeth asks to be given something, a request underscored by her repetition, "if you . . . will send her unto us . . . if you will send her unto us." But she simultaneously reciprocates with the "offer of our goodwill," which she will "make further demonstration thereof in [Sidney's daughter, Mary], if you will send her unto us." The confusion here of taking and giving makes it impossible to say who is the donor and who the recipient; as in the "marriage" of Kula artifacts, these roles are exchanged. Yet the confused give-and-take is what engenders feelings of good fellowship and surmounts the death of the child Ambrosia. Whereas God took absolutely, Elizabeth's taking is a giving. And in requesting rather than demanding the child Mary (thus granting Sidney the dignity of independence), Elizabeth allows Sidney's giving to be a taking as well: she gives him the chance to reap the heartwarming communion that comes with free giving. Any objection that such free giving is merely illusion misses the point, which lies precisely in the fostering of the illusion—call it "fiction"—of generous exchange. In such imaginative exchange, the taking of Mary as an expendable child "of very good hope" by Elizabeth results not in a loss (as when God "takes" Ambrosia) but in the very real increase of social bonding demonstrated in Mary as gift-child.

Such, then, is the total prestation of Elizabethan culture as epitomized in child exchange. We can complete our comparison to total prestation in the Kula by noticing one further facet of English child-giving: it was essentially *ornamental*. Exchangeable children were pretty trifles analogous to the personified (and named) ornaments of the Kula ring. In the process of exchange, that is, the role of children was to be "little," "toy-like," "pretty," "trivial," and yet also socially "precious." Sir Humphrey Radcliffe, for example, gave away his child precisely as if she were an ornament to be passed along with others on New Year's Day, 1561. He "brought forward his daughter Mary and laughingly presented her as a New Year's gift. Elizabeth, being in high good humour, replied graciously that she would take Mary to be one of her Maids of Honour." Radcliffe's child was thus added to the disjointed pile of personalized and inventive New Year's gifts given to Elizabeth in place of the traditional sums of gold.[41]

The key to understanding such exchanges is to realize that however metaphorical the notion of child-as-trinket, it was also substantively meaning-ful. Children given up to the fosterage system were the crowning instance of the precious, beautiful, and multifarious bric-a-brac circulating through the general network of Elizabethan gift-giving. Child-giving, for example, epitomizes the manner in which Elizabethan gift trinkets of all sorts were received at one gift-giving occasion—especially New Year's (the most important of the many gift days fostered by Elizabeth and the one tradi-tionally linked to children)—only to be passed on at yet another gift celebration.[42] Child-giving also sums up the complex manner in which many Elizabethan gifts and ornaments circulated both horizontally be-tween social equals and hierarchically between patron and client (the latter in the system of patronage or, more accurately in this case, matronage).[43] Seen in overview, that is, child-giving put the seal on the whole cosmos of trifling exchanges constitutive of Elizabethan culture—a social cosmos that at its extreme could even be seen to wear for adornment not just neck-laces and bracelets but titles, money, land, or prestige. In a sense, all such precious stuffs were ornaments precisely to the extent that they were "cul-tural" rather than only economic or political; all were exchangeable badges of distinction that manifested their transutilitarian value in being passed along to others in a seemingly offhand, free, or "generous" gesture.

Born in unformed animality, we may thus say, children were trifles whose circulation "finished" them in the way an artwork is finished. Through circulation, the child underwent a translation from mere trifle to polished ornament—from being peripheral, detached, and primitive to being central, connected, and cultivated. In short, the child acquired "civil-ity." And the ultimate reward of such civility, to be shown off as proudly as some brilliant jewel on a necklace, was the luster of civility it conferred on adult society itself. Passing children (like other precious artifacts) from fam-ily to family was one of the means by which primitiveness in Elizabethan adults—their aggression and instinct for war—was suppressed. It was the aristocracy as a whole that was "finished" in brilliant civility.

The Threat of the Irish

But the jewel of English civility had a flaw: the Irish. Here I diverge from the model of the Kula to place in play the other half of my thesis. Another way to say that England was in its own eyes a civilized country is to observe that it was determined *not* to be barbaric, primitive, or savage. England, that is, could embody but not *define* itself as a Kula-like system of gift whose universality was such that it potentially embraced all cultures without distinction between the high and the low, the "civilized" and the "primitive," *the English and the Irish*. Just as the English had to suppress the animality of their children (beating them into ornaments as socially acceptable as the jeweled whip Sidney gave Elizabeth for New Year's),[44] so too they had to put down what they saw as the barbarism of Irish child exchange, which seemed tantamount to rebellion. It was repression of Irish child-giving, we will see, that helped the English foster their own sense of "culture" as opposed to wild "nature"—a complex process of repression that activated the specter of war within the spirit of gift.[45]

Fosterage, we observe, was even more dominant in Ireland than in England. Voicing the contemporary preoccupation with Irish fosterage, Sir John Davies declared: "such a general custom in a kingdom, in giving and taking children to foster, making such a firm alliance as it doth in Ireland, was never seen or heard of in any other country of the world besides."[46] "General custom," we may note, was actually an elaborately prescribed and codified system of child-giving. In Ireland, the nobility—virtually the sole practitioners—would give away their children for the period from birth to marriageable age (around fourteen for girls and seventeen for boys). All parties to the exchange were subject to rules intricately laid out in no less than twenty-four pages of the Brehon laws. These regulations specified not only the two kinds of fosterage—"for affection and for payment" (along with amounts of payment to foster parents)—but also the kinds of food, clothing, recreation, and education the child should be given depending on his or her social rank. In addition, there were detailed regulations dealing with any disputes that might arise during the term of fosterage.[47]

Yet despite such strict legalities and economics, Irish child exchange was like its English counterpart in attempting to transcend utilitarian or market trade. While parents may have paid a fee for fosterage, the very term for that fee, "honor-price," indicates the priority given its social, rather than economic, value. Nor was the fee a payment in the sense of profit accruing to the foster parents. On the contrary, the law specifically forbade economic profit: any of the fee left over at the end of the term of fosterage, as well as any interest on the fee, had to be returned to the original parents along with the child.[48] Thus did the Irish system cleave to the primary tenet of gift exchange, wherein all increase—including in this case the growth and education of the child—must either be returned to the giver or passed along. Emblematic was the "parting gift" that foster parents presented to the child at the end of the term of fosterage. The parting gift simultaneously obliged the child to repay: he or she was expected to maintain the foster parents in their old age should they need support.[49]

Irish fosterage, then, firmly emphasized the spirit of generosity rather than of cupidity, and the social outcome of such free giving was what appeared to English observers as especially strong affective bonding. "They love tenderly their foster children," Edmund Campion reported, "and bequeathe to them a childes portion, whereby they nourish sure friendshippe, so beneficiall every way." Richard Stanihurst admired the fact that foster parents "trust [their foster children] implicitly, place all their hopes upon them and are fully acquainted with all their plans. The foster-children return this love faithfully and warmly." Again and again, we hear that the bonds cemented in fosterage surpassed even natural ties. "They love and trust their Foster Brethren more then their owne," Campion declared, and continued: "*Turlogh Leinagh Oneale* that now usurpeth, is said to repose in [his foster kin] his greatest surety." Davies affirmed that "fostering hath always been a stronger alliance than blood, and the foster-children do love and are beloved of their foster-fathers and their sept more than of their own natural parents and kindred, and do participate of their means more frankly and do adhere unto them in all fortunes with more affection and constancy." In fact, the relationship of love between foster parents and child was considered actually sacred.[50]

So strong was the bonding of fosterage that it cemented ties not only between the child and its foster parents but also between the foster parents and the natural parents. The latter bonding, we note, was at once one of "love" and of good politics. As Fynes Moryson pointed out in 1617,

> women of good wealth seek with great ambition to nurse them [foster children], not for any profit, rather spending much upon them while they live, and giving them when they die sometimes more than to their own children. But they do it only to have the protection and love of the parents whose children they nurse.

Moryson further asserts that nobles seek "to increase their power by fostering their children with the most valiant, rich, and powerful neighbours, since that people bears such strange reverence to this bond and pledge of love."[51] Thomas, earl of Ormond (to whom Spenser addresses a dedicatory sonnet in the 1590 *Faerie Queene*), understood the political advantages of fostering: when he entered into a treaty with the O'Mulrian brothers in 1557, one condition was that he give them his firstborn in fosterage.[52] Recognizing the great social and political bonds created by fosterage, nobles would compete for children of the high nobility, often offering presents in the hope of receiving the child. Children of particularly prominent parents frequently had more than one foster family and were handed from one to another, strengthening in the process the ties that bound them all together.[53]

In exchanging children, then, the Irish expressed such strong social, religious, and political ties that the net effect was intense solidarity (within particular exchange circles). This solidarity could not but be recognized by the English. After all, except for some notable differences, Irish fosterage was only an intensification of English child exchange (even such structural differences as the fact that the Irish sent their children away at birth rather than some years later could be seen to intensify rather than alter the fosterage experience).[54] Both systems transformed the expendable child into a cultural artifact by detaching it from its family and freely circulating it in an act of social communion. But to say that the English "recognized" the strength of Irish fosterage, of course, is also to say (as in the case of virtually all English observations upon the Irish) that they condemned it: it would not do for the Irish to be more English than the English. Therefore, if the virtues of Irish fosterage had to be praised, then that praise had also to castigate.

When we read English commentary on Irish fosterage, then, we find strange ambivalence. Defensiveness against the threat of the Irish model rises up even in the midst of praise. The precise threat to the English self-image, we may say, was one of absorption or inclusion. Rather than the English drawing the Irish into their centripetal cultural circle, the reverse tended to occur: the Irish absorbed English settlers into the Irish cultural round. Spenser (like most English observers) thus complained that fosterage reinforced the Irish assimilation of the English.[55] The treaty between the earl of Ormond and the O'Mulrian brothers records the method of such assimilation: English feudal lords fostered children with Irish lords. In this fashion, even the more recent English settlers of the Pale were drawn into the circle of Irish fosterage. Nicholas P. Canny notes, for example, that "Thomas Fleming, 'a gent of thenglish Pale', was a foster brother to Turlough Luineach O'Neill" (the "usurper" we saw Campion mention above).[56]

Or perhaps Irish "inclusion" of the English is not the only way to phrase the perceived threat. The equally dangerous obverse was *exclusion* by the Irish. If Irish fosterage absorbed many English settlers into the Irish cultural circle, it simultaneously shut out all other English (as well as Irish) circles

of exchange. Those within the gift ring were friends; those outside enemies. More fully: each Irish circle of exchange represented a sept or septs
centered on an overlord and bound in peace to each other but opposed in
war to everyone else. The Hibernized English feudal lords created closed
circles of child exchange on the same principle.[57]

How to meet the threat of inclusion/exclusion by the Irish? The answer
lay in expanding the faint ambivalence that was the nature of English praise
into an ideological and practical campaign against Irish fosterage. Ideologi-
cally, the English programmatically labeled the strengths of the Irish
system the cause of both internal factionalism (because each sept-circle became an island unto itself) and external warfare against England. As in the
case of the Irish nomadic life-style and "scrambling and transitory possession" of land, that is, the English propagandized against Irish fosterage by
speaking of it as yet more evidence of an against-all-comers barbarism pro-
ductive only of a fragmentary, discontinuous, and decentered culture.[58]
Practically, Elizabeth ("a louing Nurse, nay rather a kinde mother" to her
Irish subjects)[59] tried to break open the competing circles of Irish child exchange by encouraging the Irish nobility to send their children to England
for upbringing. But few, other than settlers of the English Pale, responded.
One child actually sent to England and counted as one of Elizabeth's great
successes was the earl of Ormond. Raised at court, Ormond always looked
to Elizabeth as his center of being. But such successes were offset by spectacular failures. Witness, for example, the case of Hugh O'Neill, who after
being placed as a child with the Sidneys from 1559 to 1566, subsequently set
upon the course of rebellion. Spenser, in *A View of the Present State of
Ireland,* underscored O'Neill's infamy: "was this Rebell then sett vp firste by
the Quene," Eudoxus asks, ". . . and now become so vndewtifull?"[60]

And with the word "vndewtifull," we come to the climax of the English
campaign against Irish fosterage customs. The charge of undutifulness
against O'Neill, who epitomized the unruly Irish spirit, became the great
English complaint, virtually a war cry recalling Mauss's insight into the
war normally suppressed within gift exchange. It is significant that complaints against the undutifulness of Irish foster children joined a swell of
general harping against Irish thanklessness. Barnabe Rich, for example, ex-
pounded at length in his *A New Description of Ireland* (1610):

> How many gentlemen . . . of that country birth came daily into England
> about sutes that were still begging and craving, and were continually re-
> turned from her Majesty's court back again into Ireland, laden with gifts and
> preferments that she graciously & liberally bestowed on them; who after they

had passed and possessed their grants would never come in place to say "Amen," when they heard her Majesty prayed for, but that rather, by their ill example of contempt, made others more obstinate and stubborn than otherwise they would.[61]

The English perceived both the overall Irish attitude toward English gifts and the epitome of that bad attitude—such cases of fostering-gone-wrong as O'Neill—to be so against the grain of the gift ethic that they were *ingratitude:* a rebellion and treachery against the very spirit of the gift. Elizabeth "graciously & liberally bestowed" "gifts" on the Irish; but the Irish, betraying the trust of their overseas gift partner, failed to reciprocate.

The only alternative, it would seem, was war. All the English propagandists agreed on this conclusion, though some—and here I approach the fruition of this chapter—were like Spenser in looking beyond war to a reconstruction of Ireland based on "enterminglinge" English and Irish customs.[62] Spenser's *View* suggests that the Irish be given a new sense of self—indicated by the acquisition of individual names in place of the generic sept name—but in a manner that would imply bondage to an English whole larger than the Irish sept: a circle centered on Elizabeth.[63]

Yet ultimately, Spenser's *View* is only ancillary to the goal of this chapter, which is Spenser's poetic re-presentation of the culture of total prestation. In its bloody way, we recognize, the *View* paralleled the general English response to Irish fosterage. Its plan for "enterminglinge" the Irish with the English envisioned fragmenting the Irish identity and recentering it on England through the use of force, and was thus akin to the overall English strategy of breaking up Irish factionalism, promoting the sending of Irish children to English foster parents, and enforcing the whole by war. But in advance of the *View,* Spenser had projected something like an equivalent peaceful joining of Irish and English cultures in a fiction more suggestive for our purposes because it was itself "gifted" (not only evaluatively, as we will see, but also analytically): *The Faerie Queene.* Spenser's *Faerie Queene* subsumed the ideology and practice of England's response to Irish prestation by eliding war in favor of total commitment to the spirit of the gift. Representing the intermingling of Irish and English prestation in the fairy court of Gloriana, especially as depicted in the Garden of Adonis, the poem makes the argument that it is by the principles of the gift alone that the rupture between gift cultures can be healed. Two cosmos of exchange must themselves be exchanged.

In the Garden, in short, Ireland and England can be imagined to foster a common culture. Later portions of the poem, we will see, intrude shades of a harsher view (akin to the *View*) within the gifted fiction. But for the while, the boar of war stays under the hill.[64]

The Poetics of Exchange: Spenser's Garden of Adonis

Nurtured in both England and Ireland, Spenser not unexpectedly shows in his poetry a strong concern with gift exchange and especially with child-giving. *The Faerie Queene* teems with fostered children: Arthur, for instance, "deliuered" by Merlin to Timon "to be brought vp, so soone as he was borne of the Lady Igrayne";[65] Red Cross (1.10.65–66); Ruddymane (2.2.1–2; 2.3.2); Artegall, whom as a child Astraea "did allure with gifts and speaches milde, / To wend with her" (5.1.6); the "little babe" Calepine gives to Lady Bruin (6.4.35); even Britomart, to the extent that her nurse, who calls her "my deare foster child" (3.2.33), acts as substitute mother, leaving home with her; and, of course, in canto 6 of book 3, the newborn twins, Belphoebe and Amoret. The way these latter babes are taken "to be fostered" (28) takes us straight into the book's center, the Garden of Adonis. Indeed, the exchange of the child Amoret in what we will see to be both an Irish and English version of the Kula ring provides the narrative line that will lead us not only into, but through and out of, the Garden.

We note that Spenser describes the birth of Belphoebe and Amoret in the scene immediately preceding the Garden of Adonis as a kind of free gift to their mother: Chrysogonee is impregnated "through influence of th'heauens fruitfull ray" (6). Belphoebe's birth particularly evokes the generosity and fertility associated with gift: "The heauens so fauourable were and free, / . . . That all the gifts of grace and chastitee / On her they poured forth of plenteous horne" (2). But the free gift must either be returned or passed along. Just as we saw Carre give away his children "as frelye as God haith sente or geauen them to me," so we witness Chrysogonee—albeit "vnwares" (27)—receiving her gifts only to pass them on. Venus and Diana freely take the babes from her side as she sleeps: "At last they both agreed, her seeming grieued / Out of her heauy swowne not to awake, / But from her louing side the tender babes to take" (27). The goddesses, in other words, unhesitatingly accept the children as if it were the customary thing to do.

It was. Indeed, the fact that Chrysogonee's babes are taken from her at time of birth specifically recalls the Irish as opposed to English custom of child exchange. Spenser goes on to underscore the association with child-giving (and, implicitly, with Irish fosterage). All the main features of the gift ethic are in place. We learn that Venus not only accepts the baby Amoret as if it were a gift but in essence accepts her in lieu of her own lost child, Cupid: she takes the babe "in her litle loues [Cupid's] stead" (28). But if Venus accepts Amoret in payment for "hauing lost / Her little sonne" (11), the very act of accepting the gift elicits the need to repay, and Venus does so by passing Amoret on to a third party—by taking the child to Psyche in the Garden (just as Diana takes hers to a nymph in the forest) "to be fostered" (28). The word "take" here is especially resonant. To "take" a gift is necessarily also to take it *to* someone else. In essence, "to take" is "to give." As if to make this very point, Spenser repeats versions of the verb "take" until it exchanges meaning with "give." After telling us that Venus and Diana agreed "the tender babes to take" (27), the poet declares, "Vp they them tooke, each one a babe vptooke, / And with them carried, to be fostered; / Dame *Phoebe* to a Nymph her babe betooke, / To be vpbrought" (28). The verb "tooke" becomes "vptooke," which becomes "betooke"; and the twist in the latter verb is that it means "betooke" *to* ("Dame *Phoebe* to a Nymph her babe betooke"). "Betooke," we know, had the essential meaning of "gave in charge"; and, as such, embodies within it the undecidable taking/giving of the gift.[66]

On accepting the child Amoret from Venus, Psyche herself enters the Kula ring. She must circulate the child in a system of fosterage akin to that of the Irish. Thus at the end of her time with Amoret, she acts the part of an Irish foster parent who keeps a child only to marriageable age: she brings Amoret "forth into the worldes vew" and sends her to "Faery court" (52). Significantly, however, with this last passing on of the gift to *court*, we also cross into a centripetal system of child-giving more English than Irish. Passed from her natural mother, Chrysogonee, through a chain of foster mothers (Venus, Psyche) at last to the Faery Queen, Amoret travels a route similar to that of the English foster girls I earlier mentioned, Bridget Manners and Penelope Devereux. Just as all gifts in England circled back to Queen Elizabeth as if to their source, so does Amoret. Indeed, one gets the sense of a completed circle in Psyche's sending her to court: throughout the poem, the Faery/English Queen is linked with "th'heauens fruitfull ray" that first gave Amoret her being. In Spenser's narrative of passing on Amoret, Irish fosterage joins with English child exchange to form not an Irish faction but a single, large, unbroken circle centered on Elizabeth.

Irish and English customs of child exchange are thus "entermingled," and the result is a generous increase not of factionalism and war but of culture. As in the Kula ring, where exchanged ornaments acquire cultural identity (names, personalities, religion), Amoret not only receives her name on being taken up by Venus but is cultivated through the process of being received into the gift circle. Indeed, the poem's language of generation makes the cultivation seem literal: Amoret's circulation from foster parent to foster parent engenders her growth "to perfect ripenesse" (52). Nature in the Garden *is* nurture. It grows a spirit of gift whose harvest is cultural increase. As is the rule in gift exchange, furthermore, such cultural ripeness is reaped not only by the gift-child but also by the bearers of the gift. Particularly evocative of the fruits of gift are the generosity, good fellowship, love, and trust that first blossom in the flowery language of stanza 41:

> here all plentie, and all pleasure flowes,
> And sweet loue gentle fits emongst them throwes,
> Without fell rancor, or fond gealosie;
> Franckly each paramour his leman knowes,
> Each bird his mate, ne any does enuie
> Their goodly meriment, and gay felicitie.

Venus engenders love and trust much like this by giving Amoret to Psyche "with great trust and care . . . yfostered to bee" (51). Thus is the bond sealed between the goddess of love and her lately reconciled daughter-in-law—a bond that we may take as summing up Spenser's whole vision of the cultural (i.e., social, moral, and religious) significance of fosterage. In the ring of exchange established between Venus and Psyche, the spirit of gift then culminates in readying Amoret for culture proper. Psyche teaches her "all the lore of loue, and goodly womanhead" (51) before sending her for marriage to the social and political world of the "Faery court."[67]

Nevertheless, cruel destruction (much like Venus's former aggression against Psyche) continues to threaten the Garden. We see it in such personifications as love with its "spoiles and cruelty" as well as in two imposing figures: the personified "wicked *Time*" and what might be called the counterpersonified or animalized "wilde Bore" (49, 39, 48). Time is at war with the Garden's fruits:

> Great enimy to it, and to all the rest,
>   That in the *Garden of Adonis* springs,
>   Is wicked *Time,* who with his scyth addrest,
>   Does mow the flowring herbes and goodly things,
>   And all their glory to the ground downe flings,
>   Where they doe wither, and are fowly mard:
>   He flyes about, and with his flaggy wings
>   Beates downe both leaues and buds without regard,
> Ne euer pittie may relent his malice hard. (39)

Similarly, the boar—"Which with his cruell tuske him deadly cloyd"—is "foe" to Adonis (48). With decidedly Irish pugnacity, Time and the boar threaten violence.

But unlike the Irish factions threatening the English, these enemies are peacefully incorporated in the Garden's cultural round. They are designed into the Garden's elaborate narrative of exchange in the same way, we may say, as fears and antagonisms are built into the Kula gift ceremony. The "scyth" of Time and "cruell tuske" of the boar thus menace the spirit of the gift as much as the Kula *"kudu"* or return gift in its aspect as "the tooth which bites, severs."[68] But embraced within the Garden's circle of gift, surrounded by the spirit of friendly generosity and trust, these anxieties are suppressed even as they are expressed. Even the threat of death figured in the boar—"his cruell tuske him deadly cloyd"—is held off through the acts of generosity and trust that attend the giving and receiving of Amoret. Venus thus finds her "lost" dead lover, the "boy" Adonis, at the precise narrative moment when she freely gives Amoret away "with great trust and care" (29, 46, 51). The "cruell," death-dealing boar embedded "vnderneath" the Garden's "Mount" is literally surmounted by the increase of gift exchange (48).

If we complement the literal exchange of children in the Garden with its metaphysical parallel, as Spenser does, then the Garden of Adonis may be seen to be cosmographical or universal in significance. Like Sidney's *"Idea* or fore-conceite,"[69] the Garden is a middle ground between philosophical idea (the "goodly formes" from Venus's "hous") and historical matter (the "substances" "in the wide wombe" of *"Chaos"*) (12, 36). It is a mediation, in other words, where the very foundations of existence *exchange* meanings and terms. Consider "formes," for example. When we first hear in the episode introductory to the Garden that Venus "left her heauenly hous, / . . . of goodly formes and faire aspects" (12), we naturally think of the Platonic idea of form.[70] The "naked babes" that Genius "clothes with sinfull mire, / And sendeth forth to liue in mortall state, / Till they againe returne backe by the hinder gate" (32) also seem to have Platonic parents: the incorruptible forms in Plato's wheel of creation clothed, on coming into this life, in the corruptible matter of "fleshly weedes" (32).[71] As so many critics have noted, however, within three stanzas these "formes" themselves become associated with "fleshly weedes." Their description in stanza 35 clearly evokes the earlier clothing metaphor: "Some fit for reasonable soules t'indew, / Some made for beasts, some made for birds to *weare*" (my emphases). Here the "formes" themselves are the clothes. And, as we learn in the next stanzas, they are mutable clothes, donned by the material yet eternal "substances" of *"Chaos"* (36).

A process of exchange is at work here much like that noted earlier where-in the verb "to take" assumes the character of the verb "to give." Like Platonic forms, Spenser's "naked babes" take on "fleshly weedes" and al-most immediately appear, through the rich connotations of the language, like the "fleshly weedes" they earlier put on; whereas those mutable clothes themselves take on part of the character of formal principles. In the meta-physics of engendering, form and matter are exchanged.[72]

The metaphysics of exchange in the Garden of Adonis peak in the simul-taneously sexual and transcendental exchange between Venus and Adonis on the *Mons Veneris* "Right in the middest" (3.6.43).[73] Here again the "in-consistencies" that preoccupy criticism of the Garden of Adonis episode can be explained in terms of gift exchange. Venus appears to act as a mas-culine formal principal (come from "The house of goodly formes" [12]) when she "Possesseth" Adonis "and of his sweetnesse takes her fill" (46). Yet, of course, she is female—"great mother *Venus*" (40)—and suffers asso-ciation, through her female role as *mater,* with *materia* rather than with form. Such ambiguity of gender and essence is epitomized in her ag-gressive "reaping" of Adonis (46), which likens her to the masculine grim reaper, Time, but also associates her with the feminine materiality ("fleshly weedes") in which Time clothes all creatures. Venus embodies charac-teristics of both masculinity and femininity, form and matter. But so does Adonis. As the "Father of all formes," he is associated not only with the masculine formal principle that acts upon matter but with the paternal vi-talism of the sun—"Great father he of generation" (47, 9). And yet various aspects of Adonis contradict his masculinity. He acts in the role of tradi-tional feminine passivity; he is portrayed in language echoing Spenser's description of the implicitly female materiality or "substances" of *"Chaos"*; and, as C. S. Lewis maintains, he is actually antithetical to "Great father" sun—"obstinately un-solar"—while lying "hid" in the funereal "gloomy groue" (46, 43).[74]

Venus and Adonis, I suggest, take on each other's qualities—exchang-ing form and matter, masculinity and femininity (one might add En-glishness and Irishness)—because they participate in the process of gift ex-change. Like the shells that participants in the Kula conceive as female and male principles, they "marry" at the moment of exchange, Adonis "Ioying his goddesse, and of her enioyd" (48). The "marriage" on the "Mount" with the *kudu* boar suppressed "vnderneath" (48) is a perfect emblem of gift exchange. Terms cannot be clear-cut in this liminal moment when genders as well as essences exchange identities and war is held in abeyance. To make a riddling sentence out of the paradox of the gift: S/he who simultaneously "takes" and "takes to" is "betooke" out of her/himself. In the creative act of gift exchange, of *engenderment* in more than one sense, Venus and Adonis become simultaneously givers and gifted. Each is a gift to the other: Venus *"takes* her fill" of an Adonis who "liuing *giues* to all," and vice versa (46, 47; my emphases). Encompassing all the cosmos in their round of giving, Venus and Adonis cultivate an increase in forms and matter that is also quintessentially an increase in the love, trust, compassion, and other forms and matters of the cultural cosmos, of the wedding of form and matter.

In the end, Spenser's Garden of Adonis does indeed yield a "cosmos," a universal and ornamental engenderment. It creates what I called in chapter I an ornamental vision of history. Relative to both the central Platonic "formes" of Spenser's cosmography and the main plot of book 3 itself, of course, fleshly forms and child-gifts are trifles, a mere filigree-work or ornamentation. Yet, strangely, these pretty trifles digress from the center of the universe and of the plot only to come round to an alternative centering fiction. In the Garden of Adonis episode (at once peripheral to the plot and *centered* in the cantos of book 3), Spenser does not so much narrate the true universe as elaborate an ornamental cosmos; and the function of the elaboration is to embed the cycle of exchange, seen in a filigree of trifles, into the heart of culture. We witness the engendering of a cultural whole in which the conflict between form and matter, male and female, English and Irish, civilized and savage, and, indeed, all such factional divisions born of center-periphery oppositions seem to be transcended.[75]

But a further thought, lest it be assumed that my discussion makes the Garden of Adonis only a textual copy (though idealized) of the cultural context of Irish and English child-giving, and thus *The Faerie Queene* only a spectator at a remove from the culture it participates in. In fact, the relationship between text and context in this instance is surely more complicated. For, given that the theme of the Garden of Adonis episode is the gift, a faithful mimesis of the context of gift-giving would paradoxically be *unfaithful* to the theme. To copy the gift as if in a mirror would be to deny the fact that the poetry partakes of the world it represents; it would be to make the poetry a taker of gifts that does not have the grace to render back the gift with increase. To be true to its theme, I suggest, Spenser's poetic representation must itself attempt to be giving and gifted. It must try to be a true *re*-presentation of prestation.

How does Spenser absorb the gift cosmos so as to regenerate it in the very method of his elaborate, ornamental poetry? How, that is, does he make poetic creativity a participant in the creativity of the gift that is his theme? Here it would be possible to concentrate in formal ways on the process of the poetry. But to begin preparing for the special issue of this book—the culture of subjectivity that the culture of exchange makes possible—I will frame discussion of poetic process under the problematics of the poet's "self." The Garden of Adonis episode, I suggest, attempts to represent the creative mind of a "genius" whose acts of ornamental elaboration are the ultimate dramatization of the principle of exchange. Like "Old *Genius* the porter" to the Garden's gates, the poet is the prime spirit of a cycle of give-and-take, who "letteth in" and "letteth out" into the world "A thousand thousand naked babes" (31, 32).[76] Most specifically, the poet/genius is a kind of Sidnean poet who clothes the "naked babes" of his mind—his poetic Ideas—with the "fleshly weedes" (32) of rhetorical ornaments on "deliuering them forth," as Sidney would say, to an audience. The Garden itself must thus be seen not simply as most critics have seen it (as a Platonic, Lucretian, or other philosophical model of creation) but also as a model for the poet's mind organized as a process of exchange.[77]

In its creative process, the Spenserian poetic imagination attempts to dilate beyond limited subjectivity. The self may be bounded—"girt in with two walles" (31)—but the boundary of the "I" expands to become the vehicle for the sociable communion of "we." The poet in essence opens up his mind to the ongoing process of gift exchange. Poetic self-interest certainly remains evident. As in the case of the gorgeous evocation of Time and the boar, the poet's wordplay on "tooke" calls attention to himself as self-conscious artificer. But there is a lack of self-assertion in the way one idea freely gives rise to another, as if the poet were part of the narrative of exchange rather than its generator. In fact, moments of extreme artifice in the Garden of Adonis that call attention to the poet's shaping mind (such as the "pure" art of the Ovidian flowers on the Garden's Mount) appear as a kind of living death:

> And all about grew euery sort of flowre,
>   To which sad louers were transformd of yore;
> Fresh *Hyacinthus, Phoebus* paramoure,
>   And dearest loue,
> Foolish *Narcisse,* that likes the watry shore,

Sad *Amaranthus,* made a flowre but late,
Sad *Amaranthus,* in whose purple gore
Me seemes I see *Amintas* wretched fate,
To whom sweet Poets verse hath giuen endlesse date. (45)

By the end of this stanza, the artifice of lovers "transformd" into flowers
triggers the poet's self-conscious allusion to his own art, "sweet Poets verse"
(a response, specifically, to the Sidnean *"Amaranthus"* that links these artificial flowers to Sidney's model of the poetic mind where they grow). But
as the self-absorbed *"Narcisse"* underscores, such transformations lack the
spirit of gift. They exemplify a self-contained love that rigidly preserves
rather than generously gives of the self and, consequently, kills all chance of
self-growth.[78]

In contrast to these "forced" images, the poet "seems almost to stumble
upon the Venus-Adonis image."[79] Moving from "some say" to "And sooth
it seemes they say" (46, 47), he does not impose but generously opens up
his mind. He gives himself to the poetic process. In return, he receives the
gift of vision, marked by a sudden exultant cry of inspiration: "There now
he [Adonis] liueth in eternall blis / Ioying his goddesse, and of her en-
ioyed" (48). By losing himself in the flow of thought (in a Chrysogonee-
like "vnwares" state of giving birth [27]), the poet participates with Venus
in finding the boy Adonis and achieving a vision of life-giving exchange.
The spirit of gift that effects this discovery, as in the vision itself, ensures life
in the death that is the abandonment of self: unlike the "transformd" lovers
above (or that epitome of moribund transformation, Malbecco), both the
poet and Adonis are "by succession made perpetuall, / Transformed oft,
and chaunged diuerslie" (47).

Such life-giving discovery, though conceived within the poet's creative
imagination, is thus not self-centered. It is in this sense significant that the
garden of the poetic mind, on sending its children out into the world, gives
them to a figure called "Genius" rather than, say, "poet" or "creator." The
poet sees the liberator of his art as someone other than himself (this attitude
also appears in his many invocations to his "Muse"). Indeed, Hyde argues,
to consider one's gifts to be solely of one's own making is a kind of narcis-
sism that denies growth—hence the Roman custom whereby an individual
gave gifts to his guiding spirit or *genius* on his birthday. "Respected in this
way the *genius* made one 'genial'—sexually potent, artistically creative, and
spiritually fertile."[80]

What the giving of children to "Old *Genius*" in the Garden of Adonis
fertilizes is the garden of Spenser's poetic imagination; the gift nurtures

the narrative of exchange that carries the poem's lifeblood forward. To read from this point on is to follow the perpetual increase of the gift. The giving away of Amoret to "Faery court" toward the end of the episode, for example, invokes a return gift before the canto concludes in the figure of Florimell, another "sweet flower" of the Garden.[81] And so the poem's elaborate exchange of language, ideas, things, and people continues.

To see gift exchange embedded in this way at the very heart of Spenser's poetic stance and narrative provides a more positive way of viewing what recent Spenser critics, especially those with a deconstructive thrust, consider the poet's endless substitutions and deferrals (particularly in the middle books of *The Faerie Queene*).[82] Rather than repeatedly substituting and deferring, I would argue, the poet continually exchanges and fosters. *The Faerie Queene,* in other words, is a circle of gift, an endlessly transformational round wherein all loss is gain, all giving taking, all dying living. To make yet another etymological link with the term "generosity"—which, as we saw, defined the exchange of "gender" in the Garden of Adonis—one might say that the gift is the defining principle of Spenser's "genre": chivalric romance. Generous gift exchange is an ornamental circle along which the poet generates a wandering narrative line of chivalric quest.[83] In the process of wandering toward an endlessly deferred goal (a process of error in one view but of ornament in another), the poet picks up peripheral, fragmentary, and decorative trifles that he exchanges one for another. Thus does his poetry contribute toward the cultural increase that is its theme. Culture, we may say, is precisely a deferred "goal" that systems of exchange achieve only in the *act* of wandering, of sending gifts like children along digressive paths from house to house before dedicating them finally to the court of the true Faery Queen.

The fiction of *The Faerie Queene* participates in an ideal, Elizabethan vision of commonality, of selves bound to each other in a ring of total prestation. It reaps a combined cultural and poetic increase of giftedness, and then at last is dedicated:

TO

THE MOST HIGH,

MIGHTIE

AND

MAGNIFICENT

EMPRESSE RENOW-

MED FOR PIETIE, VER-

TVE, AND ALL GRATIOVS

GOVERNMENT ELIZABETH BY
THE GRACE OF GOD QVEENE
OF ENGLAND FRAVNCE AND
IRELAND   AND   OF   VIRGI-
NIA, DEFENDOVR OF THE
FAITH, &C. HER MOST
HVMBLE SERVAVNT
EDMVND SPENSER
DOTH IN ALL HV-
MILITIE DEDI-
CATE, PRE-
SENT
AND CONSECRATE THESE
HIS LABOVRS TO LIVE
VVITH THE ETERNI-
TIE OF HER
FAME.[84]

At the Poem's Periphery: The Dedication

As we exit through the gates of Spenser's Garden of Adonis, where the poet/genius gives his children to the world, we also pass the threshold commonly connecting Elizabethan poetry and culture: the dedication. Standing on the very edge of the body of the text, the "little" dedication was in fact another peripheral fragment or trivial aesthetic alluding to history. Mimicking the typography above, we may say with emphasis that it was another poetic ORNAMENT informed by the ethics of the GIFT and, specifically, of CHILD-GIVING. Through dedications (as well as other marginal or prefatory materials), Spenser and his contemporaries delivered poetry into the world precisely as if they were "Old Genius" sending forth children: the poem was their "child." In the standard metaphor: the poem was a "child" presented as "gift" to an aristocratic patron akin to a foster parent.[85] The children of poets, in other words, were literally aesthetic artifacts.

Spenser, whose dedications virtually sang with the language of gift, specifically called his poetry a "child"-gift in the introductory poem to *The Shepheardes Calender* (1579). He tells his "little booke" to "present" itself to Sidney and to seek "succoure" from him "As child whose parent is vnkent." Sidney, in turn, in a letter to his sister, the countess of Pembroke, gave "onelie for you, only to you" "this child," the *Arcadia* (1590). So too Henry Constable presented "To the Gentlemen Readers" his "sonnes" (*Di-*

ana [1592]), who "are now / by misfortune left as Orphans: and craue desertfull / acceptance." And the printer Henry Olney declared that *Diella* (1596), given in "gift" to Lady Anne Glemnham, "is a chylde of the Muses . . . conceiued in the braine of a gallant Gentleman [probably Richard Lynche]." Olney's statement, indeed, could well remind us of Spenser's Garden of Adonis. Exchanging genders and roles, Olney imagines the masculine poet's "braine" as a kind of womb impregnated by the traditionally feminine "Muses." And like Spenser, he also visualizes a generating force in addition to the poet's self: the Muses are the counterparts to Spenser's Genius. Similarly, Thomas Lodge gave "these *infants* of mine artless brain" (*Phillis* [1595]) to the countess of Shrewsbury, whom he called "The *genius* of my muse and ragged rime" (my emphases).[86] By dedicating his child-poems to the countess, Lodge—again like Spenser in the Garden of Adonis—paid back, by passing along, the gifts of his genius.

The force of the gift ethic was such that it was natural for poets in need of patronage to dedicate not just their poems but *themselves* (and their Muse) as "children" to a foster-parent patron. Samuel Daniel thus called Lord Pembroke "the fosterer of mee and my *Muse*," and Robert Greene, dedicating *Francescos Fortunes* (1590) to Thomas Burnaby in recompense for his "many friendly, nay fatherly fauours," signed his dedication, "Your Worships adopted sonne in all humble dutie to commaund."[87] Most striking, however, is the case of Michael Drayton, who epitomizes poetry's immersion in the total prestation of child exchange. Given as a young child of about nine into the service of Sir Henry Goodere, Drayton was later "bequeathed" as a poet by Goodere to Lucy Harington (wife to the Edward Russell who was given as a child into Huntingdon's care and later became earl of Bedford). The term "bequeathed" is Drayton's own in a 1597 dedication to Bedford. Drayton begins by expressing his "love" for the families of the earl and his countess, "to whose service," he declares,

> I was first bequeathed, by that learned and accomplished Gentleman, Sir *Henry Goodere* (not long since deceased), whose I was whilst he was: whose patience, pleased to beare with the imperfections of my heedlesse and un-staied youth. That excellent and matchlesse Gentleman, was the first cherisher of my Muse, which had been by his death left a poore Orphane to the worlde, had hee not before bequeathed it to that Lady whom he so deerly loved. Vouchsafe then my deere Lord to accept this Epistle, which I dedicate as zeal-ously, as (I hope) you will patronize willingly, untill some more acceptable service may be witnes of my love towards your honour.[88]

Just as the fathers William Carre and the earl of Essex gave their children away in bequest, as we earlier saw, the already foster father/patron Sir

Henry Goodere—Drayton imagines—"bequeathed" the poet to another family. Passed in this way from one parental patron to another, the poet entered not only the household of the Russells, earls of Bedford, but also the whole Kula ring of child exchange we earlier mapped in fig. 7. Drayton's gift of poetry—his "zealously" dedicated "Epistle"—witnessed and strengthened his inclusion in this circle. His art was the counterpart of actual gift-children, who were raised in the process of exchange from trifles into aesthetic, jewel-like creatures that imaginatively bound people together in "love."

By giving his "child" *The Shepheardes Calender* to Sidney, Spenser entered the very same circle of exchange (further evidenced by his other "gift" dedications to Mary countess of Pembroke and to the Russell sisters Anne and Margaret as well as by his celebration of the Sidneys and Bedfords in *The Ruines of Time* [1591] and *Colin Clouts Come Home Againe* [1595]). It is in the dedications to the 1590 *Faerie Queene,* however, that we find the largest evidence of his participation in the cultural aesthetics of poetry as gift and as child-gift. As Edwin Miller claims, Spenser probably hoped in offering these multiple dedications—one at the beginning to Elizabeth and ten sonnets[89] at the end to the members of her court (including the Irish earl of Ormond)—to multiply his financial rewards.[90] But by surrounding his poem with dedications to principal figures of the Queen's Anglo-Irish court, he also imaged a cultural surround of gift that, as we have seen, projects much more than economics.[91] The rewards Spenser sought by addressing patrons in the language of gift included, in addition to money, the "friendship" that brought protection, personal prestige, and social and political advancement—the amity, in other words, that could foster himself and his poetry precisely as if they were gift-children. Thus in his dedication to Lord Grey, Spenser calls *The Faerie Queene* his "small guift" to the "Patrone of my Muses pupillage."[92] To gain cultural belonging, he had to submit his Muse to the status of child.

Participating through their dedications in the culture of child-giving, Elizabethan poets, like the characters in Spenser's Garden of Adonis, attempted to reap the ultimate benefits of prestation: a life-giving cultural increase accruing to both the givers and the gift. Just as the donor Essex gained a kind of continued life in giving his son to Burghley, so the gift that was Drayton's "Muse"—in danger at Goodere's death of being "left a poore Orphane to the worlde"—received sustenance in being bequeathed to the countess of Bedford. The need for succoring "life" indeed was much felt by the poets. There is almost a sense in which the poets themselves, as fathers of their child-poems, faced an anxiety of death at the moment of freely giving a poem away. In his dedication, for instance, Constable called his poems his "sonnes" and *"Orphans."* A poet is so invested in his poetry that he "dies" in giving up the poem to another. Such anxieties or misgivings of death were further aggravated by the normal social misgivings involved in giving away a poem or any gift. Drayton worried parenthetically, "(*I hope*) you will patronize willingly," and Spenser (who noted that Gosson's dedication to Sidney was "scorned") feared giving offense himself.[93] The poets' tendency to deprecate their gifts—calling them, for instance, trivial "toys" or "lowly verse"—may have been an attempt to show not only humility but also, as in the Kula ritual of belittling and throwing down ornaments, freedom from fear of rejection. But to the extent that the poets, like the givers in the Kula, *believed* in the spirit of the gift, to that extent they surmounted misgivings of "deathiness" or rejection to give generously of themselves in a sociable communion that gave life in return.[94]

Such imaginative exchange not only succored the givers and the gift but also the recipients. In one dedicatory sonnet to *The Faerie Queene,* Spenser may be a child returning "this small guift" to his father/patron Grey, "Patrone of my Muses pupillage, / Through whose large bountie poured on me rife, / In the first season of my feeble age, / I now doe liue." But in another of the poem's dedicatory "presents" (to Northumberland), Spenser, through his "Muses," "the Nourses of nobility," is the father/mother of the aristocracy and invokes them "To patronize the authour of their praise, / Which giues them life, that els would soone haue dide."[95] In such moments, poet and patron were simultaneously givers and takers, parents and children: both reaped the spiritual "life" of the gift. In this sense, gift-dedications were as much equalizers as definers of hierarchical differences: poet and patron together entered a gift circle that subsumed and dilated roles, mingling all participants in the hope of growth, peace, and culture. In Nature's words in the *Mutabilitie Cantos,* poet and patron entered a life-giving round of transformation wherein they would never die, "But by their change their being doe dilate: / And turning to themselues at length againe, / Doe worke their owne perfection so by fate" (7.7.58).

Toward the Interior Cosmos

As in the case of the exchange of children in the Garden of Adonis, in sum, Spenser's peripheral or ornamental gift-dedications expressed the perfect *ideal* of the gift. I close by emphasizing the "ideality" of the gift cosmos to prepare for a different, darker cosmos we must eventually come to. Gift exchange, it should be clear, was always innately ideal because its credo that

giving is receiving and receiving giving fostered the belief that the very act
of donation was rewarded whether or not a gift partner actually recipro-
cated.[96] Even more importantly, gift exchange was inherently ideal because
it was always less a "fact" about the way relationships are than an "idea"
about the way relationships should or might best be: an attempt to suppress
the *kudu* boar (or should we say Blatant Beast?) that threatened a culture's
vision of itself.

But such inherent idealism aside, there was something *especially* ideal
about the Elizabethan gift ethos—an overdetermination and perhaps even
hysteria of generosity that finally threatened to make apparent the fictionality, the "mere" ideality of the gift. In the concluding chapter of this book,
I will testify that the idealizing fiction of Elizabethan gift exchange arose in
reaction against an increasingly powerful estrangement sensed within the
culture and aesthetics of exchange: the market. Spenser's gift ideal, one
might say, was his attempt to guarantee continued life during the death-
threatening transformation of his age from gift, or patronage, to market
society.

The poetics of exchange thus accelerates in the middle books of *The
Faerie Queene* to match the accelerated threat of market self-interest. That
threat looms largest in the last book in the form of the primitively "cap-
italistic" brigands: a "lawlesse people" who—defying the imaginative leap
of gift exchange—cannibalistically "fed on spoile and booty, which they
made / Vpon their neighbours, which did nigh them border" (6.10.39).
The brigands, that is, embody self-interested aggression in the form of
both war and competitive economics. As such, they violently "spoyld"
(6.10.40) the ideal commonality of the shepherd society (peaking in the
Graces' jewel-like ring of exchange on Mount Acidale) in order to sell for
profit not only the sheep but the shepherds themselves.

The underworld dwelling to which the brigands take the shepherds is in
this sense the low point of the poem's engendering exchange. In fact, it is a
kind of inverted gift society. Its location on a remote "little Island" of "hollow caues" (6.10.41;42) houses the alien underside of "civilized" community. The labyrinthine and dimly lit "inner parts," which "delt / A doubtfull
sense of things, not so well seene, as felt," mirror the "disorder" of the brig-
and's fragmented, decentered, and (to English eyes) Irish-like society
(6.10.42;39). Here the individual is not subsumed in a larger whole but lost
in a murky confusion of "things." Here living beings are not passed along
in an expanding circle of exchange but traded in a self-restricting cycle of
profit: sold as "slaues . . . for no small reward, / To merchants, which

them kept in bondage hard, / Or sold againe" (6.10.43). Here competition is not ceremonial or artistic, allowing peace and life, but real and brutal, destroying all individuals and all community. In fact, the brigands, in their fight over the ornament Pastorella—"like a Diamond of rich regard" (6.11.13)—give life to Death. Their decimation makes

> way for death at large to walke:
> Who in the horror of the griesly night,
> In thousand dreadful shapes doth mongst them stalke,
> And makes huge hauocke, whiles the candlelight
> Out quenched, leaues no skill nor difference of wight.
> (6.11.16)

Significantly, such deathy language reverberates in our next vision of the great enemy to the Knight of Courtesy, the Blatant Beast. The Beast also indiscriminately wreaks "such spoile, such hauocke, and such theft" (6.12.23). Death, born of "spoile" or market self-interest, is the supreme expression of that "primitive" bestiality that only the courteous, "civilized" ideal of community can quell.

It was the market aggressiveness seen in such merchant brigands, I suggest, that was opposed by the Elizabethan idealization—a "golden-age" fiction, if you will—of poetic and cultural gift. The idealization at last succumbed under James to radically peripheral and fragmentary practices of consumption such that the commonality once manifested in the exchange of children, jewels, poems, and other trifling yet precious bric-a-brac could finally be expressed only in a kind of counter-commonality of *debased* bric-a-brac: a literal breaking apart of culture (comparable, I will argue, to the Kula's alter ego, the potlatch).

But we are not yet ready to proceed to James and the debasement of the gift ideal. The gift had a lot of life in it still to come—a life that my following chapters will translate into related concepts. Most crucially, the ideal of the gift retained its force in a domain we have yet to reach: the Elizabethan "self" as it constructed itself amid the collective bonding and identity of gift society. To complete my argument about gift exchange, that is, we need to indicate that such society also had what might be called an inner directionality. The gift that marked the displacement of aggressive self-interest at last accumulated a different kind of self-interest: subjectivity. Giving and receiving in what seemed perfectly selfless exchange, Elizabethans received a surplus "spirit" or "life" (as I have so far been calling it) whose ultimate identity was the subjectivity of the historical individual: a spirit that was itself ideal, vitalistic, never quite fixable. Of course, this did not mean that the threat to the gift ideal represented by market forces disappeared, only that it reappeared as a different kind of threat in interior form. To anticipate my full argument: the threat to gift society had its parallel in a complex tension within the Elizabethan self between public and private subjectivities. Facing outward toward the public, the self was much like the gift participants we have observed: it was ready for exchange. But facing inward toward secret privacy, the self was afraid that it was a void like the "hollow caues" of Spenser's brigands: it had nothing to give. It only consumed.

Let us follow the tale of the gift "within," then, in the same way Spenser tracked his merchanting brigands into the "inner parts" of their labyrinthine society. What we shall find—again by observing such ornamental "presentations" as gift miniatures and sonnets, dessert "voids" and masques—is that the inward is inextricably interlocked with the outward in a problematic relation of center and periphery. Public and private, public *vs.* private: the self displayed itself in an exchange of trifling ornaments each of which was at once open to social view and paradoxically locked in secret invisibility.

A signpost to the culture of inwardness we will come to occurs in the episode concluding book 3 of *The Faerie Queene:* the cave or "house" of Busirane (cantos 11-12). The house of Busirane is another marginal world symptomatic of the heightened ornamentality of the middle books of *The Faerie Queene.* Rather than climaxing or ending the narrative line of the knight's quest (as do the final cantos in books 1 and 2), Busirane's house appears to form another marginal digression. But it is a marginality that points to its own alternative center, represented as its innermost room. The cave-like house of Busirane is a periphery like the remote island "caues" of the brigands that take us to a center deep "within." Here we again find the gift-child of the Garden of Adonis, Amoret. Britomart can only approach Amoret, now grown up, by passing through two rooms each more richly ornamental than the other but also more interior and "private."[97] Only then can she finally arrive at the unadorned, most "inner roome" of intimacy where Amoret is constrained by her would-be lover, Busirane (3.12.26).

But in this unadorned room deep within, we are still in the presence of ornament, which has now become poetic: Busirane is a kind of sonneteer who "cruelly *pend*" (3.11.11; my emphasis) Amoret with "many a sad verse" of his "art" written in the "liuing bloud" of her "dying hart" (3.12.36; 31). "Ah," the poet laments in an echo of sonneteering rhetoric, "who can loue the worker of her smart?" (3.12.31).[98] Busirane's "penning" of Amoret represents the latter's fear of possession by her "true" lover, Scudamour (who proudly boasts he "bought" or "purchased" her with his sword and fetish-istically equates her with his shield [4.1.2; 10.3]).[99] Both Busirane and Scudamour, we may say, foreshadow the "me generation" of the brigands later in the poem. Within Busirane's house, however, the allegory of self-interest leads not just to an inverted gift society but into a more private world—an inner cosmos whose expressive form is not the "public" chiv-alric romance or epic but the "private" sonnet.

The private self hidden within "rooms" of public ornament and "repre-sented" by the "little" art of sonnets (and miniatures) is the subject of my next chapter.

3

Secret Arts: Elizabethan Miniatures and Sonnets

Having resolved "to open a good part of her inward mind" to Sir James Melville, ambassador from Mary Queen of Scots, and professing "a great desire" to see her "good sister" (which "desired meeting could not be so hastily brought to pass"), Queen Elizabeth led Melville into the heart of her labyrinthine state apartments at Whitehall and unveiled to him her collection of miniatures.[1] Melville's account of the 1564 incident merits quoting in full. "She took me to her bed-chamber," he recalled,

> and opened a little cabinet, wherein were divers little pictures wrapt within paper, and their names written with her own hand upon the papers. Upon the first that she took up was written, "My Lord's picture." I held the candle, and pressed to see that picture so named. She appeared loath to let me see it; yet my importunity prevailed for a sight thereof, and found it to be the Earl of Leicester's picture. I desired that I might have it to carry home to my Queen; which she refused, alleging that she had but that one picture of his. I said, your Majesty hath here the original; for I perceived him at the farthest part of the chamber, speaking with Secretary Cecil. Then she took out the Queen's picture, and kissed it; and I adventured to kiss her hand, for the great love therein evidenced to my mistress. She showed me also a fair ruby, as great as a tennis-ball. I desired that she would either send it, or my Lord Leicester's picture, as a token unto the Queen. She said, if the Queen would follow her counsel, that she would in process of time get all she had; that in the meantime she was resolved in a token to send her with me a fair diamond.[2]

This is an intensely intimate moment in a series of political maneuverings between Elizabeth and Melville over the question of Mary's marriage to

Leicester and the English succession. One gets the sense of being let in on a secret as Elizabeth penetrates outer layers of her domain—her "bed-chamber," her "little cabinet," her personally inscribed paper wrappings—to reveal her highly prized miniatures (valued equally with a ruby "as great as a tennis-ball") and her sincere feelings for Mary. The sense of secrecy as Elizabeth opens herself up to Melville is highlighted by her momentary hesitancy at revelation and by the "littleness" of the pictures that requires Melville to "press" forward and hold up his candle for more light. For a moment, we seem to spy into the most private recess of the Queen's "inward mind."

Yet Elizabeth's private self withholds something even in drawing us inward. Why does the Queen, who instigated the negotiations for marriage between Mary and Leicester, grant to Melville "a sight" of Leicester's little picture but then refuse to give away the trinket entirely, especially when an exchange of pictures in political matchmaking was the norm? Why does she answer with silence Melville's argument that she has "the original" Leicester, expressing instead her sincere affection for Mary's picture? (This evasion images Elizabeth's "*answer,* ANSWERLESS" to Parliament on the question of her own marriage.)[3] While appearing to open herself up, Elizabeth remains crucially closed—just as her reasons for arranging the Mary-Leicester marriage, which could only insult Mary, remain hidden. Indeed, each of her gestures toward sincere self-revelation is self-concealing, at once displayed and cloaked in her personal style of politics. After all, the Queen's protestations of "great desire" to meet Mary, when in fact she assiduously avoided ever meeting her; her decision to unveil specifically Leicester's and Mary's pictures; her wish that Mary "would follow her counsel": all were essentially political statements.

The uncovering of her secret self was a political "game" as intimate, earnest, and full of connivance as a game of cards between close friends. In both foreign and domestic relations, Elizabeth played on the interface between public and private self, handling threats from foreign princes by dangling the possibility of marriage with herself and managing her courtiers at home by encouraging the revival of courtly love: "Her lovers were her ministers, and her ministers were her lovers." If Elizabeth was being private with Melville, in short, she was being private *in public.* And in the process of making intimacy political and politics intimate, Elizabeth maintained an essential hiddenness: "Hir wisest men and beste Counsellors were oft sore troublede to knowe hir wyll in matters of State," Sir John Harington complained, "So covertly did she pass hir iudgmente."[4]

In the terms of my previous chapter, the Queen's interview with Melville is an episode of gift exchange in which the ultimate gift is the Elizabethan self. That is: the *double* Elizabethan self (not only of the Queen but of the aristocracy for which she was the focus). This self, I suggest, experienced a contradiction related to the split we will come to between culture as gift society and as "self-interested" market. On the one hand, the public self faced outward upon gift culture: it "gave" of itself selflessly for the increase of the commonality (or put less idealistically, for a particular regime of commonality). On the other hand, the private self faced inward toward se-crecy: it *withheld* itself from the cultural whole. Of course, a contradiction between public and private selves would not seem to be unique to the Eliz-abethan age. We thus need to be more historically particular. My argument is that the antithesis of Elizabethan public and private selves made possible a style of self-representation exactly the reverse of modern subjectivity as analyzed by Richard Sennett in *The Fall of Public Man*. Moderns, Sennett says (in an argument I will return to), have fallen into the custom of repre-senting all public experience as essentially private (so that we take the measure of a political candidate in his or her family life or love life).[5] But Elizabethans were in the inverse habit of representing private experience as inescapably public. The public self that gave outwards upon cultural ex-change was the medium of expression for a private self forever "loath" to give itself up in exchange—forever creating its very sense of itself, indeed, through acts of withholding full assent to publicness.

The history of the Elizabethan self, in short, was a history of fragmenta-tion in which the subject lived in public view but always withheld for itself a "secret" room, cabinet, case, or other recess locked away (in full view) in one corner of the house. Or rather there never was any ultimate room, cabi-net, or other *apart*ment of privacy that could be locked away from the public; only a perpetual regress of apartments. Like Elizabeth, seeming for no good reason "loath" to show Leicester's picture, the aristocratic self arose in a sort of reflex of retreat, an instinct to withdraw into privacy so pervasive even in the most trivial matters that there never could be any final moment of privacy. If "privacy" were ever achieved, then the need for *fur-ther* privacy would immediately arise. Within the "innermost" recesses of Elizabethan subjectivity, we will thus see, further recesses, cabinets, or cases kept opening up.

To come to the specific topic of this chapter: the great form of Eliz-abethan retreat was *ornament*. The Elizabethan private self withheld itself paradoxically by holding forth in ostentatious, public showcases of ornament—some as large as architecture and some as small as jeweled lockets. The literary showcase most expressive of such self-representation was the ornamental little poem of love: the "toyish" sonnet. But to assess the sonnet, I will first study an equally trifling Elizabethan art that, as Linda Bradley Salamon has recently suggested, was analogous to the little poem: the little miniature. Both showcases of Elizabethan ornament showed the self being private in public. Nicholas Hilliard and Sir Philip Sidney—the leading contemporary artists of miniatures and sonnets, respectively— crafted precious, gemlike decorations that hid the self's "secrets" behind a series of gorgeously ornate public rooms, cabinets, lockets, frames, paints, metaphors. . . .[6]

Publishing the Miniature

"In small volumes, in private manner"

An illuminating map to the Elizabethan presentation or "publication" of subjectivity in miniatures is provided by the layout of apartments in aristocratic houses.[7] We first note the co-location of miniatures and private chambers: the Elizabethan aristocracy commonly sought out the most removed or private room of the house—the bedchamber or its attached closet—to view miniatures in the company of intimates. This practice can be contrasted with the way oil paintings were presented for all to see in such relatively public or main rooms of the house as the gallery. Miniatures and oil paintings, indeed, were opposed in their very subject. Where the oil picture pulled back to view its subject publicly amidst all his or her symbols of rank and office, the miniature (called, at the time, painting "in little" or "limning") concentrated on its subject personally, focusing for the most part only on the face and shoulders, perhaps also the hands. And where the oil painting represented "a statesman, a soldier, a court-favourite in all his regalia," the miniature showed "a lover, a mistress, a wife, an intimate friend."[8] Even the Queen's limnings (at least until the 1580s) were personal by comparison with her public portraits: representations more of love mistress than of royal queen. Above all, miniatures were love tokens—presented as gifts to cherished intimates—and it is as an expression of such private emotions as love that they sought the intimacy of the bedroom.

In a regal demonstration of the close alignment of miniatures and intimate chambers, Sir Henry Unton, Elizabeth's ambassador to France, revealed a miniature of Elizabeth to Henry IV in the latter's royal bedroom in 1595. The French King had led Unton into his chamber seeking a kind of locker-room privacy to discuss his mistress, Madame de Monceaux. There, "in a privat Place" of the King's bedroom "between his Bed and the Wall," Unton mentions his own limned "Mistress," the Queen. Confidentially he tells the King,

> that if, without Offence I might speake it, that I had the Picture of a farr more excellent Mistress, and yet did her Picture come farr short of her Perfection of Beauty. As you love me (sayd he) shew it me, if you have it about you. I made some Difficulties; yett, uppon his Importunity, offred it unto his Viewe verie seacretly, houlding it still in my Hande.[9]

Unton virtually reenacts the bedroom scene in which we saw Elizabeth guardedly showing miniatures to Melville. Just as the Queen "appeared loath" to let Melville see her limnings, so Unton "made some Difficulties" to Henry. In both cases the holder of the miniature only shows the treasure upon "Importunity," offers it "verie seacretly," and never lets it leave the hand. And in both cases, too, the sense of littleness is important. As when Melville "pressed" close to see the miniature held by Elizabeth, Unton's handling of his miniature allows the littleness of the trinket to accentuate the intimacy of the private room. Offering it to Henry's view "verie sea-cretly," he demonstrates Hilliard's assertion in his *A Treatise Concerning the Arte of Limning* (written c. 1598–99) that because of its littleness the form was seen "of necessity in hand near unto the eye."[10] Viewers of the mini-ature could not stand back as disinterestedly as viewers of a large-scale painting. They had to "press" together, in Melville's phrase, so as to get close to the limning and to each other.

But before prospective viewers of miniatures could experience such inti-macy, of course, they had to get to the private room. This was by no means an easy task. The bedchamber or closet in sixteenth-century royal palaces, as well as in the great houses modeled on royal apartment plans, was in-creasingly situated at the heart of a long succession of public rooms. The outer rooms would become progressively less common as one penetrated further inward. On his way to view Elizabeth's miniatures, for instance, Melville would have passed through the highly public gallery (as well as other antechambers) where the general court gathered, through the more private presence chamber where only select courtiers entered, and through the even more private privy chamber where the chosen few assembled to discuss "the most secret transactions" of state before finally arriving at the inner sanctum of the royal bedchamber.[11] Such an experience must have registered with a double emphasis: one moved inward, but inwardness could be reached only after running a gauntlet of public outerness.

The public/private doubleness of such experience was intensified once a viewer reached the room holding the miniatures themselves. For once within the innermost room, the viewer still had to pass through something like outer "rooms" to get to the desired picture. The outermost "room" within the bedroom was a small chest or cabinet box richly ornamented for public display (Elizabeth's miniatures were probably kept in one of the "two little cabinets of exquisite work" noted by a German visitor to Whitehall in 1578).[12] Within these enclosures lay yet further enclosures usually consisting not of plain paper wrappings (like those holding Elizabeth's miniatures) but of turned ivory boxes that, while not as sumptuous as cabinets, were nevertheless still decorated for public showing. And within these latter boxes was a last, transparent enclosure—a sheet of crystal—behind which the viewer could finally see the miniature.[13]

"Publication" of the miniature, in sum, while creating a sense of inwardness—and thus appearing to respond to a real need for expressing the inner, private self—could be achieved only after submitting the viewer to a series of outer, public "rooms," whether political chambers or ornamental casings. The overall sense was of privacy exhibited in public, as if one were visiting a museum of the history of private life. Seeming to acknowledge this paradox, the miniature as early as the 1560s left the privacy of the bedroom for the arena of the court and actually began to be worn in public. Here, the contradiction between the inward and outward aspects of viewing the miniature that we saw in architecture was duplicated. Though initially introduced in court in an open frame, the miniature from the 1570s on appeared within finely enameled gold lockets (often called "picture boxes").[14] To view the miniature, one still had to penetrate the equivalent of an outer, highly social "room"—the ornamental picture-case richly decorated for all to see.

The *Armada Jewel* (fig. 8) with its miniature of Elizabeth vividly illustrates my point not only in its physical structure but in its ornamental motifs. In looking at the jewel and then opening it to get to the picture, we proceed by steps past the public image of Elizabeth, Queen of state and church, to the private one of Elizabeth, Unton's "Mistress" of beauty. Roy Strong enacts this movement in his description of the jewel:

> The outside of the case begins by an initial celebration of Elizabeth as the queen with a formal imperial profile image on the obverse together with her titles. On the reverse we progress from her secular to her ecclesiastical authority as governor of the *Ecclesia Anglicana* in the Ark of the Reformed Church sailing safely through the troubled seas. The locket opens to a contemplation of the private world of the heroine of the sonnets, a paean on her as the Lady,

8. Ascribed to Nicholas Hilliard, *Armada Jewel,* after 1588. Contains portrait of Elizabeth I dated 1580 by Hilliard, below right; outside lid, above left; front of locket, above right; inside lid, below left. 2 3/4 x 2 in. Photo: Victoria & Albert Museum (M81–1935).

as "Astraea, Queen of Beauty," whose pictured image is mirrored by the rose enamelled on the interior of the lid.[15]

Sprinkled with jewels and flowers, her ruff framing her heart-shaped face like the petals of the rose on the inside of the lid, Elizabeth the lady appears with a fresh, delicate intimacy diametrically opposed to the stony-faced, official profile of her on the outside. Yet the Queen chiselled on the outside is the only means of passage to the personal lady within.

Of course, "passage within" may at this point seem too optimistic. Perhaps a better phrasing would be that the act of passing through public enclosures forever deferred any final arrival at innermost privacy. The key fact here is that such outer coverings as the case of the *Armada Jewel* (like the many antechambers to the royal bedroom) actually protected and hid the private self more than they revealed it. In general, the elaborately ornamented cases of miniatures served this function. The *Gresley Jewel* (fig. 9), for example—thought to be a gift from Elizabeth on the marriage of Catherine Walsingham to Sir Thomas Gresley—flaunts and yet tells little of the couple's love. The overall exterior of the pendant is gold enameled in a variety of clear colors and set with table-cut rubies, emeralds, and pearls. The back sports an intricate pattern of enameled pied flowers, and the front

shows an onyx cameo of a black woman. No personal connection (master/servant, for instance) seems to have existed between the black and the married couple. Rather, busts of black persons were a convention in the jewelry of the sixteenth and seventeenth centuries, "combining the appeal of the exotic with advantageous use of the layers of an onyx."[16] They were impersonal artifice much like the enameled gold and precious jewels. In its very impersonality, such rich ornamentation hides the private love of the couple whose pictures the pendant encases. Only the two little golden cupids aiming their arrows at either side of the case point to the secret love within.

The most striking example I have found of the twinned self-revealing, self-concealing nature of the miniature cases worn at court is a curious story of a "fyne jewell" belonging to Lady Derby. Recounted to the earl of Shrewsbury by William Browne in a letter dated 1602, the story brings us back from the physical setting of miniatures to their full social setting. Browne was enclosing some verses composed by Sir Robert Cecil and set to music by Hales. He explains,

> The occasion was, as I hear, that the young Lady of Darby wearing about her neck, in her bosom, a picture which was in a dainty tablet, the Queen, espying itt, asked what fyne jewell that was: The Lady Darby was curious to excuse

9. Perhaps by Nicholas Hilliard, *Gresley Jewel*, before 1585. Contains portraits of Catherine Walsingham (c. 1580–85) and Sir Thomas Gresley (c. 1590) by Hilliard, right; closed lid, opposite right; front of locket, opposite left. 3 in. (including pearl). Pennington-Mellor-Munthe Charity Trust. Photo: Victoria & Albert Museum.

the shewing of itt, butt the Queen would have itt, and opening itt, and fynd-
ing itt to be Mr. Secretarye's, snatcht itt away, and tyed itt uppon her shoe,
and walked long with itt there; then she tooke itt thence, and pinned itt on
her elbow, and wore itt som tyme there also; which Mr. Secretary being told
of, made these verses, and had Hales to sing them in his chamber. . . . I do
boldly send these things to your Lordship which I wold not do to any els, for I
heare they are very secrett.[17]

What exactly Browne means when he affirms "these things . . . are very secrett" is itself secret. Is he referring to the love lyrics of Cecil sung to the
Queen in his bedchamber (we are told, "Some of the verses argew that he
repynes not thoghe her Majesty please to grace others, and contents himself
with the favour he hath")?[18] Or to the scene with the miniature that in-
spired this poetry? We cannot say for certain, though Browne's statement
seems all-inclusive. Certainly Lady Derby's "picture" is most secret: not
only concealed "in a dainty tablet" but hidden "in her bosom." Her attempt
to keep her miniature secret, "to excuse the shewing of itt," is precisely the
same response we saw in Elizabeth and in Unton when asked to reveal their
limnings. The reaction seems almost instinctive. There is no explanation
for Lady Derby's reluctance to uncover her miniature (it is, after all, only a
picture of her uncle) other than the fact that it is *her* miniature: a part of her
private self, her personal secret, to be revealed only to those *she* chooses.
Elizabeth violates Lady Derby's intimacy in forcing her to uncover it.

While momentarily failing her in this instance, however, Lady Derby's
"fyne jewell" had allowed her to carry a core of privacy and sincerity—her
"real" self—into the open court of artifice. Portability in this sense is as
important as the richness of the case.[19] The miniature that can be "held in
the hand" can also be "snatcht" away, "tyed" to a shoe, "walked long," and
"pinned" on the elbow. Elizabeth could thus whimsically play with Lady
Derby's little pendant, giving full expression to her own individuality. Even
in the case here of Elizabeth, however, subjectivity was "wrapt." Like the
miniature in its case, which was essentially a heart of privacy wrapped in
ornament, Elizabeth's self-expression was cloaked in ostentatious self-
display: a kind of conscious public posing, like Cecil's posing as the conventional courtly lover.

And this brings me to my crucial point. The Lady Derby/Elizabeth incident suggests that the truly "private" Elizabethan self expressed in publishing the miniature was always hidden (even from intimates) by the very
nature of the artifice that published it. For that matter, returning to architecture, even the most private rooms in Elizabethan houses (and certainly

the royal bedchamber) were sites where privacy could never be achieved. Private rooms were essentially public, readily open to servants and visitors.[20] While Elizabeth and Melville conducted their intimate interview, Leicester and Cecil conversed "at the farthest part of the chamber." (The obverse of this public rendering of Elizabeth's bedchamber is the personal denotation—"Privy"—for her political chamber.) The Elizabethan aristocracy, one might say, never really arrived at any private center in passing through its long corridor of public rooms.

Nowhere is this more evident than when the last such "room"—the ornamental chamber of the miniature case—was opened and the actual limning or picture within viewed. I refer in particular to limning style of the late Elizabethan age (from about 1570 to 1600) when miniatures became all the fashion under the impetus of Nicholas Hilliard. Having so far passed through public rooms to view the miniature case (itself publicly decorated), we must now look further inwards to Hilliard's decorative pictures. Concentrating on his innovative technique and style, we can trace in the miniature a growing artifice of secrecy that culminates in Hilliard's masterpiece, *Young Man among Roses*.

Hilliard's Secret Art of Limning

At first glance, Hilliard's limnings might seem to substantiate the notion that Elizabethans, in passing through public rooms or ornamental casings, could actually penetrate to a real, private self. In Eric Mercer's words, Hilliard's miniatures distinctly represent "a personality."[21] Or as Hilliard himself put it in his *Treatise*, he sought to "catch" the "lovely graces, witty smilings" and "stolen glances" of his sitters (p. 77).

He tried to represent such immediate intimacies by devoting himself to "the truth of the line," the unshadowed line-stroke that constituted his calligraphic style (p. 85). The *Treatise* cites in support of such style a conversation with the Queen. Elizabeth, Hilliard notes, affirmed "that best to show oneself needeth no shadow of place, but rather the open light," and therefore chose to be limned "in the open alley of a goodly garden, where no tree was near, nor any shadow at all." In concurring with Elizabeth, Hilliard's *Treatise* reasons that the "grosser line" of shadowing marred the close-in vision of limning. The argument also has a psychological and ethical dimension. Standing in an "open alley" in the clear sight of heaven signifies one's purity of soul: "For beauty and good favour is like clear truth, which is not shamed with the light, nor needs to be obscured." Shadowing, on the contrary, which "smutted" the purity of colors, is "like truth ill told" and can only signify a hidden "ill cause" (pp. 85–87). Although Hilliard uses terms like "open" and "clear" to stress the intimate truth he wishes to limn, the kind of sincerity and intimacy he describes was really at home, as we have seen, within the enclosed privacy of the bedroom or locket. Indeed, Hilliard's *Treatise* throughout insists that truthful limning was for gentlemen alone and most private: limning "is for the service of noble persons very meet, in small volumes, in private manner" (p. 65); "it is a kind of gentle painting. . . . it is secret" (p. 63).[22]

Nevertheless, if Hilliard aimed to limn such personal truths as were commonly expressed in the private room, he actually represented privacy only in eminently outward and public guise: behind a screen of ornamentation so impenetrably elaborate as at last to prevent any glimpse of a true inner self. Most of Hilliard's innovations in limning thus extended the purely ornamental qualities of limning's parent arts, goldsmithing and manuscript illumination ("limn" derives from the verb "illuminate").[23] In particular, his line-without-shadow style drew upon what was originally the goldsmith's and illuminator's calligraphic manner. Embellished and made more intricate, Hilliard's handling of the line became the basis for his ornate, busy renderings of his sitters' hair, clothes, and jewels. The portrait of an *Unknown Lady* (fig. 10) epitomizes this formalized, calligraphic style: the lady's face is framed by minutely drawn curls and a complexly patterned ruff whose design extends with variation into the ornamental tulips of her bodice and the looping gold thread of her sleeves.[24]

Hilliard then intensified the decorativeness of his patterned "lines" by adopting the fresh, bright colors of his sources. Himself both a limner and goldsmith, he passionately stressed the bond between limning colors and precious stones, insisting in his *Treatise* "that there are besides white and black but five perfect colours in the world": amethyst murrey, ruby red, sapphire blue, emerald green, topaz yellow (p. 101). He even invented new painting techniques to counterfeit jewels as well as the gloss of metals and texture of precious fabrics. While earlier miniaturists would use gold as a powdered pigment, Jim Murrell points out, Hilliard treated it as a metal, applying it thickly to the edges and inscriptions of his works and then burnishing it "so that the soft gold particles would merge together, presenting a continuous surface of gleaming metal."[25] When depicting a sitter's gems, for instance, he would build up their gold mounts in relief before then duplicating the transparency, luster, and color of the gems themselves with *trompe l'oeil* fidelity. Even his sitters' starched lace ruffs, as in the *Unknown Lady*, would be counterfeited in three dimensions, with paint dribbled in impasto

10. Nicholas Hilliard, *Unknown Lady,* c. 1585–90. 1 3/4 x 1 1/2 in.
Photo: Victoria & Albert Museum (P2–1974).

fashion onto the surface. The net product of these extensions of gold-smithing and illuminating was a decorative manner far removed from the relative simplicity of Hilliard's predecessors or followers. It was a style creative of "a highly stylized jewel-like object, whose rich variety of colours and metals became a perfect complement to the jewelled lockets in which so many miniatures were set."[26]

In their pictorial manner, then, Hilliard's limnings illustrate the way the private self lay behind a screen of ornament. The process by which Hilliard painted faces confirms the point. When we look for privacy, we discern only a face whose faint "ground" color lacks almost all definition except, paradoxically, as supplied by the ornamental hair, clothes, and background *around* the face. After meticulously grinding and washing his pigments, we know, Hilliard would first paint onto vellum the "ground" or "carnation" of his portrait. This involved a swift application of flesh color (very pale in hue) in the area destined for the face. Working from the perimeter of the head in, he would next lightly outline the visage before going on to detail the features; then he would add the background and clothing. Once the overall design was in place, ornamentation would be built up around the face in a three-dimensional manner. The only definition given the face itself came by way of "hatching" it with darker hues of the same color (rather than "shadows" of black or contrasting hues). Only faintly modeled by such "transparent hatching," facial features literally remained the ground of the portrait: flat in dimension and closest in color to the parchment base. To see the personality of the plain face, therefore, required looking to the impersonality of the built-up, outer layers of ornament all around.[27]

If we needed any further evidence that the "real" private self only existed as seen in artifice, we would now need only to look to the ground behind the "ground": to the playing card that usually backed the vellum of the simple face. Limners appear self-consciously to have chosen these cards. Backing a 1572 Hilliard limning of Elizabeth, for instance, is the Queen of Hearts.[28] In miniature painting, we may say, the private self never showed all its cards. It always had one further trick of artifice to interpose between the viewer and the heart of privacy.

As in the case of the antechambers leading to the Elizabethan private room, then, the outer layers of artifice and ornament in a limning were the unavoidable thoroughfare to the inner, truthful self—a thoroughfare that was finally blockage. Most important, the posing of the sitter behind layers of ornament emblematized the fact that the miniature glossed over true character. The intimacy of miniature portraits was "sweet" (a term in which we taste the sugar candy added to limning colors), meaning that it was a false intimacy idealizing the sitter. We see not a "true" but a flattering image. In fact, we know that Queen Elizabeth encouraged Hilliard's "line without shadow" precisely because such style masked her aging features. The intimate "lovely graces, witty smilings," and "stolen glances" Hilliard depicted in his sitters thus really amounted to "covert emotions," the emotional equivalent to Sidney's ethical *Idea*.[29] Perhaps this is why the Unknown Lady in fig. 10 so enigmatically smiles at us. Such a mysterious expression of the mouth, "depending on the sweep of the middle line, with the corners tucked up a little," effects what art historians have called a "tantalizing intimacy."[30] We catch a glimpse of the heart that in real life enlivened the plain white face (itself shaped into a heart by the intricate ornament of the limning) while the full-bodied lady lies out of reach. Like some Queen-of-Hearts playing card held close to the vest, the Unknown Lady keeps her secret.

The enigmatic smile of fleeting intimacy became a Hilliard trademark by the 1580s. It became the very signature of the fact that he was so little disturbed by the inscrutability of the private selves he painted that he began to flaunt "secrecy" itself.[31] Other ornamental devices of secrecy began to proliferate in his work. Various leaves, petals, and buds placed against a lady's breast (as exemplified in Elizabeth's portrait in the *Armada Jewel*) were early expressions of self-knowing ornamentation, of a decorativeness that almost seems to challenge us to guess its riddle. The flowers never reappeared from one miniature to another: they were unique signs with "secret significance."[32] The full flowering of this tendency toward conscious secrecy occurred in the late 1580s when many of Hilliard's miniatures showed a hand held over the heart (sometimes half concealed behind a cloak or shirt) as well as riddling mottoes in the tradition of *imprese*.[33]

Now we are prepared for the pinnacle of Hilliard's growing art of secrecy, *Young Man among Roses* (c. 1587–88), which quintessentially expresses the problematics of representing sincerity through artifice, simplicity through ornament, and secret self through public display (fig. 11).[34] *Young Man among Roses* portrays a love-sick courtier leaning elegantly against a tree within a rose briar, his cloak slung casually over his shoulder, his hand held over his heart. The lover's white face, as always in a Hilliard miniature, gives only a bare hint of expression: an abstract feeling of sadness. Full meaning is represented through the miniature's color scheme and compositional design—effects that at first glance seem to refer unambiguously to a thwarted, personal love.

In terms of color: the white of the lover's attire and face (the latter encircled by a white ruff that itself mirrors the little white roses) expresses his purity and truth. The black of his cloak and the stripes of the doublet declare his constancy in love. But the color black, of course (as well as the tawny hue woven into the doublet's stripes and buttons), is also the color of melancholy. It is the color complement to the thorns on the sweet rosebush—both emblems of crossed love. This combination of true yet thwarted love is also represented by the "crossed" lines of the picture's composition. The oval of the miniature is elongated to include the straight or "true" tree trunk—a sign of constancy drawn from books of *imprese*. The tree is paralleled by the long form of the youth as well as by his ruler-straight left leg. But we notice that the lover's right leg crosses over his left. Similarly, the patterns on his doublet crisscross his chest, a crossing motif paralleled in the way the line of his arm and raised thumb cross his breast. The design of the picture thus also shows that true love is crossed. To seal the overall image, Hilliard adds a motto. Curling in gold over the top of the lover's curly hair, crossing at one point the curving rose briar, the motto verbalizes in a single line of verse the depth of meaning conveyed by color and design. *"Dat poenas laudata fides,"* it laments: "Praised faith brings sufferings [or penalties]."[35]

This miniature is gemlike in the way it knits every detail together into a most decorative composition. It belies William Camden's ruling that in such devices the picture is "the body" and the motto "the soul." The device that is Hilliard's miniature is all body. The verbal inscription swirled in gold is as much external decoration as the ornamental little roses and other effects in the picture. All seem to point to the inner soul or heart of the lover: the *impresa's* "secretes of the minde."[36]

But to "point to" the lover's secret self is not necessarily to uncloak it. Though clearly a lyrical expression of the trials of true love, the exact self

11. Nicholas Hilliard, *Young Man among Roses,* c. 1587–88. 5 3/8 x 2 3/4 in.
Photo: Victoria & Albert Museum (P163–1910).

Hilliard was representing—the personal allusion of the motto and its accompanying picture—remains mysterious. In fact, though color and design represent the lover's meaning, they also hide his "true" love in the very process of representation. More exactly, what we again see in this miniature is privacy concealed behind public fragments or "rooms" of ornament. The outermost room is the flowery rosebush, which covers the tree and the lover's attire. Adorned by the decorative flowers and leaves, the lover's hose and cloak take on the ornamental patterns often woven into fabrics at court. This impression is reinforced by the unrealistic way Hilliard has painted the roses: they are limned *onto* the fabric, imitative of the secret flowers so often limned onto ladies' breasts. Just as the flowery roses cover the lover's constant black cloak, moreover, the now ornamented cloak becomes a public room mostly covering or enclosing his pure white hand. The plain hand then in turn becomes an ornamental room behind which hides the lover's "true" heart. As if following the corridor of rooms leading to the innermost chamber of an Elizabethan house, each successive "room" leading into the truthful heart may seem to be more private because less ornamental: we pass through the highly decorative roses to the simple but elegant cloak, and finally to the plain white hand indicating the heart within. And in the process of penetrating through this series of decreasingly ornamental coverings, the viewer may get an indefinite sense of the lover's crossed love: we, too, are frustrated. But at last (and this is our ultimate frustration) the heart we penetrate toward is as concealed as the lover's face is inexpressive: both symbolize the fact that the masks of ornamentation are never quite dropped to show the hiddenness of the lover. Even the lover's lady and intimate friends, who may have had access to some of the miniature's personal meaning, would have been denied full comprehension by the public ornamentation expressing it.

Confirming that the lover's secret truth lies hidden behind ornaments whose very nature is public display, the motto of the miniature derives from a political history: Lucan's *De Bello Civili*. The lines are spoken by the eu- ∨ nuch Pothinus, who advises Pompey's death. The lovesick pose of the courtier is thus set in a political context in which the lover is as public as Pompey the Great, whose trust made him vulnerable to betrayal. This political context can be extended even further with Strong's argument that the youth is the earl of Essex in the act of showing his flattering, secret love for the Queen (Elizabeth's colors were black and white, and the eglantine—if the roses are eglantine—was one of her symbols). What exactly the miniature would mean within this latter context remains unclear. It is difficult to

12. Nicholas Hilliard, *Man against a Background of Flames,* c. 1595. 2 5/8 x 2 1/8 in.
Photo: Victoria & Albert Museum (P5–1917).

read the motto as a prophesy of Essex's downfall, which lay some fourteen years in the future. And I do not think that, in accepting a veiled reference to Elizabeth, we need exclude an even more private love. Essex's secret marriage to Sidney's widow, we should note, also occurred about this time.[37] The point is that Hilliard and the courtier limned here would have felt as much at ease in picturing a private love through the public symbols of the Queen as in expressing the subjective experience of love through a political motto.

Everything associated with miniature painting, in sum, suggests that its habit of public ornamentation kept, rather than told, private "secrets." Bedrooms displayed closed decorative cabinets; cabinets exhibited closed ivory boxes; boxes showed off covered or encased miniatures; and, when we finally set eyes on the limning itself, layers of ornamental colors and patterns show only the hiddenness of the heart. As seen in the frequent limning of "miniatures-within-miniatures," indeed, the regress of concealing layers of ornament extended indefinitely. In Hilliard's *Man against a Background of Flames* (fig. 12), for instance, a lover appears literally to bare his burning passion. His fine linen shirt, *en déshabillé,* opens wide to reveal his white breast and an enameled gold locket hanging from a chain around his neck. Pressed against his heart, the locket undoubtedly contains a miniature of his mistress; as Hotson observes, he is "chained to the Idea of his mistress." Every decorative detail of the miniature seems to tell of his single passion: not only the other trinkets—the ring on the little finger, "the finger of lovers," and the "pendant ear-drop in the form of a true-love"—but "the white of his shirt and the nakedness of his breast [which] both show his Sincerity or Truth."[38] Most expressive of all is the flaming background, its surging rhythms growing out of the folds of the lover's shirt. "I am a martyr burning at the stake of love," the man seems to say to us. But, of course, he also warns, "My love is secret." The mistress lies *locked* within the ornamental case of the miniature he wears, just as the heart over which he holds the locket is concealed behind the white "ground" of his breast. Even if the miniature locket were opened—as his shirt is opened—it would continue to screen the truth of inwardness through its many layers of pictorial ornament. The truth of privacy cannot be represented. In the world of the court, it can only be hidden behind endless facades of public ornament. Literally, we know, there is no end to the regression of decorative facades in *Man against a Background of Flames*. Strip the man of the miniature to expose his breast, look through his breast to his heart, spy behind his heart the burning wall of flame it symbolically encases, and finally break through the background of flame itself: what would we discover to be the secret truth of this miniature? A playing card: the Ace of Hearts.[39]

Publishing the Sonnet
"Such Secret thoughts as fit not euery sight"

Having traversed the long corridor of chambers that published the heartfelt emotion of Hilliard's miniatures, we arrive almost inevitably upon love's little poem or (as contemporaries loosely defined it) the "sonnet."[40]

Elizabethan love poetry was often "published" in precisely the same architecturally peripheral or private rooms where the miniature was shown. After Elizabeth snatched away Lady Derby's miniature and played with it, we remember, Cecil (the subject of the miniature) composed love lyrics to the Queen. What we can now note is that he "published" them by having them sung to Elizabeth "in his chamber." Even aristocrats who were not actually love poets mimed the pose or language of sonneteers in their chambers. We hear that the French King, to whom Unton "verie seacretly" showed Elizabeth's miniature in the royal bedchamber, beheld it "with Passion and Admiration" and "with great Reverence . . . kissed it twice or thrice." The King was acting out a conventional image of the sonneteers:

the lover worshiping his lady like a saint. As Unton concludes in his story, love rhetoric dominated: "In the Ende, with some kind of Contention, he toke it from me, vowing, that I might take my Leave of it, for he would not forgoe it for any Treasure; and that, to possesse the Favor of the lively Picture, he would forsake all the World, and hould himself most happie, with many other most passionate Wordes."[41] Henry's kisses and "passionate Wordes" are startling in their blend of artificiality and intimacy.

Conveyed to select "intimates" in private rooms, such lyrical expressions of love were much different in spirit from more public literary forms: drama, for instance, which would have been presented to a wide audience in the hall or other main and open rooms of a house. Unlike "full-scale" dramatic action, love poetry took miniaturized snapshots of a lover. Even an entire sonnet sequence, though it may have "structure" or "movements," lacks the strict narrative continuity of drama. The sonneteer endeavors rather to catch successively heartfelt and fresh glimpses of his love: in Spenser's words, "The sweet eye-glaunces, that like arrowes glide, / the charming smiles, that rob sence from the hart: / the louely pleasance and the lofty pride."[42] The love poet was a version of Hilliard's limner—necessarily "amorous" of his sitter, Hilliard insisted—who strove to "catch those lovely graces, witty smilings, and those stolen glances which suddenly like lightning pass, and another countenance taketh place" (*Treatise*, p. 77). It follows naturally that the little sonnet manuscript, like the little vellum miniature, would have been given or shown privately, passed "in hand" between lovers and close friends. As Malcolm William Wallace observes, the showing of Sidney's love sonnets would have been even more intimate than that of his romance, the *Arcadia*, about which a contemporary affirmed, "A special dear friend he should be that could have a sight, but much more dear that could once obtain a copy of it."[43]

Love poetry, then, was guardedly "published" between intimates in private rooms. It was also kept within these rooms in ornamental cabinets or boxes. The locking of love poems in containers usually reserved for the greatest valuables belied the poets' reiterated apologies that their poems were *mere* "toys" or "youthful follies." J. C., the author of a six-line stanza sequence, *Alcilia* (1595), asserted that his poems were "vain"; but he also hoped that his lady would hide them "securely"—as if they were precious jewels—"in her secret box." Thomas Nash, justifying the piratical printing of Sidney's sonnets, argued that poetry is "oftentimes imprisoned in Ladyes casks" and has to use "some priuate penne (in steed of a picklock) to procure his violent enlargmente." So too, Sir William Alexander in *Avrora*

(1604) affirmed, "had not others otherwise aduised, / My cabinet should yet these scroles containe."[44] Did Alexander's "cabinet" also contain his miniatures? Most likely. The sonnet and the miniature probably lay side by side in the decorative little boxes and cabinets that concealed Elizabethan valuables.

In order to read a private love poem, therefore, one had to pass through the same succession of outer public "rooms"—the many antechambers as well as ornamental boxes—that allowed access to, but also kept secret, the miniature. In discussing limning, I argued that the logical extension of this fact was the miniature's appearance at court concealed within a portable "room" or ornamental casing. The love poem also traveled out to court in much the same fashion. Its smallness, even when collected in a sequence, permitted its easy portability into court as well as its secret handling. The little lyric could be hidden in a lady's pocket, like Raleigh's love poem to Lady Laiton. Or it could be "thrust" into her bosom along with the love letter in *The Adventures of Master F. I.*[45] But the closest parallel to the "publication" of the private miniature at court was the way the love poem was increasingly published in print. The poet published his private love—carrying it not only to the court but to the "commonality" of the public beyond—by enclosing his poems in what amounted to a literary locket: the "case" of prefatory letters. The function of these prefaces was to speak in wholly conventional, and thus public, terms of the betrayal of private "secrets."

In 1592, for instance, after the 1591 piratical publication of some of his sonnets together with Sidney's *Astrophil and Stella*, Daniel issued an authorized edition of his *Delia,* whose dedication to the countess of Pembroke explains:

> Although I rather desired to keep in the priuate passions of my youth, from the multitude, as things vttered to my selfe, and consecrated to silence: yet seeing I was betraide by the indiscretion of a greedie Printer, and had some of my secrets bewraide to the world, vncorrected: doubting the like of the rest, I am forced to publish that which I neuer ment. . . . I am thrust out into the worlde, and . . . my vnboldned Muse, is forced to appeare so rawly in publique.

Daniel protests that he (and by association Sidney) has suffered a mental rape. The inner temple of his "priuate passions . . . consecrated to silence" has been invaded, and his "secrets" betrayed, "forced" naked—"rawly"—into the public eye. Incessantly, the prefaces to the printed editions of sonnets described publication as a betrayal of the poet's "secrets" to the "common" public. In his preface to the Miscellany, *A Hundreth Sundrie Flowres* (1573), which contains a large number of formal sonnets by Gascoigne, "H. W." readily admits he violated the wishes of his "familiar friend Master G. T.," who "charged me, that I should use them onely for mine owne particuler commoditie." H. W. goes so far as to attach the actual letter in which, sure enough, G. T.—writing that he sends his collection to "his very friend" in order "to participate the sight therof unto your former good will"—implores "that you will by no meanes make the same common: but after your owne recreation taken therin that you wil safely redeliver unto me the originall copie." He concludes the letter by reaffirming this request: "And therfore I requier your secresie herein." William Percy's epistle to the reader prefacing his *Sonnets to the Fairest Coelia* (1594) tells a similar tale: "whereas I was fullie determined to haue concealed my Sonnets, as thinges priuie to my selfe, yet of courtesie hauing lent them to some, they were secretlie committed to the Presse, and almost finished, before it came to my knowledge." So, too, Robert Tofte frames his *Laura* (1597) fore and aft with declarations of this kind. Preceding the sequence is an "Epistle Dedicatorie" to Lady Lucy Percy "hoping your Ladiship wil keep them as priuately, as I send them vnto you most willingly." Next comes an epistle "To the Reader" in which the printer confesses he and his friend "are both too blame, that whereas he hauing promised to keepe priuate the originall, and I the copie, secret: we both haue consented to send it abroad, as common." At the close of the sequence, sealing these declarations of violated trust, is a note by another friend claiming he strove to protect the author's secret but was too late: "I came at the last sheetes printing."[46]

With such evidence in hand, we might be inclined to echo the English cry of *ingratitude* against the Irish (heard in my previous chapter) and decry the violation of the poet's trust. Yet before we too hastily conclude, "With such friends who needs enemies?" we should note that the many prefatory letters by the poets and their "friends" in fact ensured the secrecy of "priuate passions" even as they were being published. Only at first glance does the poet's claim that his love poetry is "priuate" and "secret" or that "a greedie Printer" and those very same friends "betraide" him create the sense of a door opening onto his most inner self. In actuality, the prefatory letters made it impossible to distinguish sincerity from artifice. In *Flowres,* for instance, the printer ("A. B.") accuses H. W. and G. T. of "politiquely" claiming secrecy to prevent "the daunger of misreport." He concludes, "Now I feare very muche (all these words notwithstanding) that these two gentlemen were of one assent compact to have it imprinted."[47] Yet what follows the printer's statements are published declarations to the contrary: H. W.'s letter "to the Reader" and G. T.'s letter "to his very friend H. W." entreating "secresie." One begins to get the strong impression here and throughout the sonnet prefaces of an elaborate game being played. In this sense the sonnets really were mere "toys." To the extent that this game followed recognized rules, it was public, conventional. To question the players' sincerity would have been as problematic as questioning whether Elizabeth was "really" loath to uncover her miniatures to Melville. When "G. T." or other poets protested the "secresie" of their work, we recognize, they (like the Queen) were playing out an artful pose. But their sincerity may very well have been genuine. We cannot know. The very signature of the way private sincerity hid inscrutably within public posturing was the custom of attaching secret mottoes (e.g., "*Meritum petere, gravè*" in *Flowres*) and enigmatic initials to individual poems, sequences, and prefatory apparatus. The editor, H. W., writes about the printer, A. B., and the collector, G. T. The respective title pages to *Emaricdulfe* (1595), *Diella* (1596), and *Lavra* (1597) identify the poets as "E. C. Esquier," "R. L., Gentleman," and "R. T. Gentleman." Each initial or motto hinted at a personal secret,[48] but each was also anonymous, conventional, and thus strangely impersonal. They were as pro forma in their secrecy as any purely public "Sir" or "Esquire" at the end of a letter.

The elaborate apparatus of prefatory letters and signatures attending sonnets were only the outermost ornamental "room" or "case" around the poet's love. If we enter into the text of the poems themselves, we find still more chambers of convention extending the game of secrecy.[49] Not only did the poets infuse their sonnets with conventional declarations of "secret," "hidden," and "private" affection, but—vying with Hilliard's secret mottoes—they played with amatory "riddles" and secretly published the identity of themselves and, especially, their mistresses. Repeatedly we encounter decorative anagrams or acronyms playing on a lady's name as well as special code words (Sidney's reiterated "rich," for example),[50] not to mention numerous other glances at the lady's heraldic arms, country home, etc. These conventional codes were slightly less public and more personal than the claims of "secrets bewraide" in the prefatory letters: they seem to offer closer access to the poet's "true" self and the "truth" of his love. Or at least they do to the initiated. One might say that the Elizabethan poet publishing his sonnets, like a lover "publishing" his miniature to select viewers, built up around his love a labyrinthine fun house of ornamental "rooms." One's intimacy with the poet determined how far one could pass within.

Ultimately, however, the inner sanctum of the language of love could no more be reached than in a miniature. When one penetrates inward past the outer conventions of sonnet secrecy (the title pages and prefaces) and past even the conventional emblems of secrecy within the poems (the riddles and codes of love), one is still left with the artifice of all-embracing *rhetoric*. More than any other Elizabethan sonneteer, Sidney vociferously denied but also epitomized a colorful sonnet rhetoric. In his effort to represent "true," heartfelt love, he adamantly rejected conventional "sugared" speech, just as he refused publicly to publish his sonnets. Yet in the very process of rejecting such speech, he invented "in a ground of so firme making" verbal ornaments that were precisely analogous to Hilliard's visual ornaments in hiding private feeling.[51] "Colors" of one sort or another, we may say, at once "published" love and kept it "close" (sonnet 34).

Sidney's "Ground" of Poetry

To compare the rhetorical ornament of Sidney's sonnets to the style of miniature painting, we can begin with a sonnet that explicitly invokes one of limning's parent forms. Sonnet 11 of *Astrophil and Stella* rejects surface ornament as a trivial "toy" by comparing Cupid's "boyish" fascination for Stella's "outward part" with a child's looking only at the "colourd" decorations or pictures in "some faire booke":

> In truth, ô Love, with what a boyish kind
>   Thou doest proceed in thy most serious wayes:
>   That when the heav'n to thee his best displayes,
> Yet of that best thou leav'st the best behind.
> For like a child that some faire booke doth find,
>   With guilded leaves or colourd Velume playes,
>   Or at the most on some fine picture stayes,
> But never heeds the fruit of writer's mind:
> So when thou saw'st in Nature's cabinet
> *Stella,* thou straight lookst babies in her eyes,
> In her cheeke's pit thou didst thy pitfould set,
> And in her breast bopeepe or couching lyes,
>   Playing and shining in each outward part:
>   But, foole, seekst not to get into her hart.

This sonnet, I suggest, is all about the way truth hides behind ornaments—specifically, ornaments akin to decorative miniatures. Illuminated manuscripts with "guilded leaves" and "colourd Velume," we remember, lay at the origin of miniature painting. Sidney's comparison of the child staying "on some fine picture" to Cupid settling on Stella's face and breast recalls the small portrait limnings that began appearing on manuscripts just before

the miniature departed the page to become a separate form. Hilliard illuminated two such portraits between 1581 and 1583 for a work that Sidney may
have seen: Elizabeth's now lost prayer book (fig. 13). Showing the Queen
and her suitor the duke of Anjou (Sidney was involved in the marriage negotiations), the portraits were placed one at the back and the other at the
front of the book so as to frame the intervening text in the same way that
traditional illuminations (flowers, beasts, heraldic symbols, biblical scenes)
framed individual pages of manuscripts.[52] Just so, the second quatrain of
sonnet 11 imagines ornamental pictures and decorations that fringe "the
fruit of writer's mind." Nor does the ornamental framing or encasement of
meaning stop there. The reference in the next quatrain to "Nature's cabinet" suggests by analogy that "the fruit of writer's mind" resides within a
man-made cabinet: perhaps one of the lavishly decorated cabinets enclosing Elizabethan miniatures, sonnet manuscripts, and other valuables. More
precisely, of course, this last quatrain discovers in the miniature cabinet
Stella herself. Like "the fruit of writer's mind," Stella's essential beauty is
enclosed in a box of ornament. "Nature's cabinet" encloses each of her
beautiful "outward" parts, and the outward parts in turn encase her innermost being, "her hart." In order to heed "the fruit of writer's mind" or
Stella's "hart," the sonnet says, one must penetrate layer after layer of ornament.

But the beauty of the sonnet, of course, is that it stops before peeling
away all the ornaments to get to the core of truth. What, after all, can we see
in Stella's "hart"? What, for that matter, does Sidney mean by "the fruit of
writer's mind"? (The writer's ideas? His words?) The inner truths of the fair
book and of fair Stella are not represented, despite the poet's assurance that
"heav'n" (and by implication the writer) "his best displayes." One gets at
Stella's "hart" and "the fruit of writer's mind" through ornamental displays
whose very status as distracting display makes the "best," "serious" inner
truths invisible. Playful "outward" ornament is all.

In other sonnets in *Astrophil and Stella,* Sidney comes closer to baring
"the fruit of writer's mind." I refer to his thematization of poetry itself or,
more accurately, *rhetoric.* But showy rhetoric, of course, only continues the
game of gesturing inadequately toward inaccessible "true" inwardness; it is
itself only layer after layer of ornamental display. Significantly, in the process of criticizing rhetoric, Sidney often foregrounds the likeness between
the sonnet form and the decorative miniature. Consider sonnet 3:

> Let daintie wits crie on the Sisters nine,
> That bravely maskt, their fancies may be told:
> Or *Pindare's* Apes, flaunt they in phrases fine,

13. Queen Elizabeth's prayer book with twin miniatures by Nicholas Hilliard of the duke of Anjou (formerly Alençon) at the front and Elizabeth at the back (limned between 1581 and 1583). The prayer book disappeared sometime after 1893. Photo: British Library.

Enam'ling with pied flowers their thoughts of gold:
  Or else let them in statelier glorie shine,
Ennobling new found Tropes with problemes old:
  Or with strange similies enrich each line,
Of herbes or beastes, which *Inde* or *Afrike* hold.
  For me in sooth, no Muse but one I know:
  Phrases and Problemes from my reach do grow,
And strange things cost too deare for my poore sprites.
  How then? even thus: in *Stella's* face I reed,
  What Love and Beautie be, then all my deed
But Copying is, what in her Nature writes.

As William A. Ringler, Jr., aptly observes, "Sidney here reviews the chief literary movements of his time, both on the Continent and in England."[53] At the same time, I propose, he reviews something like the jeweled lockets and ornamental style of Elizabethan miniatures. The first two lines of the sonnet at once decry and proclaim the necessity of ornamental rhetoric: "Let daintie wits crie on the Sisters nine, / That bravely maskt, their fancies may be told." "Daintie wits" only tell their private "fancies" when they are "bravely maskt"—that is, when the appearance of their heart's truth is also really a disappearance.[54] It is tempting to draw an analogy between the "daintie" poetasters of these lines and the "daintie" ladies and courtiers who "bravely maskt" their *limnings* within pretty cabinets or richly enameled gold lockets. The analogy seems called for because Sidney's sonnet goes on to mock rhetoric by comparing it explicitly to art forms such as limning: "*Pindare's* Apes, flaunt they in phrases fine, / Enam'ling with pied flowers their thoughts of gold." Rhetoric appears here as decorative gold enameled with pied flowers—a finely crafted surface much like the back of such miniature lockets as the *Gresley Jewel*. (Indeed, Sidney possibly saw this jewel, since it was given to the cousin of his close friend and future father-in-law, Sir Francis Walsingham.) Poetasting "*Pindare's* Apes" show off "thoughts of gold" much as elegant ladies and courtiers show off their private love: by encasing it in a fancy case that "flaunts," but only to "mask."

Sonnet 3 associates rhetoric not only with miniature cases but with their enclosed limnings as well. We recall that limnings were themselves lined with "gold" and "pied flowers" in lustrous colors akin to "Enam'ling." In Sidney's imagination, "lines" of verse were essentially the same as Hilliard's calligraphic "lines" of paint. The justness of the comparison will come out with special clarity if we reverse our perspective: just as Sidnean rhetoric resembles Hilliard's miniature style, so Hilliard's style resembles Sidnean rhetoric. Certainly, Hilliard's limning was generally rhetorical in effect. As we have seen, the artist's claim to "the truth of the line" did not prevent his brushstrokes from being above all decorative patterns. But I have a more specific comparison in mind with the rhetoric Sidney criticizes in sonnet 3. Hilliard's designs were often created from rich, exotic, or out of the way pigment sources that made them precisely "strange similies . . . Of herbes or beastes, which *Inde* or *Afrike* hold." The blue colors "florey" and "indigo" came from the leaves of the Indian plant, *Indigofera;* red "India Lake" derived from "the females, eggs and the exudation surrounding them" of the Indian insect "*Coccus lacca*"; and the best "velvet black" came from ivory (*Treatise,* p. 91), most of which came from Africa's beast, the elephant. (Ivory was also the material of choice for the turned boxes that cradled miniatures within cabinets.) While Hilliard drew his substances from "herbes or beastes" all over the world, in short, "*Inde*" and "*Afrike*" were major providers.[55]

Roy Strong's research into the sources of Hilliard's *Young Man among Roses* clues us to the fact that such cross-resemblances between Sidnean poetry and limning style were a consequence of the common descent of both arts from the same rhetorical ancestors. Strong suggests that one source for the *Roses* youth (painted as if enameled with decorative flowers) is to be found in the "highly stylized erotic paintings" of the Valois court: "*Triumph of Flora* epitomizes this world of sinuous elegance and courtly preciosity which, in its turn, in the scattering of flowers across the picture's surface, reflects directly the poetry of Ronsard and the Pléiade." As Ringler points out, "Ronsard and the Pléiade" were precisely what Sidney meant by "*Pindare's* Apes."[56]

Sidney's "*Pindare's* Apes," Ronsard's Pléiade, and Hilliard's youth were thus alike in enameling "with pied flowers their thoughts of gold." Of course, one cannot too exclusively enforce the analogy between sonnet rhetoric and limning. Other Elizabethan jewelry, for instance, not just the "fyne jewell" of the miniature and its case, consisted of gold enameled "with pied flowers." But the main point is clear. As in the miniature and its related goldsmithing arts, Sidney's sonnet shows poetical rhetoric to encase or "wrap" truth in decoration: "fancies" are "bravely maskt," "thoughts" enameled, "new found Tropes" ennobled "with problemes old," "each line" enriched "with strange similies." And the sacrifice of such ornamentation, again as in the miniature, is truth itself. For what is evident is that rhetorical adornment displays inner "truths" that—the moment they appear to view—are already themselves ornamental. The "new found Tropes" discovered under decorative "problemes old," for example, are themselves nothing but pieces of rhetoric. So, too, the "thoughts" discovered under "Enam'ling with pied flowers" in line 4 are cased with ornament: they are not just thoughts but "thoughts of gold." In this world, ornaments enamel other ornaments. Even "fancies," while suggestive of inner, private forces, also evokes the rich court world where an aristocrat could afford to indulge his whims.

In an effort to break through this Chinese box of ornament, Sidney turns in line 9 away from public artifice to private truth. "For me in sooth," he declares—i.e., "For myself, in truth." To paraphrase: I am but a simple man who knows only one Muse; I cannot master "phrases" and "problemes" nor pay the high cost of such rich ornament. "Strange things cost too deare for my poore sprites." (Here we might observe in parallel the great expense of miniatures and their cases, which would also have been "too deare" for Sidney in his financial straits—although that would not have stopped him from buying them.)[57] How, then, can the poet express his personal, truthful feelings? "How then? even thus: in *Stella's* face I reed, / What Love and Beautie be, then all my deed / But Copying is, what in her Nature writes." Seeking truthful self-expression, Sidney looks *into* Stella's face ("*in* Stella's face I reed")—an inward movement reinforced in his final intent to copy "what *in* her Nature writes." He turns from the artificial to the natural, from the "high" to the "plain" style, from the outward to the inward, and at last from the public to the private.

But the movement inward halts just as it begins—as if exhausted by the seduction of all the outer layers of ornamentation that the first eight lines have culled from the public domain. In essence, reading the sonnet duplicates the process of viewing a miniature: we pass inward along an endless regress of ornamental layers to a face whose meaning is inscrutable *except* as limned in the distraction of inessential decoration. To play upon the Hilliard miniature we previously examined: Sidney's sonnet is really the picture of an *Unknown Lady*. Nor, we should add, is the distraction just the fault of the rhetoric of others ("*Pindare's* Apes"). The irony of sonnet 3 and of other sonnets in *Astrophil and Stella*, of course, is that Sidney finally distracts us from inner "truth" with his *own* highly wrought elaboration upon such public rhetoric.

Sidney may claim to write "In truth" much like Hilliard claims to follow "the truth of the line." Or again—to broaden our view at this point to other sonnets—he may try to paint "in blacke and white" unmasked by rhetorical colors (sonnet 70) just as Hilliard paints in pure colors not "smutted" with shadowing. He can even picture Stella in the stance of Queen Elizabeth in

Hilliard's story: standing without "fanne's wel-shading grace" in the direct light of the sun "which open shone" (sonnet 22). Yet ultimately Sidney is also like Hilliard in failing to do more than create his own wonderful flourishes of rhetoric. William Cherubini's recent quantitative analysis of *Astrophil and Stella* confirms C. S. Lewis's statement that the work is "golden poetry." The "truthful" lines of Sidney's sonnets are shaped by a syntax "extremely rich in its variety of patterns" as well as by multiple tropes and schemes conventional to love poetry.[58] Especially responsible for Sidney's stylized, ornamental speech is his characteristic use of *epanaphora*[59]— which appears in sonnet 3 in the repetition of "Or" at the beginning of lines 3, 5, and 7. The device introduces at the left edge of the poem a weaving pattern like that of the ruff and curls encircling the face of Hilliard's lady. At the right edge, meanwhile, is the patterned rhyme that distinguishes Sidney's fourteen-line sonnets from his predecessors' more generic little poems of love.[60] In all his experiments with the form, Sidney consistently advanced the sonnet's compressed and intricate rhyme to reinforce the effect of a decorative poetic weave. Furthermore, the *colores rhetorici* of his words, though dipped in melancholy hues in the later sonnets, imitated the fresh colors of limning that Hilliard derived from actual "choisest flowers" (sonnet 55) and rare "gemmes" (sonnet 81). Sidney limned his love in "Lillies" and "Roses" (sonnet 100), in "Ivorie, Rubies, pearle and gold" (sonnet 32).

The sonnets, in sum, may gesture toward plain speech and even capture a sense of it in their concluding lines—e.g., "But, foole, seekst not to get into her hart" (sonnet 11)—but they are composed of "sweet," "sugared" phrases (two of their favorite epithets) that perfectly complement the essentially "unknown"—but "rich"—lady they address. The poet's heartfelt love cannot be known except in the "rich" ornament that screens it.

The impenetrability of the rhetorical screen in Sidney's sonnets is especially striking when we consider that the very face, heart, or identity of Stella—the referent of the poet's private love—is in fact compact of nothing but eminently rhetorical gestures toward or namings of "Stella." As we have seen in sonnets 3 and 11, the poet suggests his sincere inner love by pointing inward in his last lines: "*in Stella's* face" (line 12), "*into* her hart" (line 14). Movement inward would ideally produce "that same forciblenes, or *Energia*," which, Sidney declares in the *Apologie,* convinces ladies "that in truth they [their lovers] feele those passions."[61] But, of course, my invocation of *Energia* brings out the status of this inward gesture as rhetorical. Pointing to a face or heart that never appears, the gesture is merely a punctuation akin to a rhetorician holding up an index finger. So, too, Sidney tries to create sincerity of expression through the verbal equivalent of Hilliard's clean brushstroke: the single word. Stella's name, in particular, becomes almost a code word in the sonnets—a pure metonym—for the poet's true love. In sonnet 55, for instance, we pass by "choisest" rhetorical "flowers," but instead of turning to Stella's "hart" or "face" we turn to her "name": "For let me but name her whom I do love, / So sweete sounds straight mine eare and heart do hit, / That I well find no eloquence like it." That the poet cannot, in fact, bring himself to name Stella's name in the concluding lines of this sonnet underscores the sense in which his movement through "sugring" to "true but naked shew" (sonnet 55) conceals more than it reveals. Elsewhere in the sonnets, of course, Sidney does incessantly cry out Stella's name—but the result is just as concealing. So frequently does the word "Stella" appear that it becomes the very substance of Stella.

The poet tries to indicate the truth of his love through other single words as well. Sonnet 35, for instance, concludes by turning to the word "praise": "Not thou by praise, but praise in thee is raisde: / It is a praise to praise, when thou art praisde." One gets the feeling that Sidney is trying verbally to body forth his love by repeating over and over again the single, truthful word. Of course, he fails. His reiterated word no more represents sincere subjectivity than do Hilliard's repeated brushstrokes. On the contrary, the playful repetition of "praise" artificially patterns the poet's love so as to obscure the very sincerity it seeks to express. It forms a kind of ornamental locket or cover. The word "Stella" itself, of course, is an ornamental cover of this sort: a rhetorical "flower" that conceals "star" beneath its surface.[62]

The impenetrability of the rhetoric encasing Sidney's "true" love is further underscored by his inventive use of the poem-within-a-poem device. This device is the verbal complement to Hilliard's limning-within-a-limning, which we saw in the *Flames* miniature. Consider, for example, sonnet 80:[63]

> Sweet swelling lip, well maist thou swell in pride,
>   Since best wits thinke it wit thee to admire;
>   Nature's praise, Vertue's stall, *Cupid's* cold fire,
> Whence words, not words, but heav'nly graces slide.
> The new *Pernassus,* where the Muses bide,
>   Sweetner of musicke, wisedome's beautifier:
> Breather of life, and fastner of desire,

> Where Beautie's blush in Honour's graine is dide.
> Thus much my heart compeld my mouth to say,
> But now spite of my heart my mouth will stay,
> Loathing all lies, doubting this Flatterie is:
> And no spurre can his resty race renew,
> Without how farre this praise is short of you,
> Sweet lip, you teach my mouth with one sweet kisse.

The sonnet begins with a characteristic flourish of conventional rhetoric in which one "sweet" metaphor is piled on another. After passing through this built-up decorative praise, we come upon a different voice in the sestet that comments upon the octave as if it were a separate poem-within-the-poem. The sestet throws into relief the artifice of the octave, suspecting it to be mere surface ornament, mere "Flatterie." It presents itself instead as plain speaking. But we no more uncover the poet's "true" inwardness here than when we saw through the built-up ornaments of the *Flames* miniature to view the white ground of the lover's bared breast (fig. 12). The limned lover, we recall, exposes not his "heart" but an ornamental miniature case that locks away his love. Similarly, the poet progresses through artifice to sincerity only to reveal in the concluding line of the sonnet but another instance of conventional and flattering praise: "Sweet lip, you teach my mouth with one sweet kisse." That the elaborate praise of the first eight lines was spoken from the "heart" through the "mouth" indicates the absolute reliance of heartfelt love on artifice for rhetorical expression. In the Elizabethan court, which forms the backdrop for *Astrophil and Stella*, "truth it selfe must speake like flatterie" (sonnet 35). It is thus fitting that in the final lines it is the "mouth," the very instrument of rhetoric, that usurps all active agency to assume the role of sincere, plain speaking one normally associates with the "heart." The "heart" is silent while the poet "mouths" a love indistinguishable between truth and a taste for pure surface ornament ("Sweet lip . . . sweet kisse").

Again and again in *Astrophil and Stella*, then, we proceed through miniature-like "cases" or "lockets" of conventional rhetoric toward a private sincerity of love that we never reach. At times, the rhetorical ornaments that thus screen us from inner truth are not just public in the sense of being conventional but also political. Witness sonnet 30:

> Whether the Turkish new-moone minded be
> To fill his hornes this yeare on Christian coast;
> How *Poles'* right king meanes, without leave of hoast,
> To warme with ill-made fire cold *Moscovy*;

If French can yet three parts in one agree;
What now the Dutch in their full diets boast;
How *Holland* hearts, now so good townes be lost,
Trust in the shade of pleasing *Orange* tree;
How *Ulster* likes of that same golden bit,
Wherewith my father once made it halfe tame;
If in the Scottishe Court be weltring yet;
These questions busie wits to me do frame;
I, cumbred with good maners, answer do,
But know not how, for still I thinke of you.

This sonnet firmly supports Ann Rosalind Jones and Peter Stallybrass's claim that the poet's "supposedly 'private' sphere of love can be imagined only through its similarities and dissimilarities to the public world of the court."[64] In fact, to revive our architectural model, the poet (like the courtier seeking a private audience with the Queen) can attain private thoughts of his love only by passing through a series of outer political "rooms." He must pass through the politics of faraway Turkey, through news of the nearer lands of Poland, France, Germany, and Holland, through the affairs of England's own Ireland, and through the events of bordering Scotland—all the time nearing closer and closer to his homeland—before he can finally turn inward in the last lines to focus on his private love: "for still I thinke of you." The sense of inwardness in the sonnet is created for the most part by passage through these geographical outer "rooms" of politics. The poet's declaration itself—"for still I thinke of you"—offers little. To use the language of other sonnets, we can thus say that it is the convention of politics that provides the "publike" "Highway" leading "safeliest" to the poet's "heart" (sonnet 84). The rhetoric of Sidney's sonnets can thus express a "Great expectation" of favor (sonnet 21) simultaneously from his personal lady, Stella, and from his political lady, the Queen. It is a testament to the essentially political nature of Sidney's rhetoric that he employs a high number of such "tropes of state" in his representation of his private love: he limns his lady in the Queen's images—"Ermine" (sonnet 86) and "Roses" (sonnet 102), for example—as well as in her titles of "Majestie" (sonnet 48), "soveraigne" (song 8, line 29), "Princesse," and "Queene" (sonnet 107).[65]

To the extent that this conventional and political rhetoric not only blazons but encrypts the poet's private love (his "secretes of the minde"), we might adopt the publisher's term for the 1591 *Astrophil and Stella* and call the sonnets "devices."[66] Sidney, we know, enthusiastically exhibited devices at court tournaments and invented a number of *imprese* with stars suggestive of "Stella." The device that most fits Sidney's representation of his love in the sonnets, perhaps, is the *impresa* he displayed in the tiltyard after his uncle Leicester's newborn son deprived him of his hoped inheritance. The *impresa* stated simply "~~SPERAVI~~."[67] Combining the "word" and "picture" of the device into a single image, this *impresa* epitomized encrypted or hidden subjectivity: Sidney's personal disappointment takes the form of hope crossed out. Disappointment appears only as an invisibility limned by what it is *not*: a public display of hope. A limning analogue can be found in Hilliard's *Young Man among Roses,* where the motto of "crossed love" recapitulates the visual "crossing" of love I earlier discussed.

Sonnet 50 in *Astrophil and Stella* encrypts private truth within just such a device:

> *Stella,* the fulnesse of my thoughts of thee
> Cannot be staid within my panting breast,
> But they do swell and struggle forth of me,
> Till that in words thy figure be exprest.
>   And yet as soone as they so formed be,
> According to my Lord *Love's* owne behest:
> With sad eyes I their weake proportion see,
> To portrait that which in this world is best.
>   So that I cannot chuse but write my mind,
> And cannot chuse but put out what I write,
> While those poore babes their death in birth do find:
> And now my pen these lines had dashed quite,
>   But that they stopt his furie from the same,
>   Because their forefront bare sweet *Stella's* name.

Like Sidney's *impresa,* the above sonnet combines verbal and pictorial imagery. The lover is both painting a "portrait" and writing a text of Stella's "figure." And, as in "~~SPERAVI~~," the poet has both displayed and crossed out his love: "I cannot chuse but write my mind, / And cannot chuse but put out what I write." The different poetic voice of lines 12–14, which converts the preceding lines into another poem-within-a-poem, reinforces the sense of one subjective image standing behind or within another. Though in looking back on the "forefront" of his poem the poet stops himself from erasing his words entirely, his words in a sense continue to be "put out." We can still read the writing, but it has been crossed through in the sense that we never see a representation of Stella. All we see is the "forefront" of a poet's traditional lament that he cannot adequately "portrait" his love and his conventional claim that his love's name is "sweet." These ornamental lines (conceived appropriately as trivial "babes") "dash" out the real-life image of Stella, which can only be glimpsed behind and through them.

Nor, we should note, is it simply the reader of Sidney's verse that cannot see through such lines to their inner truth. Even Sidney and Stella themselves—i.e., the lovers in the poems—cannot penetrate "faire lines" that "write" but also "put out" the inner self they write (sonnets 71, 50). Even the lovers, that is, are like sonnet readers or limning viewers unable to know the secrecy of their own, and each other's, love. Such is especially true of the sonnets where Astrophil and Stella, as Clark Hulse argues, play the game of competing for power through language.[68] Here, the lovers write their selves for the other to read, but because they can only write their love in conventional conceits, they each become "wrapt" in cryptic fiction. The resulting difficulties of reading each other—even ultimately of fathoming their own innermost thoughts—account for the way the poet's characteristic plunge "inward" at the end of his sonnets sometimes appears ironic, conniving, or self-deluding.[69] The self does not really know what is "in" itself or its lover. It also explains Sidney's preoccupation toward the end of his sequence with another version of love crossed out: Stella's "absence" or, more accurately, her "ABSENT presence" (sonnet 106). The "real" Stella has been "absent" all along. A striking parallel appears in architecture. As we will see more fully in the next chapter, Henry VIII was commonly served dinner amidst the traditional ceremony in the royal presence chamber (fig. 1; no. 17). Elizabeth, however, withdrew inward; she ate in the privy chamber (no. 15). But all the ceremony of serving the Queen continued to be performed in the presence chamber, even though the Queen herself was not *present:* "Sayes were taken, wine and beer were poured, three courses and a dessert were served, all with full ceremony to an imaginary queen at an empty table. At the end of each serving a portion of the food or drink was taken up and carried through to the actual queen next door." This vision of conventional display serving a private and unseen queen is a perfect analogue for Sidney's sonnets. In something like the "presence" chamber that is the sonnet form, ornate rhetorical and political conventions continue to "serve" Stella even though she has withdrawn into such absolute privacy as to be really "ABSENT."[70]

We remember that in Hilliard's limnings the face of the loved one is essentially a visage of absence: a pale mask showing the pictorial "ground" amid its universe of defining ornament. On Sidney's pages, the vision of Stella's face or heart is just such a ground—unremarkable (indeed, invisible) except when seen paradoxically in ornaments that precisely *do not* display it. Significantly, Sidney himself likens Stella's face to white parchment in sonnet 102: "It is but love, which makes his paper perfit white / To write therein more fresh the story of delight." Each successive sonnet in *Astrophil and Stella* writes "fresh" the poet's love. Each sonnet re-presents the inward progress through artifice to a sincerity of self that can never—as in Elizabeth's presence chamber—be presented.[71]

In a special sense, to conclude, Sidney follows Gascoigne's advice to poets: "The first and most necessarie poynt that euer I founde meete to be considered in making of a delectable poeme is this, *to grounde it upon some fine inuention. . . . some good and fine deuise*" (my emphasis).[72] Sidney's sonnet devices are indeed grounded upon some "fine inuention." But invention is never visible except in convention. Sidney's famous first sonnet, which specifically addresses the problem of "Invention," sets the pattern for the entire sequence:

> Loving in truth, and faine in verse my love to show,
> That the deare She might take some pleasure of my paine:
> Pleasure might cause her reade, reading might make her know,
> Knowledge might pitie winne, and pitie grace obtaine,
>   I sought fit words to paint the blackest face of woe,
> Studying inventions fine, her wits to entertaine:
> Oft turning others' leaves, to see if thence would flow
> Some fresh and fruitfull showers upon my sunne-burn'd braine.
>   But words came halting forth, wanting Invention's stay,
> Invention, Nature's child, fled step-dame Studie's blowes,
> And others' feete still seem'd but strangers in my way.
> Thus great with child to speake, and helplesse in my throwes,
>   Biting my trewand pen, beating my selfe for spite,
>   "Foole," said my Muse to me, "looke in thy heart and write."

Here and throughout the sequence, Sidney seeks "to paint" his love "in truth." And he finds the "way" to "Invention, Nature's child" through conventional artifice: through the "inventions fine" of "others' leaves." Only by considering commonly used "fine" "inventions" can he make the turn inward in the last line of the sonnet toward the plain speech and sincere emotion that belong "in" his own "heart." Only through convention can he find invention. The "heart" itself, the poet's heartfelt emotion, cannot speak directly, as proved by the fact that the poet's conventional "Muse" speaks in the final line for him. Like the generic "She" that stands for the real-life Stella, the "heart" "in truth" exists more in "Idea" than actuality. It lies beyond the last line of the sonnet, or perhaps *under* all the accumulated conventions of the sonnet, in the white "ground" of the page. In this "ground of so firme making" (as we heard him say in song 11), the poet finds Gascoigne's "good and fine deuise" in the heraldic as well as the poetic sense: he invents a poetic device that conveys the *impresa*'s "secretes of the minde."

Sidney's sonnets thus perfectly complement the visual device of Hilliard's limnings. Though Sidney wrote *Astrophil and Stella* around 1581–82, a few years before Hilliard's secret art peaked, both poet and limner clearly responded to the same concern for representing subjectivity at court; and despite Sidney's attempt to reject ornament both solved the problem in a similar way: through an art of secrecy. To what extent Sidney was directly influenced by Hilliard (or Hilliardesque limning) is more difficult to determine. I have suggested that Sidney saw Hilliard's miniatures in the *Gresley Jewel* (as well as his portraits in Elizabeth's prayer book); and Sidney probably also saw a miniature of Elizabeth that Fulke Greville owned.[73] In general, Sidney would have had many opportunities to view limnings by Hilliard. Hilliard's appearance on the limning scene in the early 1570s brought him almost instant fame, ushering in a miniature craze that increased in intensity with every year of Elizabeth's reign. Everyone who was anyone at court was limned by Hilliard, including Elizabeth, Drake, Leicester, Raleigh, Essex, and Sidney's own Stella, Penelope Rich. Sidney's uncle Leicester and friend Essex were both patrons of Hilliard,[74] and through them Sidney may have met Hilliard. Or he may have met him during their joint participation in the Anjou marriage negotiations. That they did meet is certain: Hilliard in his *Treatise* reports a long conversation with Sidney (pp. 83–85). Considering their different social status, this exchange probably occurred at a sitting for a miniature, although no authentic limning of Sidney has yet been found.

Sidney's *Arcadia* (1593), specifically in the episode of the tournament held by Phalantus in book 1, provides final confirmation of Sidney's familiarity and sympathy with miniatures. Phalantus, we recall, opens the tournament by parading portraits of ladies in large-scale (each picture held by two footmen) that he has won in jousts. The disguised heroes, Musidorus and Pyrocles, whose sudden arrival brings the tournament to a climax, display their loves in notably different fashions. Though Musidorus indeed sports a picture of Pamela, the picture is not in full-scale but "in little form." It is a miniature. And the miniature is not openly displayed by servants but "covered with silk" and "fastened . . . to his helmet."[75] Unlike Phalantus, then, but very much like the Elizabethan courtiers who wore miniatures in rich cases around their necks, Musidorus publishes his love for Pamela and at the same time keeps it secret. He is the ideal companion of Pyrocles, who tells Phalantus that "if you could see it" the "liveliest picture" of his love (Philoclea) "is in my heart."[76] Musidorus's "wrapt" miniature is the outward manifestation of the inward portrait that Pyrocles hides in his heart.

After Hilliard and Sidney
"Within the loue-limn'd tablet of mine heart"

While the necessarily limited scope of this chapter precludes thorough investigation into the heritage left by Hilliard and Sidney, I should like to sketch certain ramifications and transformations of what I have dubbed their art of secrecy.[77] Particularly important are certain tensions that developed between the realms of private and public experience in the Renaissance—destabilizations that will prepare us to study other cultural and literary ornaments in the reign of James.

That the publication of Sidney's *Astrophil and Stella* in 1591 greatly influenced—indeed, triggered—the sonnet craze of the 1590s is undisputed. The fact that such enthusiasm coincided with the miniature craze suggests that the last years of the sixteenth century were ripe for "personal" arts generally. Both the sonnet and the miniature "came into being," in J. W. Lever's words, "because a new, personal attitude to experience demanded expression." Yet the two art forms, I have argued, fulfilled such demand only by frustrating it as well: they masked the person with the ornament.[78] Such equivalence between private subjectivity and public artifice became the very métier of the followers of Sidney—a generation of poets who molded the sonnet form even more closely to the miniature. Limning their "true" private loves in patterned lines, "lyvely collors," and metaphorical flowers and gems, the sonneteers became miniaturists at heart. In his *Vanytyes,* indeed (mostly composed c. 1584), Sir Arthur Gorges specifically calls on Hilliard to paint his mistress. With apparent knowledge of Hilliard's style, Gorges asks the limner to view heavenly "patterns" and "For lyvely collors reape the fresshest flowers / that in Elisas blessed fyeldes doo growe." Similarly, in a poem addressed to Hilliard in the Todd manuscript version of *Diana* (c. 1590), Henry Constable praises the limner's art. He admires a Hilliard miniature of no other than Sidney's own Lady Rich. Paying due homage to the sitter as well as the artist, however, Constable claims that it was Lady Rich's beauty that taught Hilliard the art of giving "To diamonds rubies pearles the worth of which / Doth make the iewell which you [Hilliard] paynt seeme rich."[79]

Most strikingly, the sonneteers of the 1590s explicitly spoke the language of limning. They regularly used the technical term of the miniaturist—"limn"—instead of the more general "paint" to describe their verbal portraits of their loves. When Daniel presented a sonnet portrait in "collours" to his lady, for example, he spoke of it as a limning: "Then take this picture which I heere present thee, / Limned with a Pensill not all vnworthy." ("Pensill"—a small, fine brush for delicate painting [*OED*]—also belonged to limning.) So too, the *Zepheria* (1594) poet imaged a limning love. Seemingly aware that the "richer" miniature gestured to the "heart" but projected only an *"Idea"* of inner love, he assured,

> Yet that deuine *Idea* of thy grace,
> The life-immagerie of thy loues sweet souenance
> Within mine heart shall raigne in soueraigne place:
> Nay shall it euer pourtray other semblance?
>   No neuer shall that face so fayre depaynted
> Within the loue-limn'd tablet of mine hart
> Emblemisht be, defaced or vnsaynted,
> Till death shall blot it with his pencill dart:
>   Yet then in these limn'd lines enobled more,
>   Thou shalt suruiue richer accomplisht then before.

Or again, in *Alba* (1598) Tofte's "faire and bright" limning of his love lay "hidden" "in midst of Hart":

> For though in darke she hidden doth appeere,
> Yet vnto me she faire and bright doth show,
>   My Hart's the Boord, where limnde you may her see;
>   My Teares the Oyle, my Blood the Colours bee.

Just so, Drayton, perhaps with Sidney specifically in mind, limned his love in the white "ground" of the page—"In this fayre limmed ground as white as snow"—and appropriately invoked not painting but limning in his exordium to "SWEET secrecie": "SWEET secrecie, what tongue can tell thy worth? / What mortall pen suffyciently can prayse thee? / What curious Pensill serves to lim thee forth?"[80]

But when Drayton sat for his own miniature portrait, we notice, the limner he chose belonged to the school of Isaac Oliver, not Hilliard. Drayton's choice here is important: it signaled a new movement in both limning and sonneteering. Oliver, who was second to Hilliard in popularity in the 1590s and outstripped him after Elizabeth's death, grew to reject the decorativeness of Hilliard's bright colors and patterned lines for the naturalism of muted hues and dark modeling. Whereas Hilliard's faces were white and

14. Nicholas Hilliard, *Unknown Youth,* c. 1588. 2 x 1 5/8 in. Private collection.
Photo from Reynolds, *Nicholas Hilliard and Isaac Oliver,* no. 33.

flat, Oliver's were shadowed and rounded. They were more fully represented in depth. Compare, for instance, Hilliard's *Unknown Youth* (fig. 14)
with the copy attributed to Oliver (fig. 15), both limned around 1588.[81]
From one point of view, we can see this new style of limning as more personal because it more fully figures forth the individual. Certainly Oliver's
miniatures were like Hilliard's in being associated with the private, even
secret, self. Lord Herbert of Cherbury related an incident occurring around
1600 that vividly conveys the intimacy of an Oliver miniature—specifically,
a limning of himself:

> Coming one day into [Lady Ayres's] chamber, I saw her through the curtains
> lying upon her bed with a wax candle in one hand, and the picture I formerly
> mentioned in the other. I coming thereupon somewhat boldly to her, she
> blew out the candle, and hid the picture from me; myself thereupon being
> curious to know what that was she held in her hand, got the candle to be light-
> ed again, by means whereof I found it was my picture she looked upon with
> more earnestness and passion than I could have easily believed.[82]

Yet from another point of view the psychological realism of Oliver's
miniatures made them *less* private. The more fully a sitter is realized in a
limning, the more fully his or her privacy was *publicized*. It is thus telling
that Oliver's miniature of Herbert was copied from a full-scale oil painting
by Larkin. Whereas Hilliard's limnings were noticeably different from public paintings, Oliver's limnings—though their medium was still
watercolor—were essentially oil paintings in little.[83] Here may lie the ex-

15. Ascribed to Isaac Oliver, *Unknown Youth,* c. 1588. 1 3/4 x 1 5/8 in.
Beauchamp collection, Madresfield Court, Malvern, England. Photo from
Reynolds, *Nicholas Hilliard and Isaac Oliver,* no. 123.

planation for Tofte's reference to "Oyle" colors in his limning poem. There
was a kind of split in Oliver's miniatures, in other words: they were highly
private and at the same time highly public. Such a divided personality can
be associated in literature with drama—for example, *Hamlet,* where the inner thoughts of the hero are acted out for all to see. This is not to say that
Hamlet does not remain impenetrable. His mystery, however, comes
largely from his compulsion to display himself in all his complexity. It is not
the kind of mystery—"secrecy" would be a better word—that we see in
Hilliard's miniatures and Sidney's sonnets where inwardness is only gestured at through public forms of display. Significantly, in addition to
toning down Hilliardesque ornamentalism, Oliver phased out cryptic gold
mottoes or devices bespeaking "secretes of the minde" in favor of more dramatic ways of displaying secrets. Perhaps because he lived in the Blackfriars
liberty—a haunt of the players and, for a time, home of the greatest mas-
que-maker, Ben Jonson—he frequently painted his subjects in masquing
costumes.[84]

We might remember here Spenser's allegory of Busirane's house, which
provided us with a transition into the world of privacy at the end of the last
chapter. As I suggested, Busirane's house is precisely an intimate, sonneteer's world. Britomart detours from her quest through a series of
increasingly private rooms to reach an "inner roome" secreted within the
public epic (3.12.26). In this inner room, Busirane pays court to Amoret by
writing his cruel "verse" of love (31, 36). Having toured the actual sonnet

universe of Sidney and other poets, however, we can now make a new transition by noticing a complication in the Busirane episode. The complication is a masque. For, emerging from the place of Busirane's love-making
into his most ornamental chamber of all—the room intervening between
the "inner" and "vtmost rowme" (3.11.27)—is his psychologically gripping
dramatization of "love": the masque of Cupid. The heart of the masque, as
it were, is the following representation of the inner secrets of love. Amoret
appears

> brest all naked, as net iuory,
> Without adorne of gold or siluer bright,
> Wherewith the Craftesman wonts it beautify,
> Of her dew honour was despoyled quight,
> And a wide wound therein (O ruefull sight)
> Entrenched deepe with knife accursed keene,
> Yet freshly bleeding forth her fainting spright,
> (The worke of cruell hand) was to be seene,
> That dyde in sanguine red her skin all snowy cleene.
>   (3.12.20)

What is the heart of love, of Amoret's subjectivity? No heart at all but its
absence. Amoret's breast of "iuory" is not adorned with the "gold or siluer
bright" common to jeweled miniatures, but is left a "wide wound." Or
more accurately, the wound becomes a displaced version of ornamentation
in the way it "dyde in sanguine red her skin all snowy cleene." Thus
dyed/died, simultaneously colored and made dead, Amoret's breast becomes an ornamental but empty hole. It becomes a gaping "wide orifice"
from which her inner being, her "hart," has been "drawne forth" and served
in a "siluer basin" for public "spoyle" (3.12.21; 22). Amoret's center of being,
in sum, is an ornamental "wide orifice" precisely akin to the "ABSENT
presence" of Sidney's or Hilliard's arts of secrecy, but it is so not because it is
hidden by ornament but because it has been dramatically and psychologically dished out for all to see.

Spenser's Busirane episode, I suggest, points to the secret arts of Hilliard and Sidney but also finally *past* those arts to Oliver and the sonneteers
of his time. Ornamentation is displaced in function, gaining a psychologiz-
ing thrust that threatens to expose the secret self to full public view. To the
extent that Oliver and the sonneteers after Sidney represented private love
through conventional artifices that kept inwardness hidden, they looked
back to the arts of secrecy I have traced in this chapter. To the extent, how-

ever, that they strove to dramatize inwardness for public "spoyle," they looked forward to the psychological "realism" of seventeenth-century drama and thus, as we will see, to a need for new ornamental or trivial strategies of "detachment" creating a haven for subjectivity. One can trace the dramatizing impulse of the later poets in their tendency to *describe* the limnings in their hearts rather than only gesture toward them. Shakespeare's sonnets, for example, proceed as if the poet had already penetrated to the heart and were trying to paint what he there saw, or could not see. Sonnet 24 thus depicts an internalized vision of the lover with a picture hanging at his heart. One feels in Shakespeare the modern "sense of internal experience at a distance from outward expression" that Anne Ferry argues first emerged in Elizabethan sonnets.[85] Paradoxically, internal experience is outwardly expressed as if it were not outward expression: it is dramatized as soliloquy.

Yet we must be careful in making such a summation. Indeed, we must question whether there truly is such a subject as the "modern" private self at a distance from public expression. In *The Fall of Public Man*, as I earlier mentioned, Richard Sennett offers an entirely different vision of modern society. Sennett presents the compelling argument that modern sensibility, rather than separating out the private and the public, privileges the private to the extent that the public is conceived in private terms—to the impoverishment of both aspects of self. Nowhere is this better evidenced than in our witheringly intimate gaze into the lives of political candidates.[86] To follow the line of Sennett's thesis is to realize that modern society in a way simply inverts the private/public paradox resolved through the arts of ornament in the Elizabethan period. Whereas in Elizabethan society, as we have seen in the Hilliardesque miniature and Sidnean sonnet, the private could be sensed only through the public (the ornamental, the conventional, the political); in modern society, as evidenced in political figures, the "public" can be sensed only through the private (the personal, the sexual, the familial). The result, again an inversion of the Elizabethan situation, is a masking of the "publicness" of events through the very process of displaying them in intimate terms.

Viewed in conjunction with my own study, Sennett's suggests an essential instability in the notions of "private" and "public" and in the relations between them. However much we may need to define the concepts as separate (or envision a culture *all* one or the other), "private" and "public" can only be conceived as a split unity divided along a constantly resewn seam that can never be wholly closed or absolutely parted. The history of subjectivity is the history of delicate shiftings between changing conceptions of private and public self.

I now propose to turn to the more "dramatic" literary and cultural ornaments cultivated at the beginning of the Jacobean period: specifically, the masque and its architectural "case," the Banqueting House. Here we will watch the destabilization of the boundary between private and public selves that had been so tenuously negotiated in the ornamental idiom of Elizabethan miniatures and sonnets. Seeking refuge from an all-"publishing" world, the private self sought to divide itself cleanly from the public. Yet, as if definable only in terms of that separation, it itself became divided, torn apart, estranged, and—to update Sidney's "ABSENT presence"—*void*.

4

Consuming the Void: Jacobean Banquets and Masques

Cook. Sir, this is my room and region too, the Banqueting House! And in matter of feast and solemnity nothing is to be presented here but with my acquaintance and allowance to it.

Poet. You are not his majesty's confectioner, are you?

Cook. No, but one that has as good title to the room, his master-cook. What are you, sir?

Poet. The most unprofitable of his servants, I, sir, the poet. A kind of a Christmas ingine, one that is used at least once a year for a trifling instrument of wit, or so.

Cook. Were you ever a cook?

Poet. A cook? No, surely.

Cook. Then you can be no good poet, for a good poet differs nothing at all from a master-cook. Either's art is the wisdom of the mind.[1]

As this debate between artists shows, Jonson's "trifling" masques[2] were clearly aware that their proper place lay in the venue of the cook. Increasingly, Jonson turned the traditional entrance cry of the mummery—"Room, Room"—into pointed references to the specific "room," "hall," or "place" where his masques were usually performed: the Banqueting House at Whitehall. Such keen localization culminated visually in 1623 in *Time Vindicated to Himself and to His Honors,* where a representation of the Banqueting House itself served as Inigo Jones's opening perspective scene. The year after, Jonson created his matching poetic commemoration of the masque's place: the debate between the Cook and Poet in *Neptune's Triumph.*[3]

What such self-conscious "placing" of the masque indicates, I suggest, is that Jonson's masques belonged in the Banqueting House because they were in fact precise complements to "banquets." Seen one way, they were the crowning development of a long tradition of banqueting cuisine and architecture, a sweet confection to outmatch all other dainties. Here we can pay special mind to the query that the Poet puts to the Cook in *Neptune's Triumph*: "You are not his majesty's *confectioner*, are you?" The word "banquet" in the seventeenth century designated not only a "feast," a sumptuous meal consisting of a series of many-dished courses, but—most germane here—also what was dubbed the "void": the serving after a meal, or sometimes between meals, of decorative sugar molds and sweetmeats (confectioned flowers, nuts, spices, and fruit) together with sweet spiced wines and distilled spirits.[4] By the time of the seventeenth century, voids were usually consumed in a room separated from the feast and often in a wholly separate building designed specially for the purpose. Banqueting houses arose as little, "conceited" rooms or buildings dedicated to the "void."

What did it mean for Jonson's masques to be served in James's outsize Banqueting House as an ultimate void? To understand the conjunction of the masque and banqueting traditions will require that we first explore the history of banqueting house architecture—a history of physical detachment (in favor of definitively fragmentary, peripheral, and ornamental spaces) that exaggerates the trend toward private rooms discussed in the last chapter. We will also need to observe the culinary history of actual banqueting courses or "voids." Only then will we be able to savor fully the masque served up by Jonson's poet-cook in Whitehall Banqueting House as well as the distinct aftertaste of that royal void: the Jacobean self.[5]

My argument is that the "trifling" arts of the cook, architect, and ultimately poet combined in the masque to stage a profoundly "trivial" or insubstantial Jacobean self. In the very act of communing with others, the aristocratic self in James's era absented itself—like Elizabeth from her presence chamber—to eat apart in private communion.[6] But unlike Elizabeth, it found that to pass between its public and private places it had to encounter the void in the full sense of the term: a place in the soul as dark and empty as any of the cramped, spiral staircases—wide enough for only one—leading up to a turret banqueting house in an aristocratic home (as in Hardwick Hall, Longleat, or the other residences I discuss below). The aristocratic self, in sum, experienced a breach between its public and private subjectivity so radical that it at last beheld within itself an open void.

It was this experience of emptiness, brokenness, and alienation in Jacobean subjectivity that created its dark revision of Elizabethan cultural exchange. As we will see, the engendering Kula ring of ideal commonality became its own counter-self: a cannibalistic potlatch. Centered upon a hungry void, the Jacobean aristocratic self could only give of itself in aggressive acts of tearing apart or making void.

Rooms Apart of Sweet Conceits
Toward an Aesthetics of Detachment

When did the aristocracy begin to eat alone, in privacy? When, that is, did it learn to "avoid" the public in its everyday communions?

In his *Life in the English Country House*, Mark Girouard lucidly outlines the process of architectural fragmentation and withdrawal that catered to the increasing desire for mealtime privacy.[7] Consider the principal room of the medieval house: the great hall, in which the entire household congregated and ate. By the fifteenth century, family and guests had withdrawn from the hall, leaving it to the servants, and moved upstairs to dine in a room called the "great chamber." "Now have the Rich a rule to eat by themselves," lamented Piers Plowman.[8] Almost immediately, however, a proliferation of rooms beyond the great chamber began, as well as a retreat within such rooms (which became subdivided) to ever more inward recesses of private dining. The extent of such inward flight by the beginning of the seventeenth century in English royal palaces, which set the pattern for the aristocracy's own houses, is evident from our skeletal groundplan of Whitehall (fig. 1). The hall, we see, was on the far right on the ground floor. By means of a stairway, one gained access to the great chamber, the room where Henry VII dined in his royal palaces.[9] But the great chamber had been renamed the guard chamber since being subdivided by Henry VIII to make room for the presence chamber within. The latter now took on the functions of the great chamber: Henry VIII moved into the presence chamber for most meals. But Elizabeth (as we saw in the last chapter) then out-retreated her father. For she, and James after her, usually dined in a privy chamber lying within the presence.[10] Further inwards still lay the king's withdrawing room, known as the Vane Room, and within that his bedchamber (conjecturally located on the plan), probably with yet another withdrawing room or closet beyond.[11]

If we now trace the history of the banqueting void, we find that it first followed after the main meal along a similar route of inward segmentation before taking a curious turn.[12] The medieval void was originally a way of passing the time in the hall—the sweet wine and spices eaten standing—while the tables were being cleared or "voided" after the meal. When the lord moved up to the great chamber to eat, the void naturally followed. Froissart recorded that, after dinner, noble families and friends "take other pastimes in the great chambre, and hereynge of instruments. Then a voyde of wine and spices were brought."[13] But once withdrawing chambers came into use (the fashion under Elizabeth), the void moved into them—now usually one room beyond the meal. That is, whichever of these series of rooms the meal was eaten in, the void was eaten in the room further within. After a meal, a number of guests—not everyone, only a select few—"withdrew" into the inner chamber to consume, in less formality, the void.[14]

The crucial point in its history is when the void more decisively withdrew: when it split off from the trajectory of decreasingly public rooms and was served in a special room set apart in immaculate privacy. Like the withdrawing room, the detached banqueting room began to gain widespread popularity in the second half of the sixteenth century. One usually finds these liberated architectural fragments on the extreme margin of the house: the roof. The octagonal tower that Sir William Sharington added to Lacock Abbey circa 1550, for example, housed one banqueting room atop another. Each contained octagonal stone tables, variously carved with satyrs or pagan deities, and could have admitted no more than six people. While the lower of the two rooms was proximate to the main rooms of the house (it was reached from the withdrawing room via a short passageway), the upper could be entered only by a separate staircase to the roof and a walk of some twenty-five feet along the leads (figs. 16, 17).[15] Sir John Thynne fled to the roof with even more abandon. In the late 1560s, he "scattered the roofscape at Longleat with little domed banqueting turrets, some square and some octagonal, and none of them much bigger than the rooms in the tower at Lacock" (fig. 18).[16]

We might reconstruct for ourselves the role of such banqueting turrets by looking at a particular evening's entertainment at Hardwick Hall (built c. 1590–96). Bess of Hardwick would have served supper to special guests in the high great chamber on the third floor or perhaps, for a more intimate gathering, in the drawing room within the great chamber. After the meal, rather than withdrawing further inwards with a select few, she would have led her preferred guests along the length of the adjoining gallery, through a small passageway, and up a spiral staircase in the north turret to the roof. The party would then have strolled along the leads (enjoying the air and fine view) to the south turret at the opposite end of the house. There, in "a

16. The banqueting tower built by Sir William Sharington c. 1550 as approached along the leads from the staircase door (up from his second-floor gallery), Lacock Abbey, Wiltshire. Photo: Alan Liu.

prospect-room or banqueting-house, with elaborate plaster decoration," the party would consume the void (figs. 19, 20). As this scenario dramatizes, the defensive turret of the medieval house, in which the lord held "secret house" to count his treasure, had by now become a pleasure house for private consumption.[17]

Detachment of this sort was soon exaggerated even further. In a definitive separation from public space, the banqueting room (now more accurately a "house") split off entirely from the main building and entered the garden or park. All late sixteenth- and early seventeenth-century gardens of any consequence contained a banqueting house. In some we find a trace of connection to the main house. The twin, domed pavilions at Montacute (c. 1590), for instance, were built in the same style as the main building and placed in formal relation to it some fifty yards away at either corner of the garden walls enclosing the East Court (fronting the house) (figs. 21, 22). Sometimes, as at the royal seats of Windsor, Greenwich, and The More, a gallery would connect the main structure to the banqueting house in the garden. Often, however, the banqueting house was physically more detached. Lord Exeter's banqueting house, for example, stood alone not in the front but in the back gardens of his house at Wimbledon (shown in a survey of 1609). Similarly, a timber-framed banqueting house was reared at Nonsuch in 1609–10 "in the walkes belowe the ffountayne of Diana," situated together with "a little room for the musicons" (it was rebuilt in 1621–22). With such retreats in mind, James towards the end of his reign commissioned Inigo Jones to build a banqueting house in the park of Theobalds. Approached by a flight of steps, it consisted of a small structure with one door, two windows, and a "neech" (as if imitating in miniature the "great neech" or projecting apse of the Whitehall Banqueting House, where the

17. The upper floor banqueting room inside Lacock tower with octagonal stone table delicately carved with Greek gods and goddesses. Photo: Edward Piper.

18. Turrets and banqueting houses of 1568–69 on the roof at Longleat House, Wiltshire.
Photo: Tate Gallery Archive, John Piper 285.1.3.

King sat at his masques). In this little banqueting house, James could "repose, and rest himselfe."[18]

Designed for private repose, indeed, banqueting houses could be found in especially retired or unusual sites. Lady Elizabeth, wife of Sir Thomas Berkeley, for instance, erected a banqueting house in the late sixteenth century on the edge of the great pool at Callowdon House in Warwickshire. It was to serve as "the retired cell of her soul's soliloquies to God her creator." Seeking a more secular retirement (with provision for fishing), Richard Carew planned in 1570 to build a banqueting-house island on the salt-water pond below his house in Cornwall. Ultimately, the bounds between such out-of-the-way banqueting houses and more traditional rustic retreats be-

19. The banqueting tower at the south end of the house and the approach along the leads from the north turret, Hardwick Hall, Derbyshire, c. 1590–96. The railed walkway and sloped roofing are modern additions. Photo: Alan Liu.

20. Section of the elaborate plaster decoration rimming the upper portion of the walls inside Bess of Hardwick's banqueting tower. The ceiling ornament was added by Bess's son. Photo: Alan Liu.

came confused. When at a significant distance from the main house—say, a half mile or mile—the banqueting house began to merge with the hunting lodge. "The point at which one shaded into the other," Girouard observes, "was not always clear."[19]

21. Twin, domed banqueting pavilions at either corner of the garden walls fronting Montacute House, Somerset, c.1590. Photo: Patricia Fumerton.

22. One of the Montacute banqueting pavilions as viewed from the house. Photo: Alan Liu.

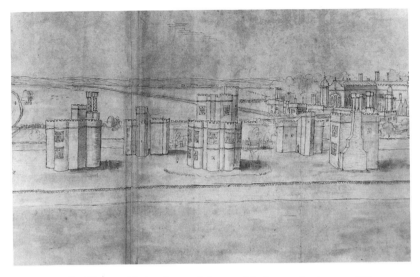

23. A. van den Wyngaerde's drawing made in 1558 of the banqueting houses of Hampton
Court, Middlesex, titled *Hampton Court Palace from the North.*
Photo: Ashmolean Museum, Oxford.

Nor was physical detachment the only way in which banqueting houses
distinguished themselves. The often striking devices adorning banqueting
rooms, houses, and lodges suggest the extent to which they also broke away
stylistically from the main house. Certainly, the ornamentation within banqueting houses was individual. We have already glimpsed the personalized
embellishment characteristic of their insides in the delicate carvings on the
octagonal tables in the Lacock banqueting rooms (fig. 17) and the elaborately decorative plasterwork of the turret at Hardwick Hall (fig. 20). Even
more striking were the actual shapes of the rooms. Carew's plan for a banqueting house was based on a complex of circles and squares; the banqueting house at Amesbury (1600) was "designed on a system of pentagons";
additional banqueting houses at Hardwick Hall were set at different angles
in the garden walls so that one appeared to be square, another triangular;
and the "fanciful turreted structures" of Hampton Court were "of various
forms, sometimes rectangular in plan and sometimes circular or polygonal"
(fig. 23).[20]

The individuality expressed by such whimsical conceits in the decoration and shapes of banqueting houses found fullest representation in Sir
Thomas Tresham's little Triangular Lodge (built 1594–97 on his estate at

Rushton, Northamptonshire [fig. 24]). The intricate artifice of the lodge celebrates the Holy Trinity. As Malcolm Airs points out,

> Each of its three sides is thirty-three and a third feet long, or a third of a hundred feet. It is three storeys high with three gables on each side and three

24. The little Triangular Lodge built by Sir Thomas Tresham c. 1594–97, Rushton, Northamptonshire. Photo: A. F. Kersting, London.

windows composed of multiples of three on each storey. The symbols and inscriptions on each side refer to one of the persons of the Trinity and each inscription is composed of exactly thirty-three letters.

The symbolism of threes in Tresham's lodge did not merely represent abstract or conventional doctrine, however. It also deeply expressed Tresham's personal identity, Très[three]-ham. "Over the doorway," Airs explains, "is the text *TRES TESTIMONIUM DANT,* which, with characteristic ambiguity, can be read as both 'There are three that bear witness' from the first epistle of St John (the doctrine of the Holy Trinity) and 'The Treshams bear witness.'"[21] So personalized, the ornament of Tresham's Triangular Lodge epitomized the singularity of expression that gave rise to the detachable room it adorned.

We see in the evolution of the ornamental banqueting house, in sum, a special place for subjectivity arising—a reverse *topos* or *un*commonplace increasingly displaced from the central places of living. Yet so far, of course, we have limned such displacement or detachment only in the banqueting house structure. We now need to enter the room and partake of the void within. What we observe is that the very ingredients, condiments, and serving utensils of the void were products of the same processes of segmentation and detachment shaping banqueting architecture. The finished creations of the void cooks were then the centerpiece of the whole architectural/culinary extravagance: what contemporaries called "banqueting stuffs" imitated the personalized conceits of the banqueting houses, modeling in a medium of petit fours the hollow place of a self set apart from the communal whole.[22]

First, we can prepare our ingredients. The crucial fact here is that the "stuff" of banqueting stuffs developed as a segregation from the melting pot of the main "feast" or "savory banquet."[23] In a typical late English Renaissance feast, abundant dishes of fish, fowl, and meat arrived with each course of the usual two-course meal. All were similarly seasoned with fruits, nuts, spices, sugar, and the vinegary tang of "verjuice."[24] All the savory feast, that is, was of one savor, though the total effect was a hodgepodge in which savoriness accented the various juices of the meats and other ingredients. With the development of void banqueting stuffs, however, savoriness clarified. While the main feast remained a miscellaneous combination of flavors and textures, a separate palette of taste finished the meal in the form of sweet wines and confectionary sweetmeats (sugared fruits, nuts, spices). Here, savoriness could be enjoyed in its pure form. Subsequently, banquets were wholly reconfigured to follow the trend of increasingly differentiated or discriminate taste. Toward the end of the seventeenth century, main feasts radically reduced spices in their major dishes to reserve savoriness for the dessert or void; and in the eighteenth century a more segregated succession of courses—soup, fish, meat, void—began to replace the practice of heaping various meats on the table.[25] Beginning with the void, then, taste separated out into discrete, detached, segmented elements.

Just so, differentiation or segmentation characterized table service. Specialized silverware, for example, was first introduced in England for the void. Just as the concentration of savoriness in the void heralded a general differentiation of courses and flavors, so separate void utensils then led the way to a general distinction among eating tools. Spoons were introduced at the void in medieval England before coming to the main table. So, too, forks turned up at voids as early as the fourteenth century before making a regular showing at main feasts at the end of the seventeenth century. Nor was silverware the only part of the service to undergo differentiation: the void also introduced specialized plateware. The use of "roundels" or little plates at voids thus led the way to replacing communal pots at main feasts (into which all hands once dipped) with individual plates. Especially fashionable in the sixteenth century were highly elaborate sets of void roundels often decorated on the back with various scenes, emblems, or verses.[26]

Whether we look at the ingredients, the order and relation of courses, or the place settings on tables, we find the same phenomenon at work that we traced in architecture: a movement toward differentiation, detachment, or segmentation. Apropos is Yi-Fu Tuan's *Segmented Worlds and Self,* which argues that the history of Western civilization is a process of progressive segmentation (of living space, food, the senses) reflecting a growing partitioning of the self from others.[27] Subdivision in all areas of experience, that is, signaled detached subjectivity. Such a trend, we recognize, was especially true of the architecture, ingredients, and utensils at the tables of the void: all intimated in their detachment and segmentation a breaking away from public experience, a discrimination of selfhood whose *reductio ad absurdum* would be a self eating alone from a private plate with private service in a private room. The self reserved a table apart from its earlier experience of communal eating. Juices—whether meat drippings or saliva— could no longer mingle.

With the ingredients prepared and table set, we can now at last sit down in the banqueting house to taste the remarkable finished creations of the void cooks. It is here that we discover the fruition of "detachment." To eat a void was to mouth whimsical shapes or "conceits" so removed in sub-

stance and style from public-feast dishes (elaborate though these could be)
that they fostered a whole aesthetics of culinary detachment, a separate,
fanciful, and ultimately private experience of gustation as *imaginary* as it
was actual. In the banqueting house, the void lost the very referent of public culinary reality: the concept of "food."[28] Thus Hugh Plat in *Delightes
for Ladies* (1603) offers a void recipe that mocks the solid, English reality of
meat dishes by concocting a *like*-meat course consisting wholly of void substance. Invent a fowl dish without the fowl, he suggests, by sculpting a
bird-shape from sugar molds dredged with crusts of bread, cinnamon, and
sugar "so they wil seeme as if they were rosted and breaded." Such will be
"a verie rare and strange deuise." Even stranger were devices that lost even
the "like" relation to actual food. A favorite void dish of the time, for example, appears in the instructions in *The good Huswifes Handmaide for the
Kitchin* (1594): "To make Snowe." So, too, there was Plat's even more popular recipe in *Delightes* for "a Marchpane [marzipan]" garnished with
"pretie conceiptes, as birdes and beasts," or shaped into "letters, knots,
Armes, escocheons beasts, birds, and other fancies." Or again, there is Plat's
recipe for a walnut in *A Closet for Ladies and Gentlewomen* (1608), a concoction like a Renaissance fortune cookie that epitomizes the fanciful essence
of banqueting stuffs. Plat describes how "To make a Walnut, that when you
cracke it, you shall find Biskets, and Carrawayes in it, or a prettie Posey written."[29]
       These curious confectionaries were in essence edible versions of the
"conceited" or fanciful banqueting rooms that housed them. At their most
restrained, the "stuff" of the void referred allusively to food much as banqueting houses referred detachedly to the main house. And at their most
unrestrained, void stuff referred by mimicry to everything but the kitchen
sink: not just snow, arms, knots, and so forth, but also (in a transliteration
of culinary into verbal media that will be important for us) poseys and letters. "Walnuts" with "a prettie Posey" inside were of a piece with banqueting houses like Tresham's Triangular Lodge with inscriptions and symbols
outside.
       While banqueting houses became detached from common living space,
then, their interior void became detached from common foodstuffs. The
ultimate significance of such detachment comes to view when we observe
that—precisely like the personalized decor of the Triangular Lodge and
other banqueting houses—decorative void cuisine created a domain apart
for personal expression. Even in aristocratic homes, we note, it was generally the lady of the house who hand-fashioned banqueting sweets. Confec-

tionary recipes often attested to such personal involvement among the highborn by qualifying instructions with a nod to individual "taste" and attributing recipes to specific aristocrats, as in "The making of manchets after my Ladie Graies vse."[30] Intimate involvement with banqueting sweets became especially notable in the early seventeenth century. It appears in the prominence of cookery books that (addressing a more general audience under the fiction that all were aristocrats) focused on banqueting stuffs for housewives rather than hired cooks. And it also appears in the proliferation of special "still-rooms," where the housewife concocted her confections and spirits.[31] Secluded within her still-room, personally fashioning ornamental conceits, the lady of the household became a kind of culinary limner painting an edible self-portrait.

Indeed, the personal attention lavished on banqueting stuffs may well remind us of the miniature. The titles of cookbooks conveyed the sense of guarded and precious objects much like jeweled miniatures: *The Treasurie of commodious conceits, & hidden Secrets . . . The Huswiues Closet, of healthfull prouision* (J[ohn] Par[tridge], 1573); *The Widdowes Treasure* ([John Partridge], 1595); *The good huswifes Iewell* (Thomas Dawson, 1587; 1596); or *A Closet for Ladies and Gentlewomen* ([Hugh Plat?], 1608). Both miniatures and banqueting ingredients (at least the prized sugar and spice) were kept locked in cabinets—the former in closets, the latter in wardrobes. Moreover, just as miniatures were enclosed in picture boxes and carried to court, so comfits were boxed or wrapped and carried about on one's person. Venus, in Jonson's *Christmas His Masque* (1616), knew the fashion: "I have cloves in my purse; I never go without one in my mouth" (ll. 139–40).[32] Finally, just as miniatures were given as personal gifts to lovers and friends, so were banqueting stuffs. "Present them," Plat advised, "to anie friende you haue for a Newyeares gift." King James was especially fond of giving presents of boxed delicacies to his intimate favorite, Buckingham.[33]

Thus the world of the void. Here, in this fantastic, detached retreat of architecture set apart from their public world and done up in lavish styles suited to their increasingly acute "taste," aristocrats came to consume. And what they consumed were sugar-and-spice constructions—all delicacy, all personalized in style, all removed from everyday sustenance—mirroring in miniature the fashion of the very rooms they sat in. All was representation. English aristocrats withdrew from publicness to like-"houses" to eat a like-"food" whose very stuff—no more than a metaphor or conceit—was void.

A final question that will bring the culinary "aesthetics of detachment," as I have called it, to bear upon aesthetics proper: how did aristocrats *enjoy* their repast in the world of the void? For example, how were their senses gratified? The answer is yet another confirmation of the detached subjectivity expressed in banqueting houses and stuffs. The senses themselves underwent a process of segmentation and detachment heightening the experience of subjectivity. In a medieval feast, we know, not only people but their senses—smell, touch, taste, sight, hearing—mingled confusedly in the large dining hall. But in the Renaissance, with its smaller, quieter feasts and new eating utensils reducing tactile contact with food, the senses began to separate out. In particular, the sense of sight came to the fore. However sweet void stuff was to the taste, after all, it melted in the mouth in seconds, like cotton candy. Void food was food primarily for the eye: a facade-food. Elaborate conceits of void birds, snow, arms, letters, and so forth were capable of filling only the hunger of vision and—the pang masked by vision—the subjective mind.

Here Norbert Elias's thesis about the civilizing process or history of manners is useful. In Elias's argument, civility comes through a kind of psychological self-seeing: the self sees itself through the judgmental eyes of others and tries self-consciously to avoid behaving rudely or shamefully in public. It does so by avoiding indiscriminate or too-near contact with the public, favoring instead a decorum of restraint and isolation. This accounts, Elias believes, for the ethos of individual servings at table.[34] Applying the thought to our topic, we can observe that in the arena of English cuisine it was the exquisitely pretty visibility of the void that most contributed to increased aristocratic self-awareness and reserve—to a *hauteur* in haute cuisine amounting to "civility." By comparison with the eye, all such accoutrements of self-conscious civility as specialized serving utensils paled. The eye was the most fastidious—the most precise and immaculate—of all serving utensils. Without the slightest danger of contagion or clumsiness, it could lap up the thinnest powdering of sugar from the finest delicacy and bring it home to the self. And it could do so with uncompromised privacy. Food for the eye was the highest of haute cuisine because in the moment of visual delectation before the first plate was touched it allowed the eating act to occur in splendid isolation from public inspection. The eye served, and the self within dined as if in a banqueting turret built for one.

Indeed, if we look from the void to the banqueting house that contained it, we notice an analogous emphasis on personal vision. Here I draw once

25. Recessional perspective scene viewed from the window of the banqueting house turret at Hardwick Hall. Photo: Alan Liu.

more upon Tuan, who argues that self-consciousness in the Renaissance was tied up with a developing interest in individualized or privatized vision—specifically, perspective.[35] Ornamental banqueting houses in our period, we find, catered simultaneously to private subjectivity and the contemporary rage for mathematically precise perspective sights. First, as we have seen, banqueting houses were physically detached from the prying eyes of the public. Second, as their alternative name—"prospect room"— suggests, they were often constructed in raised positions (in a turret approached by the leads, atop a mound in the garden/park, or as a multiple-storied structure) that offered a view of the surrounding scenery—sometimes, as at Hardwick, down a recessional vista precisely as if in a perspective painting or one of Inigo Jones's masque scenes (fig. 25).[36] The fascination with gaining a view from the private banqueting house, that is, was symptomatic of the new way of seeing. Stationed in the restricted space of a small banqueting house, the individual's vantage point came near to being the single, ideal point of observation—the vision of a particular person from a particular point—characteristic of perspective systems. The eye that savored a void course and the eye that feasted on landscape (as well as the eye that enjoyed a masque, we will later see) were the same. Both were instruments of self-service; both enjoyed an aesthetics of detachment.

In all senses, it would thus seem, banqueting houses and the food they housed nourished a subjectivity that separated itself from publicly centered forms of living. Such subjectivity was not accessible, common, or part of a whole. It was select, displaced, apart. It flourished, we may say, in an aesthetics at last wholly metonymic. Subjectivity was *a* part: a detached or merely contiguous room rather than whole house, a seasoning rather than whole meal, a feast for the eyes rather than for the whole sensorium. Between part and part, self and self, was only the void.

The Void of Self

But this is not the whole story of the void. Before we can proceed from the elementary aesthetics of sensory experience to that great aesthetic of James's Banqueting House, the masque, we must recognize that it is possible to see a void opening up *within* the part or self.

At the risk of unhinging my previous argument, I propose that we reconsider for a moment the architectural and culinary history of the void. For it may be wondered whether in tracing the detachment of ornamental banqueting houses and void stuffs we have really located subjectivity. Certainly such detachment or segmentation created the *sense* of a developing, individual self. But it was an uneasy sense troubled by the sheer obsessiveness of segmentation, of perpetually detachable rooms and eating habits. Seen in a different light, subjectivity appears unlocatable and itself segmented—in fact, self-estranged.

The very proliferation of architectural detachment implies that the desire for private consumption was never satisfied. A desire for privacy—for isolation from the public—drove medieval lords from the large hall to the more private great chamber above. And what happened? The great chamber often grew as large as the hall and even more ceremonial.[37] So the lord withdrew into a room within the great chamber. But then the withdrawing room became a dining room as well, so he withdrew for privacy further within, and within, and within. By the second half of the seventeenth century, private closets had become so public that lords and ladies were driven to add closets onto their closets, all in the search for privacy.[38] Even when in the late sixteenth and early seventeenth centuries the family split off from the great chamber to dine informally in what was called a parlor (usually located on the ground floor off the hall), here again a process of elaboration occurred by which the parlor began to vie in its handsome decorations with the great chamber itself.[39]

The banqueting house was itself subject to this recessional process by which privacy fled into ever more distanced reflections of the original place of intimacy. It was as if the self were chasing its self-image endlessly along an empty corridor of vision between facing mirrors. As we have seen in the multiple banqueting houses on the rooftop of Longleat and in the gardens of Hardwick Hall and Hampton Court, fanciful banqueting houses prolife-rated to become a labyrinth of privacy. The same was true of more remote lodges separated wholly from the main house. When Robert Cecil built his miniature castle, Cranborne Manor House, as a private lodge in 1608–11, he added a banqueting house retreat onto his retreat. Then he multiplied the banqueting house in the form of "tiny diamond-shaped lodges."[40] The Little Castle at Bolsover, where Jonson's *Love's Welcome at Bolsover* (1634) was performed, also subdivided into numerous private "houses." The Little Castle was begun in 1612 by Sir Charles Cavendish to serve, like Cranborne Manor, as a private retreat from his main house at Welbeck. Built on a lofty promontory, the completed castle consisted of a redecorated keep and a gallery added by his son William in 1629–33. One immediately thinks of the familiar banqueting-house-plus-gallery pattern. Only, as befits the "re-moved" lodge, the primary house was no where to be seen. Yet here again we find retreats within retreats. The keep itself was adorned with little orna-mental "houses," any one of which could have offered further privacy for consuming a void: on the roof, decorative domed turrets; on the top floor, the alcoved octagonal lobby beneath "a pretty cupola and lantern filled with mock-Gothic tracery"; in front, the twin entrance pavilions "deco-rated with battlements and obelisks"; and on the inside of the thick battlemented wall, where it enclosed a garden, "alcoves and little rooms, lovers' retreats." (As if underscoring the extent to which these miniature retreats were both apart from and a part of the castle retreat, one such room is embellished with "a hooded corner chimney-piece like those in the keep.")[41] Such proliferation of retreat upon retreat led to a dance of sub-division and unfixedness. The small group of guests invited to the banquet would break up into even smaller parties, each with its own "house." Or they would move from banqueting house to banqueting house, consuming within each a separate course of sweets.[42]

So, too, with the utensils and foodstuffs of the void served within the banqueting house: these were also caught up in a frustrated and endless recession of privacy. As we have seen, eating utensils multiplied: first knives; then knives and spoons; then knives, spoons, and forks; then knives, spoons, forks, and plates; and so on. (By the Victorian period, cutlery had so proliferated as to leave little room for the food itself.)[43] Matching the partitioning of the service, the void generated an even more splintered cosmos of "stuff" doled out in ornamental fragments. John Murrell's list of recipes, in *A Daily Exercise for Ladies and Gentlewomen* (1617), especially captures the dizzying variety of "conceited" banqueting stuffs: included are "collops" and "bacon"; "Buttons, Beades, Chaines"; "Snakes, Snailes, Frogs, Roses, Cheries" ("And they will be as though they grew vpon staulkes"); "Shooes, Slippers, Keyes, Kniues, Gloues"; "Letters, Knots," "double knots," "capital letters, or like claspes & eyes, or waxlights"; "a Walnut, both shell, and Kernill"; "Sugar plate"; "Cinamon stickes by Art"; and "Cinamon Letters" ("faire capitall Romane letters, according to some exact patterne").[44]

My point is not to argue that privacy could not or cannot be achieved, if by privacy we mean physical solitude or the company of a select gathering of intimates. Rather, my skepticism concerns the "self" as the *achieved identity* of privacy. The incessant segmentation and recession of rooms, "houses," service, stuff, and eating habits—all of which accelerated towards the end of the sixteenth century—record a privacy whose resident identity was forever elusive, unlocatable. In more than one sense, we may say, the "self" was void. When viewed in the context of the proliferating detachment of banqueting houses and void stuffs, the private self was a sugar-spun identity always on the verge of being consumed by an elusive and feared insubstantiality.

We can review the liminal site and structure of many banqueting houses to illustrate the kind of insubstantial identity I indicate. As rooms outside—that is, insides outside—detached banqueting houses not only lacked clear identity but were exaggeratedly vulnerable. They did not, like private chambers, lie protected within layers of outer rooms. They stood in gardens or parks detached and *exposed*. The vulnerability of such self-positioning affected the paradoxical structure of these houses. Though infinitely varied in their whimsical elaboration, the substructure of most banqueting houses was the compact, freestanding tower or turret designed for military defense. In essence, detached banqueting houses (and, as we have seen, even such attached banqueting rooms as the turret atop Hardwick Hall) were sites of pleasure-*on-the-defense*. The two-storied banqueting house that stood on a hill far off to the west of Nonsuch Palace exemplified this fragile paradox. Excavations have revealed that the ban-

26. An arbor being trained by gardeners to serve as a banqueting house. Benches and a table have been set up inside. From the front page to *The Gardeners Labyrinth* (1594), by Dydymus Mountain (Thomas Hill).

queting house was surrounded by a "retaining wall with rounded corner-bastions . . . intended to recall the form of a Tudor artillery-fort." In order to please the banqueters' sight, however, the banqueting house/fort (as described in a Parliamentary Survey of 1650) sported defenseless, large windows set "quite round the whole," and in each of the four corners "a balcone placed for prospect."[45] To please the eye and the self within, the banqueting house had to make the eye/I vulnerable.

Banqueting houses projected insubstantiality not only in the fragility of their liminal site and structure but also in the flimsiness of the substances from which they were made. While some banqueting houses detached from the main house were constructed of brick or stone, most were reared of far less sturdy stuff: timber, vines, flowers, herbs. One of the most popular banqueting house forms, for example, the arbor (fig. 26; shown being erected in Thomas Hill's *The Gardeners Labyrinth*), was especially transient. Elizabeth raised such temporary banqueting houses in her park at Greenwich "made with fir-poles, decked with birch-branches, roses, lavender and marigolds, the floors strewn with rushes and herbs."[46]

The dainties consumed within these evanescent structures further nourished their air of insubstantiality. Contemporary recipes are especially telling in this regard. Cookbooks spoke of preparing confectionary and sweetmeats as though dealing with extremely delicate and fugitive elixirs. Care in preparation was essential. The fixings and utensils had to be "best," "fine," "pure," "clean," "faire," etc. "To Candy Rose leaues as naturally as if they grew vpon the Tree," for example, Plat instructs us to take "the fayrest Rose leaues, red or dammaske" and lay them upon "faire paper" "on a Sunshine day." Then, repeatedly turning the leaves over "in the hottest of the sunne," we must sprinkle each side alternatively with "Rose water" and "thinly all ouer" with "double refined suger" beaten "very fine" and put "in a fine lawne searce." In another recipe, "To preserue Damsins," Plat demands not only that the fruit be "cleane"—wiped "one by one"—the sugar "white & good," the fire "gentle," but also that the "continuall scumming, and stirring" be done "with a siluer spoone."[47] In conclusion, we are admonished that such dainties (the most lavish, pure sugar forms appropriately dubbed "subtleties") can be "kept" only if they are sealed or boxed up tight.[48] At all times, banqueting stuffs were treated with a meticulousness that acknowledged their truly "dainty" substance.

This brings me to the point where my previous argument of detached subjectivity may seem to evaporate completely. Since we are what we eat, the "self" that found itself in banqueting houses must ultimately have been as "airy" as the dainties on which it fed. Fragile banqueting stuffs contained within fragile banqueting houses, that is, would seem to argue a mode of self-representation always on the verge of breaking up. My idiom of "breaking up" is quite literal. It was common practice at banquets not simply to consume but to "break" and "spoyle" confectionary (a fact that will have extraordinary relevance when we examine the aftermath of the Jacobean masque). Thomas Dawson, giving the popular recipe for a sugar paste to make "al manner of fruits, and other fine thinges" (including plateware), added the equally popular conclusion: "At the ende of the Banket they [the guests] may eat all, and *breake the Platters, Dishes, Glasses, Cuppes, and all other things, for this paste is very delicate and sauerous*" (my emphasis).[49] The breaking of banqueting stuffs was done with zest, even violence. Looking back nostalgically at this phenomenon in *The Accomplisht Cook* (1660), Robert May offered a sweet imitation. He proposed an elaborate sugar display figuring a mock-battle in which a castle fired artillery at a man-of-war. The sweet battle then ended with a perfumed "war," the ladies pelting each other with eggshells full of scented water.[50] Actually living in May's earlier "sugar-coated" age, John Taylor, the Water Poet, was even more militant in his enjoyment of sweets. Keenly, if satirically, he recounted the rude violence of banqueting "wars." In *The praise of Hemp-seed* (1630), he pictured "feasting fights" that riotously "spoyld" the many fanciful "Dainties" at banquets (here made by professional comfit makers):

Lip licking Comfit-makers, by whose trade,
Dainties come thou to me are quickly made;
Baboones, and hobby-horses, and owles, and apes,
Swans, geese, dogs, woodcocks, & and a world of shapes,
Castles for Ladies, and for Carpet Knights,
Vnmercifully spoyld at feasting fights,
Where battering bullets are fine sugred plums,

. . . .

Each one contending in this Candied coyle,
To take most prisoners, and put vp most spoyle.
Retiring neuer when they doe assaile,
But most aduenturously with tooth and nayle,
Raze, ruinate, demolish, and confound,
The sugred fabricke leuell with the ground.
And hauing layd the buildings thus along,
They swallow downe, and pocket vp the wrong.

. . . .

Such sweet mouth'd fights as these doe often fall
After a Christning, or a Funerall.
Thus Hempe the Comfit-makers doth supply,
From them that newly liue, and newly dye.

"Raze, ruinate, demolish, and confound." Such a decisive breaking of fast dramatized the essential nothingness of delicate sugar substances: "That who so that way afterwards doe passe," Taylor affirmed, "Can see no signe where such a Castle was."[51] The paradoxical juxtaposition of "Christning" and "Funerall," "newly liue" and "newly dye," fittingly served as final course to Taylor's account. The assertive spoiling of the dainty sweets that fed the private self reveals the stuff of "self" to be itself funereal: a sugar-spun substance, ephemeral and void.

Finally, the death blow: the essential food value of banqueting stuffs, in fact, was *nothing*. In a fashion even more radical than I earlier suggested, the culinary referent of the void was zero. By this I do not simply allude to the increasingly "representational" tendency at the courts of Elizabeth and James to economize by making banqueting stuffs out of paper (in annoyance, Elizabeth in 1601 ordered that "the banquet be of better stuff, fit for men to eat and not of paper shows"). Nor do I simply refer to Gervase Markham's term for fanciful subtleties: "*empty*" dishes, as opposed to the "full dishes" of meats "that are of substance" (my emphasis). More fundamentally, I mean what Sidney W. Mintz suggests when he argues that sugar and spice were not even considered food. Quite literally, they were substanceless.[52]

Why, then, were sugar and spice sought? Why did Elizabethans and Jacobeans consume with increasing eagerness void foods? The answer is that sugar and spice were medicines.[53] The healing powers of such beneficent stuff derived from its great expense and exoticism (by the early seventeenth century, most sugar came from the West, most spice from the East Indies).[54] So valuable and rare were spiced sugars, as we have seen, that they were locked away in cabinets as if they were jewels. Indeed, confectionary and sweetmeats were often compared to jewels (themselves supposed to have magical healing powers): jellies are "Chystall" or "orient as a Rubie"; candied sprigs of rosemary "seeme to be couered with sparks of diamonds"; pancakes "looke as yellow as golde."[55] In the fullest demonstration of this sympathy, actual jewels were often added to banquet ingredients. Dawson's recipe for "manus Christi," for example, included pearl and gold leaf.[56] Ingested with full consciousness of their rareness, the sugar and spice of void confectionary and cordial waters became a sort of ornamental talisman worn *within* the body. They were a jewel-laxative serving to "open obstructions," "purge superfluous humors," purify or "cleanse the body," aid digestion ("they are very cordiall for the stomacke"), refresh or comfort "the spirits and vital parts," and cherish "the whole Body exceedingly."[57]

The most telling catchwords here are "restore" and "preserve." Despite their fragility and ephemerality, the ingredients of banqueting stuffs and cordials were especially praised in "medical" treatises for their powers to restore and preserve the body. Cinnamon, we are told, keeps the body from "corruption and putrefaction" and "restoreth them that be appayred and decayed"; frankincense "preserueth the fleshe from putrifaction"; saffron "Preserueth all the entrals."[58] Not coincidentally, two favorite banqueting stuffs—and *the* cooking innovations of the time—were "conserves" and "preserves."[59] In *Closet for Ladies and Gentlewomen,* Plat extolled one of his marmalade preserves (ingredients included sugar, ginger, cinnamon and other spices, as well as gold leaf and pearl) as "very comfortable and restoratiue for any Lord or Lady whatsoeuer." Using "preserve" more broadly, Partridge in *Widdowes Treasure* titled a confection recipe simply "To preserue nature." Markham's concoction for an aqua vita was similarly named "A restorative of rosa solis." Not to be outdone, Dawson captioned his "restoratiue" distillation "the water of life." Many such recipes for distilled void wines (to which much sugar and spice were added) promised preservation of youth. Markham's rendition of the popular recipe for the "sovereign" "Doctor Stevens' water" concluded that it "preserveth him in good liking, and will make him seem young in old age."[60]

What sugar and spice really cured, in a word, was mortality—mortality conceived both as literal death and as a dissolving, segmenting, or breaking apart of the subjective self.[61] Though themselves "void," comfits gave comfort in face of a void, consumable self. Such comfort in the face of mortality can be detected in as basic a function as the purging of superfluities from the body. "Superfluous humors" were excremental or waste matter, which, unless purged, caused "corruption" and "putrefaction," as if the body had died.[62] In a higher sense, sugar and spice, especially when added to distilled spirits, comforted not only the mortal body but the spirit. As Leonardo Phioravante affirmed, something good became "miraculous" when distilled. This was especially true of spices, which because of their consistency as "hotte and drie thinges" were considered "spirituall" (hence the belief that the people of India "lyues onely with smelling of Odours at their nose").[63] The spirit of spices was associated with an almost Christ-like power of restoration. Not only was the wafer *manus Christi* a banquet favorite, but the seasonings in minced pie at Christmas were thought to represent the spices given by the Magi to the Christ child.[64] Needing to comfort both the self's mortal body and spirit, Renaissance cookbooks invoked a power of preservation at last divine. To cite Plat's Epistle, in *Delightes for Ladies,* they treated "of foode, sweete, fresh, and *durable* / [To] maintaine life, when all things els were spent" (my emphasis).[65]

If I seem somehow to have shifted in my discussion from emphasizing private individuality to feting the physical body (and its incorporeal spirit), it is because contemporary banqueters did. In their nervously insubstantial subjectivity, it was especially the body that gave them something tangible to hold onto. Recipes for adorning the body thus mingled freely with cookery/medical recipes. Plat's *Closet for Ladies and Gentlewomen,* for example, slid from restorative banqueting stuffs to beautifying cosmetics, and Markham's *English Housewife* from medicinal spirits to sweet-smelling perfumes.[66] Armed with such physical evidence, one might be tempted to argue that these cook/medical books sought *only* to preserve the body. Certainly the increased threat of early death towards the end of the sixteenth century, indexed by higher mortality rates, would have figured in the almost obsessive urge at this time to consume medicinal sugar and spice.[67] And yet everything that gave banqueting stuffs cultural as well as bodily meaning (the incessant privatization of rooms and eating habits, the building of insubstantial banqueting houses, the consumption of "airily" fragile confections) suggests that a more general nervousness was at work. It was not just the body but the detached—i.e., fragmented and unplaceable—

"self" reified by the body that was the source of anxiety. Renaissance banqueting houses situated a quest in which an endlessly frustrated search for private subjectivity was displaced into repetitive, ritualistic acts of preserving the flesh. Contemporaries turned for solace of their selves both to the personalized "conceits" of banqueting house architecture and, as on the title page of *good Huswifes Handmaide for the Kitchin,* to "Conceits for the preseruation of health."

James's Banqueting House and the Masque

But what about the masque conceits enacted in King James's own Banqueting House? Have we not wandered far afield from such royally housed entertainments? From aesthetics or art in the higher sense? On the contrary, I would argue, we have finally arrived. The peculiarly private/public nature of the King's Banqueting House did not make his an exception to other banqueting houses. Rather, it vividly dramatized the problematics of subjectivity that informed all banqueting houses. What contemporaries viewed through the ornamental perspective scenery and (as we will see) "sweet" conceits of masques in the Banqueting House was an exposure of the King's privacy as insubstantial fiction—as self made void—even while they saw, or hoped to see, bodily "restoratives." Before we can witness such self-*un*masking, however, we must first locate the King's personal Banqueting House and draw the connection between its masques and the void. For, actual voids were not as a rule consumed in James's Banqueting House. Masques were. Replacing the void but incorporating its spirit, language, and practices, the masque rose, like cake dough, to become the last, sweetest dessert of royal entertainment. The masque was a void proclaiming the detachment of the King's "private" self. But the very notion of "proclaiming" privacy whispered a reversal in the sense of self. James's "inside" was exposed "outside."

We can begin by placing the King's Banqueting House. Like others of its kind, it was detached from the procession of public rooms in the main residence. As shown in the plan of Whitehall Palace (fig. 1), the Banqueting House was set apart from the receding succession of principal royal chambers (the great or guard chamber, presence chamber, privy chamber, etc.). It was attached to the main rooms of the palace only by means of galleries and terraces. Physically "removed," James's Banqueting House thus stood on the very brink of breaking away entirely from publicness. Indeed, just a few yards across Whitehall Highway were the King's private pleasure spots: his bowls house, tennis court, cockpit, tiltyard, and park hunting green.

Considered stylistically, the Banqueting House went even further in the direction of detachment. This is especially true of the second Banqueting House James commissioned in 1619 after the first burned (fig. 2). Designed by Inigo Jones, the house projected pure classical lines radically diverging from the stylistic jumble of the rest of Whitehall. In Sir John Chamberlain's disapproving assessment: "the new built banketting roome . . . is too faire and nothing sutable to the rest of the house."[68] One might add that the "faire" classicism of James's Banqueting House also diverged from the style of other banqueting houses. Certainly, the comparative plainness as well as great "hall-like" size of James's building differed from the individualized ornament and relative smallness of banqueting houses like Tresham's.[69] Critics from Per Palme to Jonathan Goldberg have accordingly read the Whitehall building as designed to publicize the King's grandeur and authority.[70] Inigo Jones himself thought that building exteriors should wear a suitable public persona of "grauiti."

But Jones went on to distinguish between a building's exterior and interior "ornament," which he compared respectively to a man's outward and inward self:

> For as outwardly euery wyse man carrieth a grauiti in Publicke Places, whear ther is nothing els looked for, yet inwardly hath his immaginacy put on fire, and sumetimes licenciously flying out, as nature hir self doeth oftentymes, stravagantly, to dellight, amase us, sumtimes moufe us to laughter, sumtimes to contemplation and horror, So in architecture ye outward ornaments oft to be sollid, proporsionable according to the rulles, masculine and unaffected, wheras within the Cimeras yoused by the ancients, the varried and composed ornaments both of the house ytsuelf and the mouables within yt ar most commendable.[71]

Though still relatively grave in its lines—solid, symmetrical, plain—the interior of James's Banqueting House was like other banqueting houses in emphasizing embellishments of ornamental design. It sported not one but two tiers of decorative columns—one Corinthian, the other Ionic, "both with the entablatures enriched"—and a partitioned ceiling that by the 1630s (as we saw in chapter 1) exhibited the elaborate paintings of Rubens.[72]

But it was the "mouables" in the Banqueting House interior that were its true ornaments, its true "Cimeras" of "immaginacy" projecting the detachment of James's private self. Jones's description of inwardness as entertainment—"to dellight, amase us . . . moufe us"—points the way. The epitome of all the entertaining "mouables" in the Banqueting House

interior was the masque. Performed while the many windows of the Banqueting House were hung with tapestries to shut out the public world,[73]
James's private entertainments dramatized an alternative world of extravagant ornamentality—a whole cosmos of detached "immaginacy" working
"inwardly."

Masques were the consummate form of the whimsical ornamentality we
have already seen in the other medium of banqueting house entertainments: food. The sympathy between poet and cook was intimate. One clue,
for example, is that Jonson's verse seems almost to follow a cookbook recipe
for sugar-spun delicacies, serving up—in his own words—visions "sweet,"
"neat," "clean," "clear," "pure," "fair," "fresh," "subtle," and "airy."[74] Language in the masque had a sweet tooth. A further clue lies in the fanciful
ornament of masque costumes and dances. Richly decorated with precious
jewels, the individually tailored costumes may be said to be "spicy": not
only were jewels a common ingredient of confectionary and costumery, but
masque costumes often represented travelers from the spice Indies.[75] Similarly, costumed masquers performed dances of "curious" shapes that
mirrored the multifold sugar molds of voids and the conceited structures of
banqueting houses: circles, squares, triangles, letters, chains, knots, mazes,
and anagrams concealing personal meaning.[76]

Meanwhile, just as aspects of the masque inclined toward confectionary,
so void stuffs reciprocally leaned in the direction of masque form. As we
have seen, void confectionary was all along growing more "literate." Not
only were verses printed on the back of the individualized little plates that
first appeared in banqueting houses, and not only was confectionary
shaped into "letters," but, as in Plat's recipe to make a walnut, actual poesies
were concealed within sugar molds, or, as in the case of "frolicks," wrapped
around sweetmeats.[77] Even grand confectionary "subtleties" (or "sotelties")—the *pièces de résistance* of sweet banquets—sported verse. Subtleties were often tagged with explanatory verses called "reasons" that increasingly conveyed flattering political messages.[78] It was as if the
spectacle-food of the void ("food for the eye," I called it) was from the first
developing in the direction of the spectacle-literature of the masque.

Finally, however, it is too restrictive to describe these coincidences between the masque and the void as mere sympathy or parallel. What the clues
indicate is that there may well be a direct link in the background. The evidence lies in the masque's literal background: Inigo Jones's spectacular
stage sets. Elaborate and literate confectionaries were in fact one of the parent forms of masque scenery. Of course, in one sense Jones's scenery mirrors

not only classical architectural style and Italian stage machinery but the fancy ornamental exteriors characteristic of most banqueting houses. Gervase Jackson-Stops and James Pipkin suggest as much in discussing the mock-medieval style of Robert Lyminge's design for a banqueting house at Blickling (constructed about 1620): "its castellations and loopholes . . . can be compared with some of Inigo Jones' designs for stage sets—and indeed garden buildings were often conceived as backdrops for the masques and outdoor entertainments of the time."[79] But in another sense, masque settings descended in part from traditional court pageants, and the latter took their inspiration directly from void confectionary. Bridget Ann Henisch traces the lineage of the court pageant to banquet subtleties:

> as sotelties became more elaborate they grew larger, so large indeed that it was sometimes impossible to set them any longer on the table. Instead they had to be wheeled onto the floor of the hall, where life-size actors took the place of small-scale models. In France, the term *entremet* covered both the table ornament and its grander cousin, but in England sotelty referred only to the first, and the term *pageant* was used to cover the second.[80]

Void confectionary, that is, expanded to *become* the setting of pageants. Big enough to include whole orchestras in pies (as Richard Barber shows),[81] unwieldy enough to need floor- rather than table-space, and so complex and multiform that they allowed actors to move among them, void subtleties were one of the original patterns—the cake mold or cookie cutter—for masque scenery. Correlative evidence of the confectionary roots of the masque can be found in the many appearances within masques of edible props. "Precious gifts" of banqueting sweets, for instance ("wine, cream, jelly, beverage, cakes, spices, and other good matters"), figured in James's ill-fated Theobalds Entertainment of 1606, where they were spilled by the tipsy "Queen of Sheba" into the lap of the equally inebriated Danish King.[82]

The masque in James's Banqueting House (and elsewhere), in sum, was heir to the void. In its scenery, language, costumes, dances, and so on, it subsumed or incorporated the void. Sir Antony Weldon thought as much when he spoke of masques and voids in the same breath, almost as if they were interchangeable. Recounting the sequence of banquets associated with the masque Jonson made for Lord Hay (*Lovers Made Men* [1617]), he alternates description of voids and the masque and at one point uses language that blurs the line between masquers and consumable sweets. "The most sumptous feast at *Essex* house, that ever was seen before," he says, was followed by "a costly Voydee, and after that a Maske, of choyse Noble-men

and Gentlemen, and after that a most costly and magnificent Banquet." Like
the delectable "Voydee" and "Banquet" served after the "sumptuous feast,"
Jonson's masque is here a sweet banquet performed by deliciously "choyse"
courtiers.[83]

As if they were truly voids or sweet banquets, moreover, court masques
were regularly served in the evening after the main feasts of banquets. And
it is here that we see the issue of privacy entering. On an evening when a
masque was to be shown, James would usually have dined privately in his
privy chamber (or perhaps in one of the chambers of his courtiers). Afterwards, he may or may not have withdrawn into an inner chamber to
consume a void. The significant event occurred when he would then break
off from the entire recession of rooms in his palace to pass through the privy
gallery into his Banqueting House—there to partake of his special void: a
masque.[84] Like other aristocrats withdrawing from the main feast through
a gallery or garden to a retreat-like banqueting house, in other words,
James sought his "privacy."

That James envisaged masques in his Banqueting House as in some
sense private events, tantamount to the consuming of voids in normal banqueting houses, is evident from his response to complaints from ambassadors when they were not invited: "a Masque is not a public function,"
grumblers were informed, and therefore "his Majesty is quite entitled to
invite any Ambassador he may choose, not as an Ambassador, but as a
friend."[85] Rather than simply dismiss this statement as politicking—which
at one level it certainly was—consider that James at another level really did
want to form friendships with ambassadors. His frequent gifts of miniatures suggest the extent to which he tried to personalize public and
ceremonial relationships. John Finett, assistant master of ceremonies and
then master (whose office was devoted to handling ambassadors), recalled
one such instance: James sent the Swedish ambassador his miniature enclosed within a diamond ring worth £2,000 "as a private Toaken without
publique Ceremonie to be worne by him, not for the value, but for the
senders memory."[86] Indeed, James would often invite his ambassadorial
"friends," as Finett termed them, to dine with him in his private quarters
before departing together for the Banqueting House. Count Gondomar,
the influential Spanish ambassador, became a familiar guest: "he had his
accesses to Court, and to his Majesties Presence," Finett wrote, "as a Domestique without Ceremony, and this by the Kings own Signification of
his Pleasure."[87]

Despite the public architectural style and obvious politics of James's

Banqueting House, then—and despite the fact that actual voids were not normally consumed inside—we would still seem to be on familiar ground. The liminal location of James's Banqueting House as well as his perception of the delicious masque "mouables" within imply the privacy and detachment we have traced in other banqueting houses. But the substance of such privacy—as we previously saw—also had its hollow side. We come to the crux of our argument when we recognize that, just as in the case of other aristocratic voids held in "defensive" pleasure spots, there was something terrifyingly, mortally empty about the "privacy" of James's entertainments. There was something truly void, that is, about his sense of private self. While his entertainments seemed to project a world of intimate self-expression, they also intimated the characteristic unlocatability or insubstantiality of his, and his period's, subjectivity.

A first indication of the insubstantiality of James's wished-for "privacy" lies in the very substantialness of his Banqueting House—a paradoxical substantialness that was really porousness. The King's Banqueting House was at first glance definitely not an ephemeral structure. On the contrary, while Elizabeth had built on the same spot a temporary banqueting house made of perishable canvas and wood (decked with sweet-smelling branches, flowers, and fruits), James prided himself on building his Banqueting House of lasting stuff: what "his predecessors had left him built merely in wood," James boasted, "he had converted into stone."[88] Nevertheless, we here again find the basic infrastructure of vulnerability: a room outside, or inside outside. However solid, James's Banqueting House was profoundly vulnerable: it could not defend him against intrusions upon privacy. As we have noted, the Banqueting House sat on the very edge of the palace grounds. On one side was the palace "Inner Court" (or "Preaching Place"); on the other, across the way, the King's private pleasure spots extending to St. James's Park. But there was a vulnerability in such removal that was underscored by the abridging public Highway of Whitehall. Running north to the City James despised and south to the Parliament he opposed, Whitehall Highway was a great and dangerous divide between James's private Banqueting House and his other detached pleasure zones. It emblematized the fact that the public perpetually trespassed upon James's world of privacy.

Nor was such intrusion merely symbolic. We know that, though its windows may have been covered over during a masque showing, the Banqueting House doors literally could not keep the public out. As was commonly complained of, citizens and common gentry swelled the originally more

elite audience of aristocratic courtiers—to 600 in one estimation. The result was complete "confusion," a mob scene of the kind James intensely
dreaded for fear of his life.[89] Ironically, the "private" Banqueting House
and its masque void made James vulnerable to his greatest fear: dismemberment by a "wild," intruding public. Fear of a violent tearing apart of the
private self frequently surfaced in James's dealings with the public. "You
will never let me alone," he once complained to a petitioner. And continued: "I would to God you had first my doublet and then my shirt and
when I were naked I think you would give me leave to be quiet." Even more
tellingly: "every man runs upon me for his friends so as I am torn in pieces
amongst them." The French ambassador pictured women who publicly
gossiped about James in a similar image of dismemberment: they "tear him
to pieces with their tongues."[90] The detached privacy the King sought in
his Banqueting House and masques was perpetually sundered. It was the
personal fear of being torn apart by an unruly public that drove James incessantly to flee the court to the country in search of yet more removed privacy
in his many remote hunting lodges or "boxes"—which accordingly swelled
in size and sumptuousness.[91]

One might object that the vulnerability James experienced in his efforts
at private detachment was only to be expected. James, after all, was king.
He was necessarily a public person even when he withdrew with select intimates to a sequestered banqueting house or hunting box. But there is more
to James's plight of privacy than normal kingliness. James's inability to detach himself from his ceremonial and public role did not prevent him from
ever more urgently questing for informality and retirement—a quest
which then, in a vicious circle, *increased* his vulnerability to public exposure.
The viciousness of this circle can be seen in James's compulsion to multiply
the number of intimate palace officers. The number of gentlemen of the
privy chamber and of the bedchamber (the latter practically a new depart-
ment formed by the King) grew alarmingly under James.[92] He could not
keep the numbers down. His very need for intimacy swelled the ranks of
intimates to the point where they themselves threatened intimacy. That
was the irony surrounding James. He sought privacy with a desperation
that far exceeded Elizabeth's own drive to secrecy, yet was far less able to
locate it. Always he found instead the feared specter of violated privacy, of
an insubstantial, void place of "self."

Having observed its strangely public/private site and occasion, we can
now taste of the void-like masque itself. It was the staging of James's "private" masques that most dramatically publicized his dilemma of self-

thwarting subjectivity. As I have said, masques "proclaimed" his privacy. Or in terms of the visual analogue we will come to, they *announced* it.

Oberon in Perspective: The Annunciation of Self

My primary evidence for the masque's unmasking of subjectivity will be Jonson's *Oberon, The Fairy Prince* (1611), which I read with special attention to Jones's ornamental stage scenes and to a useful, religious parallel: Annunciation scenes. By alternately sliding Jones's masque sets and Annunciation paintings into view—like "movable" scenes—we can gain a better perspective on Jonson's poetry.

As with banquet voids, masques can be appreciated by first privileging the sense of sight. In detaching the visual from the other senses, I merely follow the masque's own habit of differentiating and segmenting experience—its habit, in other words, of participating in the proliferating withdrawals, detachments, and segmentations we have already witnessed in the architecture and foodstuffs of the banqueting house world. The masque's segmentary habit can be detected at the most elemental level of dramatic structure. Rather than represent a single cosmos, masques developed separate "outward" and "inward" worlds: the public antimasque (played by professional actors) and the private main masque (performed by a select company of court lords and ladies). This segmentation was self-perpetuating: the main masques of such later court productions as Jonson's *Pleasure Reconciled to Virtue* (1618) and *Neptune's Triumph* often underwent further subdivision through the intrusion of a second antimasque (splintering into many more antimasques under Charles).

But it was the masque's differentiation of the senses, particularly its emphasis on sight, that most dramatically acted out the problematics of self. Here I turn my spotlight on the masque's most significant experiment in sight: perspective. Jones, we know, developed perspective scenery to lead the eye of the audience "inward" from the public antimasque to the private main masque. This was especially true for the eye of James, who sat at the exact center of the three facing sides of the audience on a raised dais with rails along back and sides. As Stephen Orgel shows, this dais gave James alone the perfect vantage point from which to enjoy the perspective of his private entertainment. Yet the paradox, Orgel also suggests, is that the King thus himself became a stage watched.[93] In my terminology, he became an "inside outside." And what did James really see in perspective scenery from his "personal" point of view? He saw what amounted to an announcement of his failed search for privacy. He saw self-exposure.

Jones's early pen-and-ink designs for *Oberon* (our only full visual record), flanked by Jonson's descriptions in the text of the masque, serve well to illustrate my point.[94] *Oberon*, Jonson tells us, opened with an "obscure" outside scene in which one could detect only "a dark rock with trees beyond it and all wildness that could be presented" (ll. 1–2; fig. 27). Such "wildness," the audience soon discovered, was populated by an antimasque of primitive satyrs. Next, "the whole scene opened, and within was discovered the frontispiece of a bright and glorious palace whose gates and walls were

27. Inigo Jones, Scene of Rocks, early drawing of the first scene for Ben Jonson's masque, *Oberon, The Fairy Prince* (1611). Photo: Courtauld Institute of Art.

28. Inigo Jones, Palace within a Cavern, early drawing of the second scene for Ben Jonson's masque, *Oberon, The Fairy Prince* (1611). Also extant is a later version of the palace (*Inigo Jones*, ed. Orgel and strong, 1:217). Photo: Courtauld Institute of Art.

transparent" (ll. 97–98; fig. 28). By "transparent" Jonson appears to mean "translucent," since the final scene (the main masque) opens a further discovery (fig. 29):

> the whole palace opened, and the nation of fays were discovered, some with instruments, some bearing lights, others singing; and within, afar off in perspective, the knights masquers sitting in their several sieges. At the further end of all, Oberon, in a chariot, which to a loud triumphant music began to move forward. . . . (ll. 213–17)

What this succession of opening scenes or "discoveries" enacted was a process of penetration from the world of the public antimasque into that of the private masque. The eye of the audience was drawn through the "obscure" "wildness" of the antimasque outside, through the insubstantial ("transparent") castle walls, through the long arched corridor of receding perspective with its "nation of fays," past the more select gathering of fairy "knights masquers," and at last to Oberon—played by James's son Henry— seated in a chariot before a closed door.[95] Such an inward progression also took the form of a refining process as the rude satyrs made way for a civilized "nation" of fairies and, at the end of the recession, the fairy nation's privy courtiers and ruling prince.

29. Inigo Jones, Interior of the Palace, early drawing of the third scene for Ben Jonson's masque, *Oberon, The Fairy Prince* (1611). Photo: Courtauld Institute of Art.

30. Inigo Jones, St. George's Portico, drawing of the second scene for Ben Jonson's masque, *Prince Henry's Barriers* (1610). The first scene, The Fallen House of Chivalry, opens up to reveal the portico. Photo: Courtauld Institute of Art.

Yet at the very moment the audience's eye penetrated to Oberon "At the further end of all," his chariot began to move forward. In essence, I suggest, the eye's penetrating "discovery" of the private main masque brought the inside outside. Looking at a similar scene of outward movement in *Prince Henry's Barriers* (1610)—where the set opened upon an arched perspective recession leading to a closed door (fig. 30)—Jonathan Goldberg detects the pattern of a Roman triumph.[96] I would add that because such progressions outward in *Oberon* or *Prince Henry's Barriers* occurred only after a prior act of visual penetration, their "triumph" merely realized the victory of the audience's eye: what was so triumphally discovered (seen first and then brought forth) was interiority. Such was especially true of *Oberon*, where it was the King's son Henry who came forth from within.[97] Looking

through the arched recession of the final discovery scene down a corridor
suspiciously like James's privy gallery, the audience watched what was really
a version of the King himself coming from his privy chamber, passing down
his privy gallery, and entering the Banqueting House.[98] It watched the un-
closeting of James's privacy.

The staging of later masques similarly "discovered" royal privacy, but in
a green setting. Increasingly, masquing courtiers emerged from a closed
garden bower or arbor representing James's wish for wooded seclusion. In
The Masque of Flowers (1613), for example, the scenery opened to reveal a
walled garden. At its "farther end" stood a raised "goodly arbour" within
whose arches "the Masquers sat unseen."[99] So, too, in *The Golden Age
Restored* (1615), the masquers were "discovered" "set far within the shade
. . . in Elysian bowers" (ll. 136, 124–25). Such arboreal enclosure was then
restaged as "a glorious bower" (l. 172) in *Mercury Vindicated from the Alchemists at Court* (1616), as "the bower of Zephyrus" in *The Vision of Delight*
(1617)—which opened to discover the masquers "as the glories of the
spring" (ll. 117–18, 160–61)—and as an island tree forming an "archèd arbor" in *Neptune's Triumph* (l. 151). Leah S. Marcus has astutely read such
burgeoning garden bowers in the masque as representations of James's
desire that the aristocracy withdraw from the city to their country estates
in order to observe hospitality.[100] Such a wish, I would add, was self-
expressive: James himself, as we have seen, relished withdrawing from city
and court life to his private country retreats (extending hospitality, we
should note, only to a select circle of friends). The masque arbor was James's
locus amoenus or vision of earthly delight: a sort of garden banqueting house
transplanted to his actual, city Banqueting House. And in such transplan-
tation lay the paradox. The masques discovered—that is, at once covered
(in closed bowers) and uncovered—James's vision of retirement.

The point is that James on his dais never really *saw* in masque scenery the
retirement or detached interiority he craved, any more than he saw through
the closed doors at the recessional vanishing points in *Prince Henry's Barriers* and *Oberon* (or any more than he saw his true self in the displacement of
rule onto his unJamesian son Henry).[101] Rather, he saw the main masque
discovered *outside* the door of privacy. Similarly, the "unseen" masquers in
closed garden bowers or arbors in other masques were always finally discovered in open view beyond the pale of privacy. Thus penetrated, the
vision of enclosed privacy—of the essential mystery of subjectivity—was
punctured, dismembered, made vulnerable to public "wildness," in short,
dramatized. In *Oberon*, the transgression of private space was publicly pro-

claimed by Silenus. Pointing through the perspective scenery, he announced to James (and the rest of the audience) the "second birth" of the King's son Prince Oberon/Henry (l. 105). At this moment of piercing privacy, and of privacy pierced, the masque became a kind of secular Annunciation.

To clarify my point, indeed, I will make a brief excursion into the exemplary perspective space of Quattrocento painting, specifically pictures of the Annunciation.[102] Continental and religious in milieu, Annunciations may at first appear entirely foreign to James's Banqueting House and the transgression of private space it staged. But we have a model for our travel abroad in Inigo Jones himself, who journeyed to the Continent to study perspective in art and architecture. As in the case of Jones, our foreign journey will finally circle back home to give us fresh perspective on the masque's visual and verbal annunciation of self.

Quattrocento Annunciations, we know, figured the dissemination of the great religious precedent of mysterious subjectivity, divinity: Gabriel proclaims the engendering of the Word to the Virgin Mary. Yet all the tension of such pictures lies in the fact that they could not directly picture divinity. Indeed, divinity had to be pictured—at least at first glance—as barred or shut off from vision. Thus two topoi are commonly depicted in perspective behind the foreground scene in Annunciations: the enclosed garden (*hortus conclusus*) and closed door (*porta clausa*). Symbolic of Mary's inviolate virginity, enclosed gardens and shut doors image the fact that the picture cannot image the divine "prince" beyond the pale or portal of mortality. (The *porta clausa* is derivative of the prophet Ezekiel's reference to the Temple's shut gate, which only the "prince" can enter.)[103]

We can look, for example, at Domenico Veneziano's *Annunciation*, c. 1445 (fig. 31). Reading the picture from its margins inward: Mary is separated from Gabriel by both the checkered perspective ground-plane and the receding loggia of columns on the far right. From the left, Gabriel enters the picture having already penetrated through his matching loggia of columns. He points the lilies in his left hand (as his eyes are pointed) at Mary. Two other columns frame the archway of the central perspective recession. Within that archway, we see a path leading through an interior garden to a heavy wooden door (framed by an ivy extension of the garden). Indeed, in crossing the threshold of the central archway, Gabriel's gesture of flowers touches visually upon the interior garden. But it is to the closed door—and thus also symbolically to Mary—that the flowers (on the recessional axis) really point. For our purposes, it is this door that is most riveting. The con-

31. Domenico Veneziano, *Annunciation*, c. 1445. Photo: Fitzwilliam
Museum, Cambridge, England.

cluding door, we notice, is *drastically* closed: iron-studded and barred shut.
It is the picture's portal of essential closedness representing the mystery of
interiority.

Behind that impregnable door, symbolically on a par with Mary, is the
earthly locus of divinity. After all, it is to the heavenly counterpart of un-
seeable divinity that the announcing angel's finger points. Shut behind a
door (or barely limned in the halos of the figures or the reflected sunshine
on flowers), the Word and Light of divinity in this picture are never fully
visible. Just as Gabriel can only come to Mary through intervening visual
barriers, the role of the divine Word and Light is to be barred from view.
Alan Liu offers an intriguing commentary on this representation of closure
by comparing Renaissance Annunciations with their precedents in Byzan-
tine icons. In icons, Liu points out, the mystery of God's Word fills the
background of the paintings in the form of an expansive gold or *lux*. Thus
was infinity revealed to the eyes of finitude. But Renaissance Annunciations shut off or barred the infinitude of *lux:*

> Organizing the world into fixed "walls" of fore-, middle-, and background,
> each logically prior to its narrative fresco, Renaissance imagination saw the
> light not of infinity but of "reality." In the "worldly" Renaissance after the
> triumph of Albertian perspective, that is, anagogy was finite existence itself—
> a newly unified, planimetrically defined, and closed space so rationalized by
> geometry and the laws of the rectilinear propagation of light that an other-
> worldly *logos* or fiat of light seemed to declare itself *in* the structure of the
> world.[104]

That declaration of essential light *within* this world was also a declaration by negation of the light eternally beyond it, excluded from it. The vision of the world barred or shut the door on the infinite *lux*.

Yet, of course, the paradox is that the barring of divinity in vision must symbolize the disclosure of the Word and Light to faith. If the visible world pictured in Quattrocento Annunciations could not directly announce divinity, it had to be seen to figure, index, or lead toward the disclosure of divinity. Thus such pictures included alongside the symbolism of closed gardens and doors a supplementary symbolism—as Mary Ann Caws insightfully notices—of transgressed thresholds and pierced barriers.[105] Even in the radically closed space of the Domenico, for example, we glimpsed faint gestures toward transgression: Gabriel has crossed his loggia of columns from the left, and the flowers he holds then further cross the picture space toward Mary by visually penetrating the threshold of the intervening archway. In other words, if the axis that runs from foreground to background terminates in a shut door, the axis running from left to right qualifies such terminal closure, leaving a slight opening of symbolism through which the eye of faith can see the communication of the divine Word.

To watch the door open even wider upon a symbolic vision of divinity, we can turn from the Domenico to a picture such as Fra Angelico's *Annunciation* of 1438–45 (fig. 32). Here, we also see Gabriel penetrating on the lateral axis toward Mary's private space: he leans into the intervening column and the very sweep of his wings and clothing reinforces his forward momentum. In a radically rectilinear or arched world, indeed, his wings make an almost violent statement of angularity, cutting a sharp diagonal across several columns behind him. But for our purposes, it is at last the axis of recession from foreground to background that is even more intriguing. For in the Fra Angelico, we notice, this recession sympathizes with the action on the picture's lateral axis by transgressing further than we have yet seen into Mary's private space: her bedroom. The door in the middle distance behind Mary is open. Such openness, Caws suggests, speaks "the penetration of consciousness."[106]

But consciousness of what? The symbolism of penetration or disclosure on the recessional axis, it seems, goes only so far. Even when the shut door is opened to our eye, we penetrate inwards in the Fra Angelico only to another closed space. What we see within Mary's bedroom is nothing— nothing, that is, except the barred window at the furthest point of the central perspective line. Our perspective gaze, in effect, is literally barred.[107]

32. Fra Angelico, *Annunciation,* 1438–45. S. Marco Museum, Florence.
Photo: Scala/Art Resource, New York.

But we are not yet done with recession toward divinity in the Fra Angelico.
We notice a secondary perspective recession into the background. I refer to
the recession through landscape beyond the loggia at the left of the picture.
Here is room, perhaps, to develop the vision of divinity further, though in
this picture that possibility is at least half-blocked by the high garden fence
in the middleground.

To scale the fence, we can look to another Fra Angelico *Annunciation,* c.
1434 (fig. 33). In this picture, the penetration of Gabriel toward Mary on the
lateral axis is even more pronounced: his posture, the diagonals of his robe,
the sharp incline of his wings cutting cross the plane of the loggia, even the
golden words that pierce the column separating him from Mary—all point
toward an approaching disclosure of divinity.[108] As part of that act of disclosure, the recession to Mary's bedroom is open a further stage. Revealed
within is a curtain that provides only a partial seal; one catches a glimpse of
what is probably Mary's bed behind it. But it is to the displaced, diagonal
recession to the left of the loggia that we must at last look for full disclosure.
Along this recession, the eye passes over a noticeably *low* garden fence in the
middleground to see in the background the expulsion of Adam and Eve

from the Garden of Eden. Here at last we see divinity in the only form it can take to mortal eyes, as the *expulsion* that creates mortality in the first place and thus necessitates the redemptive mortality of the Incarnation. Here, that is, the barring of divine vision and the ability to see such vision are the same. Barred from God in the act of expulsion, Adam and Eve's very bodies (and the physical world) become the *porta clausa*. Yet it is precisely such expulsion into mortality that foreshadows the Incarnation, in which God makes his Image visible to man.

In sum, Annunciations showed a radically self-canceling vision of the divine Word or Light. Divinity only appeared as it disappeared into the forms of mortal vision; the door is opened to illumination even as it is closed in another way by generalizing the "door," by embodying it in the very physicality of the world. To clinch the point, we can look at the self-canceling vision of divinity in the Cinquecento Annunciation scenes of Tintoretto. In one such *Annunciation* (c. 1570–80) (fig. 34), for instance, the central space separating Gabriel and Mary takes the form of an archway

33. Fra Angelico, *Annunciation*, c. 1434. Diocesan Museum, Cortona.
Photo: Alinari/Art Resource, New York.

34. Tintoretto, *Annunciation*, c. 1570–80. Kaiser-Friedrich-Museum, Berlin.
Photo: Alinari/Art Resource, New York.

that looks more like a gaping hole in the wall of the middleground. Beyond, one can only obscurely detect a low-hedged garden. The overwhelming sense, in Caws's words, is of an "empty" center, an "obsessive vacuum."[109] The door is opened on a divinity that disappears even as it appears.

We can now round back to the Jacobean Banqueting House. King James and his court entertainments might seem worlds away from Annunciation paintings. But in their secular way James's masques *were* Annunciations.[110] To see the connection requires only that we superimpose the Annunciations we have seen over Inigo Jones's stage designs while transposing "divinity" into the haloed subjectivity of the royal "self." Masques, we know, often placed subjectivity *within* the divine, physically situating the private world of the masquers in an enclosure shaped like a temple or church. Oberon's palace, for example, reflected a design for a church from Serlio's *Architettura*.[111] So, too, masques often turned upon narrative actions that conformed to the basic plot of Annunciation. As we have seen in *Oberon*, a Gabriel-figure such as Silenus (or in many masques, Mercury) would announce a birth or rebirth while pointing through an exterior, public realm to a sanctified, private space. The actual son reborn in masques was played first by Henry, then by Charles. James himself, in a sense, was also the promised son because his centrally placed dais was really a kind of stage mirroring the masque stage that announced his son. In discovering Prince Oberon/Henry, James saw an image of himself. To extend the analogy even further, James can also be seen to play other Annunciation roles. He was a type of Mary because the masquers came down and out to him as if they were Gabriels leaning into the private space of virginity. Even more radically, he was God: announced in golden light, he was the very type of divinity.[112] Once the perspective scenery in *Oberon* had opened inward from the outer world of the satyrs and their mutable moon to the inner world of the King's son, Silenus declared James to be the "sun" (a pun that the masque certainly intended; l. 270).

We have now fully returned home to James's Banqueting House. For, like *manus Christi* and other restorative, jewel-adorned voids served within such structures, the sanctified sun/Son of James was announced by Silenus to be imbued with "sweetness" and "gold" (ll. 263, 268). Furthermore, we are told, such rich light, as if drawing on the power of banqueting stuffs, "preserved," "restorèd," and "Sustained" the circle of masquers, creating "a second birth" (ll. 243, 248, 251, 105). By the "sweetness of his sway" (l.263), James

> stays the time from turning old
> And keeps the age up in a head of gold;
> That in his own true circle still doth run,
> And holds his course as certain as the sun.
> He makes it ever day and ever spring
> Where he doth shine, and quickens everything
> Like a new nature; so that true to call
> Him by his title is to say, he's all.
>
> (ll. 267–74)

This celebration of rebirth through James's sweet and golden light pointed to yet another type of annunciation: Epiphany. Annunciation paintings were themselves as much epiphanies as annunciations in that they were about showing or bodying forth faith. Significantly, the Feast of Epiphany, or Twelfth Night, was the most important masquing night, commemorating the recognition of Christ's birth by the Three Magi (whose presents included such void-like precious stuffs as gold, myrrh, and frankincense). Restorative confectionary such as *manus Christi* and the spices in the

minced pie of Christmas—symbolic, as we have seen, of the Magi's gifts—
were thus all implied in the Word and Light that represented the generative
richness of James.

Yet, and here I come to the point of my comparison of masque scenery
and Annunciation pictures, what the masque at last truly announced was
the paradoxical self-cancellation of James's divine subjectivity. James's personal and genealogical vision of annunciation (focused on his son) could be
disclosed only through a scenic penetration that made his privacy disappear
even as it appeared. As symbolized by the closed doors or bowers in his
masques (a feature with clear precedents in Quattrocento painting),
disclosure was closure of another sort. It was a closing off of the very possibility of private subjectivity. The implication of James's secular
annunciations was that mystery—in this case, subjectivity—was ultimately
invisible, absent, always to be sought in a deeper or displaced recession
where, if the door or bower were ever opened (as happened when Jones's
"transparent" walls swung wide), subjectivity could only "triumph" by
marching out toward the public in an expulsion mortally fatal to it. Just as
divinity in the background of a Fra Angelico *Annunciation* can be glimpsed
only in the act that creates Adam and Eve as mortal bodies (or, in the Epiphany analogy, Christ as mortal man), so at the moment of expulsion in
James's masques when the masquers descended, the "prince" of his self, the
son representing his subjectivity, could be seen only in the triumphal action
that made him a public body.

In the masque, then, James's private self was violated in order to be incar-
nated in public form. By "violation," indeed, I signal that masques at last
staged a supremely violent and "wild" transgression of private space. A last
illustration from Annunciation painting may help. We earlier looked at a
Tintoretto *Annunciation* in which the vision of divinity disappears even as
it appears (fig. 34). A second Tintoretto *Annunciation* (1583–87) (fig. 35)
shows the violence implicit in the process of obliterating the world to
appear to the world. In this picture, Gabriel and a gang of angels, simultaneously descending from above and rushing across the pictorial scene,
appear literally to have broken down the outside wall that kept Mary inviolate, leaving behind a wake of architectural debris. As they advance through
the vast opening they have made to announce the Word (represented by the
gold-encircled dove at the point of their onslaught), Mary, at the far right,
withdraws in disquietude. But her gesture of withdrawal is futile. What
this especially aggressive *Annunciation* proclaims is privacy violated—
privacy, in fact, rendered void.

In Jones's staging of *Prince Henry's Barriers* (fig. 30), we see an enactment of just such violence: leading to an archway and closed door is a perspective line formed by architectural ruins. More generally, masques dramatized the violent transgression of privacy in the very structure and symbolics of James's perspective vision. Though his eye sought a vision of himself enclosed in civilized privacy at the end of a recession, James sat at a *vantage*— rather than vanishing—point that put him in the problematic position of being "savagely" exposed. In *Oberon*, we remember, not only was James subjected symbolically to the "wildness" of the "rude" satyrs because his line of sight had to pass through their exterior scene, but (as in other masques) he was subjected literally to wildness in the audience: his dais was raised amid an increasingly crowded and ill-assorted public. Only in and through the thick space of the public gaze—which surrounded him on three sides and found representation in the satyrs on the fourth side— could James's own gaze penetrate to his masque's private, enclosed, and sanctified inner sanctum, which then, in a mirroring of his exposed vantage

35. Tintoretto, *Annunciation*, 1583–87. School of San Rocco, Venice.
Photo: Alinari/Art Resource, New York.

point, opened to "discover," make public, and violate itself. The very act of seeing in the crowded perspective space of the masque and Banqueting House savaged James's vision of privacy.

As if to aggravate the violence of the savaging, the urge toward "discovery" that drove Oberon/Henry's chariot outward hinted at cannibalistic hunger. Though Silenus informed the audience that James could not "think within a satyr's tooth" (l. 256), the "desire" moving Oberon was part of an almost animal drive to eat the King—to satisfy the senses, we are twice told, "of tongues, of ears, of eyes" (ll. 223; 226, 233). The "discovery" of the inner sanctum was akin to a consuming of self.[113] Such violent devouring of privacy was symbolized by the ornament that Jones sketched above the exterior of Oberon's castle (see fig. 28): a stag attacked on either side by hounds and armed putti. As the satyrs confirm in their song to Diana's sign, the moon (ll. 186–205), the total ensemble may allude to the Ovidean myth of Diana and Actaeon.[114] After seeing Diana exposed in nudity, we recall, Actaeon was changed into a stag, hunted, and finally torn apart by his own hounds. George Sandys offered a representative Renaissance reading of the myth: "This fable was invented to show vs how dangerous a curiosity it is to search into the secrets of Princes, or by chance to discover their nakednesse."[115] In my terms, Jonson's masque searched into the secret *selves* of Princes. "Discovering"—or making naked—the closed world of Oberon's masquers exposed princely subjectivity to a public (all "tongues . . . ears . . . eyes") as rapacious as the hounds that dismembered Actaeon.

No wonder the poetry of the masque often seems awkward, as Orgel notes of *Oberon,* at the point where the ideal world of the main masque (what I would term the fiction of privacy) reached out to the real world of the court and its perspective-viewer, James.[116] Awkwardness arose out of nervousness. The problem was not simply the difficulty of extending an ideal fiction to a real court; it was the fear that the real selves of the court were themselves a violable, even cannibalistically consumable, fiction. Consciousness of the fugitive fragility of self thus permeated the poetry of the revels dances. In *Oberon,* the emergent masquers were so refined—constituted, indeed, of insubstantial "air" (l. 322)—that they feared exposure to the very light of day that metaphorically (in the person of James) gave them birth. Warning the fays of approaching light, Phosphorus calls them hurriedly to return to their enclosure (ll. 348–57). Similarly, cannibalistic threats to subjectivity—a final, uncanny reversion of masques to food— surface in repeated references in the revels to devouring Time. "For he

[Time] so greedy to devour / His own, and all that he brings forth," laments the Chorus of *Love Freed from Ignorance and Folly* (1611), "Is eating every piece of hour / Some object of the rarest worth" (ll. 316-19). Finally, masque revels expressed consumable transience in allusions to the danger of dancing with those on the "outside," especially the ladies. Addressing the male masquers in *Pleasure Reconciled to Virtue*, for instance, Daedalus warns, "be sweet, / But not *dissolved* in wantonness" (ll. 282–83; my emphasis).

Yet a contradiction would seem to arise here. The court ladies threatened dissolution—to the consumable self and body—by being sweeter, not less sweet, than the masquers. A similar warning in *Oberon* suggests that the outside "sweet" ladies were also threateningly more "airy" than the masquers. "It is time that we were gone," a sylvan sings, gesturing to the ladies: "Here be forms so bright and airy, / And their motions so they vary / As they will enchant the fairy, / If you longer here should tarry" (ll. 343–47). How could the ladies have embodied the sweet essence of medicinal banqueting stuffs and yet also have been dangerous? The answer, I believe, lies in the fact that delectable and refined ladies—the very makers and symbols of banqueting stuffs—also represented the feared insubstantiality of such stuffs. The court ladies personified the paradoxical nature of the void. For that very reason the masquers expressed fear not only of losing their selves to the ladies but also of losing hold of the ladies themselves. The latter fear often took the form of anxiety at stopping the dance. As the male masquers appeared to lag in *Mercury Vindicated from the Alchemists at Court* (1616), for instance, Nature spurred them on: "There is no banquet, boys, like this, / If you hope better, you will miss; / Stay here, and take each one a kiss." "Which if you can refine," the Chorus added in a direct allusion to voids, "The taste knows no such cates, nor yet the palate wine" (ll. 229–33).

"*If* you can refine." The moment of achieved masque intimacy—the kiss—became conditional upon a refining process akin to that of the cordials and "kissing Comfets"[117] that cookery/medical books said "refined" the vital spirits. One private banquet art, the masque, looked nervously to another, the void, for preservation. But the fear—already glimpsed in the self-canceling "annunciation" of self in perspective scenery—was that both were truly void.[118]

Tearing Down the Masque
Toward an Aesthetics of Consumerism

Such fear of the void stands out most starkly in the two events that closed masque entertainments. Acts of violent and ultimately cannibalistic voiding, these events revealed the consuming nothingness at the heart of the sweet aesthetics of subjectivity.

The first act of voiding, or spoiling, occurred just as the revels dance with the audience ended. Suddenly, the "wild" audience (including, presumably, the as yet unrefined lady dancers) charged the stage, tore down the perspective scenery, and stripped the masquers of their rich furnishings. A detailed description of this unsettling custom can be found in Hall's account of a precursor of the Jacobean masque: a court entertainment mounted by Henry VIII. After supper in the hall, we are told, "an arber of golde" appeared. Within were discovered the masquers (including the King) dressed in elegant garments "embroudered full of H. & K. of golde" and "poysees, made of letters of fine gold in bullyon as thicke as they might be." Dancing ensued while the pageant was conveyed to the end of the hall to await the reentry of the masquers. Suddenly, however,

> the rude people ranne to the pagent, and rent tare and spoyled the pagent, so that the lord Stuard nor the head officers could not cause them to abstaine, excepte they shoulde haue foughten and drawen bloude, and so was this pagent broken.

The masquers apparently kept their poise—until, that is, the rending turned personal. For, when they proposed "in token of liberalitie" to give their "letters" to appointed ladies and ambassadors,

> the common people perceyuyng ranne to the kyng, and stripped hym into his hosen and dublet, and all his compaignions in likewise. Syr Thomas Kneuet stode on a stage, and for all his defence he lost his apparell. The ladies likewyse were spoyled, wherfore the kynges garde came sodenly, and put the people backe, or els as it was supposed more inconuenience had ensued. So the kyng with the quene & the ladyes returned to his chamber, where they had a great banket, and all these hurtes were turned to laughying and game, and thought that, all that was taken away was but for honor, and larges: and so this triumphe ended with myrthe and gladnes. At this banket, a shipeman of London caught certayn letters which he sould to a goldsmyth for .iii.*l*.xiiii.*s*.viii.*d*. by reason wherof, it appeared that the garmentes were of great value.[119]

While Henry's ornamental arbor "deuise" and show were intended to be closed affairs, both were "broken" and "spoiled" by an Actaeon-like "rude" "common people" who—epitomized by the clutching "shipeman of London"—stripped the masquers of their precious costumes. Henry's select circle was forced physically to withdraw from the public hall to the King's private chamber. There they reassured themselves with the elite, aristocratic ethics of "honor" and "larges," and—in the spirit of fast friends "laughying"—consumed a "great banket."

The Jacobean masque suffered the same fate, but more thoroughly. Of course, James's masques were presented to a restricted audience of "friends" in a private Banqueting House rather than public hall. Certainly no common shipman would have been included. Nevertheless, as we have seen, James's audience became threateningly public as rich merchants and common gentry infiltrated the aristocratic elite. Such an invasion of James's private circle was dramatically confirmed when, as if moved by a ubiquitous "common" impulse, aristocracy and citizenry *together* tore down the masque at its conclusion. Jonson's one brief allusion to this customary ritual, in his preface to *The Masque of Blackness* (1605), recalled "the rage of the people, who, as a part of *greatness*, are privileged by custom to deface their [masques'] carcases" (ll. 6–7; my emphasis). Particularly suggestive is Jonson's term for the masque body: "carcass." Even before it was made void by the all-consuming "rage" of the public audience, the private masque was in a sense dead, a decaying corpse.[120]

A second event of violent voiding then drove the nail into the coffin (a contemporary term, we may note, for pie shell). As if in consolation for the tearing down of the masque, James now led the masquers off to consume a void. We might recall Henry VIII's similar gesture of self-comfort following the "hurtes" of his court entertainment. By the time of James, however, "comfiting" the self after a masque was itself a violent act, in essence another tearing down of the masque. Withdrawing with his select group of courtiers, James retraced his steps out of the Banqueting House, returned along the privy gallery, and entered a specified room set up with banqueting stuffs. There he toured the tables and departed.[121] What followed was not a pretty sight. "Dispatched with the accustomed confusion," Dudley Carleton recorded about the private banquet after Samuel Daniel's *Vision of the Twelve Goddesses* (1604). "So furiously assaulted that down went tables and tressels before one bit was touched," we hear of the banquet after Jonson's *Blackness*. The void, in short, became a feeding frenzy. In *Tethys' Festival* (1610), Daniel attempted "to avoid the confusion which usually attendeth the dissolve of these shewes." He did so by adding onto the revels dances another show in which Mercury summoned a guard of noblemen to escort the masquers back "in their owne forme." But such precautions merely postponed the act of tearing apart: it was the masquers themselves who went on to "viewing and scrambling" at the ensuing banquet. So, too, at the banquet after Jonson's *Oberon,* William Trumball reported that "in a moment everything was thrown down with furious haste."[122]

The kinds of foods thus spoiled were precisely the fanciful and airy delicacies of banqueting stuffs. There "were long tables laden with comfits and thousands of mottoes," a contemporary reported of the banquet following Francis Beaumont's *Masque of the Inner Temple and Grays Inn* (1613). "After the King had made the round of the tables," he continued, "everything was in a moment rapaciously swept away."[123] Most descriptive was Orazio Busino's report on the banquet following Jonson's *Pleasure Reconciled to Virtue.* The King, he wrote,

> glanced round the table and departed, and at once like so many harpies the company fell on their prey. The table was almost entirely covered with sweetmeats, with all kinds of sugar confections. There were some large figures, but they were of painted cardboard, for decoration. The meal was served in bowls or plates of glass; the first assault threw the table to the ground, and the crash of glass platters reminded me exactly of the windows breaking in a great midsummer storm.[124]

What could be a more dramatic demonstration of the fragile, self-canceling experience of privacy that sat within the sealed windows of James's "private" Banqueting House? The tradition of void banqueting, we earlier saw, had all along included a penchant for violence. We remember Dawson's proud declaration that, after eating from his sugar-spun plateware, the guests might *"breake* the Platters, Dishes, Glasses, Cuppes, and all other things, for this paste is very delicate and sauerous." Or again, "Raze, ruinate, demolish, and confound," John Taylor said. Chillingly, we now realize how well adapted such tradition was for the occasion of the tearing down of the masque. The masque and its subsequent sweet banquet—"lettered" costumes, on the one hand, confectionary "mottoes," on the other—were both voids: *both* had to be torn apart and broken. It is as if masque audience and masquers alike—the one in the Banqueting House, the other in a banqueting room—were compelled to actualize the insubstantiality of subjectivity lurking at the heart of all such "private" entertainments. Breaking and rending the facades of privacy in their orgy of communal feasting, they "discovered" the void of the self.

We can close by pausing, as if between courses, to clear our table and "appreciate" aesthetically the repast we have had. What an odd and disturbing meal! To move from the restorative sweet "conceits" of banqueting foods to the equally restorative and "sweet" conceits of the masque was to satisfy our aesthetic appetite. It was in good taste: a step up from the trivial to the more substantial, and from low to high art. But then our concluding discovery that both food and masque degenerated into rites of cannibalistic wildness brings us low indeed. "What a coarse dessert or distasteful void!" we might think. "What a descent in taste or aesthetic abasement characteristic of historicist inquiries into art!"

To prepare for the next chapter, which promises to be even more aesthetically distasteful, I append a further, revisionary appreciation of the "cannibalism" that tore down masques and also of our reactions to it.

One way to understand the specifically "wild" or "cannibalistic" aspect of tearing down the masque is to revive the anthropological analogy that allowed me to picture Elizabethan culture as a Kula ring. Private Elizabethan selves "gave" of themselves and of their children to join in a public whole. By contrast, the Jacobean culture of withdrawing selves (withdrawing into endless regressions of private rooms) emphasized what we began noticing in Elizabethan miniatures and sonnets: that commonality was *only* ideal, only a void conceit or pie-in-the-sky illusion. The private self refused to give of itself; it turned away from commonality in quest of an equally illusory counterideal of subjectivity. In the end, it tore itself apart from the public and in that tearing apart—mimed in the violent tearing down of void banquets and masques—discovered itself to be really nothing, a void. The Elizabethan Kula ring became an antimasque version of itself: the potlatch.

I refer to the potlatch of the Northwest Coast Indians (specifically, the Kwakiutl). Both masques and potlatches were "aristocratic" ceremonies that took place primarily during the winter festival season. Both were characterized by elaborate drama, song, dance, disguising, feasting, and a kind of annunciation (in potlatches, the naming of sons to their fathers' titles). Both revolved around the idea of the gift. As we saw in observing Charles's masques, the masque was a gift from the ruler to his privileged "friends." Similarly, the potlatch was a gift from one community leader to another.[125] Finally, and most significantly, both the masque and the potlatch suffered a sea change of gift-giving into violent, self-canceling, "cannibalistic" consumption. Just as audiences tore down the masque (and masquers sweet banquets), so participants in potlatches consumed a feast while rending or burning the goods they were presenting to their gift partners (blankets, coppers, and other "trifles"). Even the bodies and very houses of potlatch participants were in danger of being consumed. At the great "grease feasts," for example, "oil was poured upon the fire causing it to burn so furiously that it singed the blankets worn by the guests," "made the roof boards catch fire," and even scorched the prized house-dishes (heirloom crests).[126] As such near-cooking of the guests would suggest, the aggressive consumerism of the potlatch had its roots in cannibalism. Traces of man-eating persisted in the Cannibal Dance (one of the most important of the ceremonial dances) as well as in the language of exchange. One expression for the act of giving—that is, spoiling—goods was "I've eaten you."[127]

In the terms I have been developing, all these parallels between the "cannibalistic" masque and potlatch revolve around the paradox of "self." Just as the masque was a representation in which James wanted to see his wished-for privacy or subjectivity, so—in a variant of such "selfishness"— the potlatch was a ceremony in which community leaders wanted to see their self-importance. The potlatch was essentially different from the Kula ring in appearing to deny community, affirming instead the aggressive values of prestige, rivalry, and self-interest.[128] Masque and potlatch were both forms of expression in which the royal or aristocratic self came to the fore in splendid singleness. Yet—and here is the paradox—just as the tearing down of the masque confirmed that the masque actually voided James's subjectivity, so the destruction of goods at a potlatch ruined the notion of self. Since potlatch goods were spoiled at the very moment they were given away—when they were the property of both the self and the other—the "eating" of the other that was figured in their destruction was simultaneously an eating, voiding, or consumption of the self. Jacobean celebrants tore down their masques and banqueting tables; potlatch celebrants wrecked their goods and scorched their house and house-dishes. In both cases, the self emerged only by voiding itself and its props.

Such, then, is one way to appreciate the cannibalistic destruction of the masque and sweet banquet: the tearing down of the masque may be understood as a discrete cultural practice whose discreteness can nevertheless be appreciated more widely by comparison with alternative cultures. It may be objected, of course, that such efforts to place a cultural practice has nothing to do with "appreciation" at all, especially of an aesthetic sort able to counteract a lingering sense of artistic debasement. In comparing the tearing down of the masque to the potlatch, we have simply situated or embedded art in the field of cultural practices in a way that makes such historicist embedment *equivalent* to the loss of aesthetic discrimination. This is the seeming curse of historicist inquiry: attention to cultural situation *is* aesthetic insensitivity. Whether focused on Jacobean masquers or Northwest

Coast Indians, the camera refuses to turn off: rather than stopping when the masque itself stops—at a high moment of aesthetic transcendence—it continues filming as the masquers stumble off stage, get drunk, fall into tables, eat like savages, and (if we dared follow to the ripe corner of many aristocratic rooms of the time) relieved themselves before going noisily to bed. Thus are the masquers "embedded" in their social world like some tribal culture: their art, ceremony, and representation (in this case of the self) become indistinguishable from all the common moments of eating and sleeping that are void of either conscious art or self.

But in the last analysis, I would demur from this evaluation of historicist inquiry as equivalent to unappreciative degradation in "taste." Our comparison of the masque to the potlatch is unsatisfactory so long as we link the two only under the concept of the "low" or "savage." Just so, to take the general case, our act of historically situating art (in discrete yet broadly understandable cultural frames) is incomplete so long as we insist on seeing such situation as aesthetic abasement. I would thus like to offer one further interpretation of the tearing down of the masque that unthinks the very concept of the aesthetically low by broadening the meaning of *aesthetic*, by redeeming the low within the historical *and* aesthetic logic of cultural "triviality" that has been my method all along and that I will directly address once more in my final chapter.

Tearing down the masque (and also the potlatch), I suggest, may be viewed as itself an aesthetic act on a par with writing or staging masques. It was a cultural action at once historical *and* aesthetic, even "critical" (in the drama reviewer's sense of the word). That is, tearing down a masque—and the facades of selfhood, subjectivity, or privacy it represented—was for Jacobeans a literalization or hands-on version of what we now recognize to be artistic appreciation. It was how Jacobeans most enjoyed themselves: by consuming the masque totally. More, such was how they enjoyed themselves in a manner that was also "critical." Total appreciation—by eyes, ears, hands, mouths—meant a rending apart of costume "letters," confectionary "mottoes," and the realm of representation or facade-meaning generally. The masque was idealized but criticized, reserved for privacy but exposed to public "taste," built up but torn down. To understand this is to understand that aesthetic experience, which since the nineteenth century has seemed to us *all* about subjectivity, was in the Renaissance (and in different ways in other times) also about the voiding of subjectivity. So, too, it is to understand that aesthetic and historical experience—such acts, respectively, as viewing a masque and tearing down a masque—inhere in each other so closely that any effort to separate them would be only a duplication of James's attempt to detach privacy from the social realm.

A satisfactory understanding of the relation between historical embedment and aesthetic appreciation, in short, would recognize that it is precisely in the moment an art work is embedded in its culture (even by being vulgarly torn apart and consumed) that it is most fully appreciated. Discussing the masque as a potlatch-like "cannibalism" will seem distasteful only if we ignore the history of, and in, appreciation.

Perhaps now we are prepared to stomach even more distasteful stuff. A further question about historical situation will bring me to my concluding chapter: why did "aesthetic criticism" (as I have conceived it) in the Banqueting House take the *particular* form of tearing down the masque (rather than, say, clapping the hands)? Why did participants most appreciate the masque and its sweet banquet in the act of turning the occasion into a fit of cannibalistic consumption? Were there, after all, any actual cannibals in the Banqueting House audience who would have been disposed to transform the Kula ring of culture into a potlatch? Or more to the point, were there any "consumers" who would naturally have seen Banqueting House festivities as a celebration of conspicuous consumption?

The answer is *yes:* there *were* a species of cannibal consumers in James's Banqueting House. In particular, there were banqueters who were bankers (by the sixteenth century, "banqueter" was used for "banker").[129] As we have repeatedly had to observe, wealthy members of the middle class increasingly made their presence felt in the audiences of James's masques. The obtrusiveness of their presence can now be made clear if we add that the wealthy middle class not only infiltrated the Banqueting House but itself began building banqueting houses on its properties in imitation of the aristocracy. So, too, the middle class loved void stuffs. As early as 1587, William Harrison singled out such stuffs in observing disparagingly that merchants made a great to-do about eating aristocratic foods.[130] Meanwhile, cookbooks of the time not only expanded their market to include common gentry and husbandmen but began to interest themselves in issues of domestic economy.[131] In short, the "spices" of void stuffs were suddenly to the taste of a nouveau riche class whose riches came from coined "specie" (a word whose modern meaning originated precisely in James's reign and whose ancient meanings link it both etymologically and economically to spice).[132]

As we will see, the hunger of banqueters for masques and spiced voids was strangely similar to the consuming hunger of the financial market for

exotic spices. It was this partnership of aesthetic and financial "appreciation" that made cannabilistic consumerism—expressed in tearing down a
masque or annihilating a sweet banquet—the natural vent for artistic experience. But to "discover" beneath the masquing—and violent unmasking—of Jacobean subjectivity the coin of middle-class trade is to come to a
new topic. This topic, as well as the very notion of aesthetics as historical
topicality, is my last concern.

Art, we may say, trifles with the topics that "everybody" is talking about,
and in so doing enacts the fact that the common topics of history—floated
on a currency of gossip—are themselves trifling. But the trivial is all we
know of history and art.

5

The Veil of Topicality: Trade and Ornament in Neptune's Triumph

The text of Jonson's late, unperformed masque, *Neptune's Triumph for the Return of Albion* (scuttled by a diplomatic dispute before its scheduled production on January 6, 1624),[1] climaxes with a call for the traditional revels, in which the private masquers, "discovered" within an island arbor, were to have come forth to dance with court "nymphs" from the audience (ll. 226, 316). With strange obsession, Proteus, Saron, and Portunus (gods of sea, navigation, and ports, respectively) solicit the ladies by itemizing the rich ornament of their "dressings." Come dance, they bid:

> *Portunus.* Your dressings do confess
> By what we see, so curious parts
> Of Pallas' and Arachne's arts,
>   That you could mean no less.
> *Proteus.* Why do you wear the silkworm's toils,
> Or glory in the shellfish spoils,
> Or strive to show the grains of ore
> That you have gathered on the shore
>   Whereof to make a stock
> To graft the greener emerald on,
> Or any better-watered stone?
> *Saron.* Or ruby of the rock?
> *Proteus.* Why do you smell of ambergris,
> Of which was formèd Neptune's niece,

> The queen of love, unless you can,
> Like sea-born Venus, love a man?
> *Saron.*   Try, put yourselves unto't.

The Chorus adds: "Your looks, your smiles and thoughts that meet, / Ambrosian hands and silver feet, / Do promise you will do't" (ll. 320–39). The strangeness of this itemization lies in what may be called its oblique ornamentality, the way its exaggerated prettiness is more than normally askew to the "reality" of the masque's occasion and plot. Most obviously, the passage is peripheral to the historical topic that the masque openly (or with only slight veiling) celebrated: Charles's return in October 1623 from his unsuccessful voyage to win the hand of the Spanish Infanta.[2] Critics concerned with topical issues have found no way to bring the nymphs' "dressings" to bear on this event. Despite the noticeable length of the passage, indeed, criticism has generally ignored it.[3] Similarly, the "dressings" passage is peripheral to the masque's plot. Of course, revels dancing conventionally celebrated "love" in a decorous and decorative manner detached from any central plot function. But the revels in *Neptune's Triumph* were extreme even in relation to other masque revels. In the "dressings" passage, we dance at *two* removes: as "love" dances free from the plot, so the very language describing the nymphs' loveliness skirts the topic. Instead of naming "silk," "pearls," or "gold," the text indulges an unusually indirect style of kenning: "silkworm's toils," "shellfish spoils," "grains of ore." The nymphs can only be dressed associatively by referring to the producers or raw products responsible for their ornament: silkworm, shellfish, ore, and so on.

In short, the nymphs' "dressings" in *Neptune's Triumph* are like sequins on a dress reflecting points of light without image: they seem to have no function and to bear upon no recognizable topic. Once more we are in the presence of the fragmentary, peripheral, and ornamental.

Like Jonson itemizing the nymphs' dress, perhaps it is time for me to take stock as well. In studying the Renaissance aristocratic self, I have produced a clock, jewel, orange, gifts (and children), miniatures, sonnets, banqueting houses, voids, and masque scenery. To this list I will now add the "dressings" of masque "nymphs." Have I been frivolous? Could it be charged that I have recorded subjectivity only in fragmentary, peripheral, and ornamental impressions—as if, to draw a typographical analogy, the most significant signs of the past were erased to leave as our text only a dance of decorative glyphs, accents, and points: "*!@ #—%& (\%#}'/!!!"?

Is my argument, in short, trivial?

The answer I give, of course, is profoundly affirmative. My argument has indeed been "trivial," but no more so than the "self." Triviality was the essence of past subjectivity. Walk through the aristocratic "stately homes" of England, for example (as I have done, sometimes to distraction, in my researches), and observe the architectural version of "*!@ #—%&(\%#}'/!!!" Enter the hall and see intricately fashioned tapestries, inlaid screens, relief carvings, paintings in ornate frames, decorative plasterwork moldings, ironwork lamps, wrought andirons, embroidered chairs, armor on display, busts, trophy deer heads, and other curio-treasures pressing in upon you from every possible surface. Walk upstairs past paintings hung in the stairwell to the great chamber (much as a Renaissance guest would have done) and be assaulted by a similar army of decoration. Withdraw down the long gallery, trying to keep an even keel along the parade of elaborate chairs beckoning you to rest beneath tapestry forests and portraits bursting with intricate details of costume and jewelry. Then—in a sudden deprivation of the senses serving as foil—ascend a narrow, dark, spiral staircase up to a door that, flung open, reveals against brilliant sunlight a veritable forest of chimneys, gargoyle-like sculptures of hounds or deer, sculpted family crests, elaborate stone "strapwork" along the perimeter (like a lace fringe done in rock), and—posted at odd intervals—turret banqueting houses. Finally, walk along the leads into one of the banqueting houses and, skirting its ornamental table with stone deities beneath, approach the decoratively leaded window to look out on a perfect recessional avenue between intricate patterns of flowers, herbs, hedges, and orchards.

Trivial arts *saturate* this world with the pretty clutter of the fragmentary, peripheral, and ornamental. If the identity, the "self," of the aristocracy is to be located, it must be glimpsed here in this fantastic universe of discontinuous trivia, this gigantic miniature cabinet in which it is the artifacts that guide, regulate, and *control* the way "selves" walk, stand, sit, eat, look, and all the other actions of life. It was the trivial aesthetics of these artifacts, I have argued, that composed the fractured mirror of ornament into which the Renaissance aristocracy looked to see its identity and into which we, struggling to repiece the pretty shards together in something like their original discontinuity (for the mirror was never whole), now peer to glimpse an even more removed version of that identity.

Or again, for "fractured mirror of ornament" we might say "fractured mirror of history." As I have said in chapter 1 and implied throughout, the ornament that was the medium of the Renaissance self was also the medium of its experience of historical reality. The self *lived* historical reality in its experience of the fragmentary, peripheral, and ornamental. Cultural life was the practice of sustaining a fragile sense of identity amid decorative bits and pieces of reality that refused to cohere in a single reality, that voided identity even in the process of creating it. The history of self was the practice of social ornament.

We can return, then, to the latest item in our stock of trivia: aristocratic "nymphs" dressed in "silkworm's toils," "shellfish spoils," "grains of ore." I will conclude my argument about the aesthetic history of the Renaissance self by making Jonson's late Jacobean masque an extreme test case of the connection I assert between ornamentality and history. If the subjective experience of ornament was integral with that of history, can we also say that it was one with "topicality," the narrowest and hardest instance of the experience of history? A clock, jewel, and orange, as we saw in chapter 1, can be linked to a contemporary topic that "everyone talked about": Charles's martyrdom. But that case was easy. The site of Charles's execution was a literal *topos* linking ornamentality to a commonplace topic of contemporary history. Now take another case: can the oblique ornamentality of silk, pearls, and gold in *Neptune's Triumph* be linked to any commonplace historical topic when there seems to be no obvious connection?

If not, then we must at last reluctantly confirm the traditional division between aesthetics and history. But if so, then the "self" must be seen to inhabit a world in which aesthetics and history—specifically, ornaments and topicality—are integral no matter how oblique one is to the other. And this, I suggest, must in turn mean that we need to unthink our last resistance to marrying aesthetics and history: our residual notion that "topicality" has to do with hard and discrete events barren of art. What such recent explorations of "topicality" as Leah Marcus's *Puzzling Shakespeare* help us see is that we should abandon the assumption that ornament either is, or is not, "about something" qualitatively different from the ornament that dresses it up. A more fruitful approach will be to see that behind ornamental aesthetics in a work like *Neptune's Triumph* lies a "somethingness" of historical topicality whose essence is itself as trivial as decoration. It is historical topicality itself that is oblique to topicality because it always embraces topics *other* than that which is declared. Marcus suggests as much in her subtle analysis of the way Shakespeare used topicality "to disperse ideology prismatically so that his plays . . . would take on different colorations in different settings and times."[4] Topicality subject to "prismatic" dispersal is in and of itself ornamental and oblique. *Never* is it what it appears to be.

I propose, then, to pursue a topical approach to ornamentality in *Neptune's Triumph* with the ultimate objective—at the close of this chapter—of developing a general model of oblique topicality construing the link between historical experience and aesthetic appreciation. The topic I elect is not Charles's marriage negotiations with Spain but an associated "other" topic upsetting relations with the Spanish just before Jonson's masque was to have been put on: foreign trade. It was foreign trade—especially the East India Company's trade in spices—that supplied many of the ornaments, void stuff, and other trivia of the Jacobean aristocracy as well as an increasing proportion of its finances. Generally, indeed, it was the "selfish" market in this era that displaced the gift-culture commonality we studied in chapter 2 to subsidize the culture of "privacy." The realization that the gift ideal was in danger of being sold out came home with special force in 1623, as we will see, when news arrived that English trading ships had "barbarously" participated in the plunder of the Spanish/Portuguese town of Ormuz. What this news underscored was that the trade that increasingly supplied the living of the aristocratic "self" was also importing into that self an element so foreign to its self-image as "gifted" that it was conceptually "savage." More accurately, foreign trade exposed the fact that barbarousness had from the first been at the heart of the self insofar as that self was private (privateering, we might say with Ormuz in mind). Thus it was that "cannibals" suddenly appeared in England in the form of a bourgeois spirit (and class) infiltrating the aristocratic identity.

The question for the private aristocratic self: how to dress up in ornaments the foreign trade and bourgeois barbarousness in which it was involved so as to sustain at least the fiction of gift culture while allowing business to continue as usual? How, that is, to dress up cannibals and bankers in the Banqueting House so as to mask the fact that the "private" self was the very embodiment of such greedy consumption?

Strange Trade: Foreign Currency and the East India Company

First we need to limn a curiously split metaphor in contemporary economic thought: the "strange body," as it may be called, of Jacobean trade. As applied to the economic crisis of the time, the metaphor combined two contradictory emphases. On the one hand, "strangeness" referred to an always "mysterious," abstract, representational, or perpetually unlocatable source of economic trouble "out there" beyond perception. Something strange was happening to England's wealth, and no one knew where exactly to point the finger. On the other hand, a parallel discourse of corporeality indicated the need to reify the trouble "out there," to embody economic strangeness in particular foreign nations, peoples, or events that could be quarantined from the home trading body. But the paradox was that whenever the English actually fingered an embodied culprit responsible for economic trouble, it turned out that the English were involved. Strangeness "out there" was also "in here."

For the moment, I will focus on the discourse of economic strangeness while merely noticing that of corporeality. Especially illustrative are the abundant economic tracts of the early 1620s by Thomas Mun, Edward Misselden, Gerard Malynes, and others. This unprecedented flurry of economic theory was triggered by one of England's most severe trade depressions. The problem? England as a trading body was "costive." The country, ran the familiar complaint, lacked "vent" for the "superfluity" of its home goods (primarily woolen cloths).[5] What made such constipation especially—and literally—"strange" was the fact that the country was at the same time consuming foreign imports to excess. "Strangers," Mun remonstrated, "fill vs vp with forraine commodities, without the vent of our owne wares."[6] The foreign goods thus ingested were expensive luxury items that in other times appeared necessary (in the case of spices, even medicinal) but were now deemed excessive: "precious Stones, rich Jemmes, exquisite perfumes, costly unnecessary Spices, and rich Stuffes, which serve more for pompe and show, than for need and use." In brief: economically "vain, superfluous, unnecessary things."[7] Like tobacco, Malynes concluded, such foreign imports "shal vanish away in smoake, or be consumed and brought (as it were) vnto doung."[8] Imports, in short, were a bodily waste heaped on top of England's already costive waste.

What most caught the attention of contemporaries was the bottom line of such compound costiveness: a radical depletion of England's monetary, and especially silver, reserves. "The decay of trade outwards, and excessive consumption of wares brought in," a contemporary lamented, "have wasted and deprived us of our money."[9] Again and again, reaction to England's general economic crisis came down to dismay over the almost magical disappearance of its money (both specie and bullion).[10] Someone, somewhere was pilfering the national wealth.

How to prevent strange theft? The trade writers attempted to diagnose the strange disease that left England replete with foreign and domestic wares but depleted of money. Yet their efforts to do so produced a baffling labyrinth of inconsistencies and contradictions whose net effect was to confirm a sense of underlying strangeness.[11] All the writers agreed that England needed to trade with foreigners (termed "strangers") because the nation's monetary reserves or treasure had to be built up. All agreed as well that the only way to build up treasure was to export more goods than the country imported. Finally, all concurred that exports should be traded as much as possible for hard cash (rather than other goods). Yet the writers were spectacularly at odds on how to go about achieving these ends, and even individual authors constantly shifted their arguments. In reading the resulting pamphlets, we sense that foreign trade was a problem that simply could not be formulated, let alone solved, in contemporary terms. Indeed, the fumbling inarticulateness of the trade tracts (sometimes masked in excessive rhetoric) almost seems to parallel the symptoms of economic costiveness. In gesturing vaguely "out there" to some cause or other, the pamphleteers enacted the fact that English trade not only lacked "vent" but, to adopt the other common term for market exchange, "utterance."[12] Early seventeenth-century trade was so strange that it was at last unutterable mystery.

We can enter the "mysterious" labyrinth of the trade debate with Thomas Mun. In his early work, *A Discovrse of Trade* (1621), Mun accused those who made "clamorous complaints" against the East India Company of "not hauing as yet, discerned the mysteries of such waighty affaires." But however fresh his economic thought in many regards (as we will later see), Mun himself essentially lacked discernment in mystery. His document, in B. E. Supple's words, was a "confused amalgam of 'reasons'" for England's outflow of specie.[13] Edward Misselden added to the confusion with his *Free Trade* (1622). Focusing specifically on money, Misselden found the cause of England's costiveness in "the *Vnder-valuation* of *his Maiesties Coyne*, to that of our Neighbour *Countries*." European manipulation of currency values, he suggested, caused "abundance of Mony" to be "drawne vnto the *Mintes* of *those* Countries."[14] But no sooner had Misselden promulgated this hypothesis than it was hotly and confusingly contested by other explainers of mystery. Not "*Vnder-valuation*," Gerard Malynes thus countered in the first volley of his dispute with Misselden, *The Maintenance of Free Trade* (1622). According to Malynes, Misselden "omitted to handle *The Praedominant Part of Trade,* namely, *The Mystery of Exchange.*" The fact that English currency was undervalued and that there was a net outflow of specie, in his view, was merely a secondary consequence of the fact that foreign bankers manipulated the rate on bills of exchange to enhance a discrepancy between currency's actual and paper value. As Malynes succinctly explained in an earlier document: "If the exchange with vs here be low, so that more will bee giuen for our money being caried in *specie,* then by bill of exchange can be had, then our money is transported."[15]

Misselden promptly returned fire. Promising in *The Circle of Commerce* (1623) to make *"Malynes Oblique line . . . Right and direct,"* he defended his emphasis on the undervaluation of England's currency. Yet in doing so, he suddenly allowed his own line of reasoning to turn "oblique." Misselden shifted to the thesis that the root cause of England's monetary crisis was the balance in trade. In conspicuously elevated rhetoric, he declaimed:

> All the mysteries of other Exchanges are hidde in this mystery [the balance of trade]. All the knowledge of Commerce, is presented and represented to the life in this story, in this history. All the riuers of Trade spring out of this source, and empt themselues againe into this *Ocean.* All the waight of Trade falle's to this *Center,* & come's within the circuit of this *Circle.* This is that *Par pro Pari,* that waighe's down *Malynes* Parity, Imparity, Impurity in the Scale: & is onely worthy of the *Quaere,* or th'enquiry of a King. This is . . . the very Eie of the Eie . . . the beauty, the ornament, the complement, the accomplishment of Commerce.[16]

Unimpressed, Malynes marginalized Misselden's *Circle of Commerce* in his *The Center of the Circle of Commerce* (1623). Here he restated his accusation that Misselden did not handle "the *Mistery of Exchanges.*" Yet just as Misselden had shifted direction, so Malynes now abruptly diverted his focus to an even more "mysterious" root cause of England's depleted treasure. In fulsome rhetoric, he broke into an amoral discourse about the greedy "gainfulness" of all merchants that provided little logical explanation for the particular economic problem at hand:

> This [gain] is properly *the Scope* of Merchants, all the *Misteries* of *Personall and Prouinciall Exchanges* are comprised in this *Mistery,* which *Misselden* will make to be no *Mistery.* . . . This is that *Par pro Pari,* that waighes downe *Misseldens Ballance of Trade,* which is without a *Parallel.*[17]

Meanwhile, Mun (who had all along been the writer most concerned with balance of trade) returned to the fray to attack Malynes in his *England's Treasure by Forraign Trade* (mostly composed in the 1620s) for creating "lying wonders":

> The Author *Gerard Malynes* setteth down the admirable feats (as he termeth them) which are to be done by Bankers and Exchangers, with the use and

power of the Exchange: but how these wonders may be effected he altogether omitteth, leaving the Reader in a strange opinion of these dark mysteries.

Instead of strange "wonders" and "mysteries," Mun proposed to reveal the "common and easie business" at the root of England's loss of coin: trade imbalance. "I never knew as yet," Mun affirmed, "a decay in our Trade and Treasure for want of Merchants, or Means to employ us, but rather by excessive Consumption of Forraign Wares at home, or by a declination in the vent of our Commodities abroad."[18]

If we appear to have come full circle, back to a description of the problem rather than an explanation of its cause, it is because we have. As Supple notes, despite Mun's sophisticated understanding of the impersonal and elastic forces of supply and demand, his emphasis on the relationship between an unfavorable balance of trade and the outflow of specie was more a tautology than a causal analysis.[19] The fact is that none of the trade pamphleteers was able to penetrate beyond means and effects to an adequate analysis of cause. Or rather, their idea of analysis was "description," a mere survey of disease symptoms amid which, somewhere, an undiscovered germ hid. The result is that their ostensibly conflicting positions, because they described the same superficial signs of trouble, often overlapped in confusing ways. Each budding economist was trying to fathom the "mystery" or "wonder" of foreign trade, to penetrate to a "center" of trade's strangeness hidden paradoxically "out there" (as I have phrased it) in incomprehensible foreignness. But the resulting tangle of descriptions, not to mention the blur of positions within individual descriptions, confirmed instead a sense of centerlessness. The new market "out there" was too strange for the writers to articulate in clear, consistent theses.

Appropriately enough, therefore, the dispute of the pamphleteers came down in the end precisely to the issue of articulation, of the writer's own "utterance" or language. Misselden, for example, rebutted Malynes's *Maintenance of Free Trade* by attacking the artless metaphors Malynes used to make his case: Malynes's analogy of the parts of trade to the body, soul, and spirit of man ("admirable Oratory," Misselden mocked, "and as incomparable a comparison!"), his parable of the rudderless ship, his numerous other comparisons to square and rule, elements, clocks, ships, dials, active and passive, etc.—all came under attack.[20] The imputation was that Malynes was fictionalizing without any basis in reality. Punning on the preferred form of silver currency, Spanish rials, Misselden thus declared that "the gaine in exportation of *Reals* is reall, but *Malynes* surmises are imaginarie." Yet Misselden's equation of "story" with "history" in describing his own work emblematizes the fact that he was himself open to the charge of fiction-making ("All the knowledge of Commerce," he affirmed in his *Circle of Commerce,* "is presented and represented to the life in this story, in this history").[21] Underscoring just such fictionality, Malynes counterattacked by pointing out the unreality of Misselden's governing metaphors of "balance" and "circle": "this imaginary Ballance is without a Parallell, as his Circle is without a Center" (hence Malynes's own title, "The *Center* of the Circle of Commerce"). Malynes further called a comparison Misselden made between England's old and new economy a "vaine and a Superfluous tale" and concluded that Misselden's study of balances demonstrates "little in truth and certainty, but much in imagination and conceit."[22] As each writer told his "history" of the mystery of foreign trade, each created an artistic "story" plotted along the same, uncanny interface between the real and the imaginary.

In sum, trade was "strange" no matter how contemporaries uttered it. There was strangeness in the image of a costive trading body full of foreign and home goods but empty of money. There was further strangeness in the almost metaphysical "mystery" masking the cause of the disease. And the echo of all this strangeness hovering "out there" was the pamphleteers' preoccupation with "unreal" economic language. Trade could no longer be grasped in literal and familiar terms. It was rendered mystical and displaced into imaginative, metaphorical, or "oblique" representations.

Now we can come to the crux of our analysis of trade's unplaceable strangeness. Why had the concept of trade become so mystified that no one could articulate the crisis in the balance of trade and the value of currency except in metaphor? Most pressingly, why had the very concept of money become so strange that specie and bullion could seem to disappear from England without account—as if into thin air? Adopting a strategy that, if it will not "solve" the trade enigma, will at least place it in a comprehensible context, I call for aid at this point upon modern knowledge of the broad economic changes at the time. The mystery and strangeness with which contemporaries viewed England's woes stemmed from the fact that theory had yet to catch up with massive changes in the way commerce was actually being practiced. Specifically, the trade writers were out of date in regard to what we can call the "displacement" of the economy in both domestic and especially foreign trade—a term I now introduce to literalize the "out thereness" I have indicated. The economy was displaced away from familiar, local market mechanisms into dispersed methods of commerce that made goods and finally money itself seem—from an older perspective—as "unreal" as fiction.

We can take our first lesson from domestic trade. Even in this domain, of course, trade was at all times capable of evoking an uneasy sense of displacement from the familiar. The act of exchange required that strange wares, customs, and traders cross boundaries, if only between neighboring towns. But in England during the late sixteenth and early seventeenth centuries, as Jean-Christophe Agnew points out, this sense of displacement in trade accelerated. In effect, Agnew observes, the domestic market escaped the medieval forms of localization designed to contain market strangeness: an identifiable market*place* (tactically situated at the thresholds or crossroads between villages), reciprocal exchange of commodities carried out in the course of a single day, and the sealing of transactions with gift-giving ceremonies rooted in local tradition. With the beginnings of a full-blown money market in the late sixteenth century, transactions increasingly occurred outside ancient marketplaces and their ceremonial frames, expanding to involve several parties, extended periods of time, and—most tellingly—impersonal abstractions in the form of bills of exchange.[23] Bills of exchange were instruments that allowed the act of paying for goods to become a semi-independent, geographically separate transaction (merchants whose goods were paid for by bill of exchange did not actually receive recompense until the bill was drawn upon funds and/or commodities deposited elsewhere). Moreover, bills of exchange interposed not just a spatial break between the beginning and end of a transaction but all kinds of indirect, deferred dealings. The bills could themselves be traded or bought on the money market, and—when unsecured—could be instruments of credit rather than payment.[24] The characteristic of the new market was thus not the localization or familiarization of strange wares, customs, and traders but a "liquidity" unfixing strangeness from all moorings. The domestic way of marketing or presenting goods, we may say, had become enmeshed in alien processes of *representation*. As Agnew conceives it, this new market in which transactions could not be validated by customary person-to-person means was allied with a general rise at the time of theatrical "*mis*representation," role-playing, and maskedness.[25]

If we now turn to England's foreign trade, we find that the displacement of commerce into distanced, indirect, or representational mechanisms was even more pronounced. Like its domestic counterpart, English foreign trade in the late sixteenth century began to escape the confines of a customary, localized marketplace—in this case, the primary bilateral market first

established at nearby Antwerp and later at Hamburg. But placelessness in
the foreign theater rapidly became much more radical. It was during this
period that trade routes under the conduct of the Eastland Company, Le-
vant Company, East India Company, and so on first stretched out to remote
and exotic lands.[26] As a consequence, there arose a long, suspended chain
of detached trading places, unseen trading parties, and prolonged exchanges—an attenuation of the once localized market that had the effect of
thinning out the "reality" of the physical goods traded. Brought to market
in places farther than a telescope could spy and delayed by sea passage,
goods could almost be said to have vanished. They became the expectation
or representation of goods.

Even more distressingly, the new foreign market with its attenuated or
thin mode of transaction furthered the trend by which bills of exchange
made money itself fade into unreal, representational abstraction. One of
the givens originally underlying the debate over the disappearance of England's money supply, we remember, was the belief that fewer English-
made goods should be exchanged for foreign goods and more for real specie
and bullion—reserves that could then be imported back into the realm to
lubricate the flow of domestic capital.[27] In the new, dispersed world market, however, specie and bullion did play an increasing role—but in an
unexpectedly strange way that furthered the disappearance of English currency. Becoming themselves a kind of merchandise, specie and bullion
commodified money. Money, that is, became a specially compact and precious form of "goods" to be traded for the best (and variable) price on the
dispersed global market. Money was no longer an absolute ground of value
to be hoarded but just as abstract, mobile, and representational in principle
as bills of exchange (through which much specie and bullion were
changed). It was Mun, we might add, who best understood the commodification of money. He described complex circles of transactions by
which money could be converted from one foreign currency to another in
order to achieve a reasonable rate of exchange at the desired purchasing
point.[28]

Not accidentally, it was just this kind of flexible, over-the-horizons
thinking that also fitted Mun (though he did not grasp its full implications)
to defend the great, controversial instance of both attenuated foreign trade
and commodified money: the East India trade. Indeed, we can bring our
narration of economic strangeness to a head at this point precisely by following Mun's nose for money eastward. Under attack for exacerbating, if
not in fact causing, England's costive economy,[29] East India trade summed

up in climactic form all the mysterious "out-thereness" of contemporary commerce. It appeared to confirm the displacement of trade into mechanisms for moving goods and converting money so removed or indirect by the standards of local marketing and hand-to-hand presentation that it was beyond comprehension.

To capitalize on the etymological play that concluded my previous chapter: the East India Company exported *specie* and imported *spices* (or again, shipped out the treasure of *bankers* to bring home the stuff of *banqueters*).[30] More accurately, as K. N. Chaudhuri shows, East India trade comprised a circuit more convoluted than any two-term description of money-for-spice could comprehend. To understand the perplexities of this circuit, we can start with the original obstacle facing English traders. Native producers of spice in the tropical East Indies were naturally most interested in trading for the light-weight textiles of India rather than for what England had available: heavy woolens. Meanwhile, India itself showed little interest in English exports, thus blocking the obvious solution of a simple triangle of commerce with India as intermediary.[31] And even had markets been favorable, Chaudhuri points out, successful Asian trade required exactly the liquidity that the wool-rich but cash-poor English could not muster. Asian natives preferred to be paid in silver rather than commodities. As Chaudhuri notes, "The real price of silver, which was the current monetary standard in Asia, was much higher there than in Europe." Moreover, to add insult to injury, it was *Spanish* silver that natives wanted—so much so that there were cases where English coin was rejected as not "real" enough.[32]

So it was that by 1620 the East India Company devised its remarkable method of circumventing lack of cash: a vast, decentered network of exchange in which multiple routes of goods and plural orbits of money joined to create a sort of perpetual motion machine of deferred expenditure and delayed profit (see fig. 36).[33] A literal "currency" or ceaseless circulation of never-quite-present worth, we may say, compensated for lack of currency. To begin with, the East India Company would import to England silver bullion and specie from Seville in Spain (either directly or via ports in such countries as the Netherlands and France). The silver would be paid for in part by bills of exchange, and would be mostly in the form of Spanish rials of eight, the measurement favored by the East.[34] Now laden with Spanish silver (together with other less significant exports), an expedition would set sail for the East. The primary route would take the ships first to Surat, the Company's main trading station or "factory" in India (secondary routes might lead into the Red Sea or to other Company factories in India and

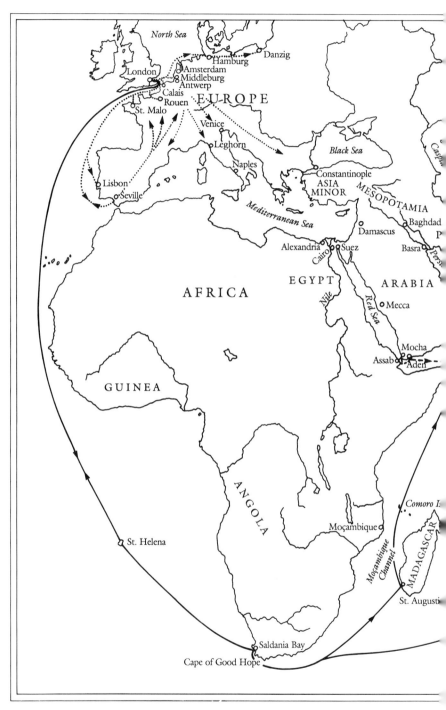

36. Map showing the trading circle of the English East India Company, c. 1620. Dotted lines indicate import routes of Spanish silver to England and re-export routes of East Indian goods from England to the Continent. Solid line traces primary sailing route to and from the East. Broken lines designate secondary trading routes in the East. Representative English trading factories are underlined.

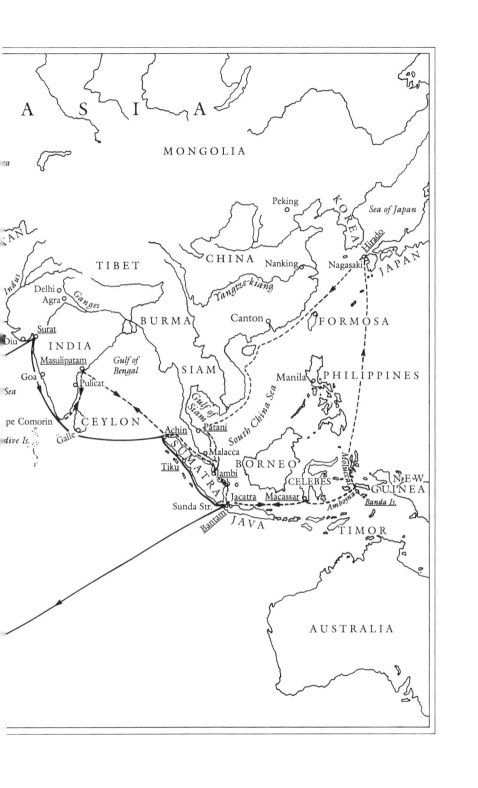

Persia). In Surat, the silver would be exchanged for indigo, calico, silk, sugar, and other goods.[35] Laden with these Indian goods, the ships would then sail for Bantam, the Company's main factory in the East Indies (and, via secondary routes, to other factories in Sumatra, Java, the Moluccas, and so on). In Bantam, part of the Indian goods would be exchanged for spices.[36] Now, laden with East Indian spices together with the remaining goods from India, the ships would sail back to England. The Company would then re-export the surplus of Eastern goods to the Continent in exchange for other commodities and (using the surplus goods to supplement bills of exchange) for Spanish silver, the latter of which—beginning the circle again—would be exported to the East.[37]

Virtually everything about this intricate circle of trade revealed East India trade to be simultaneously the most imaginative of England's commercial ventures and the most strange. Far from being bilateral, as was traditional in foreign trade, East India trade was multilateral in the extreme. It drew on markets in Europe, England, India, Persia, the East Indies, and beyond (nearly two dozen factories were established in Asia by the 1620s).[38] Far from reaping the customary quick return on goods sold, East India trade required an exceptional delay that left wealth always "out there" in the global network. Deferment of returns arose from the extended nature of the system—one way alone to or from the East took on the average seven to eight months—as well as from the huge investment of subscription funds in establishing the network.[39] Most important, far from carrying out the familiar exportation of English-made goods in direct exchange for money that could be imported back into the realm, East India trade did the exact opposite. In exchange for foreign goods, it seemed to contemporaries, the Company *exported* England's treasure (all that Spanish silver bought with all those bills of exchange!).

Ironically, Mun's defense of this strange trade, as well as the support offered by other trade pamphleteers, could serve only to heighten its alien character when compared with conventional trade. To be sure, Mun offered many assurances. He pointed out that the specie exported to the East was foreign, not English at all, and that "*India* wares hath their finall end in moneys," as in traditional foreign trade. Furthermore, he reminded his readers of the medicinal virtues of East Indian imports. Rather than being luxuries that added to England's collective costiveness, East Indian imports—when moderately consumed—were "wholesome Drugges and comfortable Spices . . . most necessary to preserue their health, and to cure their diseases."[40] (Indeed, as we saw in discussing banqueting voids, spices were the conceptual opposite of costiveness; they were purgatives.) Nevertheless, despite all his reassurances, Mun's vision of the process by which East Indian "necessities" were traded seemed to contemporaries utterly alien. Particularly strange was the recognition implied throughout his defense that East India trade was fundamentally an exchange of representational rather than "real" worth—of goods, that is, indexed upon a variable and speculative standard of value. Goods in East India trade, Mun observed, were exchanged for other goods in a transformative circle wherein the bearer of worth, money, could be both commodity and treasure and "by a continual and orderly change" convert "one into the other." Floated upon a money that was itself negotiable, the very identity of goods could seem to be unfixed. The crowning emblem of representational trade was the striking fact that, when the East India ships came home, their imports from the East could instantly be changed into "English" goods by being re-exported to the Continent.[41]

Misselden, we note, supported Mun's defense of East India trade precisely by dwelling on this latter fact. He explained that England was really exporting English goods rather than its specie—never mind that those goods were imported in the first place. "In our *Exportations,*" he said, "wee are to reckon our forraine Commodities imported, and not spent in the Kingdom, but Exported againe into forrain trade, *as the Natiue Commodities of the Kingdome*" (second emphasis mine).[42] Sir Thomas Roe similarly justified East India trade to a critical Parliament of 1641:

> Nothing exported of our own growth hath balanced our riotous consumption at home, but those foreign commodities which I call *naturalised,* that is the surplus of our East India trade, which being brought home in greater quantity than are spent within the kingdom, are exported again *and become in value and use as natural commodities.* (My emphases)[43]

King James received a like reply in August 1623 when he inquired into the vent of the "great mass of calicoes that yearly come" from the East. "Having first served his Majesty's dominions," the deputy governor of the Company explained, "the overplus is transported to foreign parts *in the nature of a home bred commodity*" (my emphasis). The Company report concluded assuringly: "The King approved exceedingly of their answer, and said that was the ready way to bring treasure into his kingdom."[44]

Though James in this instance apparently approved of the Company's response, it is clear that the government and nation as a whole were deeply suspicious. As early as June 1618, the "moneyers of the Tower" complained to the King that "they are grown poor for want of silver to coin, which is carried away by the Company." With the worsening of England's trade problems in 1620, a committee established by James riveted attention on the East India Company. The committee's plan was, first, to debase English silver coinage to prevent its exportation (a Misseldenian approach) and, second, to restrain the East India Company from paying higher prices for rials abroad than the official mint price of silver at home. But after much campaigning—and because yet another committee opposed currency manipulation—the Company was allowed to go on as before. The public, however, retained its distrust. Complaints against the East India Company arose again in the Parliaments of 1621 and—most tumultuously—1624.[45] The Company Court Minutes recorded the latter uproar:

> upon occasion of speech of the East India Company in Parliament there was a sudden motion that the East India fleet might be stayed, others cried out, "stay the money that they send out of the land," which some reported to be 80,000*l*. this year; that the heat was such that Mr. Bond, one of the burgesses of the city, did but whisper a few words to the gentleman next him and was cried to speak out else to the bar; Mr. Treasurer Bateman, another of the burgesses of London, was called up to deliver his knowledge clearly what money is to go in this fleet; he said he could not precisely satisfy them of the just sum, but that there is to be sent in these ships 30,000*l*. in ryals of eight. The house was not satisfied with that answer, and cried out, "search the books."

At this, the deputy governor of the Company "grew hot." His spirited and, by now, familiar defense was that

> the Company carry out not so much as they bring in, and not half what they are allowed to carry; it is true there is now to go some 40,000*l*., but that their returns when not interrupted are 400,000*l*. per annum in good real commodities, as calicoes, indigo, silk, and such like, whereof calicoes alone save the kingdom the expense of at least 200,000*l*. yearly; in cambric, lawns, and other linen cloth, neither is it barren in return of money; that he himself last year brought to the Mint 60 lb. weight of gold for Indian commodities exported; and that of the value of 400,000*l*. imported, about 100,000*l*. serves this kingdom, and the rest being exported, works itself home again, either in money, or commodities that would cost money.[46]

But such a complex representation of East India trade could not be appreciated. Presented with an oblique trade that so imaginatively exchanged the "real" and "rial" (commodities and commodified money, the literal and the abstract, the home-bred and the foreign), the nation continued to see in the East India Company a radical violation of the principles of England's trade. So foreign was East India exchange that even those enticed by it drew a conceptual blank. Many investors, for example, could not understand the notion of delayed financial return. The Company was thus forced to borrow money at high interest rates in order to pay dividends before any profits on investments in fact materialized.[47]

We can now look back to the rhetorical artistry of the trade tracts that told the story/history of England's wondrous foreign trade and see that they were unconscious *imitatios* of the strange trade "out there" epitomized by East India exchange. "Uttered" through imagination, conceit, and metaphor, their shifting arguments reflected what might be called a new "aesthetic" of exchange—a displaced, allusive, and oblique trade of speculative representation. The ultimate form of such aesthetics, as we will see, was the masque.

But first we must attend to the economic "body."

Eating Interests: Ormuz

In the later stages of reading economic "strangeness" above, we have already begun witnessing the pent-up need of the English to grasp strangeness by locating it in specific culprits. The English needed to blame *some* alien agent in the fuzzy "out there" of the dispersed economic world for the apparent disappearance of money. But the irony was that the someone they laid hands on turned out to be English: the East India Company in which many of the aristocracy themselves invested.[48] Herein lay a nervous realization about market forces in the Jacobean world. Once located, strangeness "out there" was discovered to be "in here" in the English identity itself.

The motif that best allows us to track this ironic realization is the economic "body," which we have already glimpsed in the symptoms of England's "unvented" "costiveness." Images of the body, of bodily actions, and—most strikingly—of dismembered body parts and cannibalism lie scattered throughout the discourse of contemporary responses to England's strange trade. What we witness in such discourse is not so much a systematic or one-to-one analogy of foreign trade with corporeality as a confusing, semi-literal/semi-metaphorical saturation of one discourse by another. Why the pell-mell convergence of economic and corporeal discourses, which seems almost to anticipate a more modern notion of "corporation"? And why did this early imagination of the corporation simultaneously evoke images of *in*corporation (cannibalism) and *dis*incorporation (dismemberment)? Though this is far from the only answer, it may be suggested that a cause of the twinning of economic and bodily discourses was precisely the need of the English to locate economic strangeness in specific culprits: it was this urgency that prompted speech about an imaginal English trading "body" whose corporate injuries could be presumed to be caused by some other national "body." But economic body-logic was problematic. The notion of competition between distinct, corporate domains ran up against the fact that when the English investigated concrete situations or events, they always found that the English economic body was monstrously conjoined with foreign bodies. As the case of the East India Company so well demonstrated, the effort to embody the mysterious, alien cause of England's economic crisis discovered no other than an English trading corporation. Strangeness thus merged with home identity, and the English body turned against itself such that corporation became its own disincorporation: the body was split within itself as if "dismembered."[49] Or again, to take the contemporary mixing of discourses about trade and body parts to its furthest stretch: if England's money was vanishing, that was because the body was "eating" itself. Market forces and the new trade they created were an ultimate incorporation or "cannibalism."

Bringing this cannibal stew of economic thought to the boiling point was a specific incident involving the East India Company—an incident that will allow us to bring our entire discussion of economics and East India trade to bear upon a single, historically discrete "topic" that "everyone was talking about." The place was London and James's court. The time: summer 1623, during the height of England's economic costiveness, the trade-tract controversy, and suspicions over the strangeness of East India trade. And the talk of the town: the homecoming of five East India Company ships laden with pepper, cloves, mace, nutmeg, indigo, calicoes, Persian raw silk[50] and—a shocking addition—confirmation of the Company's involvement in the sack of Ormuz, "the key of all India."[51]

Three of the five returning ships were actually part of the flotilla of Company vessels (well-armed to fend off attacks at sea by the Dutch) that had joined with Persian forces to attack the Portuguese/Spanish trading settlement on the Persian Gulf.[52] News of the event, which had occurred without prior sanction from Company governors, was received by a surprised London as supremely "savage" or "barbarous." The reason was not only that English sailors had leagued themselves militarily with "pagans" in an alliance of convenience but that they had actually sunk to the cultural level of pagans. Of course, sailors at the time were generally perceived to be heathenish. "The seamen that have been long in the Indies are worse than the heathens themselves," John Bickell could thus affirm to the East India Company. To Mun, such paganism was in the nature of the beast: "but take them [sailors] from their laudable and accustomed imployments, for want of voyages to Sea; we see what desperate courses they do then attempt, by ioyning, euen with *Turkes* and Infidels, to rob and spoile all Christian Nations."[53] But in Ormuz, the sailors apparently outdid themselves. As told by Eastern factors, ship captains, and others, the riotous looting by both the English and Persians was wholly barbaric. More damning: it was the *English* who led the way.

Certainly, all reporters said, the actual "perfidious Pagans" or Persians were savage in their greed.[54] Their instinct for profit together with their cannibalistic penchant for dismembering fallen victims made them something like a tribe of economic headhunters. The typical Persian, Edward Monoxe recounted, collected enemy heads, cutting "a hole either in the Eare or through one of the Cheekes, and so thrusting his finger in at the mouth and out at the hole in the cheeke, brings sometimes two, three, or foure of them before the Generall together, *in such sort that not a Butcher in East-cheape could doe it better*" (my emphasis).[55] Such cannibalistic "per capita" collection merely prepared for the collection of financial capital, which the Persians accomplished with irrepressible gusto. "Shall we sit idle, whilst the English, by stealth and strategy, exhaust all our hopes of benefits and riches?" the Persians were said to have asked their leader (identified by Sir Herbert Thomas as "the Duke"). "Wherat the Duke, glad of such advantage, replied, 'If so, go and have your desires'! Wherupon they broke open and robbed the houses and stores of what was valuable."[56] The Persians, we may say, were simultaneously cannibalistic and entrepreneurial—"raiders," in our modern corporate sense.

But the key fact, as indicated by the resentment of the Persians at sitting idly "whilst the English" had their way, was that the "perfidious Pagans" exploded into savage behavior only after being set off by English example. (Even the nom de guerre of their leader, "the Duke," made them seem imitators of the English.) According to the terms of the temporary alliance, East India Company forces and the Persians were to have split up Ormuz between them, with such areas as a monastery decreed off-limits. The plunder of the town could then have proceeded in relatively organized fashion. But a particularly unruly English sailor jumped the gun and rapaciously looted the proscribed monastery. Thomas, an eyewitness of the Ormuz siege, reported that the "rascal" sailor,

> though he knew the danger of his life and the loss of the Christian's credit; yet stole into a monastery sealed with both consents, and committed sacrilege upon the silver lamps, chalices, crucifixes, and other rich ornaments and

stuffed so full that in descending his theft cried out against him, and he was
taken by the Persians, and drubbed right handsomely.⁵⁷

It was this action by an Englishman more "sacrilegious" than actual pagans
that made the Persians turn savage in their looting and that then led to a
general descent by all forces into indiscriminate and riotous plundering.
Though the East India Company came away with good booty, in short, it
was tainted by resemblance to cannibalistic barbarians. Ormuz had not just
been plundered; it had been violently dismembered.

Variously subtle and explicit associations with cannibalistic dismemberment, indeed, continued to be heaped upon the Company as the controversy in London widened after the arrival of news about Ormuz. When the
Spanish ambassadors protested to King James in August 1623, for example,
they charged the English sailors with piratical atrocities insidiously akin to
those of cannibalistic savages. (The thinness of the line in this period between protecting trade and pirating other nations' ships on the high seas
confirms the potential resemblance between commerce and savagery.)
Pointing to the extravagance of the sailors' booty, the ambassadors initiated
a chain of incriminating metonymies by noting "that the very dishes that
the lowest and basest sort of the crew put their meat in are of silver,
stamped with the arms of many families of Portugal, whom they have mis-
erably sacked and slain." The chain of associations in this sentence suggests
an image of the English sailors feasting amid those they have murdered: we
almost see dismembered, rather than merely heraldic, "arms" heaped all
around. I hasten to add that this impression is not so farfetched. Expressing
a biting savagery in their own tone, the ambassadors continued that the
English sailors delivered up converted Persians to their pagan countrymen
"to be barbarously torn in pieces." The sailors were complicit with the
pagan orgy of literal decapitation and dismemberment. Finally, as if such
physical barbarism were not bad enough, the ambassadors then tried to
bring the uncivilized behavior of the English sailors home to James in the
most personal way possible. They went out of their way to report that on
their return voyage the ships' crews riotously celebrated the collapse of
Charles's marriage plans with Spain: "having (though falsely) heard that
the match with the Infanta was broken off," they complained, "the crew
made no difficulty to shoot off all the artillery, and for a greater demonstration of joy, the captain giving the example, threw their hats and caps into
the sea."⁵⁸

Such never-quite-logical associations between the English merchant-

37. Indian children being fed by a Spaniard to his dogs. The mother to the left has hung herself; her child, suspended from her waist, is chewed by a dog. Illustration by Théodore de Bry for Bartolomé de las Casas's *Narratio regionum indicarum per hispanos quosdam devastatarum verissima* (Frankfurt: Théodore de Bry, 1598), p. 50.
Photo: Huntington Library.

men and cannibalistic dismemberment, we may note, took place within the context of a general trend at the time to link trade (and especially sea trade) with the literal cannibalism located by contemporaries in the remote markets of alien lands (in the East Indian islands of Java and Andemaon, for example).[59] The Spanish themselves were often imaged as man-eating. Such vocal critics of Spanish acquisitiveness in the West Indies as Bartolomé de las Casas and his illustrator, Théodore de Bry, depicted the Spanish savagely dismembering Indians (hacking off legs, arms, and breasts) and feeding adult and child alike to their dogs (figs. 37, 38).[60] Closer to home, the Dutch, aggressively determined to control East India trade, were pictured by the English as "cannibals" hungrily "eating" them out of their trade.[61] And to cite just one more instance that in our context is especially interesting, the money market within England itself was increasingly imaged as a kind of literal consumerism or cannibalism.

38. An open market displays quarters of Indians for sale as food for Spaniards' dogs.
Illustration by De Bry for Las Casas's *Narratio*, p. 59. Photo: Huntington Library.

Exploitative trade in commodified money provoked an onslaught of tracts against the "biting usury" of "Long-lane Cannibals."[62] The common, derogatory term for loans that accumulated interest was "*eating* debts" (my emphasis).[63]

Ormuz, in sum, affected London with almost bodily shock in 1623 because it dramatized a contradiction that had all along been building in the notion of "foreign trade." The contradiction was that to trade with foreigners was to import the essence of "barbarousness" into civilization itself, making the home "body" a body-against-itself or body-eating-itself. Ormuz thus became an infamous paradigm for the way transactions were conducted in the new foreign market generally. Every "strange" exchange of money or goods concealed at its heart a physically imagined barbarism; every instance of foreign trade split the civil body of a nation between familiar and outlandish identities.

In this sense, the greatest example of the English civil body split between civility and barbarism was King James, whose royal "we" might be said to be corporate in personality. James's conduct regarding the rich booty looted from Ormuz demonstrates the extent to which monarchical and aristocratic identity was implicated in the contradictory economic logic of the "strange body." In essence, James wanted to have his cake and eat it too. From one perspective, he wished to distance himself from the cannibalistic barbarism of trade—i.e., to keep it definitively "out there" or "strange." The new market epitomized by foreign trade and the Ormuz incident was a global version of James's personal dread, his fear—as we saw in the previous chapter—of being torn apart or dispersed among the common public. Thus the King felt compelled to erect a barrier between barbaric economic events "out there" and civilized England by drawing on the traditional notion of the nation as a rule of patronage and *gift*. It was the spirit of the gift—of the generosity, goodwill, love, and grace we studied as an Elizabethan ideal—that barred strange trade from buying out home values.

James's use of "gift" to sweep the dirty business of market trade out of England's stately home, we may note, predated Ormuz. Bargaining over the Great Contract of 1610, for instance, by which he was to forfeit feudal revenues such as wardship and purveyance in exchange for a regular salary from Parliament, he complained that "the interest" on the crown's loans "did eat." Furthermore, even in the act of negotiating with Parliament over finances, he opposed not just the outright market cannibalism of interest but all purely financial motives. He wished to advertise that the deal he would get from Parliament was owing to him under the old customs of patronage (although here the direction of patronage is reversed). "I am loath to contract for all things," he affirmed. *"My cheif Strength I must derive from my Subjects love."* Similarly, James foregrounded the gift ethos in dealing with the next Parliament of 1614. In this case, the King began by calling upon his subjects to demonstrate their "good affections toward him" so that "this parlement might be called the Parlement of love." Then he "offered them certain graces and favors not in the way of exchaunge or marchandising, (which course he will not allow, nor cannot abide to heare of) but of meere goode will and *motu proprio.*"[64]

When it came to Ormuz, all these strategies of suppressing market forces under the cover of gift culture served James well. Dickering with the East India Company over the spoils, the King clearly showed that he wanted his split. But he wanted it presented to him and his favorite, Buckingham (in his capacity as Lord Admiral), in the familiar form of gift. Calling representatives of the Company to Whitehall, James advised them to gratify

Buckingham during the latter's absence with Charles in Spain (on the expedition to gain the Infanta's hand) "when the gift will come the more acceptably, because thereby it would appear they had been mindfull of him [Buckingham]." In the event, the Company agreed to "sweeten" Buckingham with £2,000. But James pushed for more gratification. He did so at yet another meeting by again invoking the language of reciprocation: "Did I deliver you from the complaint of the Spaniard, and do you return me nothing?"[65]

Ultimately, however, if James used "gift" to sweep away the dirty business of market forces, he did so at last only by sweeping the market under the rug—i.e., *inside* rather than outside England's grand stately home of gift culture. The profit motive kept reappearing within the ethos of patronage, and never more pointedly than after Ormuz, when James's language of gift was in the end superseded by an especially forceful expression of market consciousness. I refer to the aggressive act of profit-taking that concluded the lengthy negotiations between James and the Company (extending throughout the winter of 1623–24). During this period, the Company's 1624 fleet was preparing for departure. Anticipating Spanish retaliation for the sack of Ormuz, the Company had put together an impressive flotilla admiralled by "a ship of extraordinary 'countenance,'" the Great James. But what it had not thought to defend against was a foe nearer at hand: *King* James. When the fleet set sail in March of 1624, James forcibly stayed the ships by having them fired upon from Tilbury fort and boarded by the King's officers. Accusing the East India Company of piracy, he then arrested the fleet until £10,000 each was paid to him and Buckingham.[66]

In this single act of royal aggression, itself uncannily like piracy, James revealed his kinship to the barbarous sailors who had piratically sacked Ormuz. From beneath James's language of gift rose up his savage desire for—and even a kind of identification with—strange trade. Other aspects of James's negotiations with the Company then confirmed his keen mercantile spirit. Just a few months after holding up the East India Company for loot, for example, James came to recognize that the East India trade was a "business of state" and offered to become a member of the Company so that they could sail under his royal protection. The Company, however, turned James's scorn of merchandising against him, answering that "they cannot conceive how with his honour it may be done, the condition of partnership in trade being a thing too far under the dignity and majesty of a king."[67]

Thus we see the "strange body" of Jacobean trade. The new market forces responsible for England's economic crisis were perceived to hover perpetually "out there" in a realm of unlocatable, displaced, and unutterably foreign processes of commercial (mis)representation. But if one reaction to representation was a willingness to leave things suspended in open-ended mystery, the other reaction was a need to realize, physicalize, or embody representation. And what the English saw when they thus bodied forth the strange new economics was a monstrous version of themselves: English foreign trade was an oxymoronic "civilized barbarism."

Now we are ready at last to come to the ornament that dressed up the strange body of Jacobean trade: *Neptune's Triumph*. Composed amid the wrangling over the sack of Ormuz and scheduled for January 1624, Jonson's masque was demonstrably "about" not just Charles's voyage to Spain but the far stranger voyage of Eastern trade. Though its aesthetics were even more oblique than those of the metaphorical trade tracts of the time, the pretty dress it put on over Jacobean economics revealed as much as it hid the naked body underneath. Jonson, we may say, at once masked and unmasked (i.e., antimasqued) the topic of the day: the civilized barbarism of the market.

Dressing Up Trade
Neptune's Triumph for the Return of Albion

Gift, first of all. Like James speaking the language of gift while grabbing for loot, *Neptune's Triumph* opens and closes by erecting a facade-universe of gift culture. Jacobean masques, of course, generally projected a universal ethos of giftedness in their staging of gifts, offerings, and prayers to monarchy (as I have previously noted). But *Neptune's Triumph* virtually trumpets the gift. There is its epigraph, for example. Jonson quotes Martial: "*Omnis et ad reducem iam litat ara deum*" ("Every altar makes fair offerings to greet the returning god"). Again, there is the expansion upon this thought in the masque proper. Jonson celebrates Charles's return home from Spain by describing all England sacrificed on an "altar" burning with "pure affections, and from odorous stocks" (l. 260). " 'Tis incense all, that flames!" the Chorus cries (l. 261), a line that in the context of the Feast of Epiphany (when the masque was to have been performed) might well remind us of the Eastern frankincense that the Magi brought as a gift for the Christ child. Finally, to come to the climactic (but, as we will see, also most problematic) instance of gift ethos in the masque, there is Jonson's conclusion upon a sort of contemporary journey of the Magi: a naval expedition sent to fetch an updated version of frankincense, myrrh, and gold. Immediately after the "dressings" passage and the revels, the masque scene opens to

"discover" a view of England's ships fitted to go out and come back in an
endless circle of gift centered upon James and London. The Poet (the character in the masque) glosses the prospect:

> 'Tis time your eyes should be refreshed at length
> With something new, a part of Neptune's strength.
> See, yond' his fleet, ready to go or come,
> Or fetch the riches of the ocean home,
> So to secure him both in peace and wars,
> Till not one ship alone, but all be stars.
>
> (ll. 342–47)

Then, after a brief interruption we will need to return to, Saron (god of
navigation) itemizes the "riches" to be thus "fetched": the fleet will come
"From agèd Indus laden home with pearls, / And orient gums to burn unto
thy name" (ll. 370–71). How do we know that such items are gifts? To re-
solve any doubt, the Chorus follows Saron by confirming that the profit of
the fleet is indeed gift exchange. "But both at sea and land our powers increase," they recite, "With health and all the golden gifts of peace" (ll. 375–
76). The final dance then ensues.

Neptune's Triumph, in short, is about the triumph of the English civilization of gift. But Neptune's Triumph, we may say, is ironically also "about" or
topically grounded on the market forces that undermined such triumph.
Behind the gift-facade—and certainly behind the English fleet—lurks
trade. And it is the shadow that trade casts over the masque's universe that
allows us to grasp the ethos of giftedness for what it really is: Jonson's imitation of the way James himself tried to use "gift" to interpose a barrier
between home civility and barbarous trade—between the culture of traditional "presentation," that is, and the new market of shady dealings and
displaced "representations."

In particular, the gift ethos in Neptune's Triumph tries to defend against
the topic of trade by quarantining it in a special zone where it can be dramatized as perpetually "out there," exotic, or strange. The quarantine of the
low and topical, as in other masques, is the antimasque—the central instance of which in Neptune's Triumph thrusts us into the universe of the
market with such vividness that the sensation is almost physical. Indeed,
what the antimasque forces is precisely a physical metaphor: an extreme version of the cannibalistic body-logic of economics we earlier surveyed. After
talking for some time with the Poet at the masque's opening (beginning
with the interchange we overheard in the last chapter), the ever-visceral
Cook feels that an unruly antimasque is called for. The Poet has just finished

projecting his "device" of high allegory (l. 83): a "floating isle" and "tree of harmony" that will bear Charles and his masquers home from the "Hesperian shores [Spain]" (ll. 99, 143, 100). "But where's your antimasque now, all this while?" the Cook demands, "I hearken after them" (ll. 155–56). When the Poet confesses he has "none" (l. 156), the Cook becomes "a poet / No less than cook" (ll. 164–65) and serves forth a fantastic stew of an antimasque: a "metaphorical dish" of gossips or "Such as do relish nothing but *di stato*" in which he satirizes the rampant rumormongering occasioned by Charles's journey to Spain (ll. 169, 176).[68]

Significantly, in the process of thus lampooning vulgar gossips the Cook also satirizes a particular class of citizens rooted in the market universe: the middle class. In a manner that takes economic body-logic to the extreme, the bulk of the Cook's cannibalistic stew consists of meaty money-makers: "Grave Master Ambler, newsmaster of Paul's, / Supplies your capon," "a plump poult'rer's wife in Grace's Street / Plays hen with eggs i'the belly, or a cony," "Hogrel the butcher and sow his wife" present "bacon," and "a fruiterer with a cold red nose" performs "the artichoke" (ll. 204–5, 208–9, 210–11, 215–16).[69] Thus does the Cook serve up his delicious irony: the middle-class consumers who are part of the new world of bankers, traders, and other cannibal-profiteers of "eating interest" are themselves cannibalistically consumed. In *Gypsies Metamorphosed* (1621), it may be noted, Jonson had mocked the middle class in a similar manner. In grand banqueting style, the Devil in *Gypsies* gobbles down a hodgepodge feast: "Six pickled tailors sliced and cut, / Sempsters, tirewomen, fit for his palate, / With feathermen and perfumers put / Some twelve in a charger to make a grand salad," "A rich fat usurer stewed in his marrow, / And by him a lawyer's head and green sauce," "the mayor of a town, / With a pudding of maintenance thrust in his belly," "The jowl of a jailor, served for fish, / A constable soused with vinegar by, / Two aldermen lobsters asleep in a dish, / A deputy tart, a churchwarden pie," and much, much more (ll. 991–96, 1007–8, 1027–30). But the Cook's stew in *Neptune's Triumph* improves upon the earlier gallimaufry, intensifying the caricature of mercantilism by clarifying the hodgepodge of middle-class dishes into a single pot. Thus does Jonson attempt to quarantine (and, indeed, to sterilize by boiling) the world of the market. As emblematized by the fact that the Cook's stew is literally foreign, a Spanish "*olla podrida*" (1. 173), market forces are declared to be thoroughly "strange," beyond rational comprehension, outside the English tradition of gift.

Yet, of course, the very fact that economic strangeness is embodied cannibalistically in a class of citizens *native* to England reveals the uncanny reversal in economic body-logic. What we should finally recognize is that the barrier the masque imposes between native gift culture and barbaric market forces is porous, allowing the strange "body" of the market to be incorporated within gift civilization. If Jonson imitates James in quarantining the market from home civility, in short, he also imitates him in at last breaching the quarantine and seizing upon rich booty for the profit of civility itself. After all, the antimasque is *inside* the masque rather than at its borders; the barbaric gusto of the satirized English middle class is "contained" only by being incorporated *within*.

Nor do I mean only that the masque incorporates an encapsulated pocket of the market like a zoo. Rather, the antimasque contained in the masque is merely the largest of many signs that the masque as a whole follows the market. Here I would reverse the emphasis of Sara Pearl's reading of *Neptune's Triumph*. Pearl argues that the Cook's antimasque satirizes not just the gossips but the whole practice of topicality (James, she notes, had repeatedly issued proclamations in the early 1620s against discussing matters of state). The masque should thus be read as moving away from topicality toward a more distanced, mythic, essentially allegorical poetry.[70] But I would add that the main masque that then follows the antimasque in *Neptune's Triumph,* even while it distances itself from the topicality exemplified by middle-class gossips, suffers a return of the repressed.[71] Throughout the main masque, we find veiled or oblique references to the topic of trade. The literal is *in* the mythical and allegorical; strange trade is *in* the vision of England as gift culture.

Specifically, it is East India trade that is inside the allegory of gift. We can begin uncovering the oriental trade hidden within English gift culture by looking closely at what follows the Cook's stew: the appearance of Charles and the masquers upon a "floating isle." In essence, the island wafting Charles home from Spain and thus opening the main masque is a glorified ship, and the ship has a mainmast. As the Poet had earlier described it:

> Yes, we have a tree too,
> Which we do call the tree of harmony,
> And is the same with what we read the sun
> Brought forth in the Indian Musicana first.
> (ll. 142–45)

The tree that adorns the island is the banyan, of *Indian* origin. Why did Jonson plant a suggestion of the East so centrally in his main masque? Spain, after all, was clearly not India. In what sense could an island associated with India be said to bring Charles back from Spain? In the sense, I suggest, that the submerged thought of *Neptune's Triumph* is East India trade, which, as we saw, sent ships to Spain for rials to finance a series of exchanges culminating in the return of Eastern goods to England. (One of the East India Company's largest ships, it may be noted, was named the *Charles*.)[72]

The Indian tree is merely the leading indicator of the economics behind the main masque. What the tree points us to is the fact that the language of the main masque continually alludes to East India trade in a manner at once oblique *and* curiously precise.[73] Now we are ready to come back to the "dressings" passage upon which we began. After the island floats in to England's shore and the masquers disembark in an entry dance, the scene opens once more to discover a "maritime palace, or the house of Oceanus" (ll. 302–3). Before this setting, the masquers perform their main dance. It is then that the "dressings" passage bids the court "nymphs" join in the revels; and it is at this point, we can now fill in, that the language of the main masque precisely itemizes the stock items of East India trade. An East Indian import can be traded for each of the text's ornamental, kenning-like images: for "the silkworm's toils"—raw silk (a financially significant import by the early 1620s); for "grains of ore"—any of the costly spice imports (pepper, for example, had been used in England as a substitute for "ore" or gold); for "the shellfish spoils" and the "stock / To graft the greener emerald on, / . . . Or ruby of the rock"—the stock of jewels often imported from the East. So, too, the "smell of ambergris" can be traded for the fragrant ambergris imported to make perfume (and culinary) scents.[74]

Most tellingly, the nymphs have not only "Ambrosian hands" to receive Eastern goods but "silver feet" to fetch them. "Silver feet," of course, is a common attribute of nymphs in Jonson's earlier masques. But it is only in *Neptune's Triumph* that Jonson takes the trouble to gloss the epithet. Upon its introduction—"all the silver-footed nymphs were dressed / To wait upon him [Neptune/James]" (ll. 267–68)—the printed version of the masque devotes a note in the margin to the most obvious of explanations: "An epithet frequent in Homer and others, given by them to Thetis, Panope, Doris, etc. '*Silver-footed Thetis.*'"[75] There is something overdetermined about the fact that such a pedestrian gloss is needed at all. What Jonson's gloss masks, I suggest, is another stock-in-trade of East India trade. "Silver feet" is an oblique allusion to the silver that England acquired in Spain to initiate the Eastern trade circle. Thus it is that the masque later envisions "the silver-footed nymphs" and Nereus bringing home the rich jewels and spices of the East: "old Nereus with his fifty girls, / From aged

Indus laden home with pearls, / And orient gums." It is these *trade* goods
that are offered in "gift" to James—"to burn unto thy name" (ll. 369–71).

The nymphs of the "dressings" passage thus quintessentially represent
the greedy thought of East India trade hidden within the cosmos of gift. It
might be said that they are *personifications* of East India trade. Beneath the
oblique ornamentality of their "dress," of their veil of allegory, they—like
the "middle-class" dancers of the antimasque stew—are embodiments of
the topical. One further piece of evidence will corroborate such a reading.
How can we be sure, after all, that we should indeed peek under the "dress"
of the masque's ornamentation to see the naked market body rather than
assume that such indecencies are merely trace impurities left over in the re-
finement of gift culture? The answer lies in the brief interlude after the
"dressings" passage (and revels) and just before the conclusion. As we earlier saw, the scenery opens yet again at this point to discover the English
fleet ready to "fetch the riches of the ocean home" until "not one ship alone,
but all be stars." There is little doubt here, we can now see, that we are to
think of the *Star*—one of the ships chosen to reinforce the 1624 East India
fleet against Spanish retribution for Ormuz ("to secure him both in peace
and *wars*," the passage on the fleet reads; my emphasis).[76] Nor is this all. No
sooner is the English fleet discovered than a crucial interruption occurs just
before the masque (as we earlier saw) can then conclude by chorusing
"golden gifts of peace" fetched "From agèd Indus" and the "orient." Unruly to the last, the Cook suddenly summons up a *second* antimasque
consisting of "a dish of pickled sailors, fine salt sea-boys" (ll. 349–50), who
take the stage as if they were "taking the town." "Come away boys, the
town is ours," the old salts cry, "Hey for Neptune and our young master!"
(ll. 352–53). Taking a town and cheering Charles's return, these sailors stand
in for the actual sailors who took Ormuz and then cheered the failure of
Charles's suit for the Spanish Infanta. In short, Jonson deliberately spoils
his masque's allegory of gift culture, destabilizing or re-topicalizing it by
calling back onto stage not just trade-ship *Stars* but the whole world of the
Cook's first antimasque with its cannibalistic dramatization of the market
universe. Beneath the masque's beautiful "dressings," ironically, cavort the
ugly bodies of East India Company sailors. Behind the facade of England as
the land of gift lie the ruins of Ormuz.

We have sat down to "eat" at masques before, of course. The "dish of
pickled sailors, fine salt sea-boys" that the Cook serves the court is a less
sweet version of the fine banqueting stuffs we tasted in chapter 4: they can
be relished "like anchovies or caviar, to draw down a cup of nectar in the
skirts of a night" (ll. 349–51). Even the masquers arriving on the floating

island could be seen to be edible delicacies. As they prepare for their first figure or dance, the Chorus sings a subtle suggestion of a recipe:

> Spring all the graces of the age
> And all the loves of time;
> Bring all the pleasures of the stage
> And relishes of rhyme;
> Add all the softnesses of court,
>   The looks, the laughters and the sports,
> And mingle all their sweets and salts
>   That none may say the triumph halts.
>   (ll. 293–300)

Such cannibal stews and people-meats in *Neptune's Triumph,* we may close by saying, are the ultimate void. They tear down the masque fiction of "gift" to show the hungry void that underlay it: an *economic* as well as literal consumerism acknowledging that the spices needed for banqueting stuffs came from Eastern trade.

And a last note: as a satirist, we know, Jonson was himself frequently accused by contemporaries of being a cannibal poet. "Art not famous enough yet, my mad *Horastratus,* for killing a Player," Dekker taunted (referring to Jonson's duel with Gabriel Spencer), "but thou must eate men aliue?"[77] In fact, the word "satire" derived etymologically from a hodge-podge dish: the *lanx satura* (*OED*). Jonson's "biting" satire, therefore, was the perfect container for the two antimasque dishes in *Neptune's Triumph* (as well as the devil's people-feast in *Gypsies Metamorphosed*). Such aggressive art willing to tear into meaty topics was the other side of the oblique aesthetics that Jonson served up in his main masques.

Curtain Call: The Veil of Topicality

Once more, then, my catalogue of triviality: clock, jewel, orange, gifts (and children), miniatures, sonnets, banqueting houses, voids, masque scenery, "dressings," and so on. But now also ugly sailors, ruined Ormuz, decapitated heads, cannibals, "eating interest," and other things neither nice nor—it would seem—trivial. Has my argument come to this? Have I taken the stately home of trivial treasures that was aristocratic England in the Renaissance and, in the process of trying to understand its decorative fragments, managed to level the house to ruins? to its foundation? Have I, in other words, reduced ornamental aesthetics to the most absolute kind of "infrastructure": a view of the world as all a gigantic market? Or to expand the question in a way that retraces the course of this book: are we now to see all the Elizabethan ideal of gift and commonality reduced to Jacobean privacy; all Jacobean privacy in turn reduced to the void; and finally all void stuffs reduced to trade goods?

To the extent that my argument can appear reductive in this fashion—can seem to claim, for example, that Elizabethan culture changed irreversibly into its Jacobean successor, and that the gift was thus bought out lock, stock, and barrel by the market—precisely to that extent will it have failed. For my aim, I would like to think, has not been to hold a fire sale of culture transforming all ornamental trinkets into cash. Rather, the aim has been a more open-ended appreciation of the relation between aesthetics and history—one able to recognize that even history (economic or otherwise) has qualities of the fragmented, peripheral, trivial, and aesthetic that cannot be secured upon any absolute reality. It will be important, therefore, to close by appending a crucial qualification of this chapter's thesis.

Let me reflect on the overall nature of "topicality" as we have traced it in *Neptune's Triumph* and its context. On the one hand, any topical reading of an aesthetic work must include at some point a reductive view of what the work is "about." In such a view, for example, Jonson's masque is a naive allegory (nested within the text's own courtly allegory) whose significance is exhausted once we have lined up aesthetic ornaments with underlying economic phenomena in a one-to-one relation. Thus "silver feet" are "about" Spanish rials, "stars" about the *Star,* and so on through the inventory of adornment. But on the other hand, of course, allegory has more play in it than this. And so, too, does topicality. A fuller understanding of what an aesthetic work is "about," I suggest, would take one-to-one relations between aesthetics and history to be necessary ingredients but not the whole pie. Such relations are merely indicators. They mark out the possibility of a far more comprehensive sense of topicality—a notion of cultural relevance able to accommodate historical reality *and* aesthetic play. Topicality in this larger sense is not reductive because it is itself allegorical in a deep—indeed, bottomless—way.

Very crudely, we might think of the full topical structure of *Neptune's Triumph* in this fashion, as if setting up a double-column ledger book:

Jonson's masque:	Gift culture (main masque)	Market (antimasque)
Trade tracts:	Strangeness	Body
Contemporary trade:	Representation	Reality

A restricted or narrow view of topicality would do the accounts by looking down only one column at a time. To read the significance of the "dressings" passage in *Neptune's Triumph,* for example, we would run our finger from the gift ethos of the main masque over to the market world of the antimasque. Then, in a rapid descent of reductionism, we would immediately run our finger down the contexts in the right-hand column, detailing one-to-one correspondences as we went. With the joyful precision of a good accountant, we would see that the cannibalistic market world of Jonson's antimasques was equivalent to the economic "body" of the trade tracts and that both, on the bottom line, were displaced representations of the reality of money or goods in contemporary trade.

The larger view of topicality I have in mind would subsume such an accountant's appreciation of aesthetics within a less precise, purposely open-ended summing up. The key fact here is that while we certainly see displacement at work as we move down any single column from aesthetics and trade literature to "real" trade, so too we should see it at work on the horizontal level *between* columns. Or put another way, my whole conceit of a double-column ledger is illusional because it is in practice impossible to keep the columns distinct. Not only does the antimasque market in Jonson's work blur into main-masque gift culture, but "body"-logic in the trade tracts overlaps with "strange"-logic. Similarly, economic "reality" in actual trade overlaps with "representation." To give a full account of the topical significance of *Neptune's Triumph* in its context, therefore, is to line up not one-to-one correspondences between the masque, the trade tracts, and actual trade but the total *processes of displacement* (of what I have called "obliquity") constituting each level of text or context. Thus the important question is not, "What were individual aesthetic ornaments in Jonson's masque 'about'?" but, "What was the total process of displacement relating the main masque to the antimasque about?" What is the underlying ground, that is, of aesthetic displacement? My answer: aesthetic displacement in *Neptune's Triumph* was about the semi-aesthetic rhetoric of the trade tracts (more generally: of all kinds of contemporary economic discourse and gossip)— tracts *themselves* suspended in a process of displacement between "strange" and "bodily" manifestations of trade. And further, what in turn was this latter displacement in the trade literature about? What was *its* underlying ground? The answer must again be a further level of displacement. Obliquity in the trade tracts was about a transition or displacement in the contemporary market between representational instruments and traditional, "real" goods and monies—the "mystery," in sum, that we saw epitomized in East India trade.

It is when we reach the level of this "bottom line" in our quest for topicality that we realize that there *is* no bottom. For, what the "real" history of the East India trade showed, as we have seen, was that reality itself had the structure of bottomless allegory. Like a masque displacing trade goods into ornaments, East India trade displaced English home goods into Spanish rials, rials for Indian textiles, textiles for East Indian spices, and—at the reexportation stage closing the trade circle—East Indian (and Indian) wares for more Spanish rials to start the process all over again. Where was the ground of "reality" in this historical cosmos? When was money really money and not a commodity? Or again, at what point did a trade good become an actual or consumable "good" rather than merely a medium by which to acquire other goods? Of course, the heated controversy surrounding the East India trade was a particularly loud declaration of unstable displacements at work in historical "reality." But in quieter ways such instability affected other realms of historical experience as well. There is not a land, class, person, or other site of culture free of the transitions and tensions that unfix the security of absolute reality.

Instead of the "veil of allegory," then, perhaps we should speak of the "veil of topicality." As I previously suggested, topicality—seemingly the clearest case of history as "fact"—is never just about any one, grounded topic. It always includes within its historical base an irreducible displacement making topicality about some *other* topic perpetually about to appear over the horizon. If a masque of ornament—of fragmentary, peripheral, and trivial aesthetics—is "oblique," then that is because it was part of a world of topical history itself oblique, itself a veil of fragmentary, peripheral, and trivial truths concealing/revealing further "reality." Behind the veil of both art and history there is always another layer of reality, a more distant horizon of experience, a stranger veil of topicality.

To conclude, I would recapitulate my discussion in chapter 1 regarding the ornamental *kosmos* and Pater: history obeys the same logic of fragmented ornamentation as the aesthetic object. The task of historicist criticism, it seems to me, can only be accomplished by integrating aesthetics with history to this extent. In no other way can art be seen as a historical fact without either trivializing art in the service of respecting history or trivializing history out of respect for art. The solution is to trivialize *both* art and history—a strategy that will work if we make the commitment to *think* the "trivial," to unfold the logic of its practice of social ornament. By risking the trivializing of culture, perhaps we can recover a deeper, fuller sense of culture at the end of the wager—a culture that gives up only one of its traditional comforts, "wholeness," to gain much more than wholeness: a sense of the fragmentary part in its masque dance of attraction and repulsion with other parts.

Since the time is at hand for curtain calls, let me bring on stage for the last time the leading character in my argument about the trivial aesthetics of history: the aristocratic self. But it might be protested: where has the "self" been throughout this last chapter with its companies, corporations, and other collective entities of trade—its market transactions, in other words, necessarily involving more parties than the "self"? Do I merely reintroduce subjectivity here as a *deux ex machina* come down to bless the union of history and aesthetics? The answer, I would argue, is that throughout this chapter on trade the aristocratic self has been nowhere and everywhere.

To clarify this paradox, it will be useful to review the structure of this book, which has closed upon itself with the symmetry of an ornamental necklace or, perhaps, trade circle. After the introductory chapter, chapter 2 studied the Elizabethan gift ideal of commonality. Chapters 3 and 4 then witnessed the privatization of commonality, first within Elizabethan culture itself and then, more fully, in its Jacobean successor. These chapters saw the "self" retreat down endless corridors of secrecy toward such illusory repositories of privacy as a miniature, a sonnet, a banqueting house, or a masque arbor. Now, our final chapter completes the circle by at once pushing to an extreme the history of privatization *and,* in an uncanny way, returning us to the commonality upon which we began. We can take a lesson here from the fact that James the private king was also James the privateer seizing booty from the East India fleet. Ironically, we should realize, the world of the market was the culmination of aristocratic privatization. "Selfish" subjectivity, which found its medium of privacy in banqueting stuffs and other Eastern imports, expressed itself most secretly as the profit motive. Subjectivity, as it were, was a withdrawal into banqueting rooms that was also a financial withdrawal of funds from bankers. Yet, of course, if the global market was the true room of privacy, then that room was immensely larger than a banqueting room. The market that provided for the living of the private "self" as well as for all the ornaments expressive of that self's identity necessarily also returned the self to a common, shared cosmos—a cosmos of trade like an underworld version of the cosmos of gift exchange.

The necklace-structure of my book is thus complete. To tie the clasp, I will here leave Elizabeth and James behind to circle back to Charles. Once more, then, witness Charles's death or, as I called it, "Execution Masque." But witness that fatal performance in a way that leaves the question of whether we are really seeing subjectivity or commonality (alternatively: aesthetics or history) undecided, suspended, unwilling to reduce one to the other. We remember the clove-scented orange that Charles pocketed before stepping out of the Banqueting House onto his stage of death. Secreted on his person as if it were a last morsel of banqueting stuff, the orange could be the very emblem of his privacy. Yet, of course, the secret orange ended up in the hands of the executioner, who sold it for ten shillings. The emblem of privacy, it turns out, was really an emblem of the market.

But not quite. If the status of Charles's private "self" (with its supporting cast of gifts and ornaments) is undecidable, so too is that of the market universe around him. For the executioner, we recall, at first refused to sell the spiced orange when a gentleman approached and offered twenty shillings (twice the sum for which he later sold the prize). What was passing through the headsman's mind at this instant? Was he holding onto his new acquisition in hopes that it would appreciate in value? Or, for just a moment, did another kind of appreciation for the orange and its spice transcend all market values? Did the executioner, that is, find himself caught up in the very aura of transcendence that Charles invested in all his *gifts* (rather than goods): clock, jewel, or orange? Was the spiced orange a relic? Or was it instead a ware?

To cut my questions short: is it the aristocratic "self" that we see dramatized on that stage of death, or a prosperous transaction?

*   *   *

Envoy: Go forth, my book, which has been by me so long, a second self—fare well and prosper.

Notes

Chapter One

1. I use "aristocracy" generally throughout my book in the broad contemporary sense of "upper class," which extended from the *Nobilitas maior* of prince and titled peers down to the *Nobilitas minor* of knights, esquires, and armigerous gentry (see Sir Thomas Smith, *De Republica Anglorum: A Discourse on the Commonwealth of England* [1583], ed. L. Alston [Cambridge: Cambridge University Press, 1906], pp. 31–41). The extensive buying of titles and coats of arms under James, however, weakened this system of classification, especially at the lower stratum. For my purposes, I would thus not consider as aristocracy those in the swelling ranks of upper gentry who were not landed and who made their wealth from merchanting.

"Selfhood" and "self"—always to be read as if under quotes—are stand-ins for a number of related terms and concepts: individual, private, detached, subject. I say this even aware that "subject" will be perceived by some as the odd man out, implying an interpellated or socially determined—subjected—self opposed to any idea of individuality, privacy, or detachment. While my argument has been influenced by this position, as will become evident, I retain the use of "self" in order to foreground the need for thinking a whole, unified, and detached self (however unconscious or illusory) as much as for recognizing its actual or felt impossibility. Whatever term we adopt, we cannot get away from addressing the concept of self. The idea of selfhood is tied into the entire system of ideas from the late seventeenth century right up to the present that necessarily shapes the way we now perceive the Renaissance.

The question thus to address is: what form(s) did the notion of selfhood take in the English Renaissance, and what are the means by which we can recover that sense of selfhood given the historically intervening filters of interpretive and aesthetic assumptions through which we read the princely or poetic "I" in past texts? In addressing this question, I share the scene with many other interviewers of the past in current Renaissance scholarship. The consensus has been to speak to the self or

‚ubject through words like "subversion," "decentering," "discontinuity," and "conflict," which we might gather together under the generic name, "self-fashioning." See, for example, Catherine Belsey, *The Subject of Tragedy: Identity and Difference in Renaissance Drama* (London: Methuen, 1985); Francis Barker, *The Tremulous Private Body: Essays on Subjection* (London: Methuen, 1984); Jonathan Dollimore, *Radical Tragedy: Religion, Ideology and Power in the Drama of Shakespeare and His Contemporaries* (Chicago: University of Chicago Press, 1984); and the trigger for such studies of the self, Stephen Greenblatt, *Renaissance Self-Fashioning: From More to Shakespeare* (Chicago: University of Chicago Press, 1980). It is as if we seek to interview not so much "self" as an uncertainty about the nature of self—as if we seek to interview a ghost. What I offer as my particular approach to this common interview with the Renaissance ghostly self is the trivial.

2. Fernand Braudel, *The Mediterranean and the Mediterranean World in the Age of Philip II,* trans. Siân Reynolds, 2 vols. (New York: Harper & Row, 1972–73), 1:21.

3. Renaissance new historicism has so far avoided the issue of aestheticism out of the belief that the nature of aesthetics has been detachment from history. The result has often been the too-ready reading of textuality as historical (and of history as textual) according to a large scheme of power politics—the discourse of negotiation, subversion, and containment dominates—that blinds itself to the felt triviality of the "mere" or "ornamental" fact. Representative of the increasing suspicion of such abstracted, "transcendentalized" power is Carolyn Porter's "Are We Being Historical Yet?" *The South Atlantic Quarterly* 87 (Fall 1988): 764–65. Even when cultural historians embrace the aesthetic, under the rubric of "Marxist aesthetics," the concept (as if through predetermination) is absorbed into an abstract system: in this case, economics. Through a theory of the trivial, I mean to restate the interdependence of the aesthetic and the historical without reducing the former to a materialist scheme. Stephen Greenblatt, though clearly a proponent of power as a determining category in cultural studies, shows a beginning inquiry into this interdependence in his recent "Towards a Poetics of Culture," in *The New Historicism,* ed. H. Aram Veeser (New York: Routledge, Chapman and Hall, 1989), pp. 1–14.

4. Jeffrey Knapp, "Elizabethan Tobacco," *Representations* 21 (1988): 27–66. See also his forthcoming book, *An Empire Nowhere: England and America from "Utopia" to "The Tempest"* (Berkeley: University of California Press), which argues that the *island* nation of England developed an attachment to the negative ideal of a trifle world (whether represented by the smoke of imported tobacco or by the baubles traded with the New World Indians). His argument thus complements my own focus on the internal affairs of England: that is, on those social practices by which trivial or ornamental artifacts (including trade imports) constituted private and public subjectivity. For a more modern investment in the trivial, see Susan Willis, "Earthquake Kits: The Politics of the Trivial," *The South Atlantic Quarterly* 89 (Fall 1990): 761–85.

5. Walter Pater, *The Renaissance: Studies in Art and Poetry* (the 1893 text), ed. Donald L. Hill (Berkeley: University of California Press, 1980), p. 190.

6. The Death Warrant of Charles I, reproduced in *The Trial of Charles I: A Con-*

temporary Account Taken from the Memoirs of Sir Thomas Herbert and John Rushworth, ed. Roger Lockyer (London: Folio Society, 1959), p. 158.

7. Edmund Ludlow, *The Memoirs of Edmund Ludlow, Lieutenant-General of the Horse in the Army of the Commonwealth of England, 1625–1672,* ed. C. H. Firth, 2 vols. (Oxford, 1894), 1:218.

8. Sir Thomas Herbert, *Threnodia Carolina; or, Sir Thomas Herbert's Memoirs,* in *Memoirs of the Martyr King: Being a Detailed Record of the Last Two Years of the Reign of His Most Sacred Majesty King Charles the First (1646—1648–9),* ed. Allan Fea (London: John Lane, The Bodley Head, 1905), pp. 136–37. As Herbert's account indicates, Charles turned away most visitors, even his closest friends; see also Pauline Gregg, *King Charles I* (London: J. M. Dent, 1981; reprint, Berkeley: University of California Press, 1984), p. 443.

9. *Monday, 29th January, 1648 [old style]. A True relation of the King's speech to the Lady Elizabeth and the Duke of Gloucester, the day before his death;* an unlicensed broadsheet (which included an account by Elizabeth in her own hand) published March 24, 1649, in J. G. Muddiman, *Trial of King Charles the First* (Edinburgh: William Hodge, [1928]), pp. 137–38.

10. Herbert, *Memoirs,* p. 139; among the jewels given to Elizabeth were "two seals . . . wherein were two diamonds," *The Perfect Diurnal* (newsletter), 29th January–5th February, under the date of the 29th, in Muddiman, *Trial of King Charles the First,* p. 136.

11. Herbert, *Memoirs,* pp. 143–44. The contemporary newswriter John Dillingham, in his *Moderate Intelligencer,* mentions other parting gifts as well; he implies that they were given on the scaffold (Muddiman, *Trial of King Charles the First,* p. 152). For the gift given to Tomlinson, see *Cobbett's Complete Collection of State Trials . . . from the Earliest Period to the Present Time* [ed. W. Cobbett and T. B. Howell], 34 vols. (London, 1809–26), 5:1179.

12. Herbert, *Memoirs,* p. 143; for the handkerchief and scented orange, see Philip Howard, *The Royal Palaces* (Boston: Gambit, 1970), p. 118; also [Richard Brandon?], *The Confession of Richard Brandon the hangman (upon his death-bed) concerning his beheading his late Majesty. Printed in the year of the hang-man's downfall, 1649,* in Henry Ellis, ed., *Original Letters, Illustrative of English History . . . ,* 2nd series, 4 vols. (London, 1827), 3:341n.

13. Herbert, *Memoirs,* p. 145. The time of departure is given in Howard, *Royal Palaces,* p. 118.

14. Earl of Leicester, *Journal of the Earl of Leicester,* quoted in Edgar Sheppard, *The Old Royal Palace of Whitehall* (London: Longmans, Green, 1902), p. 207.

15. Howard, *Royal Palaces,* p. 118; also Muddiman, *Trial of King Charles the First,* p. 146.

16. Sheppard, *Old Royal Palace of Whitehall,* p. 206; Muddiman, *Trial of King Charles the First,* p. 146.

17. Herbert, *Memoirs,* p. 146.

18. Ibid., p. 146; Sheppard, *Old Royal Palace of Whitehall,* pp. 202–3; John Charlton, *The Banqueting House, Whitehall* (London: Her Majesty's Stationery Office, 1964), pp. 22, 46–47.

19. Howard, *Royal Palaces*, p. 119; the writer of a private letter, dated 30 January, also envisioned the scaffold as a "stage" (Muddiman, *Trial of King Charles the First*, p. 153).

20. Howard, *Royal Palaces*, p. 119; see also Muddiman, *Trial of King Charles the First*, p. 143.

21. The contemporary Leicester affirmed that the executioners were "disguised in saylors clothes with visards and peruques unknown" (*Journal*, quoted in Sheppard, *Old Royal Palace of Whitehall*, p. 211). However, Muddiman notes that the "close wollen frocks" of the disguises also resembled the garb of butchers (*Trial of King Charles the First*, p. 150). Much mystery and debate continues over the identity of the executioners. Ellis, for example, accepts the "confession" of the regular executioner, Richard Brandon (in Ellis, *Original Letters*, 3:341n). But Muddiman, who addresses at length the question "Who Beheaded the King?" considers the confession spurious (*Trial of King Charles the First*, pp. 167–83).

22. Howard, *Royal Palaces*, p. 119.

23. *King Charls, His Speech, Made upon the Scaffold at Whitehall-Gate Immediately before his execution On Tuesday the 30 of Jan. 1648 [old style] With a relation of the maner of his going to Execution*; the following excerpts are from Muddiman's reproduction of the printed speech (*Trial of King Charles the First*, pp. 260–64).

24. The night-cap is pictured in Fea, ed., *Memoirs of the Martyr King*, facing p. 204.

25. Herbert, *Memoirs*, p. 128; also Christopher Hibbert, *Charles I* (New York: Harper & Row, 1968), p. 255.

26. Philip Henry, eyewitness, quoted in Muddiman, *Trial of King Charles the First*, pp. 153–54.

27. Sir Roger Manley, quoted in Muddiman, *Trial of King Charles the First*, p. 155.

28. Brandon, in Ellis, *Original Letters*, 3:341n.

29. Isaac Disraeli, *Commentaries on the Life and Reign of Charles the First, King of England*, rev. ed., 2 vols. (London, 1851), 2:574n; Fea, ed., *Memoirs of the Martyr King*, p. 62 (for other "relics," see pp. 50–65). For the portrait done on hair, with crossbones and bloodied linen, see Hibbert, *Charles I*, p. 16 and facing page. For miniatures worked in hair, see Fea, pp. 61–62 (the miniature possessed by Oliver Cromwell's great-great-grandson[!] apparently attempted to capture the real-life Charles by working only the hair of the miniature with the King's own hair [p. 62]). Fea notes the talisman-like powers of such royal fragments: "so recently as 1860, a child was brought a long distance to touch these relics as a cure for the King's evil" (p. 60).

30. It has often been assumed that the traditional cry of "traitor" was raised by the second headsman; but, as Muddiman points out, the contemporary newswriter Dillingham "says that the man 'said nothing,' and of the eight other newsbook writers giving an account of the execution, not one contradicts him" (*Trial of King Charles the First*, p. 154). On Parliament's hasty and failed attempt to thwart the cry of successor, see John Bowle, *Charles I: A Biography* (London: Weidenfeld and Nicolson, 1975), pp. 332–33, 336.

31. Carol Thomas Neely, "Constructing the Subject: Feminist Practice and the

New Renaissance Discourses," *English Literary Renaissance* 18 (Winter 1988): 14; Robert N. Watson, review of *Shakespeare's "Rough Magic": Renaissance Essays in Honor of C. L. Barber,* ed. Peter Erickson and Coppélia Kahn, *Shakespeare Quarterly* 38 (Summer 1987): 251; Walter Cohen, "Political Criticism of Shakespeare," in *Shakespeare Reproduced: The Text in History and Ideology,* ed. Jean E. Howard and Marion F. O'Connor (New York: Methuen, 1987), p. 34; Edward Pechter, "The New Historicism and Its Discontents: Politicizing Renaissance Drama," *PMLA* 102 (May 1987): 301.

32. Indeed, opening abruptly with a fragmentary, paradigmatic passage is a common methodology of literary criticism, not just of the new historicism. The following collage of anecdotal openings from classicism to poststructuralism suggests the range of this practice: Horace's Foucaultian beginning to *On the Art of Poetry:* "Supposing a painter chose to put a human head on a horse's neck, or to spread feathers of various colours over the limbs of several different creatures, or to make what in the upper part is a beautiful woman tail off into a hideous fish, could you help laughing when he showed you his efforts? . . . " (in *Classical Literary Criticism: Aristotle, "On the Art of Poetry"; Horace, "On the Art of Poetry"; Longinus, "On the Sublime,"* trans. T. S. Dorsch [London: Penguin, 1965], p. 79); Sir Philip Sidney's opening anecdote to his *Apologie for Poetrie* about an advocate of horsemanship as an exemplum of speaking out for a particular vocation (in Sidney's case, poetry): "When the right vertuous *Edward Wotton* and I were at the Emperors Court together, wee gaue our selues to learne horsemanship of *Iohn Pietro Pugliano.* . . . " (in *Elizabethan Critical Essays,* ed. G. Gregory Smith, 2 vols. [London: Oxford University Press, 1904], 1:150); W. K. Wimsatt, Jr.'s, anecdotal opening to his chapter "The Chicago Critics: The Fallacy of the Neoclassic Species": "Back in the mid 1930's Professor R. S. Crane of Chicago had a conversion, from straight, neutral history of literature and ideas to literary criticism. . . ." (*The Verbal Icon: Studies in the Meaning of Poetry* [Lexington: University of Kentucky Press, 1954], p. 41); and Roland Barthes' compilation of what are essentially a series of short paradigms leading up to his concluding chapter in *Mythologies* (selected and translated by Annette Lavers [New York: Farrar, Straus and Giroux, Hill and Wang, 1972]).

33. See H. A. Taine, *History of English Literature,* trans. H. Van Laun, 2 vols. in 1 (New York, 1879). In considering the relevance of nineteenth-century thought to my thesis (and of eighteenth-century historiography below), I have been aided by conversations with Alan Liu.

34. Howard Dobin situates the new historicist anecdote specifically in the critical moment of deconstruction ("Introduction: In Defense of Anecdotes," in *Merlin's Disciples: Prophecy, Poetry, and Power in Renaissance England* [Stanford: Stanford University Press, 1990], pp. 1–18). Liu situates it as part of a larger postmodern cultural aesthetics of "detail" ("Local Transcendence: Cultural Criticism, Postmodernism, and the Romanticism of Detail," *Representations* 32 [Fall 1990]: 75–113). For a fascinating extension of the postmodern anecdote back into ancient historiography, see Joel Fineman, "The History of the Anecdote: Fiction and Fiction," in *New Historicism,* ed. Veeser, pp. 49–76.

35. Noel Henning Mayfield, *Puritans and Regicide: Presbyterian-Independent Dif-*

ferences over the Trial and Execution of Charles (I) Stuart (Lanham, Md.: University Press of America, 1988), pp. 4–7 and passim.

36. As Leah S. Marcus has noted in correspondence with me, this particular request (however sincere Charles's desire for remembrance) may have been his final display of scorn, since Puritans regarded prayers for the dead as popish.

37. William Shakespeare, *The Tragedy of Hamlet, Prince of Denmark,* in *Riverside Shakespeare,* ed. G. Blakemore Evans (Boston: Houghton Mifflin, 1974), 1.5.91. On Charles's reading of Shakespeare's plays, see Hibbert, *Charles I,* p. 255; also Hilaire Belloc, *Charles the First: King of England* (Philadelphia: J. B. Lippincott, 1933), p. 354. If the King had determined to plead his case at his trial, John Cook, solicitor general, had intended to denounce him for (among other crimes) "patronizing the stage and reading Shakespeare's plays" (Bowle, *Charles I: A Biography,* p. 325n). Significantly, in "unmasking" Charles's piety, John Milton likened him to another, more wily king in Shakespeare's plays, Richard III (*Eikonoklastes,* in *John Milton: Complete Poems and Major Prose,* ed. Merritt Y. Hughes [Indianapolis: Bobbs-Merrill, Odyssey, 1957], p. 792).

38. Shakespeare, *Hamlet,* 1.5.76.

39. On Charles's execution as theatricality (specifically, as tragedy and masque), see Nancy Klein Maguire, "The Theatrical Mask/Masque of Politics: The Case of Charles I," *Journal of British Studies* 28 (1989): 1–22.

40. Sir William Davenant, *Salmacida Spolia,* in *Inigo Jones: The Theatre of the Stuart Court, Including the Complete Designs for Productions at Court for the Most Part in the Collection of the Duke of Devonshire together with Their Texts and Historical Documentation,* ed. Stephen Orgel and Roy Strong, 2 vols. (Berkeley: University of California Press, 1973), 2:ll. 299, 294.

41. Davenant, *Salmacida Spolia,* 2:ll. 379, 360–61.

42. *The Perfect Weekly Account,* Jan. 31 to Feb. 7, 1648–49, under the date "Wednesday, January 31," in Ellis, ed., *Original Letters,* 3:346.

43. On Charles's control at the time of his execution and on the success of his kingly role, see also Maguire, "Theatrical Mask/Masque of Politics," pp. 20, 22. For an overview of the different interpretations of his injunction "Remember," see Sheppard, *Old Royal Palace of Whitehall,* pp. 219–22.

44. John Milton, quoted and translated from the Latin by William Harris, *An Historical and Critical Account of the Life and Writings of Charles I, King of Great Britain, After the Manner of Mr. Bayle. . . .* (London, 1758), p. 417.

45. Milton, *Eikonoklastes,* p. 784.

46. "When they had murdered him, such as desired to dip their handkerchiefes or other things in his blood, were admitted for monies. Others bought pieces of board which were dy'd with his blood, for which the soldiers took of some a shilling, of others half a crowne, more or lesse, according to the quality of the persons that sought it. But none without ready money" (the royalist *Mercurius Elencticus,* published on 7 February, 1649, quoted in Muddiman, *Trial of King Charles the First,* p. 155).

47. Naomi Schor, *Reading in Detail: Aesthetics and the Feminine* (New York: Methuen, 1987), p. 3. See also Liu, "Local Transcendence."

48. Steven Mullaney, *The Place of the Stage: License, Play, and Power in Renaissance England* (Chicago: University of Chicago Press, 1988), pp. xii, 60–87.

49. Herbert, *Memoirs,* p. 140.

50. Roy Strong, *The Cult of Elizabeth: Elizabethan Portraiture and Pageantry* (Berkeley: University of California Press, 1977), p. 179.

51. Thomas Carew, *Coelum Britannicum,* in *Inigo Jones,* ed. Orgel and Strong, 2:ll. 1072, 1074–80.

52. Strong, *Cult of Elizabeth,* p. 179.

53. Herbert reports that the earl of Lindsey received *Cassandra* (*Memoirs,* p. 144). For Charles's reading of *The Faerie Queene,* see Hibbert, *Charles I,* p. 250. An antimasque parody of the first episode of Spenser's book 1 appears in William Davenant's *Britannia Triumphans (1638):* echoing the Dwarf's plea to the St. George knight to flee the Wood of Error, a Dwarf in one of Davenant's antimasques calls out "Fly from this forest, squire! fly!" (in *Inigo Jones,* ed. Orgel and Strong, 2:l. 374).

54. Strong, *Cult of Elizabeth,* p. 183.

55. Charles indulged his love of the image by elaborately adorning his saint's medal (Sheppard, *Old Royal Palace of Whitehall,* p. 217). He thus took advantage of the rules of the Order, which "forbade the increased enrichment of the collar with stones and so forth" but "permitted the image to be enriched at the pleasure of the Knight" (pp. 217–18).

56. Angus Fletcher, *Allegory: The Theory of a Symbolic Mode* (Ithaca: Cornell University Press, 1964), pp. 108–46. See also Liu's application of Fletcher's concept to the convention of romantic tours (*Wordsworth: The Sense of History* [Stanford: Stanford University Press, 1989], especially pp. 10–11).

57. Stephen Orgel and Roy Strong, "Platonic Politics," in *Inigo Jones,* ed. Orgel and Strong, 1:51–52.

58. Ben Jonson, *Love's Triumph Through Callipolis,* in *Ben Jonson: The Complete Masques,* vol. 4 of *The Yale Ben Jonson,* ed. Stephen Orgel (New Haven: Yale University Press, 1969), ll. 69–93.

59. A cosmos of values was surely implied by the ornamental imagery of Charles's masques (a *Platonic* "sphere of Love," *royal* "lilies and roses," etc.). In actuality, however, the cosmos imaged by such ornament was a world-apart: small, restrictive, and removed. The larger realm of historicity—those social, political, *cultural* issues that pressed upon the minds of the royal couple and were pointed to by the antimasques—was closed off, hidden. In fact, one might question the extent to which any cosmic values were evoked by the purified masque. There is a strong sense in which Charles's masque ornament was cherished for its own sake. Its meaning lay in its ornamentality as ornamentality, and as such it replaced all historicity. This would explain why Charles did not see, or chose to gloss over, the criticisms that seem so blatant to us in James Shirley's *The Triumph of Peace* (1634). Charles demanded Shirley's masque as a show of support from the Inns of Court over the issue of ship-money. Such a demand would suggest that the King at some level acknowledged a larger, historical dimension to his ornamental masques. Yet Charles *would not see* the deeper politics of the resulting show. The antimasques of *The Triumph of Peace* clearly criticized Charles's court for granting monopolies to

"projectors" and even—when the antimasque of masque constructors (carpenter, painter, tailor, etc.) broke in, claiming their right as the real makers—for being essentially unreal (in *Inigo Jones,* ed. Orgel and Strong, vol. 2). The decorative imagery of Charles's masques *did* exclude "the real" in excluding the fullness of history. It was abstract, out of touch with his culture. But Charles did not acknowledge this criticism precisely because of the attitude being criticized. The ornament was the reality for him. It completely supplanted history. In the words of Orgel and Strong, for Charles "it is the image that is the political reality" ("Platonic Politics," 1:57).

60. Ben Jonson, *Chloridia,* in *Ben Jonson: The Complete Masques,* ed. Orgel, ll. 107–9.

61. David Harris Willson, *King James VI and I* (London: Jonathan Cape, 1956), pp. 378–79, 336. The bacchic antimasque of *Chloridia* may allude specifically to James's raucous entertainment at Theobalds (1606), satirically reported by Sir John Harington (in *The Progresses . . . of King James the First. . . . ,* ed. John Nichols, 4 vols. [London, 1828; reprint, New York: AMS, n.d.], 2:72–74).

62. Carew, *Coelum Britannicum,* 2:ll. 201–2, 253–56. See also Orgel and Strong, "Platonic Politics," 1:67.

63. Davenant, *Britannia Triumphans,* 2:ll. 8–12.

64. Pater, *Renaissance,* pp. xix–xxi.

65. Ibid., p. 188.

66. Ibid., p. xxi.

67. Carolyn Williams, *Transfigured World: Walter Pater's Aesthetic Historicism* (Ithaca: Cornell University Press, 1989), p. 59; see also pp. 1–77. This fine study unfortunately appeared too late for me fully to appreciate it in my own work. For Pater's historical "spirit," see, for example, *Renaissance,* p. xxiv.

Chapter Two

1. *The Faerie Queene,* 6.Proem.7; all Spenser quotations are from *The Works of Edmund Spenser: A Variorum Edition,* ed. Edwin Greenlaw et al., 11 vols. (Baltimore: Johns Hopkins University Press, 1932–57), hereafter *Spenser.*

2. The Graces were from classical times symbols of gift exchange. See, for example, Edgar Wind, *Pagan Mysteries in the Renaissance* (London: Faber and Faber, 1958), pp. 29–52. Spenser was well acquainted with this tradition, as is evident not only from the Mount Acidale episode of *The Faerie Queene* but also from E. K.'s gloss on the Graces in the April eclogue of *The Shepheardes Calender* (*Spenser,* 7:44). The classical mythology of the Graces can provide us only with a starting point, however. In order fully to recover the Renaissance aristocratic society constructed out of gift ornamentality (including the primitive suppressed within the decorum of civilized exchange), we will need to study anthropological models of prestation as well as contemporary practices of gift and child exchange.

3. The crucial divergence of Elizabethan exchange from the Kula will be evident when we arrive at Irish fosterage. In denouncing such a practice (uncannily like its own system of child exchange), England rejected the "primitiveness" of gift societies. That is, England could conceive of itself as a gift culture; but it could not

conceive of itself as anything other than a "civilized" gift culture that had to suppress the "primitive." Our paradigm of the Kula cannot, then, be a totalizing one. Nevertheless, even though I recognize disjunction between Kula and Elizabethan exchange, I *am* applying a model and thus could be seen to be violating my call for attention to the fragmentary, naked datum. The fact is that, as a critic seeking an interpretation, I need my explanatory models as much as the Renaissance needed its fiction of gift exchange or of detached selfhood in order to create a whole—in my case a whole "reading"—out of the fragmentary.

4. Bronislaw Malinowski, *Argonauts of the Western Pacific: An Account of Native Enterprise and Adventure in the Archipelagoes of Melanesian New Guinea* (1922; reprint, New York: Dutton, 1961), p. 93.

Argonauts is my primary source for the Kula ring. I recognize that Malinowski has suffered much criticism, especially for his macrotheory of "functionalism"— the idea that all cultural institutions function synchronically and derive ultimately from biological needs—a theory, critics argue, that fails to address problems of dysfunction and change (John Friedl, *Cultural Anthropology* [New York: Harper & Row, 1976], pp. 52–53). Malinowski's functionalism caused him to focus on traditional practices of the Kula and to neglect—although not to be unaware of —the impact of Western culture on tribal exchange, as well as to downplay the utilitarian trade that accompanied the ceremonial exchange of Kula ornaments (see especially Peter K. Lauer, "Amphlett Islands' Pottery Trade and Kula," *Mankind* [Sydney] 7 [June 1970]: 172–76; also Karl G. Heider, "Visiting Trade Institutions," *American Anthropologist*, n.s., 71 [June 1969]: 465; J. P. Singh Uberoi, *Politics of the Kula Ring: An Analysis of the Findings of Bronislaw Malinowski*, 2d ed. [Manchester: Manchester University Press, 1971], pp. 148–49; and Raymond Firth, "The Place of Malinowski in the History of Economic Anthropology," in *Man and Culture: An Evaluation of the Work of Bronislaw Malinowski*, ed. Raymond Firth [London: Routledge & Kegan Paul, 1957], p. 226). Despite these shortcomings, however, Malinowski's pioneering study of the Kula and related Trobriand exchange remains "the single best source" on primitive economies (George Dalton, "The Economic System," in *A Handbook of Method in Cultural Anthropology*, ed. Raoul Naroll and Ronald Cohen [Garden City, N.Y.: Natural History Press, 1970], p. 463n; reiterated by Firth, p. 216). Furthermore, the essentials of Malinowski's description of the Kula ring have been substantiated not only by R. F. Fortune (*Sorcerers of Dobu: The Social Anthropology of the Dobu Islanders of the Western Pacific*, rev. ed. [London: Routledge & Kegan Paul, 1963], pp. 200–234) but also by more recent contributors working to bring up to date the Malinowski-Fortune material (*The Kula: New Perspectives on Massim Exchange*, ed. Jerry W. Leach and Edmund Leach [Cambridge: Cambridge University Press, 1983], p. 533, as noted by Edmund Leach, even while warning against oversimplifying the Kula's multivariety to fit any such model, pp. 533–37). The circularity of Kula gift exchange has been further evidenced by observers of other gift systems (see Uberoi, pp. 1–2) and theorists of the gift, as my own study will illustrate. Malinowski's work simply provides the most extensive and integrated available model of the ring of gift.

5. Marcel Mauss, *The Gift: Forms and Functions of Exchange in Archaic Societies*, trans. Ian Cunnison (New York: Norton, 1967), pp. 10–12, 24, 37–41. See also Pierre

Bourdieu, *Outline of a Theory of Practice,* trans. Richard Rice (Cambridge: Cambridge University Press, 1977), pp. 4–8 and passim.

6. Malinowski, *Argonauts,* p. 97.

7. Holmes, quoted in Mauss, *Gift,* p. 31.

8. Elsdon Best, quoted in Marshall Sahlins, *Stone Age Economics* (Chicago: Aldine, Atherton, 1972), p. 158. Focusing on the Maori term, *"hau,"* Sahlins provides a comprehensive analysis of the native hunting customs (pp. 149–68). See also Mauss, *Gift,* pp. 8–10, as well as Lewis Hyde, *The Gift: Imagination and the Erotic Life of Property* (New York: Random House, 1983), pp. 18–19, and for circular giving, pp. 3–24.

9. Malinowski, *Argonauts,* p. 94; Mauss, *Gift,* p. 22.

10. Malinowski, *Argonauts,* p. 92. For Sahlins on Mauss and Hobbes, see *Stone Age Economics,* pp. 171–83; cf. Mauss, *Gift,* pp. 3, 11, 79–81. Heider observes that reciprocity between societies bridges a social "No-Man's-Land" that is "symbolically ambiguous, dangerous, and taboo" ("Visiting Trade Institutions," p. 463).

11. Mauss, *Gift,* p. 11. For the fears and antagonisms inherent in gift exchange, see Malinowski, *Argonauts,* pp. 97–99, 210, 359–60; Mauss, pp. 18, 26, 55–59, 61–62, and especially his treatment of the "agonistic" North American potlatch (a version of gift at the extreme opposite of the Kula, which we shall pursue in chapter 4), pp. 4–5, 31–45; and Peter M. Blau, *Exchange and Power in Social Life* (New York: John Wiley, 1964), pp. 106–12. Uberoi stresses the rivalries *within* rather than between groups of givers and receivers (*Politics of the Kula Ring,* pp. 97–98 and passim).

12. Mauss, *Gift,* p. 24; see also Malinowski, *Argonauts,* pp. 356–57. For ceremonial violence in the Kula, see Malinowski, especially pp. 340–49, 354, 486–87; and Mauss, pp. 23–24. See also Bourdieu, *Theory of Practice,* p. 198 n. 7.

13. Mauss, *Gift,* p. 21. Malinowski speculates that the giver disdainfully throws down his gift "to enhance the apparent value of the gift by showing what a wrench it is to give it away" (*Argonauts,* p. 353); at the same time, however, throwing down the gift—like the expression for the gift, "food left over" (Malinowski, *Argonauts,* p. 473)—serves to prove the giver's independence. "I do not need this gift," the action declares. On the gesture as a means of "role distance," see Blau, *Exchange and Power,* p. 111.

14. On the trust, generosity, and friendship in gift exchange, see Malinowski, *Argonauts,* pp. 85–86, 91–92; Mauss, *Gift,* pp. 10, 17–18, 22; Blau, *Exchange and Power,* pp. 94, 107–8; and Hyde, *Gift.* Hyde calls circular gift-giving "an act of social faith" (p. 16), which he compares to religious faith and opposes to post-Reformation usury (pp. 109–40). For a good comparison between social exchange and strict economic exchange, see Chris Gregory, "Kula Gift Exchange and Capitalist Commodity Exchange: A Comparison," in *Kula,* ed. Leach and Leach, pp. 103–17; also Blau, *Exchange and Power,* pp. 88–114; and Bourdieu, *Theory of Practice,* pp. 171–97.

15. Hyde, *Gift,* p. 25; and on the etymology of "generosity," p. 35n.

16. On the growth of Kula gifts, see Malinowski, *Argonauts,* pp. 89, 271, 504; and Mauss, *Gift,* pp. 22–24. Sahlins notes that *"Hau* and *mauri* [the talisman placed in the forest] as spiritual qualities are uniquely associated with fecundity" (*Stone Age Economics,* p. 167).

17. Hyde, *Gift,* p. 36.

18. Ibid., p. 44.

19. "Except for the honor accorded to generosity, the gift is no sacrifice of equality and never of liberty. The groups allied by exchange each retain their strength, if not the inclination to use it" (Sahlins, *Stone Age Economics*, p. 170); see also Mauss, *Gift*, and Uberoi, *Politics of the Kula Ring*.

20. Malinowski, *Argonauts*, p. 356. Hyde describes the gift circle as an expanded ego and discusses at length the nature of the "bond" created by gift exchange (*Gift*, pp. 16ff., 56–73).

21. On the confused merging of givers with their gifts, see Mauss, *Gift*, pp. 10, 11–12, 22–24. For the etymological link between "generous" and "gender," see the *OED*, which traces the roots of both words to the Latin *genus*. For the "total prestation" of gift exchange, see Mauss, *Gift*, pp. 1ff., and Malinowski, *Argonauts*, pp. 85–86, 167.

22. *The Oxford Dictionary of English Etymology*, s.v. "decorate"; also in this entry is "decorous," suggesting simultaneously the beautiful and the proper.

23. Recent trends in the law courts have acknowledged that art is not the same as utilitarian property ("The 'Moral Rights' of Artists," *Time*, 14 March, 1988, 59).

24. Malinowski, *Argonauts*, p. 96.

25. Bronislaw Malinowski, *Coral Gardens and Their Magic: A Study of the Methods of Tilling the Soil and of Agricultural Rites in the Trobriand Islands*, 2 vols. (London: George Allen & Unwin, 1935), 1:456; for criticisms that Malinowski in *Argonauts* underplayed utilitarian trade, see note 4 above.

26. Bourdieu, *Theory of Practice*, pp. 194–95.

27. "Fosterage" also refers to the custom among the nobility of sending babies to peasant wet nurses for the first 12 to 18 months. My concern, however, is with the *exchange* of children after nursing: with the custom among households of generally comparative social standing of giving and receiving minors for upbringing. On this kind of fosterage, in particular, see Grant McCracken (who focuses on hierarchical exchange), "The Exchange of Children in Tudor England: An Anthropological Phenomenon in Historical Perspective," *Journal of Family History* 8 (Winter 1983): 303–13; Lawrence Stone, *The Family, Sex and Marriage in England, 1500–1800* (New York: Harper & Row, 1977), pp. 6, 107–14; Ivy Pinchbeck and Margaret Hewitt, *Children in English Society*, 2 vols., *From Tudor Times to the Eighteenth Century* (Toronto: University of Toronto Press, 1969–73), 1:10–13, 25–33; Lloyd DeMause, ed. *The History of Childhood* (1974; reprint, New York: Harper & Row, 1975), pp. 32–34; and A. L. Rowse, *The Elizabethan Renaissance: The Life of the Society* (London: Macmillan, 1971), p. 97. On fosterage for girls, especially, see Pinchbeck and Hewitt; Dorothy Gardiner, *English Girlhood at School: A Study of Women's Education through Twelve Centuries* (London: Oxford University Press, 1929), pp. 114–29; Kenneth Charlton, *Education in Renaissance England* (Toronto: University of Toronto Press, 1965), pp. 209–10; and for the placing of girls in Queen Elizabeth's service, Violet A. Wilson, *Queen Elizabeth's Maids of Honour and Ladies of the Privy Chamber* (London: John Lane, The Bodley Head, 1922).

Although child exchange declined toward the latter half of the sixteenth century in favor of sending children away to school, the custom continued well into the seventeenth century, especially for girls, who could not attend university. Furthermore, the shift for boys from education in another household to education at school was less of a break than it might at first seem. At the same time that parents increasingly gave their boys to schools rather than to foster parents, the schools themselves—grammar and university—increasingly acted, as Stone observes, *"in loco parentis"* (p. 165). The result of this new parental school was "a childhood prolonged into an adolescence from which it was barely distinguished," declares Philippe Ariès, in *Centuries of Childhood: A Social History of Family Life*, trans. Robert Baldick (New York: Alfred A. Knopf, 1962), p. 262. (The expression "to matriculate," with its root in the Latin *matrix*, meaning "womb," takes on new meaning.) For the growing importance and parental character of schools, see Ariès, pp. 137–336. Also see Stone, pp. 3–218, where he traces a gradual development in the sixteenth century from the "Open Lineage Family" of child exchange to the "Restricted Patriarchal Nuclear Family" (dominating, he argues, from about 1580–1640), which continued to pass around children, but between closer relatives (p. 124) and with greater emphasis on the family, the state, and education.

28. Stone, *Family*, pp. 106, 116, 177; Ariès, *Centuries of Childhood*, p. 39. I have met with considerable resistance from some modern readers (seemingly in direct correlation to the number of children they have) to my claim that Renaissance children were considered trivial. The facts of the "mereness" of the child are on my side. Our resistance to accept them suggests the problematics of historical gaps. It is as if we, for whom children (especially in infancy) are so dear, cannot accept the Renaissance expendability of the child. The problem of breaching such a great historical divide is akin to the problem faced by the period itself of investing coherence in the detachedness of the child. The answer to both problems, I believe, lies in aesthetics.

29. For convenience I have located the families at their traditional family seats, although they owned and often resided at other places.

30. On Robert Tyrrwhit and Bridget Manners, see Wilson, *Queen Elizabeth's Maids of Honour*, pp. 194 and 187–88, respectively; on the Bedford children and Rutland's sister, see Claire Cross, *The Puritan Earl: The Life of Henry Hastings, Third Earl of Huntingdon, 1536–1595* (New York: St. Martin's, 1966), pp. 58–59; and on Mary Sidney, see James M. Osborn, *Young Philip Sidney, 1572–1577* (New Haven: Yale University Press, 1972), pp. 311–12. Claude Lévi-Strauss argues that the woman given in marriage, like Mary Sidney, is "the supreme gift" (*The Elementary Structures of Kinship*, trans. James Harle Bell, John Richard von Sturmer, and Rodney Needham, rev. ed. [Boston: Beacon, 1969], p. 65; see also pp. 52–68). Hyde also stresses the tie between women and gifts (*Gift*, pp. 93–108). In point of fact, each of our five families above is linked through the exchange of women, or marriage, as well as through the exchange of children. For example: the second earl of Rutland's widow (stepgrandmother to Bridget Manners) married Francis Russell, the second earl of Bedford; Anne Russell married Huntingdon's brother-in-law Ambrose Dudley; Sir Henry Sidney married the countess of Huntingdon's (and Dudley's) sister Mary; and Pembroke married Sidney's daughter Mary.

31. On the giving of Penelope Devereux, see William A. Ringler, Jr., ed., *The Poems of Sir Philip Sidney* (Oxford: Clarendon Press, 1962), pp. 437–38. On the placing of Bridget at court and Elizabeth's thank-you letter, see Wilson, *Queen*

Elizabeth's Maids of Honour, pp. 188–92. Wilson says Bridget was twelve at this time (p. 195); Pinchbeck and Hewitt say she was thirteen (*Children in English Society,* 1:11).

32. On Anne Russell, see *Lives of Lady Anne Clifford countess of Dorset, Pembroke and Montgomery (1590–1676) and of her parents, summarized by herself,* ed. J. P. Gilson (London: Hazell, Watson and Viney, 1916), p. 19. On George Clifford, see G. C. Williamson, *George, Third Earl of Cumberland (1558–1605), His Life and His Voyages: A Study from Original Documents* (Cambridge: Cambridge University Press, 1920), pp. 2–6. On the granddaughters of Bedford (daughters of Lady Elizabeth Russell), see Wilson, *Queen Elizabeth's Maids of Honour,* p. 219.

33. Elizabeth, speaking to her 1563 Parliament, quoted in J. E. Neale, *Elizabeth I and Her Parliaments, 1559–1581,* 2 vols. (London: Jonathan Cape, 1953), 1:109.

34. On Rutland's motive in obtaining the Tyrrwhit wardship, see Wilson, *Queen Elizabeth's Maids of Honour,* p. 194. Lawrence Stone implies the Queen's motives in the case of the Clifford wardship (*The Crisis of the Aristocracy, 1558–1641* [Oxford: Clarendon Press, 1965], p. 252).

35. Williamson, *George, Third Earl of Cumberland,* p. 12.

36. The most comprehensive study of the Court of Wards is Joel Hurstfield's *The Queen's Wards: Wardship and Marriage under Elizabeth I* (Cambridge: Harvard University Press, 1958). Hurstfield's analyses of Burghley and Cecil, Burghley's son and successor in the Court of Wards, are particularly suggestive (see especially pp. 260–82, 297–325, 329–52). Whereas Burghley was firmly allied to the ancient system of gift, Hurstfield implies, Cecil looked forward to a modern market economy: he strove to raise the official price of wardships, for instance, and, with the death of Elizabeth in 1603, forbade his officers to accept gifts (pp. 310–14). (That too-low fees in the granting of wardships during Burghley's term of office actually nurtured the seeds of corruption in the 90s—corruption that burgeoned during James's reign—is one of the ironies of a gift system hovering on the threshold of a market economy.) For Burghley as the concerned and generous guardian of aristocratic crown wards, see Hurstfield, pp. 241–59; also Rowse, *Elizabethan Renaissance,* p. 97.

37. For the giving of Lady Hoby as a child to the Huntingdons, see *Diary of Lady Margaret Hoby, 1599–1605,* ed. Dorothy M. Meads (London: George Routledge & Sons, 1930), p. 5; for the reported offers of children to Hoby, in turn, see pp. 166 and 202; Sydenham is quoted in Stone, *Family,* pp. 111–12; for Carre, see Gardiner, *English Girlhood at School,* p. 118.

38. Pinchbeck and Hewitt, *Children in English Society,* 1:27.

39. Wilson, *Queen Elizabeth's Maids of Honour,* pp. 187–88; Cross, *Puritan Earl,* p. 59.

40. Quoted in Osborn, *Young Philip Sidney,* pp. 311–12.

41. Wilson, *Queen Elizabeth's Maids of Honour,* p. 41; dated on p. 38. For the special value attached to Elizabeth's New Year's gifts, see Peter Burke, "Renaissance Jewels in Their Social Setting," and Janet Arnold, "Sweet England's Jewels" (both in *Princely Magnificence: Court Jewels of the Renaissance, 1500–1630* [London: Debrett's Peerage, in association with the Victoria & Albert Museum, 1980], pp. 10–11 and 37–40, respectively). Even when sums of gold were given, the exchange belied Paul Johnson's complaint of the "mechanical and mercenary" nature of New Year's giv-

ing. "Members of the nobility and senior officials," Johnson observes, "presented her [the Queen] with purses of gold, according to their wealth and station; in return they got carefully graded quantities of silver-gilt plate" (*Elizabeth I* [New York: Holt, Rinehart, and Winston, 1974], pp. 210, 209). There does appear to have been understood guidelines for the amounts given: earls gave around £20, lords around £10, and so on. A quick glance at the gift lists, however, reveals that the sums varied considerably from person to person and year to year (see the selected lists in John Nichols, *The Progresses . . . of Queen Elizabeth . . .* , 3 vols. [London, 1823; reprint, New York: Burt Franklin (1963)]). Amounts may have been "carefully graded," but, as in the Kula ring, the exact quantities of the gifts and the countergifts were left up to the givers.

   In fact, the exchange of New Year's gifts observed all the gift conventions noted in the Kula ring: not only undiscussed values but also a delay between the initial gift (given in the morning) and its repayment (in the afternoon), as well as, of course, the primary ethical obligations to give, to receive, and to repay. The occasion thus fostered, in the spirit of gift, feelings of generosity, trust, and good fellowship that cemented a social bond—even while reinforcing a political hierarchy of power—between the ruler and her court.

   42. Louis Adrian Montrose touches on a number of these gift-giving occasions, including New Year's, in establishing the sociopolitical context of a performance for the Queen ("Gifts and Reasons: The Contexts of Peele's *Araygnement of Paris*," *ELH* 47 [Fall 1980]: esp. 447–57). For a discussion of giving gifts to Elizabeth on her royal progresses, see also his "'Eliza, Queene of shepheardes,' and the Pastoral of Power" (*English Literary Renaissance* 10 [Spring 1980]: 159–60, 176, 178). In this latter article, Montrose observes that the mingling of images and ideas in such prestations to the Queen is akin to pastoral poetry as exemplified by Spenser's *The Shepheardes Calender.* I hope further to explore the connections between Elizabethan gifts and poetry. While Montrose underscores the idea of reciprocity, however, I am concerned primarily with the circulation of gifts, like the circulation of Elizabeth herself on one of her progresses: that is, with the *narrative* of exchange.

   43. See McCracken, "Exchange of Children in Tudor England," p. 310. Burke draws an explicit parallel between Renaissance patronage and the Kula gift ring ("Renaissance Jewels in Their Social Setting," pp. 9–10).

   44. A full description of Sidney's gift was entered in the New Year's gift-list, 1581: "a jeuell of golde, being a whippe, garnished with small diamondes in foure rowes and cordes of small seede pearle" (Nichols, *Progresses . . . of Queen Elizabeth,* 2:301). The gift alluded to Sidney's recent opposition to the Anjou marriage proposal (Ringler, ed., *Poems of Sir Philip Sidney,* p. 440). In the gift of the little jeweled whip, however, hostilities have been suppressed, translated into an aesthetically pleasing ornament expressive of "civilized" exchange.

   45. Greenblatt similarly argues that the forceful oppression of an alien Other, such as the "barbaric" Irish, was necessary in the sixteenth century to fashion the identity of English civility (*Renaissance Self-Fashioning,* especially pp. 184–88). He sees Spenser figuring this act of power in *The Faerie Queene,* particularly in the Bower of Bliss (pp. 169–92); in my own view, as the following analysis will illustrate,

Spenser rewrites such violence in his poetry through the civilizing fiction of gifts—an ideality that suppresses the very fact of force.

46. Sir John Davies, *A Discovery of the True Causes Why Ireland Was Never Entirely Subdued . . . until the Beginning of His Majesty's Happy Reign,* in *Ireland under Elizabeth and James the First: Described by Edmund Spenser, by Sir John Davies, . . . and by Fynes Moryson . . .* , ed. Henry Morley (London, 1890), p. 296. A selection from *Discovery* and many other contemporary works on Ireland can be found in *Elizabethan Ireland: A Selection of Writings by Elizabethan Writers on Ireland,* ed. James P. Myers, Jr. (Hamden, Conn.: Shoe String, Archon, 1983).

47. *Ancient Laws of Ireland,* ed. W. Neilson Hancock et al., 6 vols. (Dublin, 1865–1901), 2:xliii–xlvi, 146–93. We cannot be sure to what extent Elizabethan Irish actually observed these ancient native laws. Though Brehon law continued to be assiduously studied in the sixteenth century, there was an evident gap between theory and practice (Kenneth Nicholls, *Gaelic and Gaelicised Ireland in the Middle Ages* [Dublin: Gill & Macmillan, 1972], p. 44). The Brehon laws of fosterage may well have had considerable lasting influence, however, since evidence shows that the great prominence they gave to fosterage extended into later, Elizabethan practice. On Irish fosterage, see Nicholls, p. 79; P. W. Joyce, *A Social History of Ancient Ireland . . . ,* 2 vols. (London: Longmans, Green, 1903), 2:14–18; Myles Dillon and Nora K. Chadwick, *The Celtic Realms* (New York: New American Library, 1967), pp. 100–101; and David Beers Quinn, *The Elizabethans and the Irish* (Ithaca: Cornell University Press, 1966), pp. 84–85.

48. *Ancient Laws of Ireland,* ed. Hancock et al., 2:153, 163.

49. Ibid., 2:xlv, 191–93; Joyce, *Social History of Ancient Ireland,* 2:16.

50. Edmund Campion, *A Historie of Ireland (1571)* (New York: Scholars, 1940), p. 14 ("childes portion": a legacy equal to that given their own children); Richard Stanihurst, *On Ireland's Past,* in Colm Lennon, *Richard Stanihurst the Dubliner, 1547–1618: A Biography with a Stanihurst Text, On Ireland's Past* (Blackrock, County Dublin: Irish Academic, 1981), p. 157; Campion, p. 19; Davies, *Discovery,* p. 296. On the sacred nature of foster ties, see Joyce, *Social History of Ancient Ireland,* 2:17.

51. *The itinerary of Fynes Moryson,* selections from Moryson's 1617 travel account, in C. Litton Falkiner, *Illustrations of Irish History and Topography, Mainly of the Seventeenth Century* (London: Longmans, Green, 1904), pp. 318, 244.

52. Nicholls, *Gaelic and Gaelicised Ireland,* p. 79.

53. Campion declares "that commonly five hundreth kyne and better are given in reward to winne a noble mans childe to foster" (*Historie of Ireland,* p. 14). For the parallel Kula practice, see Malinowski, *Argonauts,* pp. 98–99; and Mauss, *Gift,* pp. 25–26. For multiple Irish foster parents, see Joyce, *Social History of Ancient Ireland,* 2:16–17.

54. The same could be said about the very un-English system of inheritance behind Irish child exchange; it intensified the fosterage experience. The English generally observed the law of primogeniture in inheritance. The cultural bonds created by English fosterage thus lacked intensity to the extent that they did not significantly influence the transfer of land and power (excepting perhaps the three-party exchange of wardship, wherein the court or guardian had a say in the ward's

marriage, and hence certain control over the alliance of estates). But the Irish did not observe primogeniture. The Irish gathered together in communities or "septs," usually bound to a superior sept, but each governed by an extended family which owned land in common and from which a leader would be chosen on the basis of status and power rather than priority of birth. Such a system of inheritance intensified the fosterage experience because the alliances consolidated by Irish fosterage both within and between septs could directly determine territorial rule. For the Irish system of land tenure and rule, see Nicholls, *Gaelic and Gaelicised Ireland,* especially pp. 21–30, 56–67; also G. A. Hayes-McCoy, "Gaelic Society in Ireland in the late Sixteenth Century," *Historical Studies* 4 (October 1963): 45–61.

55. Spenser, *A View of the Present State of Ireland* (*Spenser,* 10:39–231, especially 117, 119, 209). On the fear of absorption, see also Greenblatt, *Renaissance Self-Fashioning,* pp. 184–87.

56. Nicholas P. Canny, *The Elizabethan Conquest of Ireland: A Pattern Established, 1565–76* (Hassocks, Sussex: Harvester, 1976), p. 27. Despite repeated statutes against fostering with the Irish, the practice continued even after the "conquest" of Ireland in 1603 (Quinn, *Elizabethans and the Irish,* p. 84).

57. Canny, *Elizabethan Conquest of Ireland,* pp. 20–28; see also Nicholls, *Gaelic and Gaelicised Ireland,* pp. 3–5, 12–20.

58. *Plantation of Ulster: A Letter from Sir John Davies to Robert Earl of Shrewsbury, concerning the State of Ireland* (1610), in *Ireland under Elizabeth and James the First,* ed. Morley, p. 386. For English attitudes to the Irish, see also Quinn, *Elizabethans and the Irish,* especially pp. 7–13; and *Elizabethan Ireland,* ed. Myers, pp. 15–16.

59. Barnabe Rich, Dedication to *A short svrvey of Ireland. . . . With a description. . . . No lesse necessarie and needfull to be respected by the English, then requisite and behoouefull to be reformed in the Irish* (1609), sig. A2r.

60. *Spenser,* 10:167. On fostering Irish boys in England, including O'Neill, see Quinn, *Elizabethans and the Irish,* pp. 154–55. On Thomas Butler, tenth earl of Ormond (or Ormonde), see the *Dictionary of National Biography,* and Canny, *Elizabethan Conquest of Ireland,* p. 3.

61. Quoted in Quinn, *Elizabethans and the Irish,* p. 156. Quinn notes the prominence of Irish suitors at Elizabeth's court (pp. 155–56).

62. Spenser, *View* (*Spenser,* 10:212). One should also recognize that, though the propagandists advocated war, there was also a strong contingent of English Catholics who were pro-Irish.

63. Spenser, *View* (*Spenser,* 10:214–15). With new individual identity would come the individual ownership of land, held according to "English lawe"–including the law of primogeniture—under the sovereignty of the crown (pp. 207–9).

64. As I earlier intimated, a different view of such ideal poetic fictions as the Garden of Adonis would bring the boar out from under the hill. But I delay such a view for later in my book, where the boar will appear in the guise of "trade," the true threat to the ideal of the gift.

65. "A Letter of the Authors expounding his whole intention . . . to the Reader . . ." (*Spenser,* 1:167).

66. *OED,* s.v. "betake"; Emile Benveniste (*Indo-European Language and Society,* summaries, table and index by Jean Lallot; trans. by Elizabeth Palmer [London:

Faber & Faber, 1973], p. 66) notes that "in Indo-European the notions 'to give' and 'to take' converged, as it were, in gesture (cf. English *to take to*)."

67. See Thomas P. Roche, Jr., *The Kindly Flame: A Study of the Third and Fourth Books of Spenser's "Faerie Queene"* (Princeton: Princeton University Press, 1964), pp. 125–28; also Donald Cheney, *Spenser's Image of Nature: Wild Man and Shepherd in "The Faerie Queene"* (New Haven: Yale University Press, 1966), pp. 138–39.

68. Mauss, *Gift*, p. 24. See also note 12 above.

69. Sir Philip Sidney, *An Apologie for Poetrie*, in *Elizabethan Critical Essays*, ed. Smith, 1:157.

70. Although even here, as Robert Ellrodt argues, "formes," linked with "hous" and "aspects," also conjures up astrological associations, perhaps passed on by the earlier reference in stanza 2 to "th'*Horoscope*" of Belphoebe's "natiuitee" (*Neoplatonism in the Poetry of Spenser* [Geneva: Librairie E. Droz, 1960], p. 90).

71. See Harry Berger, Jr., "Spenser's Gardens of Adonis: Force and Form in the Renaissance Imagination," *University of Toronto Quarterly*, 30 (January 1961): 137.

72. Though proposing a single philosophical model for the Garden of Adonis—the Neoplatonic idea of "seminal reasons"—James Nohrnberg reveals a keen sensibility to the Garden's processes of "reciprocity": "a Garden of Forms must enjoy a liminal relation with a Chaos of Matter" (*The Analogy of "The Faerie Queene"* [Princeton: Princeton University Press, 1976], p. 555). On the confusion of the clothing image, and of form and matter, see, for example, Berger, "Spenser's Gardens of Adonis," pp. 137–38; William Nelson, *The Poetry of Edmund Spenser: A Study* (New York: Columbia University Press, 1963), p. 216; and Cheney, *Spenser's Image of Nature*, pp. 127–28.

73. For the anatomical geography of the Garden of Adonis, see Nohrnberg, *Analogy of "The Faerie Queene,"* pp. 525–33, and John Erskine Hankins, *Source and Meaning in Spenser's Allegory: A Study of "The Faerie Queene"* (Oxford: Clarendon Press, 1971), pp. 239–55, as well as Hankins's note to earlier critics, p. 240, n. 2.

74. Among those critics who see Venus as form are John Upton (*Spenser*, 3:260); and, more recently, C. S. Lewis (*Studies in Medieval and Renaissance Literature*, collected by Walter Hooper [Cambridge: Cambridge University Press, 1966], p. 155); and Humphrey Tonkin, "Spenser's Garden of Adonis and Britomart's Quest," *PMLA* 88 (May 1973): 412. On mother/*mater*/*materia*, see Roche, *Kindly Flame*, p. 125.

Among those who see Adonis as form are Roche, p. 123; William C. Johnson ("'God' as Structure in Spenser's Garden of Adonis," *English Studies* 63 [August 1982]: 305); and Judith C. Ramsay ("The Garden of Adonis and the Garden of Forms," *University of Toronto Quarterly* 35 [January 1966]: 191ff.). On Adonis's passivity, see Tonkin, p. 412, and Cheney, *Spenser's Image of Nature*, p. 137. Berger points out the verbal links between Adonis and the matter of Chaos ("Spenser's Gardens of Adonis," pp. 142–43), and Ramsay notes his associations with death (p. 202). For Lewis on Adonis's un-solar character, see p. 156.

75. Such transcendent cultural wholeness out of ornamental exchange, we should add, fulfills the political strategy by which Elizabeth sought to rise above her unwedded state. The Garden, that is, brings to fruition Elizabeth's verbal habit of wedding herself to herself by exchanging genders and roles (as in calling herself

"Prince"); see Leah S. Marcus, *Puzzling Shakespeare: Local Reading and Its Discontents* (Berkeley: University of California Press, 1988), pp. 53–66; also Montrose, "'Eliza, Queene of shepheardes,'" especially p. 159. The resultant image of the Queen is sexually, monarchically, and transcendentally "whole": Elizabeth is both participant and central "mother" in an Anglo-Irish circle of child exchange without herself ever having to marry and bear children.

76. In conversation with me A. Kent Hieatt has pointed out that the give-and-take between the good Genius and the outside world that occurs at the threshold to the Garden of Adonis can be directly contrasted with the rejected gift relationship between the bad Genius and Guyon at the threshold to Acrasia's garden: when Genius offers Guyon his "bowle of wine," Guyon overthrows it "disdainfully" (2.12.49).

77. Sidney, *Apologie*, 1:157; in "Spenser's Gardens of Adonis," Berger also argues that the narrative enacts the creative processes of the poet's mind or imagination. Many of Berger's views are consonant with my own—especially his emphasis on poetic form achieved in, and through, a process that recognizes violence—although I place more emphasis on the subsuming of force by form (the circular form of gift exchange) and, as we will see, on the poet giving himself up to this process.

78. On the deadly stasis of this artifice, see Berger, "Spenser's Gardens of Adonis," p. 141; and Ramsay, "The Garden of Adonis and the Garden of Forms," pp. 201–2. On the associations of "*Amaranthus*" with Sidney (as well as with Thomas Watson's *Amyntas*), see A. C. Hamilton, ed., *The Faerie Queene* (London: Longman, 1977), p. 363n.

79. Berger, "Spenser's Gardens of Adonis," p. 143.

80. Hyde, *Gift*, p. 53.

81. Hamilton, ed., *The Faerie Queene*, p. 347n.

82. The most striking example is Jonathan Goldberg's *Endlesse Worke: Spenser and the Structures of Discourse* (Baltimore: Johns Hopkins University Press, 1981). See also Patricia A. Parker, *Inescapable Romance: Studies in the Poetics of a Mode* (Princeton: Princeton University Press, 1979), pp. 3–15, 54–113; Maureen Quilligan, *The Language of Allegory: Defining the Genre* (Ithaca: Cornell University Press, 1979), especially pp. 224–61; and, on the Garden of Adonis, in particular, Robert A. Brinkley, "Spenser's Gardens of Adonis: The Nature of Infinity," *Massachusetts Studies in English* 4, no. 4 (1974): 3–16.

83. I draw for my vocabulary here from Tonkin, who argues that Spenser unites in Britomart both line (the quest, linear and severe) and circle (the garden, cyclical and kinetic), and so "takes the basic paradox of romantic chivalry—the martial pursuit of love—a stage further" ("Spenser's Garden of Adonis and Britomart's Quest," p. 408; see also pp. 413–16).

84. Dedication to the 1596 *Faerie Queene*, (*Spenser*, vol. 1).

85. On giving of books, see Natalie Zemon Davis, "Beyond the Market: Books as Gifts in Sixteenth-Century France," *Transactions of the Royal Historical Society*, 5th ser., 33 (1983): 69–88.

86. Spenser, "To His Booke," ll. 1–6, prefacing *The Shepheardes Calender* (*Spenser*, vol. 7); Sir Philip Sidney, Dedication to *The Countesse of Pembroke's Ar-*

cadia, facsimile edition, intr. Carl Dennis (Ohio: Kent State University Press, 1970), sig. A3v&r (and appearing in all subsequent editions of the poem); Henry Constable, "To the Gentlemen Readers," prefacing *Diana. The praises of his Mistres, in certaine sweete Sonnets*, in *The Poems of Henry Constable*, ed. Joan Grundy (Liverpool: Liverpool University Press, 1960), p. 110; R. L. [Richard Lynche?], Dedication to *Diella, certaine sonnets, adioyned to the amorous poeme of Dom Diego and Gineura*, sig. A4v&r; Thomas Lodge, "The Induction" to *Phillis: Honored with Pastoral Sonnets, Elegies, and Amorous Delights*, in *Elizabethan Sonnet-Cycles*, ed. Martha Foote Crow, 4 vols. (London, 1896–98), 1:12.

87. Samuel Daniel, *A Defence of Ryme, Against a Pamphlet entituled: 'Obseruations in the Art of English Poesie.'* . . . , in *Elizabethan Critical Essays*, ed. Smith, 2:356; Robert Greene, Dedication to *Francescos Fortunes: Or, The second part of Greenes Neuer too late.* . . . , in *The Life and Complete Works in Prose and Verse of Robert Greene*, ed. Rev. Alexander B. Grosart, 15 vols. (London, 1881–86), 8:115, 117 (see also his valedictory to Burnaby in *A Qvip For an Vpstart Courtier: Or, A quaint dispute betvveen Veluet breeches and Cloth-breeches.* . . . [1592]: "Your duetifull adopted sonne" [*Works*, 11:210]).

88. Quoted in Bernard H. Newdigate, *Michael Drayton and His Circle*, corr. ed. (1941; reprint, Oxford: Basil Blackwell, 1961), pp. 74–75. On the early giving of Drayton to Goodere, see pp. 32–33.

89. Seventeen in subsequent printings.

90. Edwin Haviland Miller, *The Professional Writer in Elizabethan England: A Study of Nondramatic Literature* (Cambridge: Harvard University Press, 1959), p. 120. Multiple dedications, which appeared increasingly in the 1590s, point to what James C. Scott has called "the growing role of marketplace criteria" within the patronage of the gift ("Proto-Corruption in Early Stuart England," in *Comparative Political Corruption* [Englewood Cliffs, N.J.: Prentice-Hall, 1972], p. 45).

91. Indeed, observing the ethic of gift, Spenser echoed his contemporaries' fear of appearing to give poetry "for gaine and commoditie" (1579 Letter to Harvey [*Spenser*, 10:5]). He also imitated their vague way of referring to past or expected "furtheraunce," eschewing open requests for weighed amounts (Dedicatory Sonnet to the earl of Essex [*Spenser*, 3:192]).

92. *Spenser*, 3:194.

93. 1579 Letter (*Spenser*, 10:6). Like Kula gift partners, Spenser also at times complained of insufficient return gifts. Some of his more vocal protests can be found in the October eclogue of *The Shepheardes Calender*, ll. 7–18, 31–36 (*Spenser*, vol. 7), as well as in *Mother Hubberds Tale* (1591), ll. 895–908, and *Prothalamion* (1596), ll. 5–9 (both in *Spenser*, vol. 8). For the Kula complement to this, see Malinowski, *Argonauts*, pp. 97–98, 359.

94. Though a late expression of such belief and one, to an extent, undercut by obvious profit motives (despite protests to the contrary), the printers of the first folio offered the "trifles" of Shakespeare's plays as a "present" to the earls of Pembroke and Montgomery in the spirit of life-giving exchange: "We haue but collected them, and done an office to the dead, to procure his Orphanes, Guardians; vvithout ambition either of selfe-profit, or fame: onely to keepe the memory of so

worthy a Friend, & Fellow aliue, as was our SHAKESPEARE, by humble offer of his playes, to your most noble patronage" ("The Epistle Dedicatorie," reproduced in *Riverside Shakespeare,* ed. Evans, pp. 61–62).

95. Spenser, 3:194, 191.

96. See Mauss, *Gift,* p. 34.

97. See Alastair Fowler, *Triumphal Forms: Structural Patterns in Elizabethan Poetry* (Cambridge: Cambridge University Press, 1970), pp. 48–49.

98. On the evocations of sonnet conventions in the masque authored by Busirane, which emerges from the innermost room, see Roche, *Kindly Flame,* p. 78.

99. A. C. Hamilton, *The Structure of Allegory in the "Faerie Queene"* (Oxford: Oxford University Press, 1961; reprint, 1964), p. 182.

Chapter Three

1. *Memoirs of Sir James Melville of Halhill, 1535–1617,* ed. A. Francis Steuart (New York: E. P. Dutton, 1930), pp. 92–94.

2. Melville, *Memoirs,* p. 94.

3. Isaac Disraeli, *Curiosities of Literature,* 6th ed., 3 vols. (London, 1817), 1:491.

4. Marville, quoted in Disraeli, *Curiosities,* 1:485; Sir John Harington, *Nugae Antiquae; Being a Miscellaneous Collection of Original Papers in Prose and Verse. Written in the Reigns of Henry VIII, Queen Mary, Elizabeth, King James, Etc.,* ed. Henry Harington, Jr., 3 vols. (London, 1769–79), 2:217.

5. Richard Sennett, *The Fall of Public Man* (New York: Alfred A. Knopf, 1977; reprint, New York: Random House, Vintage, 1978).

6. Since the sixteenth century loosely applied the term *sonnet* to any small or "short" poem (George Gascoigne, "Certayne notes of Instruction concerning the making of verse or ryme in English, Written at the request of Master *Edouardo Donati*" [1575], in *Elizabethan Critical Essays,* ed. Smith, 1:55), I shall include in my literary discussion general reference to love lyrics; my goal, however, is the formal fourteen-line sonnet that increasingly figured in the 1590s. For Linda Bradley Salamon's comparison of miniature and sonnet, see "The Art of Nicholas Hilliard," in *Nicholas Hilliard's Art of Limning: A New Edition of A Treatise Concerning the Arte of Limning, Writ by N. Hilliard,* transcription by Arthur F. Kinney, commentary and apparatus by Salamon (Boston: Northeastern University Press, 1983), pp. 104–6. Numerous art historians of miniatures have made passing reference to sonnets as well: for example, Roy Strong, "From Manuscript to Miniature," in *The English Miniature,* ed. John Murdoch et al. (New Haven: Yale University Press, 1981), p. 73; John Pope-Hennessy, *A Lecture on Nicholas Hilliard* (London: Home and Van Thal, 1949), p. 19; and Carl Winter, *Elizabethan Miniatures* (1943; reprint, Harmondsworth, Middlesex: Penguin, 1949), p. 8.

In addition to the above works, my study of miniatures is especially endebted to: Nicholas Hilliard, *A Treatise Concerning the Arte of Limning,* bound with Edward Norgate, *A More Compendious Discourse Concerning ye Art of Liming,* ed. R. K. R. Thornton and T. G. S. Cain (Ashington, Northumberland: Mid Northumberland Arts Group in association with Carcanet New Press, 1981); Orest Ranum, "The Refuges of Intimacy," in *Passions of the Renaissance,* ed. Roger Chartier, trans. Arthur Goldhammer, vol. 3 of *A History of Private Life* (Cambridge, Mass. and London:

Harvard University Press, Belknap, 1989), pp. 248–50 (unfortunately, this series appeared too late for me to make full use of it in my study of privacy); Mary Edmond, *Hilliard and Oliver: The Lives and Works of Two Great Miniaturists* (London: Robert Hale, 1983); Roy Strong, *The English Renaissance Miniature* (New York: Thames and Hudson, 1983), and his *Nicholas Hilliard* (London: Michael Joseph, 1975); Roy Strong and V. J. Murrell, *Artists of the Tudor Court: The Portrait Miniature Rediscovered, 1520–1620* (London: Victoria & Albert Museum, 1983); Jim Murrell, *The Way Howe to Lymne: Tudor Miniatures Observed* (London: Victoria & Albert Museum, 1983); Leslie Hotson, "Queen Elizabeth's Master Painter," *Sunday Times Colour Magazine,* 22 March 1970, 46–53; Daphne Foskett, *British Portrait Miniatures: A History* (London: Methuen, 1963); Eric Mercer, "Miniatures," in *English Art, 1553–1625,* ed. Eric Mercer, vol. 8 of *The Oxford History of English Art* (Oxford: Oxford University Press, 1949–78), pp. 190–216; Graham Reynolds, "The Painter Plays the Spider," *Apollo* 79 (April 1964): 279–84, as well as his *English Portrait Miniatures* (London: Adam & Charles Black, 1952) and his *Nicholas Hilliard and Isaac Oliver: An Exhibition to Commemorate the 400th Anniversary of the Birth of Nicholas Hilliard* (London: Ministry of Education, 1947); Erna Auerbach, *Nicholas Hilliard* (London: Routledge and Kegan Paul, 1961); Torben Holck Colding, *Aspects of Miniature Painting: Its Origins and Development* (Copenhagen: Ejnar Munksgaard, 1953); and John Pope-Hennessy, "Nicholas Hilliard and Mannerist Art Theory," *Journal of the Warburg and Courtauld Institutes* 6 (1943): 89–100.

Susan Stewart considers miniature paintings specifically in terms of privatization and textuality (*On Longing: Narratives of the Miniature, the Gigantic, the Souvenir, the Collection* [Baltimore: Johns Hopkins University Press, 1984], pp. 125–27); for the intimate connection between the idea of the miniature and children, see p. 44.

7. The title of this section is quoted from Hilliard, *Treatise* (the English ed.), p. 65. Both because of my topic in this book and because the miniature was a peculiarly aristocratic fashion, I look specifically to the houses of the upper class. (In her landmark biography of the two major miniaturists of the English Renaissance, Edmond convincingly counters past views that the miniature, from the 1570s on, became "democratized" [*Hilliard and Oliver,* p. 101]; see also Mercer, "Miniatures," p. 197).

8. Mercer, "Miniatures," p. 196. For the public placing of oil paintings in the gallery, see Roy Strong, *The English Icon: Elizabethan & Jacobean Portraiture* (London: Routledge and Kegan Paul, 1969); also Mark Girouard, *Life in the English Country House: A Social and Architectural History* (New Haven: Yale University Press, 1978; reprint, Harmondsworth, Middlesex: Penguin, 1980), pp. 101–2. The exception that proved the rule were large erotic paintings: the blown-up scale of these paintings is more a sign of inflated (and taboo) intimacy than of publicness. However physically large they were, Ranum surmises, erotic paintings were "presumably exhibited in small, secret rooms, where no confessor or devout relative was likely to see them" ("Refuges of Intimacy," p. 252). For the terms "miniature," "limning," and "painting in little," see, for example, Foskett, *British Portrait Miniatures,* p. 33; for "miniature," in particular, see Colding, *Aspects of Miniature Painting,* pp. 9–19.

9. "Sir H. Unton to her Majesty, from Coucy, Feb. 3, 1595–6," in William Cecil Burghley, *A Collection of State Papers Relating to Affairs in the Reign of Queen Elizabeth, from the Year 1571 to 1596*, transcribed by William Murdin (London, 1759), p. 718.

10. Hilliard, *Treatise* (English ed.), p. 87. Future citations of Hilliard's treatise will be to this edition and will appear in the body of my text.

11. Rowse, *Elizabethan Renaissance*, pp. 40–41. See also Johnson, *Elizabeth I*, p. 80; Peter Thornton, *Seventeenth-Century Interior Decoration in England, France and Holland* (New Haven: Yale University Press, 1978), pp. 57–60; and Girouard, *English Country House*, who traces from medieval times the progressive retreat within proliferating rooms (a phenomenon we shall return to in the next chapter). Such withdrawal enacted the common sixteenth-century metaphor for self-examination, noted by Anne Ferry in *The "Inward" Language: Sonnets of Wyatt, Sidney, Shakespeare, Donne* (Chicago: University of Chicago Press, 1983), pp. 46–48. (Ferry's objection to the generally accepted thesis that the increasing interest in private rooms in the sixteenth century indicates growing interest in the private self [pp. 47–55] will be answered in the course of this chapter.) For architectural inwardness or perspective as a representation of sexual intimacy, see Donald Keith Hedrick, "The Ideology of Ornament: Alberti and the Erotics of Renaissance Urban Design," *Word and Image* 3 (January–March, 1987): especially pp. 113–20.

12. J. F. Hayward, *English Cabinets in the Victoria and Albert Museum* (London: Her Majesty's Stationery Office, 1964), p. 3. For the placing of cabinets "in the main chamber or bedroom," see Doreen Yarwood, *The English Home: A Thousand Years of Furnishing and Decoration* (New York: Scribner's, 1956), p. 90.

13. Strong, "Manuscript to Miniature," pp. 73, 76.

14. Ibid., p. 76. Not until the 1630s would the miniature reside again primarily in the cabinet box—and then as part of the connoisseur's collection in a cabinet room (pp. 80–84). See also Strong's "Introduction: The Tudor Miniature: Mirror of an Age," in Strong and Murrell, *Artists of the Tudor Court*, pp. 9–10.

15. Strong, "Manuscript to Miniature," p. 73.

16. *Princely Magnificence: Court Jewels of the Renaissance, 1500–1630* (London: Debrett's Peerage, in association with the Victoria & Albert Museum, 1980), p. 62, catalogue no. 46. Originally the gold cupids at the sides of the case were also black.

17. Edmund Lodge, *Illustrations of British History, Biography, and Manners, in the Reigns of Henry VIII, Edward VI, Mary, Elizabeth, and James I: Exhibited in a Series of Original Papers, Selected from the Manuscripts of the Noble Families of Howard, Talbot, and Cecil . . . with Numerous Notes and Observations*, 3 vols. (London, 1791): 3:146–47.

18. Ibid., 3:147.

19. Reynolds, *Nicholas Hilliard and Isaac Oliver*, p. 13.

20. Ferry, *"Inward" Language*, pp. 48–49.

21. Mercer, "Miniatures," p. 199.

22. "Limning emerges," remarks Strong in *English Renaissance Miniature*, "full of covert tricks and recipes passed secretly from master to pupil" (p. 8). See also his "Manuscript to Miniature," p. 60; and Jim Murrell's "The Craft of the Miniaturist," in *English Miniature*, ed. Murdoch et al., p. 7.

23. See, for example, Mercer, "Miniatures," p. 199; for goldsmithing, in particu-

lar, see Colding, *Aspects of Miniature Painting,* pp. 26–40. Colding posits a third influence in the medal (p. 40); also Foskett, *British Portrait Miniatures,* pp. 33–34. For limning and illumination, see especially Strong, "Manuscript to Miniature."

24. Pope-Hennessy, in *Lecture on Nicholas Hilliard,* particularly stresses Hilliard's concern with "line" (p. 20) and, in specific reference to the *Unknown Lady,* with "pattern" (pp. 21–22). See also his "Nicholas Hilliard and Mannerist Art Theory," pp. 96–97.

25. Murrell, "Craft of the Miniaturist," p. 6. Murrell provides the best analysis of limning techniques and materials. I will be quoting primarily from this work, but much of what he says there reappears in *Howe to Lymne* and in his chapters in Strong and Murrell, *Artists of the Tudor Court* (pp. 13–32).

26. Murrell, "Craft of the Miniaturist," p. 9. For Hilliard's gem- and lace-work, see pp. 6–8.

27. I have deduced Hilliard's limning procedure primarily from Murrell, "Craft of the Miniaturist," pp. 5–14; and Hilliard, *Treatise.* Some of the "flatness" of Hilliard's faces comes from the fading of fugitive flesh tints; as Mercer points out, however, Hilliard's style of limning here worked with time ("Miniatures," p. 201).

28. On playing cards, see Murrell, "The Art of Limning," in Strong and Murrell, *Artists of the Tudor Court,* pp. 14–15. On the card backing Elizabeth's limning, see Philip Norman, ed., "Nicholas Hilliard's Treatise Concerning 'The Arte of Limning,'" *The Walpole Society* 1 (1911–12): 54.

29. Pope-Hennessy, "Nicholas Hilliard and Mannerist Art Theory," p. 99. For sugar candy in limning see, for example, Murrell, "Craft of the Miniaturist," p. 11. For Elizabeth's limning "mask of youth," see especially Strong, *English Renaissance Miniature,* pp. 118–22.

30. Auerbach, *Nicholas Hilliard,* p. 103; Pope-Hennessy, *Lecture on Nicholas Hilliard,* p. 23.

31. Hilliard's attitude to artifice can be contrasted with that of an artist such as Alberti, who was also concerned with secrecy and ornament. As Hedrick shows, in his "Ideology of Ornament," Alberti wrestled with the troubling relation between beauty conceived as essence and ornament conceived as addition: i.e., with the problem that "beauty is whatever *cannot be improved* by addition or subtraction, but that ornament is whatever is *needed to improve* beauty." Hedrick observes, "this reversible hierarchy of oppositions constitutes precisely what Derrida terms the 'logic of the supplement', that threatens to undo difference, whereby that which is in the 'supplement' or dependent category on the one hand appears *superfluous* and on the other appears *necessary for completion*" (p. 125; for Derrida's recent treatment of the supplement in relation to painting and specifically to ornament, see Jacques Derrida, *The Truth in Painting,* trans. Geoff Bennington and Ian McLeod [Chicago: University of Chicago Press, 1987], especially pp. 12–147). Since ornament for Alberti was necessary chiefly to conceal defects—"painting and concealing any Thing that was deformed" (p. 130)—and since he linked architecture to the human body (both having "facades"), the threat of ornament "undoing" the center led Alberti to associate excessive ornament with the erotic, subversive, and deceptive power of the individual. In Alberti's "public-minded" thinking, ornament thus had to be con-

tained. Hilliard, on the other hand, embraced just such reversibility between essence and ornament (as between center and periphery) in the service of the erotic self or lover. While shadowing signified a hidden "ill cause," ornament in its purity supplemented in the sense of adding onto the truth of subjectivity. Like the intricate line of architectural rooms leading to an inner chamber, ornament pointed to the desiring self as central. As we have seen, it also finally revealed that true self to be hidden or absent; but, again, Hilliard showed no uneasiness with this fact. In Hilliard's "private-minded" thinking, secreting ornament was to be avidly cultivated.

32. Reynolds, "Painter Plays the Spider," p. 283.

33. For Hilliard's turn to more private representation, see especially Auerbach, *Nicholas Hilliard*, pp. 97–110. For the influence of tournament *imprese* on Hilliard, see especially Strong, *English Renaissance Miniature*, pp. 95–99; also his "Manuscript to Miniature," pp. 68–73; "Tournaments and Masques," in Strong and Murrell, *Artists of the Tudor Court*, pp. 133–38; and for the *Roses* miniature, in particular, *Cult of Elizabeth*, pp. 75–78.

34. I treat *Young Man among Roses* as the zenith of Hilliard's limning, though from another perspective it could also be considered the beginning of the end. Because the five-by-three-inch miniature depicts the sitter in full-length, Mercer ("Miniatures," pp. 206–8) argues that it foreshadows the decline of private limning.

35. See Strong, *Cult of Elizabeth*, pp. 68–77; also Leslie Hotson, *Mr. W. H.* (London: Rupert Hart-Davis, 1964), pp. 208–12. Hotson argues, unconvincingly I believe, that the miniature pictures not love but friendship (Shakespeare's for William Hatcliffe), and he receives tentative support from Edmond, *Hilliard and Oliver*, pp. 89–91. The majority of art historians, however, agree with Strong in seeing the youth as a lover. For the added association of tawny and black with melancholy, see, for example, Strong, *English Icon*, p. 34.

36. Epistle of "N. W." prefacing Paolo Giovio, *The Worthy Tract of Paulus Iovius* 1585), trans. Samuel Daniel; bound with Giovio's *Dialogo dell'imprese Militari et Amorose*, facsimile ed. (Delmar, N.Y.: Scholar's Facsimiles and Reprints, 1976). Camden is quoted by both Strong, *Cult of Elizabeth*, p. 77, and Hotson, *W. H.*, p. 208.

37. On the Pompey allusion, see Strong, *Cult of Elizabeth*, pp. 77–78; and Hotson, *W. H.*, pp. 212–13ff. On Essex as the *Roses* youth, see Strong, *Cult of Elizabeth*, pp. 60–83; Edmond, who does not accept Strong's identification, argues that the roses are not eglantine (*Hilliard and Oliver*, pp. 89–91). Essex secretly married Sidney's widow in 1590 (*Dictionary of National Biography*).

38. Hotson, *W. H.*, p. 206. Strong, in the catalogue of Strong and Murrell, *Artists of the Tudor Court*, argues that the miniature is by Isaac Oliver, not Hilliard (p. 109); all other art historians, so far as I can find, attribute it to Hilliard.

39. Noted, for example, by Hotson, *W. H.*, p. 206.

40. Section title quote from "A pretie Poeme" (no. 20), in Nicholas Breton et al., *The Arbor of Amorous Devices, 1597*, intro. Hyder Edward Rollins, facsimile ed. (Cambridge: Harvard University Press, 1936), p. 19. On the loose definition of sonnet as a small poem and its evolution into a specific kind of poetic smallness (characterized by fourteen lines of intricate rhyme, rhetorical elaboration, etc.), see note 6 above.

41. "Sir H. Unton to her Majesty," p. 718.

42. Edmund Spenser, sonnet 17, *Amoretti* (1595), in *Spenser,* 8:201–2. On the structural "movements" of sonnet sequences, see Carol Thomas Neely, "The Structure of English Renaissance Sonnet Sequences," *ELH* 45 (Fall 1978): 359–89.

43. Edmund Molyneux, quoted in Malcolm William Wallace, *The Life of Sir Philip Sidney* (New York: Octagon, 1967), p. 225.

44. J. C., prefatory Latin poem to *Alcilia: Philoparthen's Louing Follie (1595): From the Unique Exemplar in the Town Library, Hamburg,* ed. Rev. Alexander B. Grosart (St. George's, Blackburn, Lancs., 1879), p. 6, trans. in introduction, p. xii; Thomas Nash, preface to Sidney's *Astrophel and Stella* (first quarto ed., 1591), in *Elizabethan Critical Essays,* ed. Smith, 2:224; William Alexander, "Sonnet 1," *Avrora. Containing the first fancies of the Authors youth,* sig. A3r.

45. Lyric 3, *The Poems of Sir Walter Raleigh,* ed. Agnes M. C. Latham (London: Routledge and Kegan Paul, 1951), pp. 4–5; [George Gascoigne], *A Hundreth Sundrey Flowres: From the Original Edition of 1573,* ed. Ruth Loyd Miller, 2d ed. (Port Washington, N.Y.: Kennikat, 1975), p. 122. On the secret handling of love letters, see Ranum, "Refuges of Intimacy," p. 246.

46. Samuel Daniel, dedication to *Delia. Containing certayne Sonnets: with the complaint of Rosamond,* in *Poems and A Defence of Ryme,* ed. Arthur Colby Sprague (London: Routledge and Kegan Paul, 1950; reprint, Chicago: University of Chicago Press, 1965), p. 9; "H. W. to the Reader" and "The letter of G. T. to his very friend H. W. concerning this worke," in Gascoigne, *Flowres,* pp. 117 and 118, 120–21, respectively; William Percy, "To the Reader," in *Sonnets to the Fairest Coelia,* sig. Ayr; R[obert] T[ofte], "The Epistle Dedicatorie . . . ," "To the Reader . . . ," and "A Frends iust excuse about the Booke and Author, in his absence," in *Lavra, The Toyes of a Traueller. Or. The Feast of Fancie. Diuided into three Parts,* letters reprinted in Robert Tofte, *Alba: The Month's Minde of a Melancholy Lover* (1598), ed. Rev. Alexander B. Grosart (St. George's, Blackburn, Lancs., 1880), pp. xxvi, xxvii, xlii.

47. "The Printer to the Reader," in Gascoigne, *Flowres,* p. 113.

48. The secret inscriptions and tantalizing initials invited readers to play the game of guessing identity. Literary critics have gladly complied. See the "guesses" of the editor of *Flowres* (p. 5) on the identity of H. W., G. T., and on the author behind the "*Meritum petere, gravè*" inscription (most now believe all are Gascoigne); also Bernard M. Ward's chapters in *Flowres,* pp. 28–34, 75–89. J. W. Saunders, in another light, views secret inscriptions, along with initials and protestations of betrayal, as ways of bypassing the stigma of printing ("The Stigma of Print: A Note on the Social Bases of Tudor Poetry," *Essays in Criticism* 1 [April 1951]: especially 143–46).

49. Convention, we have noted, is ornamental in the sense that, like artifice, it is public and anonymous, and thus theoretically "external" to or detachable from the idea of privacy. But convention is also more exactly ornamental in Fletcher's sense of the word, as we discussed it in chapter 1. Fletcher, we recall, argues that ornament points allusively or allegorically to history. So does convention. As Alan Liu explains, conventionality constitutes a mark or token which is taken for granted and thus appears to signify nothing. In fact, however, it points to deep social meaning, to the "beauty" of social history or civilization. "Imagine this composite painting of a tour," suggests Liu: "nature dominates the foreground; toward the back of the

foreground, there is a mark composed of historical synopses, a mark like Brueghel's Icarus that seems ornamental because it points to no signified in the foreground; but the mark is crucial because its conventionality establishes the very perspective system, the social history or overall conventionality of vision within which foreground nature can be seen as a 'delightful' beauty in the first place. No jewel without its setting: without history in the background, after all, a landscape is not a landscape; it is wilderness" (*Wordsworth*, pp. 10–11). The strange character of conventionality as ornamentality in the sonnet and miniature, I would add, is that it marks not only such beautified social history but also, at a more embedded level, the history of subjectivity alien to such ideal commonality.

50. An allusion, of course, to Penelope Rich—Sidney's Stella—in sonnets 9, 24, 35, and 37 of *Astrophil and Stella* (composed c. 1581–82; published 1591), in *Poems of Sir Philip Sidney*, ed. William A. Ringler, Jr. (Oxford: Clarendon Press, 1962).

51. Sir Philip Sidney, *Astrophil and Stella*, song 11, l. 4, in *Poems of Sir Philip Sidney*, ed. Ringler; all future citations to the sonnets and songs of *Astrophil and Stella* will be to this edition and will appear in the body of my text.

52. For the portrait miniature's descent from illuminated manuscripts, see Strong, "Manuscript to Miniature," pp. 25–45; for portrait miniatures *on* manuscripts, see, for example, pp. 41 and 58. Hilliard, notes Strong, limned in 1571 "a booke of portraitures" (quoted p. 48). For Elizabeth's prayer-book limnings, see Auerbach, *Nicholas Hilliard*, pp. 77–83; also Edmond, who most fully treats Hilliard's involvement in the Elizabeth/Anjou marriage negotiations (*Hilliard and Oliver*, pp. 61–63). For Sidney's involvement, see Wallace, *Life of Sir Philip Sidney*, pp. 203 and 216–19.

53. Ringler, ed., *Poems of Sir Philip Sidney*, p. 460.

54. The use of the adjective *daintie* reinforces the sense of a rich ornament that hides. *Daintie* suggests "fine" or "delicate," perhaps overly delicate: "fastidious." As the expression *to be dainty of* implies, moreover, the "daintie" person can also be "chary" or "sparing" (*OED*). He keeps to himself. He is private. This is how G. T. used "daintie of" in making public the identity of Gascoigne in *Flowres:* "I will now deliver unto you so many more of Master Gascoignes Poems as have come to my hands, *who hath never beene dayntie of his doings, and therfore I conceale not his name . . .*" (my emphasis). Sidney himself seems to associate *daintie* with concealment in sonnet 41. The poet, having won a court tournament, lists suggestions advanced by onlookers for his success before turning to the true cause of his victory—"*Stella* lookt on." Among the wrong guesses is that of a "daintier judge": "Horsemen my skill in horsmanship advaunce; / Towne-folkes my strength; a daintier judge applies / His praise to sleight, which from good use doth rise." The "daintier judge" rejects the indelicate reasons for victory—"skill in horsmanship" and brute "strength"—and turns instead to the idea of "sleight." *Sleight* itself can mean "skill," but, as the *OED* notes, its common meaning down to the seventeenth century was "craft or cunning employed so as to deceive; deceitful, subtle, or wily dealing or policy; artifice, strategy, trickery" ("frequently contrasted with *strength, might,* or *force*"). Akin to the "artifice" of hiddenness and ornament, "daintie wits" both display and craftily mask their "fancies" in bravery.

55. See editors' introduction to Hilliard, *Treatise*, p. 43; for the source of ivory,

see Alfred Maskell, *Ivories* (Rutland, Vt.: Charles E. Tuttle, 1966), p. 25. For more on limning pigments and their sources, see Murrell, *Howe to Lymne,* pp. 67–70.

56. Strong, *Cult of Queen Elizabeth,* p. 60; Ringler, ed., *Poems of Sir Philip Sidney,* p. 460. Hilliard, when in France (1576–78), apparently met Ronsard (*Treatise,* p. 69).

57. Mercer, "Miniatures," p. 197. While the normal charge in Elizabeth's reign for an uncased miniature was £3, notes Strong, "When Hilliard provided the setting the price could soar." A jeweled miniature of James, for instance, cost in 1615 £35 (*Nicholas Hilliard,* p. 17). A more extravagant example is James's gift to the duchess of Lennox: "a fair chain of diamonds with his picture on it, valued by the jewellers at £8,600" (quoted in Burke, "Renaissance Jewels," in *Princely Magnificence,* p. 11). For Sidney's money difficulties and lavish spending, see Wallace, *Life of Sir Philip Sidney,* p. 126.

58. William Cherubini, "The 'Goldenness' of Sidney's *Astrophel and Stella*: Test of a Quantitative-Stylistics Routine," *Language and Style* 8 (Winter 1975): 56.

59. Ibid., p. 52. *Epanaphora* is "the repetition of the same word or words at the beginning of several successive sentences or sentence members" (*Princeton Encyclopedia of Poetry and Poetics,* ed. Alex Preminger, Frank J. Warnke, and O. B. Hardison, Jr., enl. ed. [Princeton: Princeton University Press, 1974], s.v. "anaphora").

60. See note 6 above.

61. Characteristically, notes Jean Robertson, Sidney throws the weight of the sonnet "on to the final line" ("Sir Philip Sidney and His Poetry," in *Elizabethan Poetry,* Stratford-upon-Avon Studies, no. 2 [London: Edward Arnold, 1960], p. 125). For Sidney on *energia,* see his *Apologie,* 1:201. Since forcible sincerity in *Astrophil and Stella* exists in and through conventional ornament, Sidney's *energia* in practice comes closer to the combined concepts of *energia* and *enargia* enumerated by George Puttenham in *The Arte of English Poesie. Contrived into three Bookes: The first of Poets and Poesie, the second of Proportion, the third of Ornament* (1589): "This ornament then is of two sortes, one to satisfie & delight th'eare onely by a goodly outward shew set vpon the matter with wordes and speaches smothly and tunably running, another by certaine intendments or sence of such wordes & speaches inwardly working a stirre to the mynde. The first qualitie the Greeks called *Enargia,* of this words *argos,* because it geueth a glorious lustre and light. This latter they called *Energia, of ergon,* because it wrought with a strong and vertuous operation" (in *Elizabethan Critical Essays,* ed. Smith, 2:148). The "outward shew" or "glorious lustre" of Sidney's ornament (recalling Hilliard's demand that the artist imitate the "proper lustre" of colors [*Treatise,* p. 91]) itself points within, "inwardly working a stirre to the mynde" of the poet and his audience. *Through* the outer layers of built-up ornament in *Astrophil and Stella* we get a sense of forcibly penetrating into the poet's sincere inner "passions."

62. See also Ferry, *"Inward" Language,* pp. 142–43.

63. For the poem-within-a-poem in *Astrophil and Stella,* see Ferry, *"Inward" Language,* pp. 143–47, who also discusses sonnet 80 (pp. 143–44); also Barbara Herrnstein Smith, *Poetic Closure: A Study of How Poems End* (Chicago: University of Chicago Press, 1968), pp. 149–50.

64. Ann Rosalind Jones and Peter Stallybrass, "The Politics of *Astrophil and*

Stella," Studies in English Literature 24 (Winter 1984): 54. See also Arthur F. Marotti, "'Love is not Love': Elizabethan Sonnet Sequences and the Social Order," *ELH* 49 (Summer 1982): 396–406; and Clark Hulse's "Stella's Wit: Penelope Rich as Reader of Sidney's Sonnets," in *Rewriting the Renaissance: The Discourses of Sexual Difference in Early Modern Europe,* ed. Margaret W. Ferguson, Maureen Quilligan, and Nancy J. Vickers (Chicago: University of Chicago Press, 1986), especially pp. 285–86.

65. See Cherubini, "'Goldenness' of Sidney's *Astrophel and Stella,*" p. 55. On the virtual identity of sonnet heroine and Queen, see especially Jones and Stallybrass, "Politics of *Astrophil and Stella,*" pp. 63–68. The poet's turning to public service at the end of the sequence in sonnet 107 is thus not an eschewing of his private love for public *"Ambition"* (sonnet 27) because he never really left public service in serving his personal lady, his "Queene" (sonnet 107). We should here also recall Puttenham's noted analogy between the artifice of the poet and the politics of the courtier. Since Sidney's passageways of ornament that point to the heart are conventional or public, they are inherently political and, like the politics of the courtier, "dissembling"; see Puttenham, *Arte of English Poesie,* 2:182–87.

66. The publisher's precise term was "famous device" (Albert Feuillerat, ed., *The Complete Works of Sir Philip Sidney,* 4 vols. [Cambridge: Cambridge University Press, 1912–26], 2:369. Hulse similarly likens the sonnets to *imprese* ("Stella's Wit," p. 274).

67. William Camden, quoted in Katherine Duncan-Jones, "Sidney's Personal *Imprese," Journal of the Warburg and Courtauld Institutes* 33 (1970): 323; for stars in Sidney's *imprese,* see p. 322.

68. Hulse, "Stella's Wit." See also his argument that in Shakespeare's sonnet "portraits" the poet's self is "self-made . . . through the simultaneous concealment of that self from and revelation of it to the world, as the self is broadcast and then drawn back to itself" ("Shakespeare's Sonnets and the Art of the Face," *John Donne Journal* 5, no. 1 [1986]: 13).

69. On Astrophil's manipulation and problems of self-definition, see, for example, Richard A. Lanham, *"Astrophil and Stella:* Pure and Impure Persuasion," *English Literary Renaissance* 2 (Winter 1972): 100–115; Andrew D. Weiner, "Structure and 'Fore Conceit' in *Astrophil and Stella," Texas Studies in Literature and Language* 16 (Spring 1974): 1–25; Alan Sinfield, "Astrophil's Self-Deception," *Essays in Criticism* 28 (January 1978): 1–18; Daniel Traister, "Sidney's Purposeful Humor: *Astrophil and Stella* 59 and 83," *ELH* 49 (Winter 1982): 751–64; and Thomas P. Roche, Jr., *"Astrophil and Stella:* A Radical Reading," *Spenser Studies* 3 (1982): 139–91.

70. Girouard, *English Country House,* p. 110. Mary E. Hazard cites numerous other historical and rhetorical instances of "ABSENT presence," a tradition within which, she argues, both ruler and subject could find personal expression ("Absent Presence and Present Absence: Cross-Couple Convention in Elizabethan Culture," *Texas Studies in Literature and Language* 29 [Spring 1987]: 1–27). For a different version of Stella's "ABSENT presence," see Murray Krieger, "Poetic Presence and Illusion I: Renaissance Theory and the Duplicity of Metaphor," in *Poetic Presence and Illusion: Essays in Critical History and Theory* (Baltimore: Johns Hopkins University Press, 1979), pp. 3–27.

71. On the poet's re-creation of self in each sonnet of a sequence, see also Richard A. Lanham, *The Motives of Eloquence: Literary Rhetoric in the Renaissance* (New Haven: Yale University Press, 1976), p. 124 and passim. I would substitute the "space" repeatedly gestured at through penetration for Charles Altieri's interesting but "horizontal" "space of rhetorical performance" that balances "distance with desire, freedom with submission, and intellectual control with passionate obsession," as well as ideal with real ("Rhetorics, Rhetoricity and the Sonnet as Performance," *Tennessee Studies in Literature* 25 [1980]: 4, 13).

72. Gascoigne, "Certayne notes of Instruction," 1:47.

73. Greville's miniature is mentioned in "Wilson to the Queen," 11 June 1577, in *Calendar of State Papers, Foreign Series, of the Reign of Elizabeth, 1558–1582*, ed. Joseph Stevenson, Allan James Crosby, and Arthur John Butler, 16 vols. (London, 1863–1909), 11:596.

74. The names of Hilliard's last three surviving children—Lettice, Penelope, and Robert—testify to the patronage of the Leicester-Essex circle (see Edmond, *Hilliard and Oliver*, p. 84).

75. Sir Philip Sidney, *The Countess of Pembroke's Arcadia* (1593), ed. Maurice Evans (New York: Penguin, 1977), p. 166; I am assuming that Musidorus wears the miniature in the same fashion as the knight from whom he took it.

76. Sidney, 1593 *Arcadia*, p. 167.

77. Section title quote from "canzon" 14, *Zepheria*, 1594 (Manchester, 1869), p. 18.

78. J. W. Lever, *The Elizabethan Love Sonnet* (London: Methuen, 1956), p. 103. In conjunction with the emergence of personal secret arts, there arose a personalized institution of secrecy. I refer to the Secret Service, which emerged as a fully operational body under Elizabeth (never to be matched by the Stuarts). The organization was personally founded by Sidney's father-in-law, Walsingham, who operated out of his own pocket and his own home, which he turned into a school for forgery (R. A. Haldane, *The Hidden World* [London: Robert Hale, 1976], pp. 60–61 and 65). Sidney himself may have attended some classes—we know he presented Elizabeth with a cipher he devised (Wallace, *Life of Sir Philip Sidney*, p. 270). He also went on an informal spy mission for the Queen (Wallace, p. 173). While Elizabeth's secret service was obviously a political organization, its way of working through private individuals as well as its inherent concern with secrecy linked this new development to the developing interest in a secret self that we have seen in Sidney's sonnets and Hilliard's limnings. Significantly, Hilliard's miniatures were often involved with spy missions. Constable, for instance, operating in 1588 as an agent at James's court in Scotland, made intriguing reference in code to his miniature of Lady Rich. And we hear of a Catholic plot against Elizabeth in 1591 that involved getting hold of a Hilliard miniature of Lady Arabella Stuart (see Edmond, *Hilliard and Oliver*, pp. 94–95, 114–18).

Art historians take pains to discount Hilliard's culpability in these operations, and I have no reason to suspect else. What is fascinating, however, is that Hilliard's miniatures were considered somehow appropriate for this kind of undercover work. Miniaturization of size clearly promoted portability for a spy. But I suspect the very art of secrecy Hilliard limned would have furthered their candidacy. Hilliard's miniatures were intricately part of a secret and yet also political self. For the very same reason, I believe, the "small guilded coffer" of Mary Queen of Scots, which was produced at her trial for treason, contained not only eight enciphered letters but also twelve sonnets (Johnson, *Elizabeth I*, p. 165; Haldane, who notes that the letters were enciphered [p. 64], reproduces the cipher used [p. 63]). Sidney's sonnet devices and Hilliard's limning devices are in a way themselves "ciphers": encoded transmissions of very secret loves offered not only to private ladies but also to her majesty, the Queen (for ciphers and *Astrophil and Stella*, see Hulse, "Stella's Wit," pp. 278–79). Both poet and limner in developing arts of secrecy were "On Her Majesty's Secret Service."

79. "Sonnett" 75, *The Vanytyes of Sir Arthur Gorges Youthe*, in *The Poems of Sir Arthur Gorges*, ed. Helen Estabrook Sandison (Oxford: Clarendon Press, 1953), p. 74; "To Mr. Hilliard, vpon occasion of a picture he made of my Ladie Rich," Todd MS (MS. Dyce 44), in *The Poems of Henry Constable*, ed. Grundy, p. 158.

80. Samuel Daniel, sonnet 34, *Delia*, p. 27; "canzon" 14, *Zepheria*, p. 18; Tofte, *Alba*, p. 23; Michael Drayton, "amour" 14 and 46, *Ideas Mirrour. Amours in Quatorzains* (1594), in *The Works of Michael Drayton*, ed. J. William Hebel, 5 vols. (Oxford: Basil Blackwell, 1931–41), 1:104, 121. On limning pencils, see, for example, Murrell, "Craft of the Miniaturist," p. 12. Claire Pace notes the new tendency for the poet to inscribe his lover's portrait in his heart ("'Delineated Lives': Themes and Variations in Seventeenth-Century Poems about Portraits," *Word and Image* 2 [January–March 1986]: 4).

81. For Oliver's style in relation to Hilliard, see Edmond, *Hilliard and Oliver*, p. 111 and passim; Murrell, *Howe to Lymne*, pp. 38–46; Strong, "Manuscript to Miniature," pp. 62–68; Mercer, "Miniatures," pp. 210–14; Auerbach, *Nicholas Hilliard*, pp. 235–54; and Reynolds, *Nicholas Hilliard and Isaac Oliver*, pp. 13–17. Auerbach (pp. 103, 236) specifically contrasts the two limnings of the *Unknown Youth;* see also Reynolds (p. 16). On the immediate followers (and actual sons) of Hilliard and Oliver—Lawrence Hilliard and Peter Oliver—see especially Strong, *English Renaissance Miniature*, pp. 186–88. The miniature of Drayton, attributed to Peter Oliver, is reproduced on the frontispiece to Bernard H. Newdigate, *Michael Drayton and His Circle* (corr. ed.) (Oxford: Basil Blackwell, 1961).

82. *The Autobiography of Edward, Lord Herbert of Cherbury*, ed. Will H. Dircks (London, 1888), p. 87.

83. Mercer, "Miniatures," p. 210; on the Herbert copy, see Herbert, *Autobiography*, p. 86. It was Herbert who attributed the large-scale painting to Larkin, though the editor of his autobiography notes that "Larkin" (now unknown) may have been Nicholas Lockie.

84. For Oliver's rejection of Hilliardesque inscriptions, see, for example, Edmond, *Hilliard and Oliver*, p. 111. Strong, especially in "Tournaments and Masques," aligns Hilliard with the former (pp. 133–38) and Oliver with the latter (pp. 138–42); see also Edmond, p. 152. For the residence of Oliver and Ben Jonson in Blackfriars, see Edmond, pp. 138–39 and p. 152, respectively. Pace traces in seventeenth-century portrait poems "a shift away from the iconic, pictorial and largely descriptive tradition characteristic of the Renaissance, to a greater interest in rendering psychological depth" ("'Delineated Lives,'" p. 3).

85. Ferry, *"Inward" Language*, p. 3.
86. Sennett, *The Fall of Public Man*, pp. 4–5.

Chapter Four

1. Ben Jonson, *Neptune's Triumph for the Return of Albion* (1624), in *Ben Jonson: The Complete Masques*, vol. 4 of *The Yale Ben Jonson*, ed. Stephen Orgel (New Haven: Yale University Press, 1969), ll. 13–26; all future citations of Jonson's masques will be to this edition and will appear in the body of my text.

2. Jonson often judged masques to be "most unprofitable" because "trifling": that is, useless, superfluous, *trivial* (this even though he was well-paid for his contribution—on the average of £40 per show). Anxiety over his art's triviality concentrated in criticisms voiced by his characters about the antimasque buffoonery: best "vrom de purpose," insisted Vangoose in *The Masque of Augurs* (1622), l. 244; "Mere by-works, and at best outlandish nothings," affirmed the Poet of *Neptune's Triumph*, l. 160. Attempting to detach himself from such superfluity, Jonson made distinctions between the poet's "inward parts" and the architect's "outward celebration or show": the spectacular costumes and scenery of Inigo Jones (a tastepleaser like the Cook above); see *Hymenaei, or the Solemnities of Masque and Barriers at a Marriage* (1606), ll. 11–14. Unfortunately, Jonson's contemporaries were less discriminatory. Francis Bacon dismissed masques in general as "but Toyes" that smacked of "Petty Wonderments" and "childish Curiosity" ("Of Masques and Triumphs," from his *Essays*, in *Francis Bacon*, selected and edited by Arthur Johnston [New York: Schocken, 1965], p. 124). A satirist of like mind pictured James being made "fatt" on the "masks and toyes" of his "merry boys" (quoted in David Norbrook, "The Reformation of the Masque," in *The Court Masque*, ed. David Lindley [Manchester: Manchester University Press, 1984], p. 101). Even other masque writers concurred. Acknowledging the court taste for triviality, Samuel Daniel concluded that, rather than fattening, masques were "hungry shadows, which no profit breed" (cited in Joan Rees's Introduction to Daniel's *The Vision of the Twelve Goddesses* [1604], ed. Joan Rees, in *A Book of Masques: In Honour of Allardyce Nicoll* [Cambridge: Cambridge University Press, 1967], p. 21). Daniel thus gladly deferred in his masques to the man of "show," Jones. Thomas Campion took Daniel's stance a step further: he envisioned his masque poetry not being adorned by, but "adorning," Jones's "art" (*The Lords' Masque*, ed. I. A. Shapiro, in *Book of Masques*, l. 180). He thus aspired only to please the contemporary counterpart to childish "boys," court ladies. As Jonas A. Barish aptly summarizes, for Campion the masque was "a sugarplum to melt in a lady's mouth" (*Ben Jonson and the Language of Prose Comedy* [(1960); reprint, New York: Norton, 1970], p. 271).

3. In *Time Vindicated*, it may be noted, the Poet (Jonson) and Cook (Jones) were already at odds. Though Jones designed as the first scene for the masque an *outdoor* "prospective of Whitehall, with the Banqueting House," Jonson intended the opening scene to take place *indoors;* see l. 45 (Orgel, ed., *Ben Jonson: The Complete Masques*, pp. 502–3). For Jones's sketch of the Banqueting House scene, see *Inigo Jones*, ed. Orgel and Strong, 1:356–57.

4. *OED*, s.v. "banquet"; see also "voidee" and "void," sb.[2] As late as 1616, Lane

used the word "void" to describe the serving of "praeserves in silvern plate" (quoted in *OED*, s.v. "void," sb.²). Towards the end of the sixteenth century, however, the term "banquet" increasingly supplanted "void" (a sign of the void's growing elaboration). When Thomas Cogan in 1588 used the word "banquet," he had a sumptuous void in mind: "and after supper for feare lest they bee not full gorged, to have a delicate banquet, with abundance of wine" (*OED*, s.v. "banquet"). The double meaning of "banquet"—savory meal and sweet course—could lead to confusion. As we will see, however, the architectural placing of the sweet banquet separated out its meaning. By the end of the seventeenth century, such detachment would result in an independent term for the sweet banquet— "dessert."

5. On the intimate alliance between court entertainments and banquets (both savory and sweet), see Allardyce Nicoll, *Stuart Masques and the Renaissance Stage* (London: G. Harrap, 1938; reprint, New York: Arno, 1980), pp. 29–32; and Per Palme, *Triumph of Peace: A Study of the Whitehall Banqueting House* (London: Thames and Hudson, 1957), pp. 128–35. As Palme notes, James's Banqueting House traditionally housed a savory meal once a year (celebrating the Order of Saint George); nevertheless, as we shall more fully see, the Whitehall building and the masques served within it actually originated out of the void. For a more general discussion of Jonson the playwright as poet-cook, see Jonas A. Barish, "Feasting and Judging in Jonsonian Comedy," *Renaissance Drama* 5 (1972): 3–35.

6. See my discussion in the previous chapter.

7. See Girouard, *English Country House*, especially, pp. 1–118.

8. Ibid., pp. 30–31; see also pp. 38–40.

9. Henry VII, of course, did not live in Whitehall. Whitehall (previously known as York Place) only became a royal palace in 1529 after Henry VIII seized it from Thomas Wolsey, archbishop of York; until then, the primary royal residence in London was the Palace of Westminster (George S. Dugdale, *Whitehall through the Centuries* [London: Phoenix House, (1950)], pp. 5–9).

10. Girouard, *English Country House*, p. 110. Palme adds that James as a rule dined in the privy chamber (*Triumph of Peace*, p. 112). "Privy" suggests the process of privatization here; in fact, the privy chamber was originally so named because it was the room in which the monarch prepared himself to void excrement (Girouard, p. 57). It should be noted, however, that James also revived the ancient custom Elizabeth let slide of dining in state in the presence chamber; see E. K. Chambers, *The Elizabethan Stage*, 4 vols. (Oxford: Clarendon Press, 1923), 1:15. Such a dual culinary thrust by James—inward and outward—implies a divided personality, which we shall pursue.

11. G. P. V. Akrigg has placed James's bedchamber at the northeast corner of the privy garden in the privy gallery, although he admits that the bedchamber, and the adjoining withdrawing rooms, could also have lain catercorner to this site in the north end of the stone gallery (*Jacobean Pageant; or, The Court of King James I* [Cambridge: Harvard University Press, 1962], p. 398). See also Palme, *Triumph of Peace*, p. 112.

12. Girouard provides the most sustained (though still relatively brief) architectural history of the void, to which much of the following discussion is indebted (*English Country House*, pp. 104–8). See also G. Bernard Hughes, "The Old English

Banquet," *Country Life* 117 (February 17, 1955): 473–75; and Gerard Brett, *Dinner Is Served: A History of Dining in England, 1400–1900* (Rupert Hart-Davis, 1968; reprint, Hamden, Conn.: Archon, 1969), pp. 28, 31.

13. Hughes, "Old English Banquet," p. 473.

14. On the sixteenth-century importance of withdrawing rooms and the tendency to retire into them with only a chosen few, see Girouard, *English Country House,* pp. 94, 99–100. See also Gervase Jackson-Stops and James Pipkin, *The English Country House: A Grand Tour* (Boston: Little, Brown, 1985), p. 139.

15. *Lacock Abbey, Wiltshire* ([London]: National Trust, 1979; rev. ed. 1990), pp. 12–13; also Girouard, *English Country House,* p. 106.

Here and elsewhere in my discussion of banqueting houses and their relation to aristocratic residences, I supplement information in the literature with my own observations from visits to Lacock Abbey, Longleat House, Hardwick Hall, Montacute House, the Triangular Lodge at Rushton, and other sites. I wish to thank the administrators and librarians of several of these stately homes (Janet Burnett Brown, Administrator of Lacock; Kate Harris, Librarian and Archivist to the Marquess of Bath, Longleat; and I. St.C. Hughes, Administrator of Hardwick), who were kind enough to give me access to the roofs, guide me along the intricate routes to the banqueting houses, and answer my questions.

16. Girouard, *English Country House,* p. 106.

17. Mark Girouard, *Robert Smythson and the Elizabethan Country House* (New Haven: Yale University Press, 1983), p. 157. The floor plan of the house is given on p. 155 (the third floor is there labeled, in accordance with European usage, the second floor). See also Girouard, *English Country House,* pp. 116–18. The scenario I describe is further based on my own visit to Hardwick. Another, more informal, version of this scenario: Bess could have dined in the low great chamber on the second floor or in the attached smaller dining chamber (perhaps originally only an anteroom to the low great chamber). After the meal, instead of retiring into her withdrawing room to consume the void, she could then have lead her special guests out onto the landing of the north staircase and, from thence up to the roof and along the leads to the banqueting room in the south turret. On the tradition of "secret house" and the translation of the defensive turret into the private pleasure spot, see Girouard, pp. 76, 78.

18. For Montacute, see Ralph Dutton, *The English Country House,* 2d ed. (London: B. T. Batsford, 1943–44), pp. 96–97 (supplemented by my own observations). For the banqueting houses connected by galleries at the royal seats, see *The History of the King's Works,* 6 vols., ed. H. M. Colvin et al. (London: Her Majesty's Stationery Office, 1963–82), 3:325; 4:105, 165. (References to royal banqueting houses appear throughout this collection.) On the intimate relationship between long galleries and gardens, see Jackson-Stops and Pipkin, *English Country House,* p. 107. For Exeter's banqueting house, see J. Alfred Gotch, *Early Renaissance Architecture in England: A Historical and Descriptive Account of the Tudor, Elizabethan, and Jacobean Periods, 1500–1625, for the Use of Students and Others,* 2d ed. (London: B. T. Batsford, [1914]), pp. 150, 148. For the Nonsuch and Theobalds banqueting houses, see *History of the King's Works,* 4:203, 277.

19. Girouard, *English Country House,* p. 106. Even when the lodge was relatively

large, its function as a private retreat linked it to the banqueting house. Around 1610, for instance, Lord Exeter built at Wothorpe a lodge on the plan of a Greek cross about a mile or so from his primary seat "to retire to out of the dust while his great house [Burleigh] was a sweeping" (p. 108).

20. Girouard, *English Country House,* p. 106; Reginald Blomfield, *A History of Renaissance Architecture in England, 1500–1800,* 2 vols. (London, 1897), 1:78; my own observation of Hardwick's gardens (of the four garden pavilions, we know that the one in the southeast corner was probably used as a banqueting house and that the one in the northeast corner was possibly so used); *History of the King's Works,* ed. Colvin et al., 4:138.

21. Malcolm Airs, *Tudor and Jacobean: A Guide and Gazetteer,* vol. 1 of *The Buildings of Britain* (London: Barrie & Jenkins, 1982), pp. 17–18.

22. My French ("petit fours') is not mere affectation; or rather, it is the affectation of the English Renaissance elite. French cuisine became *the* fashion in James's reign. See Stephen Mennell, *All Manners of Food: Eating and Taste in England and France from the Middle Ages to the Present* (Oxford: Basil Blackwell, 1985), p. 116ff. The sweet delights of the void were most likely modeled on the French "collation" (itself of Italian influence) introduced to France by Catherine de Medici in the sixteenth century. On the French collation, see Barbara Ketcham Wheaton, *Savoring the Past: The French Kitchen and Table from 1300 to 1789* (Pennsylvania: University of Pennsylvania Press, 1983), pp. 51–52, 108, 131–32, 144–45, 147–48; on its Italian and Portuguese origins, see C. Anne Wilson, *Food & Drink in Britain from the Stone Age to Recent Times* (London: Constable, 1973), p. 301.

23. On the relation of the terms "savory banquet" (or main feast) and "sweet banquet" (or void)—both subsumed under the general category of "banquet"—see note 4 to this chapter.

24. See, for example, Gervase Markham's "Ordering of great feasts," in *The English Housewife: Containing the Inward and Outward Virtues Which Ought to Be in a Complete Woman; As Her Skill in Physic, Cookery, Banqueting-stuff, Distillation, Perfumes . . . and All Other Things belonging to a Household* (1615; rev. eds. by Markham, 1623, 1631), ed. Michael R. Best, using the 1631 edition as copy-text (Kingston and Montreal: McGill-Queen's University Press, 1986), pp. 121–24; Markham's cookery recipes, pp. 60–121 (which reflect many new fashions, such as the taste for "sallats"); and Best on Markham's seasonings, pp. xxxvi–xxxvii. See also, for example, Wilson's description of Elizabethan and Jacobean stews (*Food & Drink in Britain,* p. 133); and Jean-François Revel, *Culture and Cuisine: A Journey through the History of Food,* trans. Helen R. Lane (1982; reprint, New York: Da Capo, 1982), p. 94, and on "verjuice," pp. 96–97.

25. Wilson, *Food & Drink in Britain,* pp. 106, 297, 223–24. Mennell nominates La Varenne's *Le Cuisinier François* (1651) as the leader of the new taste for discrimination in cooking (*All Manners of Food,* pp. 71–74ff.). However, he attributes subsequent changes in England less to such courtly *nouvelle cuisine* than to a bourgeois "economy, plainness, and hostility to French cookery" (perceived as extravagant); p. 96. See also Revel, *Culture and Cuisine,* p. 106.

26. For the first appearance of spoons at the void, see Katie Stewart, in collaboration with Pamela and Maurice Michael, *The Joy of Eating: A Cook's Tour of History,*

Illustrated with a Cook's Section of the Great Recipes of Every Era (Great Britain, under the title *Cooking and Eating,* [by Pamela and Maurice Michael]: Hart Davis, Mac-Gibbon, 1975; reprint, Owings Mills, Md.: Stemmer House, 1977), pp. 68–69. For the void fork, see Bridget Ann Henisch, *Fast and Feast: Food in Medieval Society* (University Park: Pennsylvania State University Press, 1976), p. 186; and Major C. T. P. Bailey, who describes combination forks/spoons for eating sweatmeats and locates the general use of table forks in the late seventeenth century (*Knives and Forks: Selected and Described with an Introduction* [London: Medici Society, (1927)], pp. 5, 8). For the void plate, see Stewart, p. 99; Henisch, p. 161; and, for the dishing up of decorations, Brett, *Dinner is Served,* p. 78, as well as Hughes, "Old English Banquet," p. 474. Samples from two sets of decorated "roundels" or void plates (both dated c. 1600) are in the Victoria & Albert Museum. Diners would eat their sweets from the plain side of these roundels before turning them over to appreciate the inscriptions.

27. Yi-Fu Tuan, *Segmented Worlds and Self: Group Life and Individual Consciousness* (Minneapolis: University of Minnesota Press, 1982).

28. I concentrate on void stuffs here, but in extending my thesis that the void lacked substantive reference to "food" I will later discuss void cordials and sweet wines as well.

29. [Hugh Plat], *Delightes for Ladies, to adorne their Persons, Tables, closets and distillatories. With Beauties, banquets, perfumes and waters. . . .*(1603), sig. B4r (recipe no. 10); *The good Huswifes Handmaide for the Kitchin. Containing Manie principall pointes of Cookerie . . . Hereunto are annexed, sundrie necessarie Conceits for the preseruation of health. Uerie meete to be adioined to the good Huswifes Closet of prouision for her Houshold* (1594), p. 40v; Plat, *Delightes for Ladies,* recipe no. 18; [Hugh Plat?], *A Closet for Ladies and Gentlewomen, Or, The art of preseruing, Conseruing, and Candying. With the manner howe to make diuers kinds of Syrups: and all kind of banqueting stuffes. Also diuers soueraigne Medicines and Salues, for sundry Diseases* (1608), p. 33 (though the authorship of this last work is uncertain, I shall for convenience cite Plat).

30. *good Huswifes Handmaide for the Kitchin,* p. 52v. On the aristocratic gentlewoman's personal hand in creating such void stuffs, see Wilson, *Food & Drink in Britain,* p. 301. Of course, as Wilson also notes, sweetmeats could be purchased in the towns from professional confectioners as well (p. 302). On the allowance for personal taste (despite the author's often commanding tone—"you must," "take," etc.), see, for example, Plat's recipe for the aforementioned walnut: "then put what you please into the nut" (*Closet for Ladies and Gentlewomen,* p. 34).

31. Both the latter phenomena lend support to Don E. Wayne's claim that the idea of the nuclear "home" was now emerging. See *Penshurst: The Semiotics of Place and the Poetics of History* (Madison: University of Wisconsin Press, 1984), p. 75. For the prominence of the still-room in the seventeenth century, see Girouard, *English Country House,* p. 208.

It makes sense to broaden our discussion from the aristocracy proper to gentry and husbandmen in studying the recipe books of the sixteenth and seventeenth centuries because of the fiction in these books that their audience was entirely polite. On the class issues involved in this fiction, see my discussion below.

32. On locking up spices, see Wilson, *Food & Drink in Britain*, pp. 285, 293. The fashion for carrying comfit boxes developed in France by the close of the sixteenth century (Frederick W. Hackwood, *Good Cheer: The Romance of Food and Feasting* [London: T. Fisher Unwin, 1911], p. 287).

33. Plat, *Delightes for Ladies*, sig. Dllv (recipe no. 66, under heading: The Arte of Preseruing, conseruing, candying, &c.); Philip Gibbs, *The Reckless Duke: The Romantic Story of the First Duke of Buckingham and the Stuart Court* (New York: Harper & Brothers, 1931), p. 103.

In several senses, personalized confectionary was actually more intimate than the ornamental miniature. First, as we have seen, sweet conceits were definitively displaced from the main practices of living. They were not, like miniatures, located at the center of public rooms or of the court. They were detached. Second, such sweet fancies (although they could be bought in comfit shops) were as a rule fashioned by housewives. They were not, like miniatures, the province of professionals. They were personally made. Finally, an obvious but important point: when eaten, confectionary literally became the consumer. The keen literalism with which the Renaissance observed this fact led to what one might call an "identity principle" of consumption. In an essential way, subjectivity was fed by private foods.

34. Norbert Elias, *The History of Manners*, vol. 1 of *The Civilizing Process*, 2 vols., trans. Edmund Jephcott (New York: Urizen, 1978; reprint, New York: Pantheon, 1982), pp. 78, 104–8, and passim.

35. Tuan, *Segmented Worlds and Self*, pp. 106–7; 114–15ff.

36. We have seen turrets at Lacock, Longleat, and Hardwick; a three-storied banqueting house in Tresham's Triangular Lodge; and a raised banqueting house in James's little house approached by a flight of steps in Theobalds' park. For an example of a banqueting house built on a mound, see Gotch's discussion of the 1587 survey of Holdenby (*Early Renaissance Architecture in England*, pp. 85–86).

The vista seen today from the Hardwick banqueting turret is obviously not exactly the same as it would have been in the Renaissance. As Mark Girouard notes, however, the basics remain the same: "The arrangement of courts and orchards around the New Hall [as opposed to Hardwick's Old Hall nearby] is contemporary with the building of the house [c. 1590–96], and they form an integral part of the design" (*Hardwick Hall* [London: National Trust, 1989], p. 90). Certainly, geometrical garden designs (often more elaborate than that seen today from the Hardwick banqueting turret window) were common in the Renaissance.

37. Girouard, *English Country House*, pp. 90–93.

38. Thornton, *Seventeenth-Century Interior Decoration*, p. 299.

39. Girouard, *English Country House*, p. 104; for the parlor's location, see pp. 59, 103–4.

40. Airs, *Tudor and Jacobean*, p. 56.

41. Olive Cook, *The English Country House: An Art and a Way of Life* (London: Thames and Hudson, 1974), pp. 95, 98. For the alcoved lobby beneath the cupola, see in addition Girouard, *Robert Smythson*, p. 244. See also his description of the Little Castle, pp. 206–10, 234–45, 260–69.

42. Wheaton, *Savoring the Past*, p. 49; Gervase Jackson-Stops and James Pipkin, *The Country House Garden: A Grand Tour* (Boston: Little, Brown, 1987), pp. 188–89.

43. Tuan, *Segmented Worlds and Self*, p. 48.

44. John Murrell, *A Daily Exercise for Ladies and Gentlewomen. Whereby they may learne and practise the whole Art of making Pastes, Preserues, Marmalades, Conserues, Tartuffes, Gellies, Breads, Sucket Candies, Cordiall waters, Conceits in Sugar-workes of seuerall kindes. As also to dry Lemonds, Orenges, or other Fruits. . . .* (1617), recipe nos. 75, 76, 77, 78, 79, 80, 81, 84, 89. The title to Murrell's cookbook itself projects the splintered void cosmos of which the above choice tidbits are parts.

45. *History of the King's Works,* ed. Colvin et al., 4:202. See also Gotch, who describes the building as three-storied (*Early Renaissance Architecture in England,* p. 150).

46. Philippa Pullar, *Consuming Passions: Being an Historic Inquiry into Certain English Appetites* (Boston: Little, Brown, 1970), p. 124. Other examples can be found in the more naturally "grown" bowers "smelling of sweet flowers and trees" that Leicester created at either end of his new garden at Kenilworth, or in the new arbors James had constructed in the great garden at Theobalds, 1612–13 (Cook, *English Country House,* p. 80; *History of the King's Works,* ed. Colvin et al., 4:275).

47. Plat, *Closet for Ladies and Gentlewomen,* pp. 17, 12–13. Murrell, in "To preserue Cherries," required the same "siluer spoone" for the four-fold skimming of his syrup "very cleane" (*Daily Exercise for Ladies and Gentlewomen,* recipe no. 13). The same meticulousness pervades Dawson's recipe for a sweetmeat ("To preserue Quinces whole"):

> Take a pottle of faire water, and put it into a cleane panne, and beate iii. pound of fine suger, and put into it, then set it on the fire, and when you haue skimmed it, put in twelue spoonefuls of rosewater, then take x. faire Quinces, and pare them, and core them cleane, then put them into your syrup, and so couer them verie close for the space of two houres with a faire platter, and let them boyle a good pace at the two houres, and vncouer them, and looke whether you finde them tender, and that they haue a faire crimson colour, then take them vp and lay them vpon a faire platter, couering your syrruppe againe, And let it seeth while it be somewhat thicke, then put your Quinces into your syrrup againe, and so haue a faire gallie pot, and put in both your syrrup and quinces as fast as you can, and couer your potte close that the heate goe not foorth, you must not put them in a glasse for it will breake. (*The good huswifes Iewell. Wherein is to be found most excellent and rare Deuises for Conseites in Cookerie. . . . Newly set forth with Additions* [1587], pp. 36–37).

On the great skill and attentiveness as well as the special equipment demanded in confectionary cookery, see also Wilson, *Food & Drink in Britain,* p. 302.

48. See, for example, Dawson's recipe in the preceding note; also Plat's conclusion to a recipe: "put it in fine Christall Glasses, and keepe it all the yeare" (*Closet for Ladies and Gentlewomen,* p. 31). Or again, John Murrell: "then box it vp and keepe it all the yeare" (*A Delightfull daily exercise for Ladies and Gentlewomen. Whereby is set foorth the secrete misteries of the purest preseruings in Glasses and other Confriction-aries. . . . Whereto is added a Booke of Cookery* [1621], recipe no. 5). We shall more fully pursue the phenomenon of "subtleties" (or "sotelties") later in this chapter.

49. Thomas Dawson, *The Second part of the good Hus-wiues Iewell. Where is to be found most apt and readiest wayes to distill many wholsome and sweet waters. In which likewise is shewed the best maner in preseruing of diuers sorts of Fruits, & making of Sirrops. With diuers conceits in Cookerie with the Booke of Caruing* (1597), pp. 39–40.

50. Cited in Richard Barber, *Cooking and Recipes from Rome to the Renaissance*

(London: Allen Lane, 1973), pp. 131–32. May's nostalgia is for the prerevolutionary reigns of Elizabeth, James, and Charles I. See also Sydney Anglo's report of a 1522 entertainment: seeking to free beautiful ladies held captive within a castle, Henry VIII ("Ardent Desire") and his companions assaulted the jailers with dates, oranges, and other "fruites made for pleasure"; the defenders returned fire with a hail of rose water, comfits, and other trifles (*Spectacle, Pageantry, and Early Tudor Policy* [Oxford: Clarendon Press, 1969], pp. 120–21).

51. *The Works of John Taylor the Water Poet*, reprinted from the folio ed. of 1630, part 3 (Spenser Society, 1869), p. 66 (first of two p. 66s). I am grateful to Jon Reed for pointing out this passage to me.

52. Ian Dunlop, *Palaces & Progresses of Elizabeth I* (London: Jonathan Cape, 1962), p. 69; Markham, *English Housewife*, p. 123; Sidney W. Mintz, *Sweetness and Power: The Place of Sugar in Modern History* (New York: Viking Penguin, 1985; reprint, Penguin, 1986), p. 78ff.

53. Thomas Aquinas resolved the twelfth-century debate over whether spiced sugars were food (and therefore constituted a violation of a fast) by declaring them medicinal rather than nutritive (Mintz, *Sweetness and Power*, p. 99). The debate over the food value of sugar and spice resurfaced in the sixteenth and extended into the nineteenth century; until the late eighteenth century, the medicinal powers prevailed (pp. 101–8). So strong was the equation between spiced sugars and medicine that the popular banquet recipe for hippocras—distilled wine mixed with honey and spices—was originally prepared by an apothecary (Hackwood, *Good Cheer*, p. 125). Not coincidentally, then, the Latin verb *curare* signifies to dress a dinner as well as to cure a disease (noted by Hackwood, p. 235).

54. Mintz, *Sweetness and Power*, p. 234 n. 39; K. N. Chaudhuri, *The English East India Company* (London: Frank Cass, 1965), pp. 140, 167.

55. Murrell, *Daily Exercise for Ladies and Gentlewomen*, recipe nos. 44, 47, 61; J[ohn] M[urrell], *A New Booke of Cookerie. Wherein is set forth the newest and most commendable Fashion for Dressing or Sowcing, eyther Flesh, Fish, or Fowle. Together with making all sorts of Iellyes, and other made-Dishes. . . . Hereunto also is added the most exquisite London Cookerie. . . . Set forth by the obseruation of a Traueller* (1615), p. 30 (pp. 30 and 31 are repeated; reference is to second p. 30).

56. Dawson, *good huswifes Iewell*, pp. 23r–24v.

57. Guilielmus Gratarolus, *A Direction for the Health of Magistrates and Studentes. . . . Written in Latin*, trans. T[homas] N[ewton] (1574), sig. Miii(verso); [Thomas Lupton], *A Thousand Notable Things, of sundrie sortes. . . .* (1579), p. 90; [Hugh Plat], *The Accomplisht Ladys Delight In Preserving, Physick, Beautifying and Cookery* (n.d.), p. 71 (recipe no. 89, under heading: Excellent Receipts in Physick and Chirvrgery) and [John Partridge], *The Widdowes Treasure. Plentifully furnished with sundrey precious and approued secrets in Phisicke and Chirurgery, for the health and pleasure of Mankinde. Heereunto are adioyned, sundry prittie practises and conclusions of Cookerie, with many profitable and wholsome Medicines, for sundrie diseases in Cattell* (1595), sig. C4r; Murrell, *Delightfull daily exercise*, recipe no. 72; Plat, *Accomplisht Ladys Delight*, p. 18 (recipe no. 77) and Markham, *English Housewife*, p. 57; Plat, *Accomplisht Ladys Delight*, p. 18 (recipe no. 77).

58. Gratarolus, *Direction for the Health of Magistrates,* sig. Miiir; Leonardo Phioravante, *A Compendium of the rationall Secretes, of the worthie Knight and moste excellent Doctour of Phisicke and Chirurgerie. . . . hetherto neuer set out before,* [translated by John Hester] (1582), book 3, p. 38; Henry Buttes, *Dyets Dry Dinner: Consisting of eight seuerall Courses. . . . All serued in after the order of Time vniuersall* (1599), sig. O5v.

59. Sugar and spice alone made up the void in medieval times; as part of the growing separation of all savoriness from the main feast and consequent elaboration of void stuffs in the Renaissance, however, conserves (sugar-coated spices, nuts, flowers, etc.) and preserves (fruits cooked in sugar and spice) also entered the scene. See Revel, *Culture and Cuisine,* p. 141.

60. Plat, *Closet for Ladies and Gentlewomen,* pp. 44–45; Partridge, *Widdowes Treasure,* sig. E6r; Markham, *English Housewife,* p. 57; Dawson, *good huswifes Iewell,* pp. 49r, 48v; Markham, pp. 56–57.

61. To this list I would also add "departing." An early version of the moment of exiting from one room to another to consume a void was the drinking of a void just before departing from a house or retiring from a room for the night (*OED,* s.v. "voidee"). It is in this context that we should consider Charles's drinking of a cordial before leaving his private chambers to meet his death.

62. See, for example, Lupton on the effects of his "Electuary of lyfe" and of sugar (*Thousand Notable Things,* pp. 89–90, 129); also Gratarolus on cinnamon (*Direction for the Health of Magistrates,* sig. Miiir); and Phioravante, *Compendium of the rationall Secretes,* book 1, pp. 2, 23–24, and passim. Significantly, spices were burnt at feasts to mask the smell of decomposing animal skins when the cooked meat was stuffed back into the carcass for "show" (Revel, *Culture and Cuisine,* p. 134).

63. Phioravante, *Compendium of the rationall Secretes,* book 3, pp. 110, 66; Lupton, *Thousand Notable Things,* p. 38.

64. Peter Farb and George Armelagos, *Consuming Passions: The Anthropology of Eating* (Boston: Houghton Mifflin, 1980), p. 147; also Betty Wason, *Cooks, Gluttons & Gourmets: A History of Cookery* (Garden City: Doubleday, 1962), p. 170. Henisch notes the association of the delicate wafer with manna (*Fast and Feast,* p. 77).

65. Plat, *Delightes for Ladies,* sig. A2r. The fashion of consuming confectionary and sweetmeats in the English Renaissance was thus an intense moment in a long tradition by which cultures endured death-threatening separation by eating sweets. We can see literal representations of this phenomena in the sugar-forms of the present day: the candy skulls, tombs, and wreaths celebrating All Saints' Day in Mexico (reproduced by Mintz) as well as the candied treats memorializing funerals in much of Europe. While Mintz contrasts such bittersweet consumption with the eating of confectionary at Easter, I would argue that all of these sugar rituals address the same desire and fear: the hope of preservation in the face of death (*Sweetness and Power,* back of page facing p. 184). Sir Thomas Elyot, I would further add, was thinking along the same lines when he recommended spices for curing melancholy caused by ingratitude, loss, or death (*The Castell of Helth Corrected, and in some places augmented* (1572), pp. 67v–70r).

66. Plat, *Closet for Ladies and Gentlewomen,* pp. 45–46; Markham, *English House-*

wife, pp. 132–36. As Markham's modern editor notes, many of his distillations "would have been simple perfumes derived from herbs high in essential oils" (p. xxxi).

67. The death rate in London almost doubled at the end of the sixteenth century (and was even higher in other areas of England); see Andrew B. Appleby, "Diet in Sixteenth-Century England: Sources, Problems, Possibilities," in Charles Webster, ed., *Health, Medicine and Mortality in the Sixteenth Century* (Cambridge: Cambridge University Press, 1979), p. 114. At the same time, pepper and spice consumption increased dramatically. Between 1500 and 1620, notes C. H. H. Wake, the trade in Moluccan spices appears to have grown by as much as 500% ("The Changing Pattern of Europe's Pepper and Spice Imports, ca 1400–1700," *Journal of European Economic History* 8 [1979]: 393).

68. Palme, *Triumph of Peace,* pp. 102, 288ff.; John Chamberlain, *Letters,* ed. Norman Egbert McClure, 2 vols. (Philadelphia: American Philosophical Society, 1939; reprint, 1962), 2:367.

69. Jones's classicism, however, did prefigure a later banqueting-house style. See, for example, Jackson-Stops and Pipkin, *Country House Garden,* pp. 189–90, 191. Resemblances to the public hall were strongest in the first Banqueting House of 1606 (Palme, *Triumph of Peace,* p. 116).

70. Palme, *Triumph of Peace,* p. 288 and passim; Jonathan Goldberg, *James I and the Politics of Literature: Jonson, Shakespeare, Donne, and Their Contemporaries* (Baltimore: Johns Hopkins University Press, 1983), pp. 39–40.

71. Quoted in Palme, *Triumph of Peace,* p. 92.

72. On the severe "sameness" of the building's interior, see Palme, *Triumph of Peace,* p. 178. On the decoration of columns, see p. 192 and, for a full discussion of the interior decoration, including an interpretation of Rubens's paintings, pp. 225–88. Roy Strong offers an alternative reading of the paintings in *Britannia Triumphans: Inigo Jones, Rubens and Whitehall Palace* (New York: Thames and Hudson, 1981).

73. Palme, *Triumph of Peace,* p. 285. Palme argues that, on each side of the ground floor, four of the seven windows were permanently closed or "bastard" windows. The sequence of open and closed windows would have been a-bb-a-bb-a (p. 217).

74. The following is but a random sampling. "Sweet," "sweeter," "sweetness(e)," "sweets": *The Masque of Beauty* (1608), l. 97; *The Masque of Queens* (1609), l. 395; *Oberon, The Fairy Prince* (1611), l. 263; *The Golden Age Restored* (1615), l. 183; *The Vision of Delight* (1617), l. 138; *Pleasure Reconciled to Virtue* (1618), l. 282; *Neptune's Triumph for the Return of Albion* (1624), l. 299; *Timber; or, Discoveries . . . of the Times* (composed c. 1623–35), in *Ben Jonson,* ed. C. H. Herford and Percy and Evelyn Simpson, 11 vols. (Oxford: Clarendon Press, 1925–52), 8:566, 587, 626, 639. "Neat": *News from the New World Discovered in the Moon* (1620), l. 94; *Discoveries,* 8:620. "Clean": *News,* l. 94. "Clear," "clearest," or "clears": *Hymenaei* (1606), ll. 139, 784; *Love Freed from Ignorance and Folly* (1611), ll. 34, 256; *Vision,* l. 164. "Pure," "purer," or "purity": *The Masque of Blackness* (1605), ll. 135, 230; *Beauty,* l. 300; *Love Freed,* l. 229; *Golden Age,* ll. 94, 155, 172; *Neptune's Triumph,* l. 260; *Discoveries,* 8:620. "Fair," "fairest," "fairer": *Blackness,* ll. 120, 138; *Hymenaei,* l. 412; *The Haddington Masque* (1608), l. 110; *Love Freed,* ll. 30, 91, 285, 286, 302; *Vision,* l. 1; *Pleasure Reconciled,* ll. 155, 189, 259, 274. "Fresh," "refresh," "refreshed": *Mercury Vindicated from the Alchemists at Court*

(1616), l. 176; *A Masque of the Metamorphosed Gypsies* (1621), l. 1327; *Vision*, l. 158; *Neptune's Triumph*, l. 342. "Subtle," "subtile," "subtly," "subtlest," or "subtlety" ("subtilty," "subtility"): *Blackness*, l. 279; *Beauty*, l. 182; *Hymenaei*, ll. 279, 554; *Oberon*, l. 278; *Pleasure Reconciled*, l. 271; *Discoveries*, 8:589, 611. "Airy": *Hymenaei*, ll. 229, 596; *Oberon*, l. 344; *Golden Age*, l. 145; *Lovers Made Men* (1617), l. 96; *Gypsies*, l. 1338.

75. Travelers specifically from the Far East arrive, for instance, in *Love Freed*. On masquing garbs of both the East and West Indies, see Nicoll, *Stuart Masques*, pp. 194–98.

76. See, for example, the circles, squares, and triangles danced in Daniel's *Vision of the Twelve Goddesses*, l. 174; the letters and chain in *Hymenaei*, ll. 283–85; the circles in *Oberon*, l. 278; the "curious" knot and maze in *Pleasure Reconciled*, ll. 225, 233; and the anagram of Charles James Stuart ("*Claims Arthur's Seat*") in *For the Honor of Wales* (1618), ll. 347–48.

77. For "frolicks," see Jonson's *The Devil is an Ass* (performed 1616), in *Jonson*, ed. Herford and Simpson, 6:2.7.73; and the accompanying note (*Jonson*, 10:239).

78. "Reasonable" confectionary was designed to delight and teach through literally sweet persuasion ("sweet" and "persuade" derive from the same root, *swād;* Mintz, *Sweetness and Power*, p. 155). Subtleties also quintessentially represent the segmentation and detachment of savoriness from the main meal in the form of banqueting stuffs. While subtleties originally ushered in the separate courses of savory banquets, they then separated off, along with spiced sugars, in the singular taste of the void (Wilson, *Food & Drink in Britain*, pp. 336–37). On the attached verses or "reasons," and their political significance, see Barber, *Cooking and Recipes from Rome to the Renaissance*, p. 101; Hackwood, *Good Cheer*, p. 108; and Mintz, pp. 88–90.

79. *Country House Garden*, p. 189.

80. Henisch, *Fast and Feast*, p. 234.

81. Barber, *Cooking and Recipes from Rome to the Renaissance*, pp. 101–2.

82. Sir John Harington, cited in *Progresses . . . of James the First*, ed. Nichols, 2:72. For appearances of comfits in Elizabethan masques as well, see Chambers, *Elizabethan Stage*, 1:164–65.

83. Cited in *Jonson*, ed. Herford and Simpson, 10:566. I am assuming that the last service was a sweet rather than a savory banquet; it was customary under James (as we shall more fully pursue) to complete a masque entertainment with a void.

84. Palme, *Triumph of Peace*, p. 130.

85. Cited in *Jonson*, ed. Herford and Simpson, 10:447.

86. John Finett, *Finetti Philoxenis: Som Choice Observations of Sir John Finett Knight, and Master of the Ceremonies to the Two Last Kings, Touching the Reception, and Precedence, the Treatment and Audience, the Puntillios and Contests of Forren Ambassadors in England* (1656), p. 45. The urge for personalization as much as for political subterfuge might also explain James's highly irregular and informal system of sending "ambassadorial" representatives abroad (see David Harris Willson, *King James VI and I* [1956; reprint, London: Jonathan Cape, 1959], pp. 142–48).

87. Finett, *Finetti Philoxenis*, pp. 8, 62.

88. G. Topham Forrest and Montagu H. Cox, *The Parish of St. Margaret, Westminster*, 2 vols., originally published for the London County Council as vols. 10 and

13 of the Survey of London (London: B. T. Batsford, 1926–30; reprint, New York: AMS, 1971–79), 2:116–17, 118. Actually, James's Banqueting Houses (both the one built in 1606–7 and the other in 1619–22) were built of brick and stone (and woodwork still decorated their insides); see *History of the King's Works*, ed. Colvin et al., 4:323, 330–31.

89.Orazio Busino (chaplain to the Venetian embassy) provides this head count of the audience at the masque *Pleasure Reconciled* (englished in Orgel and Strong, eds., *Inigo Jones*, 1:282). Glynne Wickham notes that the problem of overcrowding at such entertainments largely arose from the expansion of the "understood" elite entitled to attendance according to the rules of precedence and social etiquette. Such muddied "understanding" of position became acute by James's reign, due (I would add) to massive selling of titles (*Early English Stages, 1300–1660*, 2 vols. [New York: Columbia University Press, 1963–72], 1:200). The expansion of the court audience to include "country" ladies and even wealthy citizens (especially their wives) is mocked in Jonson's *Love Restored* (1612), ll. 97–99, 107–13. Daniel, with clear disgust, states that usually "inferiour sort" even mixed in with "great Personages" as part of the show (*Tethys Festival: or, The Qveenes Wake* [1610], in *The Complete Works in Verse and Prose of Samuel Daniel*, ed. Rev. Alexander B. Grosart, 5 vols. [1885–96; reprint, New York: Russell & Russell, 1963], 3:ll. 417–20). Complaints of the "confusion" created by the great crowds pressing in to see the show are incessant. See, for example, Dudley Carleton's account of the mob scene at *Blackness* (quoted in *Jonson*, 10:449). As we shall see, disturbances of this sort definitively concluded the masque and ensuing banquet.

90. David Harris Willson, *King James VI and I*, pp. 195, 434, 196. The French ambassador here secularizes as gossip the language of blasphemy (thought to re-tear the body of Christ); see Leah Sinanoglou, "The Christ Child as Sacrifice: A Medieval Tradition and the Corpus Christi Plays," 48 *Speculum* (1973): 497.

91. David Harris Willson, *King James VI and I*, pp. 183–84. On the problematics of such country withdrawal for a king, see also Philip Howard, *The Royal Palaces* (Boston: Gambit, 1970), pp. 9–10, and for the term "hunting-box," p. 8.

92. Chambers, *Elizabethan Stage*, 1:52–53. The proliferation of numbers extended to other offices as well (David Harris Willson, *James VI and I*, p. 190).

93. Stephen Orgel, *The Illusion of Power: Political Theater in the English Renaissance* (Berkeley: University of California Press, 1975), pp. 10–16; see also Palme, *Triumph of Peace*, p. 151.

94. Though Jones's early designs do not represent his final sketches for the masque (mostly missing), they are close approximations and offer a rare glimpse of a complete sequence of perspective scenes. For all extant designs, see Orgel and Strong, eds., *Inigo Jones*, 1:210–20.

95. I presume that the door is closed, though it is possible that the sketch represents a dark doorway. In either case, the doorway is closed to vision and acts as what I will later call a *porta clausa*.

96. Goldberg, *James I*, p. 40. My analysis of the discovery of the masquing self converges with Goldberg's along a number of lines: we both see masques as being about the "mystery" of the kingly self, and we both find such selfhood realized in acts of dramatization. Goldberg's broader argument that privacy was thus indis-

tinguishable from the public or political, however, diverges from my own. My goal is to open up a space for withdrawal and intimacy even as such privatized space was transgressed in the act of being publicized.

97. In *Prince Henry's Barriers,* Henry did not (as he would do in *Oberon*) proceed through the opening of the portico; his challengers did. The Prince and his cohorts were concealed in a pavilion in front and to the right of the receding perspective scenery. From this pavilion, they emerged to await their opponents (Orgel and Strong, eds., *Inigo Jones,* 1:164, 167). Henry's position thus offered "another stage / And scene" (ll. 164–65) rivaling his father's stage/dais from which to watch the show. The implication was that the son's gaze mirrored and yet diverged from that of his father. Indeed, the war-loving Henry (whose "self" was dramatized in the ideal of knighthood that issued from within St. George's Portico to engage with him) could never be fully aligned with the peace-loving James (see below and note 101).

98. Significantly, the "room" of the Banqueting House structurally resembled an extension of James's privy gallery: "The axis of the hall," Palme notes, "is the undecided extension of a gallery or corridor, not the qualified and directive axiality of a ceremonial hall" (*Triumph of Peace,* p. 180).

99. Anon., *The Masque of Flowers,* ed. E. A. J. Honingmann, in *Book of Masques,* ll. 292–94, 303.

100. Leah S. Marcus, *The Politics of Mirth: Jonson, Herrick, Milton, Marvell, and the Defense of Old Holiday Pastimes* (Chicago: University of Chicago Press, 1986), chapter 3, especially pp. 69–70. See also her article (under Leah Sinanoglou Marcus), "City Metal and Country Mettle: The Occasion of Ben Jonson's *Golden Age Restored,*" in *Pageantry in the Shakespearean Theater,* ed. David M. Bergeron (Athens: University of Georgia Press, 1985), p. 36.

101. On the lack of sympathy between kingly father and princely son, see David Harris Willson, *James VI and I,* p. 281; see also note 97 above.

102. I am indebted throughout my analysis of Annunciation pictures to discussions with Alan Liu as well as to his own work on Annunciations in *Wordsworth,* pp. 67–74 and passim.

103. Frederick Hartt, *History of Italian Renaissance Art: Painting, Sculpture, Architecture,* 2d ed. (New York: Harry N. Abrams, 1979), p. 69.

104. Liu, *Wordsworth,* pp. 71–74.

105. Mary Ann Caws, *The Eye in the Text: Essays on Perception, Mannerist to Modern* (Princeton: Princeton University Press, 1981), pp. 109–15.

106. Ibid., p. 114.

107. The same barred window appears twofold in Giotto's *Annunciation* in the Arena Chapel (Hartt, *History of Italian Renaissance Art,* pp. 221, 69). It is also doubly suggested in the Domenico above (fig. 31) in the form of the blackened windows on either side of the central archway that leads to the barred door.

108. The verbal signs of this Annunciation mark a significantly more definitive intercourse with divinity than the characteristic pointing upward (to the medallion representing God in the archway above and to the light-inbued dove of Christ hovering over Mary's head).

109. Caws, *Eye in the Text,* p. 112.

110. In making this statement, of course, I am abbreviating a much fuller argument that would need to be made to embed James's masques in a pictorial tradition. Such an argument would retrace the ways in which the masque was invested with the iconography of religious stasis generally, that is, with the great scenes of dogma, including not only the Annunciation but the Transfiguration, Mother and Child, Adoration, Epiphany, Crucifixion, etc. Together, these scenes (characteristically set in closed architectural spaces) provided the masque with its vocabulary of visual space. I shall pursue the masque's analogy between scenes of Annunciation and Epiphany below.

111. Orgel and Strong, eds., *Inigo Jones,* 1:212.

112. On James (and, by extension, the poet) as both creator-father and -mother of the masque, see Goldberg, *James I,* p. 88.

113. See also *Vision*—"We see, we hear, we feel, we taste, / We smell the change in every flower" (ll. 127–28); *Gypsies,* which directly addresses the senses of James; and *Time Vindicated,* where the antimasque is populated by the Curious devourers after news (the Eyed, the Eared, and the Nosed).

114. Orgel and Strong, *Inigo Jones,* 1:210; I am also indebted to James Winn for drawing my attention to the visual detail of the stag.

115. G[eorge] S[andys], *Ovid's Metamorphosis Englished, Mythologiz'd, And Represented in Figures, An Essay to the Translation of Virgil's Aeneis* (1632), p. 100. Glossing Sandys, Louis Adrian Montrose adds a political interpretation: "To 'discover' the nakedness of the prince is both to locate and to reveal—to demystify—the secrets of state" ("The Elizabethan Subject and the Spenserian Text," in *Literary Theory/Renaissance Texts,* ed. Patricia Parker and David Quint [Baltimore: Johns Hopkins University Press, 1986], p. 328). Sir John Chamberlain invoked the same myth in reporting contemporary criticisms over Sir Edward Coke's "too too busie" investigation of James's favorite, the earl of Somerset: Coke, we are told, "dived farther into secrets than there was need, and so perhaps might see *nudam sine veste Dianam*" (*Letters,* 2:14).

116. Stephen Orgel, *The Jonsonian Masque* (Cambridge: Harvard University Press, 1967; reprint, New York: Columbia University Press, 1981), p. 88; see also p. 87.

117. A popular recipe. See, for example, Murrell, *Delightfull daily exercise for Ladies and Gentlewomen,* no. 71.

118. Anxiety over the presence of such a void can be further seen in the compulsion to "fill" all void or empty places in the stage sets. Describing Jones's landscape scene for *Blackness,* for example, Jonson affirms that every "void place" was "filled with huntings" (l. 21). See also Mark Breitenberg's discussion of the state pageantry celebrating Elizabeth's entry into London ("'. . . the hole matter opened': Iconic Representation and Interpretation in 'The Quenes Majesties Passage,'" *Criticism* 28 [1986]: 13–14, 17).

119. *Hall's Chronicle; Containing the History of England, during the Reign of Henry the Fourth . . . to the End of the Reign of Henry the Eighth. . . . Carefully Collated with the Editions of 1548 and 1550,* ed. Sir Henry Ellis et al. (London, 1809), pp. 518–19.

120. In the same passage, Jonson attempted to distinguish between such mortality and enduring "spirits" of the masque (as, elsewhere, he differentiated between its "outward" and "inward" parts). As with banqueting stuffs, however, the

masque's inwardness and spirituality were grounded on the body. Jonson's use of the word "sense" is illustrative. Inevitably, to adopt the Bowl-bearer's pun in *Pleasure Reconciled to Virtue,* the word developed "two senses" (l. 60): physical sense and its opposite, idea or meaning. In *Hymenaei,* for instance, Jonson begins by distinguishing between things "subjected to understanding" ("the inward parts") and those "objected to *sense*" ("the outward celebration or show") but goes on to declare that, in the former, "their *sense* or doth or should always hold on more removed mysteries" (ll. 1–17; my emphases). The other version of this doubling pun was the interplay between the "nonsense" of the antimasque and the "non-sense" of the main masque. In *Oberon,* for example, the gesture inward toward the non-sensical "air" of masquers required passing through the nonsensical "rude" banter of the satyrs (ll. 322, 237). It was in the fullest dramatization of this interdependence that the annunciation of self concluded with Oberon's chair moving outward as if in a "desire" physically to devour James, the twice-told "wonder of tongues, of ears, of eyes" (ll. 223, 226, 233). Thus even the "achieved" inwardness and spirituality of the masque were conceived of as consumable goods. Even before made void by the "rage" of the "public" audience, the private masque was being consumed. In fact, as we have seen in the nervous references to ephemerality in the revels, though the masque sought restorative sweets, it was—like a carcass—subject to *mortal* consumption.

121. Chambers, *Elizabethan Stage,* 1:206–7.

122. *Dudley Carleton to John Chamberlain, 1603–1624; Jacobean Letters,* ed. Maurice Lee, Jr. (New Brunswick, N.J.: Rutgers University Press, [1972]), p. 56; Chambers, *Elizabethan Stage,* 1:207, 3:282–83; Orgel and Strong, eds., *Inigo Jones,* 1:206.

123. Chambers, *Elizabethan Stage,* 3:235.

124. Busino, cited in Orgel and Strong, eds., *Inigo Jones,* 1:284.

125. Helen Codere, *Fighting with Property: A Study of Kwakiutl Potlatching and Warfare, 1792–1930,* Monographs of the American Ethnological Society, no. 28 (New York: J. J. Augustin, [1950]), pp. 5–6. For consistency of tense in this chapter, I speak of the potlatch in the past tense; it should be noted, however, that this practice of gift exchange, like the Kula, goes on even today.

126. Codere, *Fighting with Property,* pp. 77–78; on the destruction of coppers (the equivalent of "bank notes of high denomination"), see pp. 75–77; on the kinds of goods potlatched, see pp. 90–91.

127. Eli Sagan, *Cannibalism: Human Aggression and Cultural Form* (New York: Harper & Row, 1974), pp. 112–17, 112. On the Cannibal Dance, see also Stanley Walens, *Feasting with Cannibals: An Essay on Kwakiutl Cosmology* (New Jersey: Princeton University Press, [1981]), pp. 15–16, 141–48, 154–63.

128. Anthropologists from Mauss to Bourdieu have extended the potlatch's agonistic character to gift exchange generally (see Mauss, *Gift,* pp. 3–5 and passim; and Bourdieu, *Theory of Practice,* p. 194 and passim). I do not deny the presence of aggressiveness in the Kula any more than I deny the value of community in the potlatch (argued for by Walens, *Feasting with Cannibals,* especially pp. 16–17, 32–35, 148–49). The question is to what extent aggressive values are overtly affirmed in exchange as opposed to suppressed and aestheticized in favor of community values? The answer for any particular gift system is necessarily comparative. Kula and pot-

latch, in this sense, stand at opposite ends of the same spectrum. Put another way, they are opposite sides of the same coin: the one extends the tale of community; the other projects the face of self-interest.

129. *OED*, s.v. "banqueter."

130. "To be short, at such time as the merchants do make their ordinary or voluntary feasts, it is a world to see what great provision is made of all manner of delicate meats from every quarter of the country, wherein, beside that they are often comparable herein to the nobility of the land, they will seldom regard anything that the butcher usually killeth, but reject the same as not worthy to come in place. In such cases also geliffes [jellies] of all colors, mixed with a variety in the representation of sundry flowers, herbs, trees, forms of beasts, fish, fowls, and fruits, and thereunto marchpane wrought with no small curiosity, tarts of divers hues and sundry denominations, conserves of old fruits, foreign and homebred, suckets, codiniacs, marmalades, marchpane, sugarbread, gingerbread, florentines, wild fowl, venison of all sorts, and sundry outlandish [foreign] confections, altogether seasoned with sugar (which Pliny calleth *mel ex arundinibus,* a device not common nor greatly used in old time at the table but only in medicine, although it grew in Arabia, India, and Sicily), do generally bear the sway, besides infinite devices of our own not possible for me to remember" (William Harrison, *The Description of England,* ed. Georges Edelen [Ithaca: Cornell University Press, for Folger Shakespeare Library, 1968], p. 129).

131. Barber, *Cooking and Recipes from Rome to the Renaissance,* p. 104.

132. The first usage of "specie" as "coin" was in 1615. As Jack Goody notes, Latin *species*—for precious commodity—was the etymological origin of "spice," and it was spice that the Romans traded for precious metals. See *OED*, s.v. "spice" and "specie"; and Goody, *Cooking, Cuisine and Class: A Study in Comparative Sociology* (Cambridge: Cambridge University Press, 1982), p. 105.

Chapter Five

1. The masque was canceled due to a dispute between the Spanish and French ambassadors over which one should be invited; see *Jonson,* 10:659–60.

2. See, for example, the notes to the masque in *Jonson,* 10:658, 665–66, and in Orgel, ed. *Ben Jonson: The Complete Masques,* pp. 413–14, 504–5. More recent localizations of *Neptune's Triumph* in the return of Charles from his Spanish marriage expedition include Sara Pearl, "Sounding to Present Occasions: Jonson's Masques of 1620–5," in *Court Masque,* ed. Lindley, pp. 69–71; Jerzy Limon, *Dangerous Matter: English Drama and Politics in 1623–24* (Cambridge: Cambridge University Press, 1986), pp. 20–39; John Loftis, *Renaissance Drama in England and Spain: Topical Allusion and History Plays* (Princeton: Princeton University Press, 1987), pp. 163–64; and David Cressy, *Bonfires and Bells: National Memory and the Protestant Calendar in Elizabethan and Stuart England* (Berkeley: University of California Press, 1989), p. 100. Cressy's study well illustrates how an event considered "mere" from the *long durée* of history can at the time of its occurrence be charged with major national importance.

3. The notable exception is Orgel, who shows keen sensitivity to the almost

"greedy" piling up of images in the passage (*Jonsonian Masque,* pp. 98–99); such an accumulation of riches, we shall see, is the topic or topicality veiled by the pretty artifice of the masque (i.e. *trade*).

4. Leah S. Marcus, *Puzzling Shakespeare: Local Reading and Its Discontents* (Berkeley: University of California Press, 1988), p. 218. In my discussion of topicality I am guided generally by Marcus's exploration of the topic.

5. See, for instance, T[homas] M[un], *A Discovrse of Trade, From England vnto the East-Indies: Answering to diuerse Obiections which are vsually made against the same* (1621), in *A Select Collection of Early English Tracts on Commerce, from the Originals of Mun, Roberts, North, and Others,* ed. J. R. McCulloch (London, 1856; reprinted for the Economic History Society, 1952), p. 41. Just as unpurged superfluities in the physical body were thought to corrupt and mortify, so unexported products in the trading body created a *"Decay"* and "generall *Dampe* and *Deadnesse* in all the *Trades* of the *Kingdome*" (Edward Misselden, *Free Trade. Or, The Meanes to Make Trade Florish. Wherein, The Causes of the Decay of Trade in this Kingdome, are discouered: And the Remedies also to remooue the same, are represented* [1622], Reprints of Economic Classics [New York: Augustus M. Kelley, 1971], p. 29). Body metaphors for England's trade are common in the tracts (B. E. Supple, *Commercial Crisis and Change in England, 1600–1642: A Study in the Instability of a Mercantile Economy* [(Cambridge): Cambridge University Press, 1959], p. 175).

6. Mun, *Discovrse of Trade,* p. 43.

7. Lewes Roberts, *The Treasure of Traffike or a Discourse of Forraigne Trade. Wherein is shewed the benefit and commoditie arising to a Common-Wealth or Kingdome, by the skilfull Merchant, and by a well ordered Commerce and regular Traffike* (1641), in *Early English Tracts,* ed. McCulloch, p. 76; contemporary quoted in Supple, *Commercial Crisis,* p. 93. Other imports included silks, cambrics, tobacco, and wine (Supple, p. 93).

8. Gerard Malynes, *The Maintenance of Free Trade, According to the Three Essentiall Parts of Traffique; Namely, Commodities, Moneys and Exchange of Moneys, by Bills of Exchanges for other Countries. Or, An answer to a Treatise of Free Trade, or the meanes to make Trade flourish, lately Published* (1622), Reprints of Economic Classics (New York: Augustus M. Kelley, 1971), p. 96.

9. Quoted in Supple, *Commercial Crisis,* p. 176.

10. The term "money" as used by contemporaries and historians of the period can be confusing. Money usually referred to coins or specie, and such will be my usual reference as well, but it also included uncoined bullion (which also circulated). Thus "money," "specie" and "bullion" were interchangeable. In all cases, however, money designated "hard," or what contemporaries would call "real," currency as opposed to token or paper currency such as bills of exchange (the increasingly important role of the latter in foreign trade, we shall see, in large part accounts for trade's perceived strangeness).

11. The most complete summary of the trade debate and the positions of the individual economic thinkers is Supple, *Commercial Crisis,* pp. 198–221.

12. "Vent" and "utter" were interchangeable terms. Consider, for example, Misselden's assessment of England's costive trade: "a *Common-wealth* that excessiuely spendeth the *Forreigne* Commodities deere, and vttereth the *Natiue* fewer and

cheape, shall enrich other *Common-wealths,* but begger it selfe. Where on the contrary, if it vented fewer of the *Forreigne,* and more of the *Natiue,* the residue must needes returne in treasure" (*Free Trade,* p. 13).

13. Mun, *Discovrse of Trade,* p. 6; Supple, *Commercial Crisis,* p. 213.

14. Misselden, *Free Trade,* pp. 8, 18. As a solution, Misselden proposed that England raise the valuation of English coin and abate foreign coin to equal value (p. 103).

15. Malynes, *Maintenance of Free Trade,* Dedication; Gerrard De Malynes [Gerard Malynes], *A Treatise of the Canker of England's Common wealth. Diuided into three parts: Wherein the Author imitating the rule of good Phisitions, First, declareth the disease. Secondarily, sheweth the efficient cause thereof. Lastly, a remedy for the same* (1601), p. 34. Cf. *Maintenance of Free Trade,* pp. 14, 36–37. See also pp. 2–3, where Malynes grounds his argument upon a body metaphor wherein commodities are the body, money is the soul, and exchange is the vital spirit of trade. Such a trading body was to be regulated by the King: specifically, the government, Malynes argued, should legislate exchange transactions to ensure par value for English money (p. 84). The concept of "bills of exchange" will be treated more fully below.

16. Edward Misselden, *The Circle of Commerce. Or The Ballance of Trade, in defence of free Trade: Opposed to Malynes Little Fish and his Great Whale, and poized against them in the Scale. Wherein also, Exchanges in generall are considered: and therein the whole Trade of this Kingdome with forraine Countries, is digested into a Ballance of Trade, for the benefite of the Publique. Necessary for the present and future times* (1623), Reprints of Economic Classics (New York: Augustus M. Kelley, 1971), pp. 59, 142.

17. Gerard Malynes, *The Center of the Circle of Commerce. Or, A Refutation of a Treatise, Intituled "The Circle of Commerce," or "The Ballance of Trade," lately published by E. M.* (1623), The Epistle Dedicatory, A3v, p. 55. The importance of gain as a causative factor could be seen emerging as early as Malynes's *Maintenance of Free Trade;* see for example, pp. 82–83.

18. Thomas Mun, *England's Treasure by Forraign Trade. Or, The Ballance of our Forraign Trade is The Rule of our Treasure* (1664), in *Early English Tracts,* ed. McCulloch, pp. 167, 164, 174, 180. Though this document has in the past been attributed to the 1630s, Supple notes, "it is now clear that the most important parts of Mun's theoretical analysis derive directly from the 1622–23 controversy on treasure and the exchanges." Mun's memoranda submitted to the trade commission in 1623 contain "the arguments, the technical advice, and much of the wording which comprise the significant portions of the later book" (*Commercial Crisis,* pp. 211–12).

19. Supple, *Commercial Crisis,* p. 218.

20. Misselden, *Circle of Commerce,* pp. 19–24 and passim. Over the trilogy of body/spirit/soul Misselden preferred the Aristotelian duality, matter/form; see pp. 7–13.

21. Ibid., pp. 27, 142.

22. Malynes, *Center of the Circle of Commerce,* pp. 5, 56, 60.

23. For the sake of clarity, I suppress the fact that not just bills of exchange but the growing use of money itself (instead of commodity-for-commodity exchange) can be seen as a sign of increasing abstraction. We shall see the representational quality in "money" below in the contemporary innovation manifesting such abstraction most fully: money's commodification. I privilege bills of exchange here in order to

bring out money's new role: bills of exchange were the premier instruments of such commodification.

24. For the various contemporary uses of the term bill of exchange, see OED, s.v. "Bill," *sb.*[3], subheading no. 9, "Bill of Exchange." The first recorded usage of this term is precisely in our period: 1579.

25. Jean-Christophe Agnew, *Worlds Apart: The Market and the Theater in Anglo-American Thought, 1550–1750* (Cambridge: Cambridge University Press, 1986), especially pp. 27–31, 41–46. On theatrical *"mis*representation," see p. 60. Agnew associates role-playing and maskedness with privacy as well, a topic I will pursue later in this chapter.

26. K. N. Chaudhuri, *The English East India Company: The Study of an Early Joint-Stock Company, 1600–1640* (New York: Reprints of Economic Classics, 1965), pp. 5–8. As we will see, East India trade epitomized the new market displacement.

27. The need for continuous supplies of liquid capital in its domestic economy made England especially dependent on the infusion of money into the country through foreign trade (Supple, *Commercial Crisis*, p. 13).

28. See, for example, *England's Treasure*, pp. 167–68; also pp. 174–75.

29. Shafaat Ahmad Khan, *The East India Trade in the Seventeenth Century in Its Political and Economic Aspects* (New Delhi: S. Chand [1975]), pp. 51–53.

30. See the conclusion to the previous chapter. On the English export of silver specie for exotic spices, see Chaudhuri, *English East India Company*, especially pp. 111–36. As we have seen, such spices were crucial ingredients in banqueting stuffs.

31. Ibid., pp. 14, 117, 136–38. The expansion of access to Persia opened up some vent for English clothes and other commodities; Chaudhuri, p. 138 and Mun, *Discovrse of Trade*, pp. 14, 18. The Company secured its Persian trade in 1622 with the conquest of the Portuguese/Spanish town of Ormuz strategically located in the Persian gulf. At the same time, however, as we will see in the next section, such a "barbaric" seizure unmoored English anxieties over the "strangeness" of its foreign trade.

32. Chaudhuri, *English East India Company*, p. 118. For the first East India Company voyage, Queen Elizabeth tried to supplant Spanish with English silver: she ordered the minting of a special coin for exportation of about the same silver content as the Spanish rial but "stamped with the emblem of the portcullis on one side and the Arms of England on the other." The natives of the East Indies, however, would accept no substitute, and the Company was forced to return to exporting only Spanish silver (Chaudhuri, pp. 125–26).

33. My sketch of East India trade draws on Chaudhuri's map of English factories in the East as of 1617 (frontispiece, *English East India Company*) as well as on his detailed description of the network of East India exchange (pp. 14–19 and passim). I have also consulted the accounts of the early voyages of the East India Company in vols. 2–5 of Samuel Purchas, *Hakluytus Posthumus; or, Purchas His Pilgrimes. Contayning a History of the World in Sea Voyages and Lande Travells by Englishmen and others* (1625), 20 vols. (Glasgow: James MacLehose and Sons, 1905–7). I am indebted to Simon Hunt for helping me compile the above information and produce the map.

The map illustrates the primary route of East India trade c. 1620 as well as the secondary routes (including the routes of local or "country" trade) traveled in the course of developing and strengthening the primary route. It should be noted, however, that the map and the accompanying summary are meant to be representative, not definitive. Not every possible permutation is sketched. Once in the Indian Ocean, for instance, an expedition headed for Surat on the west coast of India might split up and send some of its ships into the Red Sea, or up the east coast of India, or down to the East Indies. Or the entire expedition might sail directly to Bantam in the East Indian island of Java, where it would meet up with ships from another English expedition sailing down from Surat. With the full development of the East India trade, the two different trading regions served by Surat and Bantam (known to the Company as "Northwards" and "Southwards," respectively) became mutually interdependent (Chaudhuri, p. 17). (When Bantam was closed in 1620, the factory was moved to nearby Jacatra [present day Jakarta]; Andrews, *Trade, Plunder and Settlement: Maritime Enterprise and the Genesis of the British Empire, 1480–1630* [Cambridge: Cambridge University Press, 1984], p. 269). Furthermore, much of the secondary country trade in the southern and northern regions was carried out by the Company's local representatives, or "factors," in anticipation of the arrival of expeditions from England. Certainly no single expedition would travel more than a few of the secondary routes. Finally, routes varied tremendously and could change on the spur of the moment due to varying winds, market conditions, and unstable relations with the Dutch, Portuguese, and natives.

34. Chaudhuri, *English East India Company*, pp. 124–29, 136. As Chaudhuri indicates, primary markets for silver in the Netherlands were Middleburg and Amsterdam; in France: St. Malo, Rouen, and Calais. Another port of export was Leghorn in Italy. To a great extent, we can observe, the bills of exchange used to buy Spanish silver were akin to credit. They were drawn on funds deriving not just from previous profits but from shareholder investors expecting a return. The importance of the Company's "own" cash or profit-monies was then further diminished by the fact that bills of exchange paid for only a portion of the Spanish silver needed to start an expedition. As I mention below, the remainder of the Spanish silver was paid for with trade goods carried back from earlier ventures to the East (although even these goods could in some cases be transferred by bills of exchange). The overall effect was that a relatively small amount of the Company's "own" "treasure" was needed to start up the trade system.

35. Secondary exports by the Company included not only English woolen cloth, lead and tin, but also commodities from all over Europe (ibid., p. 114). For imports from India and Persia, see ibid., especially pp. 176 and 203.

36. Sumatra, Java, and the Moluccas were the chief suppliers of spices; these consisted primarily of pepper, cloves, nutmeg, mace, cinnamon, and ginger (ibid., pp. 14 and especially pp. 140, 167).

37. Although the re-export of commodities from overseas represented only 6 percent of England's total exports by 1640, it constituted the most rapidly expanding area of foreign trade (W. E. Minchinton, ed., *The Growth of English Overseas Trade in the Seventeenth and Eighteenth Centuries* (London: Methuen, 1969), pp. 20–21. As we shall further see, contemporary defenses of the East India Company focused on this aspect of the exchange circle and especially on the "Englishness" of the re-exported goods.

38. See Chaudhuri's map, *English East India Company,* frontispiece. As mentioned in note 32 above, the factory at Bantam shown on the map was temporarily moved to Jacatra in 1620. It should also be noted that, due to financial and political difficulties, the Company was forced to abandon the Siam and Japan factories in 1623 (p. 17).

39. Ibid., pp. 107, 26, 56–57. On the difficulties of financing, see especially pp. 207–23. Another cause of deferred returns was the hijacking of English ships by the Dutch, a frequent complaint in the trade tracts.

40. Mun, *Discovrse of Trade,* pp. 17–18, 23, 8.

41. Mun, *England's Treasure,* p. 137; *Discovrse of Trade,* pp. 45–46.

42. Misselden, *Circle of Commerce,* p. 124; see also pp. 34–36.

43. Cited in Chaudhuri, *English East India Company,* pp. 142–43.

44. *Calendar of State Papers, Colonial Series, 1574–1660* (hereafter *CSP, Colonial*), ed. W. Noël Sainsbury et al., 40 vols. (London: Her Majesty's Stationery Office, 1860–1939; reprint, Vaduz: Krauz Reprint, 1964), 4:134.

45. Court Minutes of the East India Company, June 12, 1618, *CSP, Colonial,* 3:170, cited in Chaudhuri, *English East India Company,* p. 130; Chaudhuri, pp. 130–31 (see also Supple, *Commercial Crisis,* pp. 184–85).

46. *CSP, Colonial,* 4:256–57.

47. Chaudhuri, *English East India Company,* pp. 56–57. Compounding the problem was the investors' reluctance to meet their part of the bargain and make regular payments into the share-capital; see especially pp. 219–20.

48. The Company, we know, became a popular court investment (Ibid., pp. 35–36); in 1619, gentlemen tried unsuccessfully to stage a coup against the Company (p. 37).

49. In our own times, it is the "multinational corporation" that embodies such paradoxical, self-but-other corporate identity.

50. *CSP, Colonial,* 4:120, 126, 127, 144; see also Beckles Willson, *Ledger and Sword; or, The Honourable Company of Merchants of England Trading to the East Indies (1599–1874),* 2 vols. (London: Longmans, Green, 1903), 1:146.

51. *CSP, Colonial,* 4:64 (Ormuz was the contemporary English spelling of today's Hormuz). News about the taking of the town, which surrendered in April, 1622, had reached Spain overland as early as December of that year and from thence, in the form of Spanish complaints, traveled to the English Court (see 4:79); but it was not until the following summer that full, on-site documentation arrived in London on board the returning ships.

52. The three ships that took part in the fighting were the London, Jonas and Lion (Charles Grey, *The Merchant Venturers of London: A Record of Far Eastern Trade & Piracy during the Seventeenth Century,* ed. Sir George MacMunn [London: H. F. and G. Witherby, 1932], p. 153). The Company reported all three arriving back in England on July 18, 1623 (*CSP, Colonial,* 4:123). The other two ships that returned that summer were the Lesser or Little James and the Palsgrave.

53. *CSP, Colonial,* 3:416–17; Mun, *Discovrse of Trade,* p. 29.

54. The phrase "perfidious Pagans" appears in the report of Sir Herbert Thomas, cited in Grey, *Merchant Venturers,* p. 159.

55. "Relation of the late Ormuz businesse, gathered out of the Journall of Master Edward Monoxe the Agent for the East Indian Merchants trading in Persia," in Pur-

chas, *Hakluytus Posthumus*, 10:358. The report continued: "But if (as commonly it happeneth) that these Heads of their Enemies so taken in the warres be sent to the view of the King of Chan, then they are no lesse cunning to flea off the skinne of the whole head and face and stuffe the same with Straw like a football, and so send them by whole sackfuls together" (p. 359).

56. Cited in Grey, *Merchant Venturers*, p. 159.

57. Cited in ibid., p. 159.

58. Spanish Ambassadors, the Marquis de La Ynojosa and Don Carlos Coloma, to King James, *CSP, Colonial*, 4:139.

59. See John Stow, *Annales, Or, A Generall Chronicle of England. Begun by John Stow: Continved and Augmented with matters Forraigne and Domestique, Ancient and Moderne, vnto the end of this present yeere. By Edmvnd Howes* (1631), p. 993; and Purchas, *Hakluytus Posthumus*, 10:110.

60. For recriminations by Spaniards like Las Casas of their nation's savage dismemberment of natives to feed its devouring greed, see Tzvetan Todorov, *The Conquest of America: The Question of the Other*, trans. Richard Howard (New York: Harper & Row, 1984), pp. 138–42. On England's effort to distance itself from such aggressive consumerism, see Richard Helgerson, "The Voyages of a Nation," in *Forms of Nationhood: The Elizabethan Writing of England* (forthcoming, University of Chicago Press, 1992).

Attempting to explain the excessiveness of Spanish barbarisms, Todorov distinguishes between the cannibalistic Aztecs and the voracious Spanish in terms of sacrifice-societies on the one hand, and massacre-societies on the other (pp. 143–45). However, the two societies interface in the double-edged sword of "consumerism."

Such twinning is dramatized by the Spanish massacre that occurred during an Aztec sacrifice. The Spanish had allowed the Aztecs to proceed with their ritual honoring their god only on condition that "in their sacrifice shoulde no mans bloud bee spilte, nor yet to weare any weapon." The ceremony consisted of a masque-like display of song and dance performed by Aztec "Gentlemen" costumed in rich attire "wrought with precious stones, collers, girdles, bracelettes, and many other Jewels of golde, siluer, and aliosar, with gallant tuffes of feathers on their heades." Despite the Spanish prohibition against spilling blood, the ceremony also consisted of a sacrifice—not by the Aztecs but by the Spanish themselves. For, feeding their eyes on the riches adorning the celebrants, Spaniards suddenly broke into the show and committed the very act of violence they had prohibited. They sacrificed the Aztecs to their own god of greed: "seeing them so richly attired, they [the Spaniards] coueted their Gold and Jewels which they ware, and besieged the Temple with tenne Spaniardes at each doore, and the Captaine [Alvarado] entred in with fiftie men, and without any Christian respect slewe and murdered them all, and tooke from them all their treasure." The violence of dismemberment and cannibalism elided from the Aztec's sacrifice was re-inscribed by the Spaniards' massacre/sacrifice to "divine" consumerism (*The Pleasant Historie of the Conquest of the West India, now called new Spaine. Atchieued by the most woorthie Prince Hernando Cortes, Marques of the Valley of Huaxacac, most delectable to reade*, trans. T[homas] N[icholas] [London, 1596], pp. 260–61). See also the contemporary Aztec engraving showing Spaniards hacking off the limbs and heads of the temple celebrants in Todorov (p. 122).

61. See, for example, *CSP, Colonial,* Dec. 14, 1623, 4:209, 208; and 2:419; also John Keymers, "Observations made upon the Dutch Fishing, About the Year 1601" (cited in Khan, *East India Trade,* p. 26); and Sir Thomas Overbury, cited in Beckles Willson, *Ledger and Sword,* 1:84n.

62. Agnew, *Worlds Apart,* p. 45; Don K. Hedrick, "Cooking for the Anthropophagi: Jonson and His Audience," *Studies in English Literature* 17 (Spring 1977): 237.

63. Robert Ashton, *The Crown and the Money Market, 1603–1640* (Oxford: Clarendon Press, 1960), p. 34.

64. Report of an anonymous parliamentary diarist and letter from John Pory to Sir Ralph Winwood, in *James I by His Contemporaries: An Account of His Career and Character as Seen by Some of His Contemporaries,* ed. Robert Ashton (London: Hutchinson, 1969), pp. 74 and 72, respectively; John Chamberlain, *Letters,* 1:525.

65. *CSP, Colonial,* 4:124, 125.

66. *CSP, Colonial,* 4:143, 125 (see also pp. 254–55). For the Tilbury firing upon and boarding of the fleet, see Beckles Willson, *Ledger and Sword,* 1:147.

67. *CSP, Colonial,* 4:324, 323, 335.

68. The rumor-mill was jump-started by the bumbling secrecy with which the journey got underway. See Roger Lockyer, *Buckingham: The Life and Political Career of George Villiers, First Duke of Buckingham, 1592–1628* (London: Longman, 1981), p. 136.

69. The "Gentleman of the Forest," who "presents pheasant" (l. 207), would seem to be the significant anomaly here. It should be noted, however, that in June of 1623 an under-keeper at Theobalds Park, Henry Field, was apprehended for stealing and selling the King's deer (Chamberlain, *Letters,* 2:502). While a "lewde fellow," according to Chamberlain, the market-serving Field was a royal forester and may well have suggested the "Gentleman of the Forest" included in Jonson's mercantile gallimaufry of 1624. If so, the "gentleman" not only mixes well with his fellow bourgeois ingredients but also savors of the aristocracy's own involvement in strange trade.

70. Sara Pearl, "Sounding to Present Occasions: Jonson's Masques of 1620–5," in *Court Masque,* ed. Lindley, pp. 60–62, 69–71.

71. As will be clear later, my disagreement here with Pearl is not absolute. There is a perspective from which topicality and avoidance of topicality are identical.

72. The Charles weighed in at 1,000 tons; the average weight of an East India Company ship was about 500 tons (Chaudhuri, *English East India Company,* pp. 232–33).

73. Thus the island's association with classical myth—it is called "a Delos" (l. 131)—would seem to purify the foreign (and thus make it so unforeign in our period as to be an essential part of England's gifted, or Muse-inspired, aesthetics), but it at the same time contains allegorically the topical foreignness of East India trade.

74. For raw silk, see Chaudhuri, *English East India Company,* pp. 203ff. For the use of pepper as money, see Betty Wason, *Cooks, Gluttons and Gourmets: A History of Cookery* (Garden City: Doubleday, 1962), p. 125. For the importing of diamonds and rubies, see, as example, Beckles Willson, *Ledger and sword,* 1:87 n.2; also *CSP, Colonial,* 2:lviii, lix. For ambergris (as well as jewels and spice), see, as example, 3:495.

75. Printed in appendix by Orgel, ed., *Complete Masques,* p. 554.

76. *CSP, Colonial,* 4:143. I do not mean to deny other possible allusions: one of the ships in the English fleet that was sent to bring Charles back from Spain, for instance, was called "The Seaven Starres" (Nichols, *Progresses . . . of King James the First,* 3:924). But the specific context of the "stars" reference in the masque would seem to point more pressingly to the East India ship, the Star. That context includes not only oblique references to East India trade goods in the nymphs' dressings immediately preceding the "stars" reference but also, as we shall see, more pointed references to war and the taking of a town (suggestive of Ormuz) immediately following it. Such an "allegorical" layering of referentiality is an essential characteristic of topicality.

77. Spoken by the character Tucca to Jonson's stand-in, Horace, in Thomas Dekker's *Satiro-mastix. Or the Vntrussing of the Humorous Poet* (1602), cited in *Jonson,* ed. Herford and Simpson, 1:19n.1. On Jonson's "taste" for cannibalism in his works, see Hedrick, "Cooking for the Anthropophagi"; and Maggie Kilgour, *From Communion to Cannibalism: An Anatomy of Metaphors of Incorporation* (Princeton: Princeton University Press, 1990), pp. 102–18.

Index

Sonnets, 27, 170, 201, 232 n. 49; appeared at court, 87; Cecil's lyrics sung to Elizabeth I, 76; "detached" from public, 109, 163; formal, 96, 226 n. 6; and inaccessibility of inner love, 90; location in house where "published," 85–87; and miniatures, 70, 72, 86, 90–110 passim; prefaces to, 87–89; privacy/secrecy of, 66, 85–90 passim, 205, 236 n. 78; within public "rooms," 87, 89; published private love in print, 87–90; rhetorical artifice of, 90; "sincerity" and "truth" of, 88–89; "sonnet: as any small poem, 85, 226 n. 6; Spenser's Busirane as sonneteer, 65, 107–8; and the trivial, 2–3, 86–87. See also *Astrophil and Stella*

Sonnet sequences: *Alba* (Tofte), 105, 106–7; *Alcilia* (J. C.), 86; *Amoretti* (Spenser), 86; *Avrora* (Alexander), 86–87; *Delia* (Daniel), 60, 87–88, 105; *Diana* (Constable), 59–60, 62, 104; *Diella* (Lynche), 60, 89; *Emaricdulfe* (E. C.), 89; *Ideas Mirrour* (Drayton), 105; *Lavra* (Tofte), 88, 89; *Phillis* (Lodge), 60; *Sonnets to the Fairest Coelia* (Percy), 88; *The Vanytyes of Sir Arthur Gorges Youthe* (Gorges), 104; *Zepheria,* 105. See also *Astrophil and Stella*

Spain (and Spanish), 173, 197, 198–99; cannibalistic greed of, 191, 258 n. 60; and massacre/sacrifice of Aztecs, 258 n. 60; and Ormuz, 188, 190, 194; Spanish silver, 181, 199, 202, 204, 255 n. 32, 256 n. 34

Specie: depletion of, 174; origin of term, 166, 252 n. 132. See also Money

Spencer, Gabriel, 201

Spenser, Edmund, 31, 37; complained of insufficient return gifts, 225 n. 93; feared dedication would offend, 62; gift ethic of, 225 n. 91; his poem as child-gift, 59. Works: *Amoretti,* 86; *Colin Clouts Come Home Againe,* 61; *Mother Hubberds Tale,* 225 n. 93; *Mutabilitie Cantos,* 62; *Prothalamion,* 225 n. 93; *The Ruines of Time,* 61; *The Shepheardes Calender,* 59, 61, 214 n. 2, 220 n. 42, 225 n. 93; *A View of the Present State of Ireland,* 48, 49, 222 n. 63 —*The Faerie Quenne,* 20, 27, 49–50, 63, 220 n. 45; its narrative of exchange, 57–58; and dedications, 46, 58–59, 61, 62; "Letter of the Authors," 50; book I, 20, 50, 65, 213 n.

53; book 2, 50, 65, 220 n. 45, 224 n. 76; book 3, 50, 65–66, 107–8, 224 n. 83; book 5, 50; book 6, 29–30, 50, 63–64, 65, 66, 214 n. 2

Spice, 125, 134, 174, 245 n. 62, 256 n. 36; in Charles I's orange, 16, 206; considered spiritual and Christ-like, 135; East Indian import, 181, 184, 188, 199, 201, 204; of the Magi, 16, 135, 155–56, 195; market in, 166–67, 173; as medicinal, 134–36, 174, 184–85, 244 n. 53; more consumed with higher death rates, 246 n. 67; mortality cured by, 134–36, 245 n. 65; not considered food, 133, 244 n. 53; separation from main meals, 122–23, 247 n. 78; and "specie," 166, 181, 252 n. 132; in void foods, 112, 122, 155–56, 201, 245 n. 59, 255 n. 30. See also Voids

Stallybrass, Peter, 99

Stanihurst, Richard, 46

Star (East India Company ship), 200, 202, 260 n. 76

Stewart, Susan, 227 n. 6

Still-rooms. See Rooms

Stone, Lawrence, 36, 218 n. 27

Strange, concept of: and East India trade, 180–81, 184–85, 186–87; and economics, 173–88 passim; in masques, 169–70; reified as particular foreignness, 174, 187–88, 195, 203; and topicality, 204; as unlocatable, 173–74, 177, 178, 180–81, 187, 194–95, 203. See also Trade

Strong, Roy: on allegorization of Saint George, 21; on Charles I's masques, 214 n. 59; on James I's Banqueting House, 246 n. 72; on miniatures, 72–74, 83, 94, 228 n. 22, 230 n. 38, 233 n. 57

Stuart, Lady Arabella, 235 n. 78

Subjectivity. See Self, concept of

Sugar, 125, 134, 245 n. 59; East Indian import, 184; as medicinal, 134–36, 244 n. 53, 252 n. 130; mortality cured by, 134–36, 245 n. 65; not considered food, 133, 244 n. 53; separation from main meals, 122, 247 n. 78. See also Voids

Sumatra, 183 (fig;. 36), 184; a chief supplier of spice, 256 n. 36

Supple, B. E., 175, 177, 253 n. 11, 254 n. 18

Surat, India, 181, 183 (fig. 36), 184, 256 n. 33

Sydenham, Roger, 41, 42